Feminist
Research Methods

About the Book and Editor

Feminist inquiry has affected the nature of research in all the social and natural sciences over the past decade, but much contemporary writing on feminist methods simply offers a critique of traditional methods. This book, one of the first to offer a practical guide to conducting research informed by feminist methods, is based on the premise that abstract discussion of methodological issues is most meaningful and instructive in conjunction with examples of actual research.

A comprehensive and far-reaching introduction defines feminist research and explains how it differs from traditional methodology in the social and natural sciences. In a beautifully clear style, Dr. Nielsen guides the reader through a number of philosophy of science, history of science, and sociology of knowledge issues that are fundamental to understanding the nature of scientific method in its traditional sense and the role of feminist scholarship in the larger intellectual movement that is transforming and redefining scientific methodology. Part One presents the best of feminist commentary on both feminist and traditional methods. Part Two consists of readings that illustrate particular feminist methods, including oral history, linguistic analysis, feminist anthropology informed by feminist literary criticism, and reinterpretation and reanalysis of empirical data from a feminist perspective. Substantive issues addressed in the readings include women's suffrage in the United States, women as shamans, sex differences in suicide rates, sex differences in cognitive abilities, gender dominance through conversation, gender and public policy, and public-private sphere dichotomies.

Joyce McCarl Nielsen is associate professor of sociology at the University of Colorado–Boulder. She is the author of *Sex and Gender in Society: Perspectives on Stratification.*

Feminist Research Methods

Exemplary Readings in the Social Sciences

EDITED BY

Joyce McCarl Nielsen

University of Colorado–Boulder

WESTVIEW PRESS
Boulder, San Francisco, & London

The diagram on page 22 is reprinted from George Ritzer, *Sociology: A Multiple Paradigm Science* (Boston: Allyn and Bacon, 1975), p. 3. Used by permission of Simon & Schuster, Inc. The editorials and articles on pages 123, 124, 124–126, and 130 are reprinted from the *New York Times.* Copyright © 1912 by the New York Times Company; reprinted by permission.

Published in 1990 in the United States of America by Westview Press, Inc., 5500 Central Avenue, Boulder, Colorado 80301, and in the United Kingdom by Westview Press, Inc., 13 Brunswick Centre, London WC1N 1AF, England

Library of Congress Cataloging-in-Publication Data
Feminist research methods : exemplary readings in the social sciences /
   edited by Joyce McCarl Nielsen.
      p.   cm.
   Contents: Gender and science / Evelyn Fox Keller — Feminist
criticism of the social sciences / Marcia Westkott — Knowledge and
women's interests / Judith A. Cook and Mary Margaret Fonow —
Beginning where we are : feminist methodology in oral history /
Kathryn Anderson . . . [et al.] — Laura Ellsworth Seiler : in the
streets / Sherna Berger Gluck — The vision of a woman Shaman / Anna
Lowenhaupt Tsing — Between two worlds : German feminist approaches
to working-class women and work / Myra Marx Ferree — Women and
suicide in historical perspective / Howard I. Kushner — How large
are cognitive gender differences? / Janet Shibley Hyde —
Interaction : the work women do / Pamela M. Fishman — A new
approach to understanding the impact of gender on the legislative
process / Lyn Kathlene.
   ISBN 0-8133-0604-3. — ISBN 0-8133-0577-2 (pbk.)
   1. Women's studies—Methodology. 2. Feminism—Research—
Methodology. I. Nielsen, Joyce McCarl.
HQ1180.F465 1990
305.42'072—dc20   89-29019
                                                                                  CIP

Printed and bound in the United States of America

The paper used in this publication meets the requirements of the American National
Standard for Permanence of Paper for Printed Library Materials Z39.48-1984.

10   9   8   7   6   5   4   3   2   1

Contents

v

Preface

Editing this book was both a difficult and a satisfying experience. Writing the Introduction gave me an opportunity to develop and integrate a number of disparate themes, thoughts, and impressions that had been on my mind for some time. The first such idea was the power of the women studies paradigm itself; as director of a women studies program I had witnessed the sheer generative impact of focusing on women in all the disciplines. Mainstream knowledge seemed constricted, as if in an intellectual straitjacket, compared to the expansiveness and richness of feminist work. A second idea was that feminist scholarship can be conceptualized as part of the larger postpositivist academic stage, about which I knew just enough to want to know more.

Third, as both a student and a teacher of research methods, I have always thought that the best way to learn methods was by example. Early in my postgraduate education in the Sociology Department at the University of Washington (where positivism was stressed), I noticed that those we jokingly called "real scientists" (biochemists, physicists, geologists) did not take separate methods courses per se. They might have a section on a specific laboratory or field technique, such as tissue culture or radioactive dating, but the basics of the approach (for example, making controlled comparisons) were taught as an assumed, or given, part of the subject matter. Students in those disciplines were not asked to read *about* the value of scientific method; they saw it concretely in the work they studied every day. They absorbed it along with the subject matter in an integrated, holistic fashion.

This is not to say that I think reading about methods is not worthwhile— but in order to learn a discipline's methodology, the more direct and compelling approach seems to me to be learning by the example of its best work. Studying Durkheim's *Suicide* in detail, for example, will help a student learn statistics in a way that a methods text cannot. Likewise, feminist research, which is still being developed and defined, imparts knowledge about feminist research methods.

Finally, as both a student and an instructor, I have become familiar with and have done research using a variety of theoretical approaches, each with its implied and distinctive methodology—including participant observation, quantitative statistical analysis, survey research, laboratory and field experimentation, and even operant conditioning of social behavior. As a result, I experienced firsthand the incommensurability of paradigms that Kuhn wrote about. And yet I was always looking for the "crucial experiment" that would rule out competing, alternative theories or explanations of a given phenomenon, as if theories *were* commensurable. Perhaps the juxtapositioning of these contradictory stances generated dialectical tension for me. The process of thinking through such contradiction and integrating it with the general themes expressed above, and elaborated on in the Introduction, was indeed satisfying.

Identifying good examples of research that expressed the power of a feminist perspective was relatively easy. My goals were clear: to represent as many different disciplines in the social sciences and as many different methodological strategies as possible; and to include articles that would be readable by students who may not necessarily have a background in the discipline represented by the chapter. The most important criterion for inclusion was that the work contribute to the scholarly literature and at the same time either be practical or have practical implications for the larger goal of women's liberation—in short, it had to be feminist research at its exemplary best.

Joyce McCarl Nielsen

Acknowledgments

My thanks go to Jeana Abromeit, Eleanor Hubbard, Glenda Sehested, and Sarah Nathe for their helpful discussions of the issues raised in the Introduction. I am grateful also to Alan Franklin, Martha Gimenez, Elizabeth Moen, and especially Marcia Westkott for their careful reviews of earlier versions of the Introduction.

More than any other person, Barbara Ellington of Westview Press has seen me through the completion of this book. She encouraged and bolstered me when interest, enthusiasm, and motivation waned; she disciplined me with a firm hand when necessary; and, early on, she recognized the importance of the subject matter.

J.M.N.

Introduction

JOYCE McCARL NIELSEN

Feminist research methods is an exciting, emergent, and potentially revolutionary academic subdiscipline, but by its very nature it is also controversial. Some writers and researchers have questioned whether it is possible to identify certain methods as distinctly feminist; some have suggested that the expression itself may be a contradiction in terms. As Parlee (1986:5) observed, "The notion of 'feminist methodology' strikes some of us as absolute nonsense while others take it for granted as a useful concept."

To understand this controversy, we must first understand what traditional social scientists mean by *methods*. In the first part of this Introduction, I describe scientific method as it is usually formally presented and show that, at first glance, it does seem contradictory to feminist-based inquiry. In the second section I demonstrate that there is an identifiable feminist approach to research that is grounded in both an older positivist-empirical tradition and in a newer postempirical one.[1] I argue, too, that feminist methods (in the broadest sense of that term) is part—perhaps the best part—of a larger intellectual movement that represents a fundamental shift away from traditional social science methodology. Thus feminist research is contributing to a transformation of what traditionally has been called methods in the same way that feminist scholarship has transformed substantive academic disciplines and subdisciplines from literary criticism to history, anthropology, and psychology.[2]

SCIENTIFIC METHOD AS A WAY OF KNOWING

Most people understand the term methods to mean the scientific method; the scientific method, in turn, is best seen as one of the ways people (especially scholars) have tried to answer the question, "How do we know what we know?" When we say, for example, that the earth is round, that aggression is a common response to frustration, that women have a distinctive moral developmental history, that men excel at math, or that human infants need love and care in order to thrive, on what grounds do we base these assertions? What would we consider evidence or proof for such statements if they were challenged, as these particular statements have been at one time or another?[3] Do we most trust self-reflective knowledge, practical reasoning, or traditional authority as the final arbiter of what is right and what is real?

The history of Western philosophy shows that some fairly well-defined schools of thought—what philosophers call epistemologies, or theories of knowledge—have characterized different historical times and places. Examples are Greek rationalism, which posited logic as the final test of truth; seventeenth- and eighteenth-century empiricism, which held sense perception to be the sole source of valid human knowledge; Hegelian dialectics, where thought proceeds by contradiction and the reconciliation of contradiction; dialectical materialism, the method of Karl Marx, who regarded knowledge and ideas as reflections of material conditions; and mysticism, which holds that knowledge is communicable only in poetic imagery and through metaphor, if at all. Certainly the unquestioned authority of the scientific method as the best way to study both natural and social-cultural phenomena has characterized our own time.

Two distinguishable and dominant tendencies within the scientific tradition of method are, of course, rationalism and empiricism. The dominance of pure reason or logic (to the point of virtual absence of interest in observation) is the earlier mode. In discussions about the nature of the physical world, for example, early Greek philosophers made such statements as "What is, is," and "What is not, is not," or "Thou canst not know nor utter what is not—that is impossible" (Parmenides, cited in Jones, 1970:21). An example of seventeenth-century (versus classical) rationalism is Descartes's famous statement, "I think; therefore, I am." This statement is considered true because it would be a contradiction in terms to both think and not be. The first part of the statement makes the negation of the second part illogical. The fact that Descartes's ontological reality (his sense of existence or being) was grounded in thinking rather than, say, feeling or loving—he did not say "I feel (or love); therefore, I am"—illustrates an extraordinary trust in rational thought.

Empiricism, the second dominant theme, is probably more familiar to modern readers. This is the process of directly observing, recording, or monitoring the social and natural world. Contemporary physical scientists, for example, use sophisticated and elaborate measuring instruments to examine and manipulate aspects of the natural world. Although there are other ways to justify what we think we know (for example, divine revelation), the combination of rationalism (which now often takes the form of logic) and empiricism in modern science captures the dominant trends in Western thinking.

In spite of changing dominant epistemologies, one issue—which we will call "objectivism versus relativism" for now—has characterized the Western discourse on knowledge. Because of its importance to understanding feminist methods, I will outline this issue. Its relevance to the definition of feminist methods, how feminist inquiry is both similar to and different from other ways of knowing, and how feminist research fits into the particular historical context of contemporary epistemology will become clear.

At least since Plato's time there has been a tendency to take an either/ or position about whether it is possible to obtain absolute or indubitable knowledge about the world. At one extreme are the many well-known philosophers (for example, Descartes, Kant, Spinoza, Hegel, Schopenhauer) who spent much of their lives searching for a foundation or basis for arriving at absolute knowledge. This search has mainly taken the form of assuming that there is some objective (that is, independent of the knower) world that is knowable. At the other extreme are those (like the Greek sophists or contemporary philosopher of science Paul Feyerabend) who answer the question "How can we be sure of what we know" with a despairing "We can't, not really." Their argument is that there is no final, ultimate measure of truth that all can agree on. The modern version of this kind of skepticism is relativism, which asserts that all knowledge is culture-bound, theory-bound, and/or historically specific—that is, understandable and valid only within a specific time, place, theory, or perspective.[4] Some distinguish between cognitive and moral relativism, arguing that we *can* be certain about scientifically based knowledge of the natural world but that moral or ethical judgments are relative—that is, dependent on one's values, which are culture-bound. Others say that everything we know (including knowledge about the physical world) is contextual. Some relativists argue further that because there are no sure grounds for choosing between competing explanations or theories, such different and sometimes contradictory ideas, thoughts, or claims are equally good or valid. This idea is sometimes called pluralism.

The dilemma of how we can be sure of our knowledge has been with us a long time. Yet it takes on new urgency and seriousness in contemporary society because of the recent loss of faith in science by social scientists and the redefinition of scientific method as we have understood it. This point will be elaborated on later.

SCIENTIFIC METHOD IN TEXTBOOKS

Even though most people have some sense of what is meant by doing something "scientifically," it is surprisingly difficult to say exactly what makes science scientific. This is partly because what is now called science developed over a period of several hundred years. During this time it evolved from a small reform movement (against authority based on tradition) characterized by little specialization and minimal division of labor into a large-scale, government- and military-sponsored, bureaucratic and specialized complex.

A second reason it is difficult to define what science essentially is arises from the claim that science is a method, or a way of knowing, that different disciplines have in common rather than a subject matter. Although people often think of science as comprising those disciplines that deal with the physical/natural world (astronomy, physics, geology, chemistry), philosophers of science and scientists themselves define science more abstractly as comprising disciplines that use scientific methods to gain or develop knowledge. We can tentatively and briefly define scientific method as including an appeal to empirical evidence, experimentation (defined as the purposeful manipulation of physical matter or events in order to gauge their effects), and the use of inductive and deductive logic. (Deduction is inference that follows necessarily from premise to conclusion; induction is inference from the particular—usually an observation—to a more general statement.)

But as Bernstein (1976), Harding (1986), and others pointed out, it is difficult to find a procedure or combination of procedures common to all of the disciplines we now call scientific. Astronomy, geology, and math, for example, are not primarily experimental, whereas physics is. And, of course, people who do not call themselves scientists routinely use empirical evidence as well as deductive and inductive reasoning.

Even more interesting is that physics is considered the model of science— "the most real of sciences" to use Haraway's (1981:475) phrase. Yet it is unlike the different disciplines we call scientific, at least in terms of (1) its considerable use of experimentation and formal logic, (2) the comparative simplicity of its subject matter, which is neither self-reflective nor intentional (as is human behavior, which is, of course, the subject matter of the social sciences), and (3) its minimal use of interpretation (Harding, 1986). This is significant because the social sciences, in their quest for academic respectability during their formative years, adapted physics and its methods as a model. Thus they not only made the assumption that the social world could be explored and studied in the same way as the physical world, but they also chose to emulate a form of science that is not very representative.

The argument I make in this chapter (shared by many others) is that on close analysis of what scientists actually do as opposed to what they and others say they do, the scientific method is inherently less distinguishable from other ways of knowing than previously thought. I will demonstrate this by first considering the scientific method that is endorsed by social scientists in their methods textbooks.

Most texts list a set of interrelated assumptions that are shared by social scientists who adopt a naturalistic approach to social phenomena but that are usually unstated and/or nonconscious in their particular works. The first assumption is that the social world is knowable (in the certain, nonrelativistic way discussed earlier) and in the same way that the natural world is knowable— that is, through observation and recording of what appears as "objective" reality by a subjective (independent) researcher. This is the "objectivity" assumption—that there is an objective (independent of the subjective knower) reality to be known. This assumption presumes, in turn, a distinction or separation between the subjective knower and the objective to-be-known world. This second assumption is referred to as the subject-object separation assumption. An extension of this is the idea that the subjective should not infect objective truth—that evaluative concerns of the subjective knower should be excluded.

A third assumption, called the empirical assumption, is that verification of one's claims about the social world should be based on the use of the senses, which, it is assumed, will give accurate and reliable information about human behavior. We observe through touch, sight, smell, hearing, and seeing, though sometimes indirectly with the use of measurement; information gained through the senses is considered the way to be "objective." The key word here is observe. It is also assumed that different observers exposed to the same data will come to more or less the same conclusions; thus intersubjective verification is not only possible but desirable.

The fourth assumption is that there is order in the social world, that social life is patterned, and that this pattern takes a predominantly cause-and-effect form. In other words, things don't just happen. This is called the cause-and-effect assumption, and it is reflected in the overall goal of the social scientist (in the naturalistic tradition, at any rate): to develop universal laws about the social world or social behavior—that is, generalizations that hold true across time and place and in many different conditions or situations. Notice that this purpose assumes that in spite of historical and cultural variation there is something permanent and regular about social life that can be captured in generalizations and abstract laws. This is a rationalist assumption—that social life is orderly, rational.

The fifth and final assumption is that there is a unity of the sciences (including the social sciences) insofar as they all share the same method of going about learning about the world, and that it is the best, if not the only, legitimate way to ground knowledge. Methods texts also assert that scientific conclusions—that is, the body of scientific knowledge at any given time—are always tentative (open to subsequent modification) and that the rules and procedures of science minimize subjectivity and personal bias.

These assumptions, then, are associated with a knowledge-generating approach that emphasizes rationality ("no contradictions"), impersonality ("the more objective, the better"), and prediction and control of events or phenomena studied. That is, it is a short step from discovering regularities to predicting them and then to controlling them. Indeed, this seems to be the end product of much science. In the natural sciences prediction and control are used presumably for human benefit. The social sciences have been less successful in this regard, yet the goal of much research is to explain and thereby solve what are defined as social problems. (An indeterminate world view, in contrast to a deterministic [cause and effect] one, means some degree of unpredictability or lack of pattern, thus making control and intervention difficult, if not impossible.)

THE FEMINIST CHALLENGE:
A FIRST LOOK

Oakley's (1981) study of the transition to motherhood for fifty-five women is a good starting point for understanding feminist research. She discovered quickly that textbook advice about interviewing (for example, to maintain a certain distance between yourself and the interviewee, to "parry," or avoid, answering questions so as not to influence the answers of the interviewee, and so on) not only would not work but would also limit her ability to communicate with respondents in a way that would generate worthwhile and meaningful information. She asks how one can parry questions like "Have you got any children?" "Did you breast feed?" "Do you think my baby's got too many clothes on?" and "Why do some women need caesareans?" (p. 42). It would be obviously rude to evade or dodge such questions and then turn around and ask the respondents to answer similarly personal and matter-of-fact questions. Her successful research strategy turned out to be quite the opposite of what textbooks advocated. She not only answered questions, thereby becoming an important source of information and reas-surance about the unknowns and anxieties related to childbirth, but established and continued to maintain a friendship with over a third of the women participants even after the study was over. In short, she got involved. The obviously successful consequences of her involvement directly challenges the subject-object separation referred to earlier.

A second example of feminist research—Freeman's (1975) study of the women's movement of the 1960s—also illustrates the lack of relevance of traditional scientific methodology to high-quality research.[5] I cannot capture all the complexity and richness of this study in a short space, but the gist of her argument is that two branches of the women's movement (the younger and the older) were involved in creating the conditions that led the movement to emerge at the time that it did. These conditions included a cooptable communication network (established in part by the New Left movement), a crisis (the circumstances surrounding passage of Title VII of the 1964 Civil Rights Act), and a sense of relative deprivation (when rewards are perceived to be incommensurate with effort or contribution). More important for our discussion is how she arrived at this assessment: Her research depended heavily on her participation in the movement. She traveled to and attended both informal and formal meetings and conventions; she interviewed key persons in different factions of the movement and recorded their talks; she monitored the movement through newspaper accounts and did library research to check relevant historical and legal documents. In brief, the work was multimethodological and required the researcher's personal involvement—hardly the recipe for "objective," scientifically sound work in the ideal sense described earlier.

These are not unique examples. Others have described feminist research as contextual, inclusive, experiential, involved, socially relevant, multimeth-odological, complete but not necessarily replicable, open to the environment, and inclusive of emotions and events as experienced (Reinharz, 1983). Feminist inquiry is much more than this list of characteristics, but for now the point is that given the obvious contrast between it and textbook definitions of scientific research, the expression "feminist research methods" does seem to be a contradiction in terms. It would seem that feminist research cannot be methodological in the sense of scientific method as presented thus far. My argument, however, is that the sketch (given earlier) of the scientific method as presented in textbooks is a false or at least incomplete picture of the scientific research process as we now know it. To elaborate, I will first outline what is referred to as the crisis in contemporary philosophy of science and then trace some of the events that led up to this crisis. In this context, then, we will take a second and closer look at the nature of feminist inquiry and expand on its part of this contemporary drama.

THE POSTEMPIRICAL CRISIS IN KNOWLEDGE

Considered the only way to sure and respectable knowledge, science as a way of knowing has dominated modern life. In the past 25 years, however, we ·have seen the development of what philosophers of science call the postempirical period, which is characterized by the realization that the scientific method is not the ultimate test of knowledge or basis for claims to truth that we once thought it was. This realization is critical because there seems to be nothing to replace science—what can we depend on, if not science? Without some agreed-upon foundation for knowing we are extremely uncomfortable. I should add, however, that the sense of crisis is expressed more by philosophers, historians of science, epistemologists, sociologists of knowledge, and those in related disciplines than by practicing social scientists, and even less by practicing natural scientists. Though many factors have contributed to this new skepticism and ensuing crisis in knowledge, several are particularly important here. These include two traditions of thought in the social sciences: the interpretive and the critical.

The Hermeneutic Tradition

The interpretive, or hermeneutic, tradition can be defined briefly as a theory and method of interpreting meaningful human action. Those working in this tradition represent an exception to the dominant trend in the social sciences because they question the wholesale application of natural science methods to the study of social life, even though they share some of the textbook assumptions listed earlier. Specifically, they are concerned with the importance of meaning in social interaction and argue that limiting research to observable human action misses the most important part of the story. To explain and understand any human social behavior, they argue, we need to know the meaning attached to it by the participants themselves.

Nevertheless, it is important to note that they endorse the subjective-objective distinction. Max Weber, for example, whose work initially inspired development in this tradition, argued that studying social phenomena involves studying conscious human agents who attach sense or meaning to their actions. Thus the social sciences are inherently different from the natural sciences, and a full understanding of social action must involve *verstehen* (empathetic understanding). At the same time, he believed that although true objectivity is impossible, the social scientists should attempt to remain value-free. Notice here the implicit acceptance of the subjective-objective distinction, which distinguishes these earlier critics of the scientific method (as applied to social phenomena) from later critics who not only reject the subjective-objective distinction but question whether traditional scientific method is the appropriate description of what both natural and social scientists do.

Schutz (1967), who has probably done the most to develop and legitimize an interpretive method in the social sciences (especially for sociologists), made a strong case for the importance of meaning and its inseparability from human action. As Bernstein (1976:145) said, for Schutz, "[Human] action is intrinsically meaningful; it is endowed with meaning by human intentionality, i.e., by consciousness. . . . We are continuously ordering, classifying, and interpreting our ongoing experiences according to various interpretive schemes." But how can we, as subjective, meaning-producing persons ourselves, be objective about the subjective meanings of others?

Schutz argued that social scientists must "bracket"—that is, hold in abeyance or set aside temporarily—the pragmatic and private concerns that dominate their own everyday lives and thus assume the attitude of a disinterested observer. In other words, by suspending their own subjectivity, researchers can be "objective" about the subjectivity of others. This way of acknowledging and studying subjective meaning objectively, then, illustrates endorsement of the subjective-objective dichotomy. Whether researchers are actually able to bracket their own subjectivity in the way Schutz described, however, is a question we will consider later.

The value of work in this tradition is that it has provided alternative research models—especially during a period of otherwise naturalistic hegemony. Participant observation, for example, which is a research strategy of direct participation in and observation of the community, social group, or event being studied, characterizes research in this tradition. Indeed, the two examples of feminist research I presented earlier could have been labeled interpretive as well as feminist. If it sounds contradictory to say both that these research projects benefited from the investigators having gotten involved and that they fit a research style modeled on the basis of a disinterested researcher-observer, it is partly because there is some question about whether a researcher can ever be really disinterested. In any case it is difficult to determine what it is to be "disinterested."

As you will see, feminist work has an interpretive dimension that attempts to transcend or move beyond concerns about personal prejudgments. Furthermore, there is a gap between the way research is presented and the way it is executed on a daily basis. A number of published case histories or "inside" stories of research projects illustrate this point rather well (for example, Becker, 1971; Horowitz, 1976; Bell and Newby, 1977; Roberts, 1981). This point is important because it buttresses the argument made earlier that traditional conceptions of science, especially as depicted in textbooks, are somewhat inaccurate.

In any case, in the context of the positivist (scientific) tradition, research strategies (for example, interviewing, participant observation) used by phenomenologists generate data that are considered less "objective" than that produced by physical scientists,[6] yet they are considered "scientific" to the extent that they share with positivism the underlying assumption that there is indeed an objective reality that is separate and separable from the (subjective) researcher. Thus phenomenologists differ more from positivistic social scientists with respect to their belief in how one can best know and understand that reality than with the assumption that it is objectively knowable.

The overall effect of the interpretive tradition is that it has kept alive the critique of (but not replaced) the natural science model that stresses objectivism, which is still the majority view. It has provided a legitimate alternative for those who want to stay within the scientific tradition, but incorporate the subjective into their research.

Critical Theory

Critical theorists (also referred to as the Frankfurt School) have also argued against the wholesale use of a science model for social inquiry and at the same time have been critical (in a debunking sense) of the practice of natural science itself. Criticism in this tradition means more than a negative judgment; it refers to the more positive act of detecting and unmasking, or exposing, existing forms of beliefs that restrict or limit human freedom. Thus it differs from the hermeneutic tradition in its purpose. To adopt Habermas's (1970) trichotomous identification of the cognitive interests that generate the different research/knowledge traditions considered here, we can say that the positivists' goal is to predict and control, the hermeneutics' is to understand, and the critical theorists' approach is to emancipate—that is, to uncover aspects of society, especially ideologies, that maintain the status quo by restricting or limiting different groups' access to the means of gaining knowledge.

Thus, theory is "critical" because it departs from and questions the dominant ideology, creating at least the possibility of being "outside" of that ideology. The dominant ideology in this context is usually that of capitalistic political and economic organization. Take, for example, the beliefs that individuals are naturally competitive and that people get pretty much what they deserve; ideas like these help to justify the status quo, so that social patterns such as extreme individualism, competitiveness, and poverty appear to be inevitable or natural.

What does critical theory have to do with our discussion of methods and feminist inquiry? In direct contrast to the positivism that goes with the endorsement of the scientific method, the critical tradition rejects the idea that there can be "objective" knowledge. Proponents of the tradition argue that there is no such thing as an objectively neutral or disinterested perspective, that everyone or every group (including themselves) is located socially and historically, and that this context inevitably influences the knowledge they produce. Knowledge, in short, is socially constructed.[7]

This assertion brings us back to the perennial issue of methods, introduced earlier as the issue of foundationalism (the belief in a basis for absolute knowledge) versus relativism. The question is, if every group's knowledge is grounded in history and social structure, then whose view should prevail? And what criteria should we use to decide? Writers in the critical tradition have provided several answers to this question, but I will elaborate on only one because it is relevant to feminist inquiry—this is the notion of standpoint epistemology.

Standpoint Epistemology

Briefly described, standpoint epistemology begins with the idea that less powerful members of society have the potential for a more complete view of social reality than others, precisely because of their disadvantaged position. That is, in order to survive (socially and sometimes even physically), subordinate persons are attuned to or attentive to the perspective of the dominant class (for example, white, male, wealthy) as well as their own. This awareness gives them the potential for what Annas (1978) called "double vision," or double consciousness—a knowledge, awareness of, and sensitivity to both the dominant world view of the society and their own minority (for example, female, black, poor) perspective. For example, given that blacks in our culture are exposed to dominant white culture in school and through mass media as well as in interaction with whites, we can see how it is possible that blacks could know both white and black culture while whites know only their own. The same might be said about women vis-à-vis men.

To the extent that women as a group are socially subordinate to men as a group, it is to women's advantage to know how men view the world and to be able to read, predict, and understand the interests, motivations, expectations, and attitudes of men. At the same time, however, because of the division of labor by sex found in all societies and sex-specific socialization practices, sex segregation, and other social processes that guarantee sex differences in life experience, women will know the world differently from men. It is almost as though there is a separate women's culture, which is certainly not the dominant one. Feminists use terms like "underground," "invisible" or "less visible," or "the underside" to describe women's culture, history, and lives. This does not mean that all women are acutely aware of what they share with other women. But members of the subordinate group in any dominant-subordinate relational system will have the potential for this awareness.

The standpoint notion is based on several premises outlined by Hartsock (1983). The first is that one's material life (what one does for a living and related facts such as the quality of one's material surroundings) structures and limits one's understanding of life. Being a coal miner, for example, would lead to quite a different understanding (standpoint) than being chief executive officer of a corporation. A second premise is that members of more powerful and less powerful groups will potentially have inverted, or opposed, understandings of the world. Third, the dominant group's view will be "partial and perverse" in contrast to the subordinate group's view, which has the potential to be more complete. The dominant group's view is partial and perverse because, according to Hartsock, so long as the group is dominant, it is in the members' interest to maintain, reinforce, and legitimate their own dominance and particular understanding of the world, regardless of how incomplete it may be.

Hartsock gave the example of the worker's versus the owner's view of the process of production. The owner sees it as a matter of exchange: the purchase and sale of labor power. The worker has the potential to see—is in the position to see—the real point of production, which is, in the final analysis, the continuation of the species. Jagger (1983) even more dramatically contrasted evaluations of the social order from the viewpoints of owner and worker in Western capitalistic society, using the terms "Eden" and "hell" to represent their respective viewpoints. These examples illustrate that the standpoint of the more politically powerful group is considered by these analysts as being more superficial than false. It does not get to a deeper or underlying meaning of social life, which is accessible to the subordinate. A final but important point made by Hartsock is that the less powerful group's standpoint has to be developed or acquired through education (including, presumably, consciousness-raising); its conscious distinctiveness from the usually more widely shared dominant group's view cannot be taken for granted. Without conscious effort to reinterpret reality from one's own lived experience—that is, without political consciousness—the disadvantaged are likely to accept their society's dominant worldview. Indeed, because the less advantaged are often denied access to formal education, they are likely to be less knowledgeable than the dominant group. The point, however, is that according to standpoint epistemology—which has the main premise that one's everyday life has epistemological consequences and implications—the disadvantaged have the potential to be more knowledgeable, in a way, than the dominant group.

We will say more about standpoint epistemology in relation to "feminist" standpoints later. For now, the point is that the methodology of the critical tradition has provided an alternative to the otherwise dominant view of the scientific method and its assumptions.[8] And, as you will see, both Marxist and socialist feminists have built on this tradition in ways that are directly relevant to our question about the definition of feminist research methods.

Conclusion. These two alternative traditions, the interpretive-hermeneutic and the critical, are easily distinguishable from each other in terms of subject matter focus, purpose, specific methodologies, level of analysis, and so on. Yet they have both contributed to postempirical epistemology by providing the impetus and inspiration for developing a satisfactory alternative to empirical-analytical social science. More recent developments along these lines by Bernstein (1983), Gadamer (1975, 1980), Habermas (1984), and Hekman (1986), as well as by feminists, are delineated in a later section of this chapter.

To be discussed next are two events, one from within the practice of science itself and one from the history of science, which have also contributed to an erosion of the philosophers' and social scientists' endorsement of scientific methods. This erosion challenges the assumption of objectivity within the study of the natural world itself.

Science as Paradigm Shifting

In 1962 Thomas Kuhn published *The Structure of Scientific Revolutions.* Based on a historical analysis of the progress and success of Western science, his book redefined science in a way that had the effect of demythologizing it as pure truth in an ultimate sense. Until recently, most people thought of science as a cumulative process of the discovery of increasingly correct descriptions of the physical world. That is, there seemed to be an increasingly better fit between the theories of science and what we thought of as an independent, physical reality. The phenomenal success of scientific inquiry seemed to be a function of continuously testing increasingly accurate theories about nature against what was considered a given empirical reality. Kuhn's analysis challenged this conception of science, describing it instead as a social-historical process of paradigm transitions.

Paradigms are defined in two basic ways. First, as "the entire constellation of beliefs, values, techniques and so on shared by members of a given [scientific] community" (Kuhn, 1970:175). An example of such a constellation is the mechanical worldview of Newtonian physics. Second, paradigms are defined as concrete puzzle solutions that are like schema and are used as models to complete the full development of a particular theory. The mathematical expression, $f = ma$, for example, has various transformations that are similar in form but slightly different in content. That is, its specifics change as it is used to describe the movement of a simple pendulum, a gyroscope, or a vibrating string. Thus the use of this equation is an example of a puzzle-solution in physics. A paradigm shift, then, is a process whereby new ways of perceiving the world come to be accepted. According to Kuhn, paradigms function as maps or guides; they dictate the kinds of problems or issues that are important to address, the kinds of theories (explanations) that are acceptable, and the kinds of procedures that will solve the problems defined. At least they function this way until a new paradigm succeeds the old.

For example, it took several hundreds of years for scientists to exhaust all the possibilities presented by Isaac Newton's laws of motion, the paradigm that replaced Aristotelian laws of motion. Thus the work done in the aftermath of Newton's laws was carried out in the context of a single, widely accepted paradigm until Albert Einstein's work led to a rather different worldview and a new paradigm.

How do these transitions come about? Two conditions prompt them, according to Kuhn. The first is the presence and awareness of anomalies— that is, phenomena that either do not fit, contradict, or cannot be explained by the existing dominant paradigm. What is important is not only that they exist (because at any given time there are always anomalies) but that scientists take note of them and define them as counterinstances that challenge the truth or accuracy of the dominant paradigm, rather than defining them as irrelevant, bothersome, and unimportant minor deviations.

The second condition necessary for a paradigm transition (or what amounts to a scientific revolution) is the presence of an alternative paradigm, one that can account for both the phenomena that the earlier paradigm explained *and* the anomalies that it did not. During periods of what Kuhn called normal science, there is widespread agreement about the veracity of a paradigm, and the scientific work consists mainly of "mopping up" operations because it is primarily elaborating on and developing the implications of the paradigm. The work that occurs during transition or crisis periods, when two or more paradigms compete (for example, Galileo's heliocentric worldview versus the earth-centered model it replaced; Einsteinian versus Newtonian models of time/space) is called extraordinary science.

Kuhn's argument can be summarized by saying that data or observations are theory-laden (that is, the scientist only sees data in terms of their relevance to theory); that theories are paradigm-laden (explanations are grounded in worldviews); and that paradigms are culture-laden (worldviews, including ideas about human nature, vary historically and across cultures).

Kuhn's work and the discussion it generated contributed to the development of the postempiricist crisis of knowledge in several ways. First, it challenged the idea that the scientific process itself should not be examined in the same way that other phenomena are—that is, scientific statements themselves are now seen as more relative or specific to a given historical period and/or paradigm rather than as universals, as they are presented in science texts. As Bloor (1977) discussed, even mathematical principles are socially and historically grounded. Though the truth or correctness of "one plus one equals two" seems immutable, the meaning and interpretation of the number "one," for example, was different for the Greeks than it is for us. As Harding (1986) notes, they regarded one as the first (in the sense of a generator) of a lineage but not as an odd (as opposed to even) integer as we do.

Second, though Kuhn may not have intended it, his work challenged the idea of a fixed, absolute reality against which we test our notions about the natural world. Given Kuhn's description of science, it seems that objective reality changes with changing paradigms. After a scientific revolution, said Kuhn (1970:135), "The data themselves had changed. . . . Scientists work in a different world" because what they take to be the empirical world is shaped by the paradigms they use to understand it.

Third, Kuhn's work has prompted a closer look (if not just at the physical world) at what criteria are actually used to decide which of several competing paradigms about the natural world is more correct. Of course, scientists continue to use traditional criteria such as a paradigm's or theory's predictive accuracy, reliability, scope, consistency, fruitfulness, simplicity, or elegance. But Kuhn's analysis showed, in addition, the importance of agreement, or consensus, on the part of the scientific community, especially during a period of extraordinary science. Rather than clear-cut criteria and critical empirical tests, the criteria used were based on shared values, reasoned judgment, and the convincingness of an argument.

For example, the notion of the crucial experiment—one that produces results such that one of two or more competing theories can be ruled out—was seriously challenged. Again, because theories are incommensurable—they are grounded in distinct or separate frames of reference—there are no fixed criteria for determining one as more correct than the other. Theories and paradigms are comparable, of course, but the criteria are "open," and that openness includes discourse with other scientists. This idea poses a problem for some people because of its potential to lead to an inescapably relativistic view of our knowledge about the world. The question is whether subsequent paradigms are really progressive improvements compared to their predecessors or just different. Are all theories equally valuable and the dominance or acceptance of any one dependent on the outcome of scientists' talk and persuasion? There is a hermeneutic or interpretive dimension to science, which is increasingly being recognized by philosophers and historians of science (Giddens, 1982:14; Hekman, 1986; Heelan, 1983; Lyotard, 1984; Toulmin, 1982).

Quantum Physics

Another series of events that occurred within science itself has contributed to the questioning of the infallibility of scientific knowledge. This series was an even more direct challenge to the distinction between a subjective knower and an objective to-be-known world. That this scenario comes from physics is significant because of its adaption by the social sciences as a model for research.

During the first 30 years of the twentieth century experimental physicists discovered that subatomic particles (called quanta by Einstein and now known as photons) manifest both what had earlier been called wave-like (spread out over a large region of space) characteristics and particle-like (confined to a small volume) characteristics. Whether wave or particle likenesses emerged depended on the experimental situation—that is, the measuring apparatus and the experimenter's decision about the direction of the spin of the electron.[9] These experiments suggested that atomic objects do not have properties that are intrinsic to themselves and independent of their environment. Rather, what characterizes them is their interconnections, not their properties. As Capra (1982:80) said, "Subatomic particles have no meaning as isolated entities. . . . They can be understood only as interconnections or correlations between various processes of observation and measurement. Capra (1984:124) cited Niels Bohr, who wrote, "Isolated material particles are abstractions, their properties being definable and observable only through their interaction with other systems." Notice that there is a shift from single objects as the unit of analysis to relationships as the unit to be studied—in other words, things (objects) are defined by their relation to other things rather than as entities in and of themselves.

The development of quantum theory to account for these observations (which are anomalies in the Kuhnian sense) has helped us to question the idea of an external physical reality as independent, spatially separated events.

It also helped to introduce a new view of physical reality that is described as organic, holistic, ecological, systemic, and indivisible, replacing an older, more mechanistic worldview that underlies the assumptions of both Newtonian physics and traditional scientific methods. Furthermore, in quantum theory, events do not always have well-defined causes; they occur spontaneously (though not necessarily arbitrarily), and their occurrence seems to depend on the dynamics of a system rather than on a single cause.[10] There is a part/whole interconnectedness that seems to characterize the subatomic system.

The crucial feature of this interpretation of quantum mechanics (Keller, 1985) that is relevant to our discussion is that an observer is necessary to reveal the properties of subatomic phenomena—that is, the decision about how to observe these phenomena will determine the electron's properties to some extent. Thus the sharp division between mind and matter and between observer and the observed that is inherent in the assumed subject-object dichotomy referred to earlier could no longer be maintained.

What does all this have to do with feminist research? If Kuhn is right about science as it is actually practiced—that theory or paradigm choice depends to a considerable extent on normative consensus in the scientific community—then the physical and social sciences are not so different after all. This is because the physical sciences, having an interpretive dimension, are actually more like the social sciences rather than because the social sciences have successfully emulated the methods of the physical sciences. In the postempirical period we can paraphrase Hesse (1980:280–281), who said that in both the social and natural sciences, data are not detachable from theory; theories are models of the way the facts themselves are seen. Further, natural and social phenomena are interpreted by scientists in a language that is irreducibly metaphorical, and meanings are understood by theoretical coherence rather than by correspondence with facts. In other words, distinctions among different sciences or kinds of inquiry are moribund, and both the natural and social sciences have an interpretive or hermeneutic dimension.

We can summarize the impact of Kuhn's work and developments in quantum physics by noting first that the subject-object distinction in the physical world is being questioned. Thus, it is even more reasonable to do the same in the social sciences because the social sciences adapted this distinction from physics in the first place. Second, Kuhn's work made it clear that data do not necessarily speak for themselves; what is factual (what is regarded as data) greatly depends on the substantive content of one's theory. Theory, in turn, depends at least partly on one's social location, social identity, and research purposes.

To illustrate this last point, let's take a second, longer look at the nature of the feminist challenge to the assumptions of the scientific method as they are traditionally described. Like Kuhn's work on the nature of science and quantum mechanics in physics, feminist work has contributed to the growing crisis of knowledge.

THE FEMINIST CHALLENGE:
A SECOND LOOK

The nature of the feminist challenge is perhaps best illustrated by Harding's (1986) and Haraway's (1978) discussions of androcentric and feminist accounts of the origin of human society—that is, the evolutionary transition from the collective social life of nonhuman primates to that of prehominids and then to that of humans. These theories all acknowledge a major transition from forest to savanna life and, of course, the development of the unique characteristics of human physiology and anatomy that accompanied this transition (bipedalism, upright posture, tool use, development of symbolic communication). And they all hypothesize connections between savanna life, technology, diet, social organization, and selective processes. But here the similarity ends.

The most well-known androcentric theories stress the importance of hunting as an adaptation to the environment, regardless of whether the focus of the theory is on reproduction (Sir Solly Zuckerman); or production (Sherwood Washburn) (cited in Haraway, 1978). Zuckerman's argument, for example, is that human animals are basically solitary because life depends on competition for scarce resources. In this regard, males dominate females and males compete for females in order to maximize their own reproduction. He acknowledged that for humans some form of continuous association with others is necessary for survival, and that male dominance, therefore, is necessary to maintain order. His theory included references to several classically sexist claims: that female prostitution originated during this period and consisted of trading sexual favors for competitively scarce goods; that the harem is part of our evolutionary history and thus has biological roots; and that females are a threat to the social order precisely because of their sexual (reproductive) value.

Washburn's man-the-hunter theory is similar but focuses on the productive process as much as on the reproductive one. He also argued that male aggression toward females is adaptive because it allows them to mate more and thus have more offspring, and that natural selection pressures favored increased tool use, which facilitated a hunting way of life, the evolution of a larger brain, and language. Further, the consequences of hunting as an adaptation included increased curiosity, mobility, pleasure in hunting and killing, and the importance of the male (hunting) group because of its interdependence and cooperation.

Notice that in these theories, males as hunters are seen as responsible for most of our uniquely human traits and social life. One begins to wonder, as Hubbard (1979) did, how females evolved at all! Tanner and Zihlman (1976) developed the most complete account of human evolution that includes females as active agents in the evolutionary process. Like Washburn, they stressed production rather than reproduction, but their reconstruction was quite different. Their hypothesis was that gathering (both plants and animals) was the major dietary specialization of savanna living, and that this encouraged tool use and bipedalism, all of which interrelates with two important female activities: maternal socialization and female choice in sexual selection.

They argued that it is likely that female gatherers developed digging sticks, food containers, and, of great importance, baby-carrying devices. Gathering or foraging activity itself required knowledge about what was and what was not edible, where the best foods were found, and details of the local ecology—requirements that would have constituted selection pressure for the development of symbolic communication.

Survival in the savanna setting, then, would have depended on cunning, not fighting, and on cognitive processing, not aggression. And because human babies are hard to raise (the socialization process is much longer than it is for primates), females would choose friendly, nonthreatening males as mates, and there would have been selection for bisexual cooperation regarding child-raising. Notice their stress on female sexual choice versus the androcentric theories' stress on female passivity in reproduction.

It is important to note that both feminist and androcentric accounts operate within the context of scientifically sound modern physiology, genetics, and social theory. They are both "scientific." The Tanner and Zihlman account is more consistent with the most recent evidence we have about early human social life. This evidence arises from several sources, including studies of contemporary foraging societies (for example, the !Kung in the Kalahari Desert) and of the social interaction of chimpanzees. The use of chimps (versus baboons) as models is justified on the grounds that they are more like the stem population that preceded apes and hominids. That female chimps use tools more often than male chimps, that chimp social structure is flexible rather than rigid and hierarchical, that social continuity flows through females (through child socialization and close mother-child ties), and that female chimps choose their sexual partners all constitute evidence to support Zihlman and Tanner's reconstruction. In short, the feminist account reveals the androcentric bias of the earlier argument and is itself a more inclusive, less restrictive understanding of the earliest human foraging societies—even if it is not the final word on the subject.

Harding (1986) used a similar contrast between these androcentric and feminist accounts to pose a paradox that challenges our traditional understanding of the scientific method. She asked, How can work that is frankly political—the feminist researchers in this case were reacting to previous work that devalued women and were looking specifically for women's contributions—be more plausible, more acceptable, and more supported by the evidence than the so-called objective work of earlier researchers, which now looks blatantly androcentric in comparison? Though the feminist work was well in the context of traditional scientific methods, it was also purposely political. As Haraway (1978:56–57) described, Zihlman and Tanner appropriated sociobiology for feminist purposes. The question is, How can blatantly political research better fit the "facts" and now seem so acceptable?

One could argue, as Longino and Doell (1983) did, that the previously androcentric account was just not "good" science, that increased objectivity on the part of the researchers would have eventually resulted in a fairer treatment of women. But, as Harding pointed out, such an argument, which she calls "feminist empiricism," suggests that objectivity in science depends on the researcher as much as on the method. This contradicts the depiction of science as a more or less foolproof procedure that relies on observation to test theories and hypotheses about the world. The procedure itself is purported to guarantee that such testing can be done by any competent person (Theodorson and Theodorson, 1969). (This is the assumption of intersubjective verifiability that was mentioned earlier.) If objectivity depends on the researcher, how can it be guaranteed? If androcentric results are just bad science to be replaced eventually by good or better science, why is it that androcentric theories like man-the-hunter last as long as they do (why did no one notice evidence against it earlier), and why is it that they are now being corrected not by androcentric scientists themselves but by feminists with conscious intent to change this androcentrism? The central question is, How can feminist consciousness produce better science than androcentric scientists? Explaining such different theories of the same phenomena in terms of bad versus good science, then, implies that using data or observation as the ultimate criterion to prove or disprove theories does not guarantee objectivity after all.

It is important to realize that the dilemma posed by the relativist position—that is, the lack of agreement about criteria for sure knowledge—is a problem that is also shared by feminist scholars. They must either justify the feminist alternative by appealing to some accepted or shared standards or accept a pluralistic stance. But as Harding (1986) noted, feminists, after all, are not interested in having their work be *part* of a broader relativism, one of many multiple realities. Their goal is to *replace* patriarchal models with feminist ones. Nevertheless, in feminist work as a whole there seems to be some tension between the desire to replace nonfeminist with feminist models and a tolerance for plurality (see Stanley and Wise's [1983] discussion of false consciousness and related terms). All of this raises the question of what criteria we should use to prove that feminist explanations are more adequate than others and to decide which among the many feminist approaches are the best.

Feminist work has contributed to the questioning of scientifically based knowledge as absolute by providing numerous examples of work in different disciplines that both highlight the bias of previous work and provide alternative explanations that are more complete and more comprehensive, albeit from the feminist's own "biased" perspective. This, indeed, is the strength of the feminist contribution to postempirical philosophy of science. It provides exemplars that concretely and specifically illustrate the weaknesses of explanations produced by traditional social scientists and at the same time provides alternatives to those explanations.[11]

Because of this exemplary work, the feminist challenge can be considered as more significant, more critical, and also more potentially reconstructive than other critical traditions (Bowles, 1984). Bernstein (1983:121) described phenomenologists, for example, as having "a tendency to talk constantly about phenomenology and what it can achieve, rather than . . . *do* phenomenological analysis" (emphasis in original). That feminist inquiry does more than talk about the problems and limitations of traditional science is, I think, its most significant achievement. The purpose of this book, consisting of exemplary feminist work, is to underscore and highlight this contribution.

FEMINIST INQUIRY AS A
PARADIGM SHIFT

The importance of feminist scholarship in the present context, then, is that it has contributed to the development of a solution to the contemporary epistemological crisis. This impact can be seen more clearly by first considering the new scholarship on women as a paradigm shift in the Kuhnian sense. Then I will discuss how feminist research has informed more abstract philosophical discussions of postempiricist epistemology.

Many writers (Evans, 1983:223; Farnham, 1987; Klein, 1983:97–99; Stanley and Wise, 1983:154–156; Tetreault, 1985) have indicated (though sometimes in passing) the paradigmatic implications of feminist scholarship. Indeed, it is so assumed that Stacey and Thorne (1985) referred to a "missing revolution" in the discipline of sociology precisely because it has not been as deeply transformed by feminist work as some other disciplines.[12]

In attempting to develop this theme I have drawn two conclusions. One is that the development and growth of women studies as a body of scholarship and an academic discipline provide a useful test of the very abstract paradigm shift concept. Thus we can ask both how or to what extent women studies constitutes a paradigm shift *and* how adequate the paradigm shift notion is for describing the reality of women studies scholarship. Juxtaposing this reality against the concept seems especially useful because of the considerable ambiguity, confusion, and disagreement about the word paradigm. Indeed, one reason for this confusion is that there are so few widely agreed-upon examples of paradigms (as opposed to theoretical perspectives) in the social sciences that we have trouble identifying what does and does not constitute a paradigm shift.

In this respect, Kuhn did eventually limit his originally broad and multifaceted definition of paradigm to two aspects: the general worldview idea and the puzzle-solving formula presented earlier. Yet his substantive examples are all from the physical and natural sciences. Though he described the social sciences as preparadigmatic, the term paradigm is used loosely in the social sciences to mean perspective, worldview, metatheory, assumptions about reality, schema, and theoretical orientation, all of which are more like the first definition given by Kuhn than the second.

A second conclusion that arises from considering feminist scholarship as a paradigm shift is that the irreducible element in all feminist analysis is its focus on the distinctive experience of women—that is, seeing women rather than just men in center stage, as both subject matter of and creators of knowledge. As Stimpson (1983:1) said, "The study of women is important." The full sense in which this is a paradigm shift becomes clear only after considering all of its implications. This seemingly simple but obviously important shift from male-centered perspectives influences what is studied (what a discipline's problematics are, as the philosophers of science say) and how it is studied.

Consider the problematics of the discipline of women studies, for example. In the same way that scientists after 1895 began to see x-rays where they had not seen them before (Kuhn, 1970:58), the feminist perspective has generated the study of phenomena previously not extensively considered by social scientists—for example rape, wife abuse, heterosexuality, childbirth, housework, incest, sexual harassment, pornography, and prostitution. Each of these reflects a theme of sexual politics not previously articulated. Other examples include the gendered nature of language, environmental policy, technology, body language, everyday talk, and advertisements.[13] What was previously invisible (sometimes not yet even named) has become visible. In this text we include Fishman's "Interaction: The Work Women Do" and Kathlene's "A New Approach to Understanding the Impact of Gender on the Legislative Process" as examples of studies that show gender relevance in substantive areas where it was previously invisible. Fishman nicely exposes otherwise unnoticed ways in which everyday conversation operates to maintain male dominance. Kathlene's paper suggests gender differences in social policy formation on the part of state legislators.

To consciously adopt a woman's perspective means to see things one did not see before and also to see the familiar rather differently. So an obvious but important way in which feminist research constitutes a paradigm shift is exemplified by the many reinterpretations, reconstructions, and reanalyses of existing data from the new perspective. Examples include Weiner's (1979) reexamination of Trobriand kinship (to compare to Bronislaw Malinowski's earlier well-known study of this group) and Gough's (1971) reexamination of Nuer kinship (vis-à-vis E. E. Evans-Pritchard's work on the same subject). In this book, Howard Kushner's reanalysis and reinterpretation of suicide data and Janet Shibley Hyde's reanalysis of data on sex differences in verbal and mathematical abilities exemplify this type of feminist work.

Feminist inquiry has also successfully generated anomalies—data or observations that do not fit received theory. The best example is Kelly-Gadol's (1976) work in history, which showed that the Renaissance was not a renaissance after all, at least for women. And once this anomaly was realized, other standard historical periods in history were challenged in the same way. That is, historians started asking, Does the labeling of a period adequately reflect the experience of the female half of the population? Another well-known example of anomalies generated by the feminist perspective is Gilligan's (1982) work on moral development. She showed that middle-class women do not accurately fit the model that Lawrence Kohlberg has assumed was universal. The alternative theory that she developed to adequately account for the moral development of women is an example of another aspect of the larger process of paradigm shift. Her theory provides a specific, alternative, substantive explanation that is more inclusive than the earlier one. Another example of feminist research along these lines that is reprinted in this text is Myra Marx Ferree's summary of research on German working women. It transcends the distinction between public and domestic spheres of life, a dichotomy that has been assumed and unquestioned in family and occupational research and even emphasized in earlier feminist work (for example, Rosaldo and Lamphere, 1974; Rosaldo, 1980). All of these examples illustrate a final aspect of paradigm shifting also recognized by Kuhn: that the new paradigm contains both old and new elements.

Two other features of the paradigm shift model described by Kuhn, resistance and conversion, can be seen in feminist research. The resistance to feminist work in both formal and informal everyday interaction and in published work (as described by Aiken et al., 1987) parallels Kuhn's description of the tendency of scientists to ignore anomalies and maintain received theories for as long as possible.[14] Kuhn used the word conversion to describe the process by which individuals eventually endorse the new paradigm. Likewise, a conversion of sorts frequently occurs after exposure to feminist scholarship. Note that many (usually younger and/or less traditional) researchers do not need to go through a conversion because the new view had become the received one during their professional lifetimes and was thus part of their professional training. They essentially "grew up" with the new view.

This last point underscores another parallel between Kuhn's description and the emergence of women studies as a discipline: that paradigm shifts are more likely to occur at the margin of a society or discipline. Kuhn noted that some researchers—younger people and those in between different disciplines—are more likely to formulate as well as adopt new paradigms. This pattern is seen in women studies, a discipline characterized by young, nontenured, female, interdisciplinary scholars.

Another interesting but perhaps more controversial aspect of feminist scholarship that fits the paradigm shift model is the increasing tendency of women studies scholars (for example, Stanley and Wise, 1983:154–156) to describe some aspects of feminist work as *normal* scholarship—that is, the filling out, completing, "mopping up" operations (as Kuhn called them). Indeed, much feminist scholarship flows rather predictably from the initial shift. That is, once the commitment to study women is made, scholarship is somewhat predictable. For example, one can ask of almost any theory in psychology, history, sociology, and so on, "Does this work for women?" and generate new scholarship. Such a query becomes a challenge (an anomaly) to the theory if the experience of women does not fit, a confirmation of it if it does, or an elaboration of it if it does in some ways and not in others. The possibilities are seemingly endless, which is, of course, one reason women studies scholarship has expanded so rapidly.

These obvious directions in some respects constitute the Kuhnian mopping up operations of normal science. This term should not be construed as belittling because it is precisely through such work that anomalies become apparent and the discipline grows, develops, and matures. A case in point is the recent realization on the part of feminist scholars that their theories excluded nonwhite women and men. If the paradigm shift process is accurate, this realization would not have happened without the cumulative development of women's scholarship in the normal sense.

Another way of illustrating the normal and extraordinary sides of women studies is to differentiate ongoing normal scholarship (that is, work that answers the paradigmatic questions outlined above) from the extraordinary conversion processes that occurred earlier in the discipline's history and now seem to reoccur during what are called women studies integration projects. These projects are somewhat formal, organized efforts that consciously and purposively juxtapose the "men's studies" that is in the minds of most faculty members with the new scholarship on women. Such juxtapositioning sometimes leads to resistance (Aiken et al., 1987) but it also leads to gradual, and sometimes not so gradual, conversion. Of course, these processes are not easily delineated in life, and the attempt to describe women studies in these terms illustrates what many have realized when discussing the implications of *The Structure of Scientific Revolutions:* that the distinction between normal and extraordinary is not nearly as sharp as Kuhn suggested. Nevertheless, we can recognize a normal component of women studies that is different from the initial gestalt-like shift in perspective. It is not surprising, then, that MacKinnon (1982:519) defined consciousness-raising as "the major technique of analysis, structure of organization, method of practice, and theory of social change of the women's movement."

Using women studies as a sort of test of Kuhn's concept, however, brings out some interesting limitations of his model, though one might conclude that his analysis is more incomplete than wrong. Probably most important is the almost total absence of discussion about events external to the scientific enterprise. It is perhaps obvious by now that a closer look at the political and economic context of periods of scientific revolution would help to explain (at least as well as the internal factors that Kuhn cited) scientists' acceptance of a new theory.[15] Feminist research, for example, began as a result of consciousness-raising that would not have occurred without the women's movement that began in the 1960s.

In this regard, consider Ritzer's (1975) diagram of the paradigm shift process:

Paradigm 1⟶Normal Science⟶Anomalies⟶

Crisis⟶Revolution⟶Paradigm 2, and so on.

Using this diagram to describe women studies requires an added factor called feminist consciousness, or focus on women, a factor that came from outside the respective disciplines. Thus:

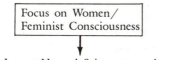

Paradigm 1 ——▶Normal Science——▶Anomalies ——▶

Crisis——▶Revolution——▶Paradigm 2, and so on.

In other words, this revolution did not originate within the process of research and scholarship. An interest in women produced anomalies rather than the other way around. We now know that studying women *had* produced anomalies in several well-known studies, but they were not recognized as such. In David McClelland's work on achievement, for example, the responses of women subjects confounded results based on the responses of male subjects, so he essentially eliminated female subjects from the process of theory development. Similarly, in Lawrence Kohlberg's work on moral development, female subjects differed from male subjects and were thus defined by him as less developed morally. In short, feminist consciousness juxtaposed with knowledge of traditional disciplines is leading to new substantive theories and paradigms based on women's inclusion.

An important implication of describing feminist research as a paradigm shift is that it indicates a nontextbook approach to teaching feminist methods. I agree with Kuhn (1970) and Polanyi (1958) when they questioned the value of abstracting methods from specific research studies and then formally presenting them in textbooks. Their argument is that paradigms, theories, methodologies, and specific research strategies are so interrelated that the better way to learn the methods of a discipline (whether feminist or not) is by becoming acquainted with exemplars or models of its best work. Knowledge of this sort is tacit rather than formal. Partly for this reason most of this text consists of exemplars of feminist methods, and only a few articles are about feminist methods in the abstract—but even these (the Westkott, Cook and Fonow, and Anderson et al. chapters), are not limited to a discussion of specific methodologies per se, but stress the importance of methodology informed by feminist perspectives and purposes.

My preference to exemplify rather than lecture about feminist methods also partly explains why all the research articles in this volume have an empirical component. I want students to see firsthand the interconnection between what we call theory and what we call data. Another reason for the empirical emphasis is that feminist methods, as I said earlier, is still developing. We do not know yet what it will look like in the future. In the meantime, however, feminist instructors would like to teach and students would like to learn how to do feminist research that has an empirical component. Teaching by example helps to satisfy this need. A final reason for the empirical emphasis in this text is that there are already many good feminist theory texts and readers available, and although some of these illustrate the intricate interconnection of paradigms, theories, and data, such connections are not often the main point.

You will notice that the empirical works in this book all nicely illustrate feminist research but might not be included in a list of the most-cited or best-known works in women studies. I purposely selected high quality but "routine" (normal?) research in women studies in order to emphasize the power of the shift we have been discussing. Notwithstanding the brilliance, hard work, and sound scholarship of the researchers themselves, the shift itself has generated new knowledge that is worth rereading.

FROM PARADIGM SHIFT TO FEMINIST STANDPOINTS AND DIALECTICAL PROCESSES

If feminist inquiry represents a paradigm shift, it is a shift toward what Hartsock (1983), Harding (1986), Jaggar (1983) and others called feminist standpoints.[16] Standpoint is defined by Jaggar as "a position in society from which certain features of reality come into prominence and from which others are obscured" (p. 382). Feminist standpoints begin with but do not end with women's experiences, and as in the case of other standpoint epistemologies, they are more than perspectives. They involve a level of awareness and consciousness about one's social location and this location's relation to one's lived experience. In this section I develop more in depth the nature of feminist standpoints.

Following Hartsock (1983), we first note that much of women's work in modern industrial societies (childrearing and housework, but also some market work) (1) involves an emphasis on change (versus stasis); (2) is characterized by interaction with natural substances (versus work that separates one from nature); (3) emphasizes quality versus quantity; and (4) involves in most activities a mind/body unity that is not found in administrative, intellectual, and managerial work. In short, traditional women's work involves everyday contact with material necessities (clothes, meals, bodies) and attention to natural changes in natural substances. I should add that these aspects of women's work are also often characteristic of the work of working-class and blue-collar men.

Further differences between women's work and most men's work include the fact that women simply work more (that is, more hours per day); that a greater proportion of their work is unpaid; that it is structured more by repetition; and that it is sensuous. Finally, women's reproductive work (childbearing and childrearing) involves more body involvement and is more relational and interpersonal. Smith (1979) made a similar distinction between women's work as being in the "bodily mode" and men's work in the "abstract, conceptual mode."

Given these differences in everyday work activities as well as in socialization experiences by sex,[17] women's and men's perspectives are not only (potentially) very different, but inverted, or at odds with each other. The premise here is: You are what you do. Further, Hartsock and feminist standpoint advocates argue that women are more able to see the viewpoints of both men and women, and thus a woman's understanding is potentially more complete, deeper, and more complicated. The implication for developing a specifically feminist epistemology is that a woman's perspective (if transformed through consciousness-raising) will lead to more accurate, more complex knowledge.

This last aspect of the standpoint concept is what makes it both promising and problematic. On the one hand, the potential for transcendence is there— that is, the perspective of a more complex understanding of social relations could promote change for the betterment of all or have a liberating effect. On the other hand, the standpoint concept implies that one group's perspective is more real (better or more accurate) than anothers. And "more accurate" implies that there are some criteria for accuracy. So again we are confronted with the problematic idea of an objective reality.

A second problem with standpoint epistemologies in general and feminist standpoints in particular is that they imply that the more oppressed or more disadvantaged group has the greatest potential for knowledge construction. If the group's view is less superficial and more encompassing than others', its knowledge should prevail. When carried to its logical conclusion, however, the implication of this notion is that the greater the oppression, the broader or more inclusive one's potential knowledge is, a conclusion that few scholars can agree with. This conclusion leads one into a discussion that is not very productive about who is more oppressed (and how to prove it) and therefore potentially more knowledgeable.

Dialectical processes. More relevant for our purposes is Westkott's (1979) description and analysis (which appear in this book) of the dialectical tension that characterizes both women's experience and feminist research. As developed by Westkott, *dialectical* refers to discontinuities, oppositions, contradictions, tensions, and dilemmas that form part of women's concrete experience in patriarchal worlds—dilemmas that are realized only with a feminist consciousness.

Consider, for example, that according to tests that measure popular, ideal sex stereotypes such as the Bem Sex Role Inventory (Bem, 1976), a woman in our society who is gullible and yielding is conforming to a feminine ideal. Yet these same attributes would limit one's ability to be effective in the world at large. Or consider the normative expectation that women (and, earlier, U.S. Blacks) present themselves as smiling and cheerful. Compliance means conforming to a stereotyped role and some degree of social invisibility. Noncompliance means risking being labeled bitchy, difficult, or angry (Frye, 1988). Similarly, a young woman's decision about being sexually active puts her in a no-win situation: If she chooses to be active, she risks social censure as well as pregnancy and/or the side effects of dangerous contraceptives. If she chooses not to be sexually active, she risks being defined as prudish or frigid. Also consider a woman's conformity to body-damaging and body-limiting fashions such as high heels, girdles, panty hose, tight skirts, and so on. Nonconformity is better for her body but it means she appears different and even weird. As Westkott put it, women "oppose the very conditions to which they conform."

Westkott's examples of dialectical tension focus on the contradictions of women scholars and researchers—for example, that women feminist scholars are both "inside," or part of, their disciplines and "outside" of them due to their feminist perspectives, and that women's creativity often expresses a discontinuity between consciousness and action. The notion of dialectical tension and the creativity it generates is well developed in the Westkott chapter in this book. The point is that dialectical processes characterize feminist inquiry in many different ways and at different levels. This is evident in many of the contributions to this book. Sometimes it is explicit, as in Anderson et al., who illustrate the importance in obtaining oral history of gently probing and listening for a woman's subjective meanings of her behavior, which are often at variance with the meanings internalized from the larger society. A dialectical theme is also evident in Tsing's account of Induan Hiling, a female shaman in the Meratus Mountains of Indonesian Borneo, who endorsed and used the spiritual tradition of her culture yet simultaneously challenged and revised it. The dialectical theme is even more dramatically or forcefully expressed in Ferree's report of working-class women in Germany who are neither completely in the public nor the domestic sphere, but stand precariously between the two. Finally, Kushner's reinterpretation of the meaning of suicide for women (and men) suggests that when a woman takes her own life it may be a behavioral way of rebelling against the situation she is in, though this theory contradicts the assumed nonaggressive nature of women.

FROM FEMINIST STANDPOINTS TO
FUSION OF HORIZONS

I said earlier that feminist inquiry is contributing to a transformation of methodology and resolution of the epistemological crisis by producing exemplary research in a reconstructive postempirical context. The postempirical period has been characterized by many efforts to identify and delineate research strategies that are alternatives to positivism—for example, Gergen (1982) and Reason and Rowan (1981). Most of these efforts are best described as "contextual" in that they are variations of the relativistic theme we outlined earlier. They are satisfying and sophisticated because they build on the recognition that social knowledge itself is socially constructed in context and in interaction with others. But they do not directly answer the lingering question, How do we know what we know? In other words, they do not explicitly lead the researcher out of the "either (objectivism)/or (relativism)" dilemma with which we began this Introduction. Without agreed-upon, demonstrable criteria, how does one argue for a given feminist interpretation?

Yet out of the postempirical context, such criteria are being developed. As a tentative guideline, we can adapt Bernstein's (1976:xiv) formula: "An adequate, comprehensive . . . social theory must be at once empirical, interpretive, and critical." Empirical, interpretive, and critical: These are our criteria for now. Several other writers (Bowles, 1984; Farganis, 1986; Kasper, 1986; Wolff, 1975) have explicitly proposed the integration of epistemological aspects of feminism with the hermeneutic and critical theory traditions. And though they did not consider feminist inquiry, both Hekman's (1986) and Bernstein's (1983) syntheses of major contemporary writers in these traditions can be appropriated for our purposes.

Bernstein argued first that we (postempiricist researchers) can move "beyond relativism and objectivism" to endorse a new approach to knowledge and research. By this he meant that we are now abandoning (and rightly so) the either/or stance about irrefutable knowledge that I described at the beginning of this Introduction. In other words, there is something in between a foundation for irrefutable knowledge and relativism with all its problems: a synthesis of several major ideas from the traditions we outlined earlier.

To begin this synthesis, consider the problem of anthropologists studying another culture. To understand a culture other than their own, researchers can relate to the object of understanding (the other culture) in several possible ways. The first is to study the other culture using the standards or norms of the researchers' own cultures as criteria against which the other society is evaluated. This, of course, is ethnocentrism at its worst and is considered unacceptable, although Western researchers are often nonconsciously ethnocentric. A second possibility is for the researchers to do as Schutz advocated and "bracket" (that is, hold in abeyance) their own judgments, beliefs, norms, and standards while studying the other culture. But this is what more recent hermeneutic thinkers have said is impossible. Gadamer, in particular, argued the opposite of earlier writers, asserting that one cannot escape from one's own assumptions or worldview. He said that there is no such thing as knowledge outside of a frame of reference.

A third possibility is to adopt the view of the alien culture—to "go native" as anthropologists say. Though not always practical, going native can be considered a form of relativism—that is, acknowledging the coexistence and legitimacy of different perspectives. It tends, however, to lead to the skeptical position described earlier: that there is no way to decide which interpretation of a culture is "better," and thus all are equally correct.

Bernstein likened the dilemma of trying to study another culture without being ethnocentric or going native to that of choosing among alternative paradigms or theories in the natural sciences and to considering alternative interpretations of works of art or literature. These are both different manifestations of the same problem because the processes involved (choosing, judging, weighing evidence for or against a given argument, and so on) and the outcome are partly determined on the basis of dialogue with other members of the scientific or academic community.

One could argue that there is no need to determine one view as more correct, that a plurality of views could prevail. But at some point—such as when important decisions have to be made—some view of reality must be endorsed. To develop a policy about abortion, for example, one would have to take a stance in an area where there are conflicting, seemingly irreconcilable views. Or consider the practice of introducing or imposing Western technology and normative standards—exploitive factory-based manufacturing and other forms of commercialization—into non-Western cultures. The British government's outlawing and eventual eradication of suttee (the practice of burning or burying women alive with their deceased husbands) in Hindu India is another case in point.[18] Whose standards of rationality, meaning, or ethics should prevail? During an official state visit, former First Lady Rosalyn Carter walked behind the then President Carter in order to conform to the host country's norms. Yet that behavior contradicted another normative standard: that women and men be treated equally. Though this is a single instance, it is a public, visible example of the issue at hand. So the question is not just whose standards should prevail but what criteria we use when different groups' standards conflict, compete, or differ. In these cases, decisions have to be made and they inevitably reflect assumptions, or theories, about human nature and social relations between children and adults and men and women.

The dilemma, then, is that once one rejects objectivism, the alternative seems to be a kind of relativism that is not very satisfying. This problem involving the various possible relations between the researcher and the researched captures the crisis in modern epistemology. Further, these examples illustrate the extent to which ethical and practical policy issues are part of the larger process of knowledge formation.

Let us go back to the argument that one cannot separate oneself from one's own historical, cultural context. Gadamer (1976), building on (but differentiating himself from) the hermeneutic tradition, argued that it is precisely through the interplay between one's existing cognitions or values (what he called prejudgments) and the elements of other cultures or new theories that one develops knowledge. In other words, one's prejudgments, or prejudices, makes one more open-minded than closed-minded when one puts these prejudgments at risk, testing them through exposure to and encounter with others' prejudgments. Prejudgments, in Gadamer's (1976:9) words, "constitute the initial directedness of our whole ability to experience. Prejudices are biases of our openness to the world. They are simply conditions whereby we experience something—whereby what we encounter says something to us. . . ."

Prejudgments, then, are the means by which one reaches the truth. Gadamer argued further that prejudice is the ontological condition of humans in the world. Rather than bracketing them, we should use prejudgments as essential building blocks or components for acquiring new knowledge. To know, one needs to be aware of one's own prejudice but one cannot, indeed, should not, try to transcend them. It is necessary to go back and forth between the old and new theories, paradigms, cultures, or worldviews to create a new synthesis. (In fact, one of the weaknesses of earlier [Schutzian] phenomenology is that the emphasis on individual intent in order to find the meaning of behavior makes it difficult to develop and acknowledge the fact that meaning is intersubjective, negotiated, and therefore collective rather than individual [Hekman, 1986].)

This back and forth process is captured in Westkott's characterization of feminist inquiry as dialectical and in Gadamer's notion of "fusion of horizons," which we can now use to more completely describe feminist inquiry. *Horizon* in this context refers to the full range of one's standpoint and includes the particulars of one's situation (for example, historical time, place, culture, class; any number of contextual variables are appropriate here). The *fusion* results from seeking knowledge while grounded in a perspective (in this case, feminism) that cannot be bracketed or held aside during the inquiry process. So one's horizon is described as necessarily limited and finite. At the same time, however, it is open to relating or connecting with horizons other than one's own (for example, feminist work does not ignore men the way androcentric work ignores women). The resulting fusion represents an enlargement, broadening, or enrichment of one's own horizon (as when feminist work is more inclusive than previous work).

The fusion of horizons concept carries the double, or dual, vision and dialectical notions a step further than do standpoint epistemologies because it indicates a transcendent third and new view, or synthesis. This next step in knowledge generation is captured in expressions like beyond- or post-feminism. Too often, such expressions are used by people who show no indication of ever having had a feminist perspective. Even so, some contemporary feminist writers hint at a "next step." Support for a beyond-feminism notion, for example, can be found in results from some women studies integration projects (described earlier as organized, formal programs designed to integrate the new scholarship on women into the curriculum, usually via faculty development). Faculty are expected to become familiar with the new scholarship and revise a targeted course accordingly. Evaluation of these projects supports the notion that faculty often move through a series of stages, from male-centered to increasingly female-centered ways of thinking, with the final stage variously described in post-feminist terms (Nielsen and Abromeit, 1989; Tetreault, 1985). This pattern is similar to what is described by the fusion idea, where one's view is enlarged and broadened by the clashing of two cultures; in this case, however, it is male-dominated versus feminist paradigms that clash.

To further clarify this fusion notion and at the same time incorporate more fully the critical and emancipatory element of feminist inquiry, I will use a metaphor: Consider an ordinary everyday conversation between two people. If the context or setting is free enough—if the two people respect and trust each other and are roughly equal in materialistic terms—then both are free to engage in unlimited dialogue, and the resulting conversation is potentially very constructive, creative, and somewhat indeterminant (that is, not very predictable). Even if one of the parties has an agenda (or prejudgments, to use Gadamer's term), the course of the conversation and its outcome are not predictable. Because verbal interaction is so dynamic, the discussants' ideas, thoughts, beliefs, and statements get developed, modified, and expanded in the course of being juxtaposed with other ideas, thoughts, theories, and so on.

This is what happens (or can happen if the process of knowledge development is completely free) in our pursuit of knowledge. To the extent that knowledge formation is a dialogic process, as we have seen, it is an open process that requires a context of equality. Knowledge construction requires the material and social conditions that promote freedom and equality and that have no obstacles to open dialogue. It is in this way that we incorporate a critical dimension into our blueprint for knowledge. Feminist work is emancipatory in that it identifies obstacles to the kind of equality necessary for dialogue. Our agenda for knowledge construction, then, includes removing the structural features and barriers that distort or limit open, free dialogue.

Addressing the emancipatory element of feminist work more directly, Smith (1977, 1979), Westkott (1983), and others have argued that feminist research is *for* rather than *about* women. We should not forget that the original impetus for feminist inquiry was to find an educational strategy for eradicating sexism. Our goal after all is women's liberation, and we assume that creative and scholarly work can contribute to reaching it. As Westkott (1983) said, we cannot leave out the emancipatory element—that is, the opposition to as well as understanding of sexism, the judging of as well as seeing sexism. Both theory and "praxis" (the inseparable action component of critical theory)[19] are vital to feminist inquiry. Westkott talked about the importance of holding criticism (of sexism in society) in tension with vision (a new feminist worldview) as well as the importance of the interaction between social knowledge and self-knowledge, which produces both anger about and distance from knowledge of women's subordination. In a phrase, "The personal becomes intellectual, and the intellectual, personal" (Westkott, 1983:211).

The feminist scholarship included in this text is implicitly or explicitly critical. Two chapters describe women's active involvement in both organized and individually motivated efforts for social change (the chapters by Gluck and Tsing). Two chapters describe and criticize male-only perspectives in documentation and the research process itself: Kushner criticizes the stereotypes that inform statistics on suicide, and Hyde criticizes how statistically derived but miniscule sex differences in cognitive ability are misused. Fishman's analysis of how women do the work of everyday conversation between intimates is more implicitly critical, as is Kathlene's elaboration and implied celebration of a contextualist approach to public policy formation.

So far we have talked about some of the interpretive and emancipatory aspects of feminist research. We can now broaden our characterization of feminist work to include its empirical aspect by justifying empirical as a criterion. Throughout this Introduction, I have been somewhat inconsistent in my presentation of empiricism. On the one hand, I presented it as part of the classical, objective tradition that many are saying has run its course. On the other hand, I said that one criterion I used for choosing the articles for this book was empirical content—that they include at least some data or observations relevant to the writer's argument. As Haraway (1981) pointed out, it is contradictory to expose bad science (that is, biased work that is presented as objective truth)—thereby implicitly showing the constructed character of all science—and then to produce feminist science with its own facts. If *all* facts are theory-laden and thus laden with value and history, how can we say feminist facts are any truer than androcentric or nonfeminist ones? To the extent that it is more complete, more inclusive, more comprehensive, and more complex, feminist work comes closer to realizing, or at least better exemplifying, the fusion of horizons process we have described here. Further, there are several reasons for preferring some form of empiricism to presentations that are empty of empirical reference.

First, it would be archaic to endorse a return to nonempirical inquiry. In this respect, I would argue that we should retain the element of empiricism in any definition of what good inquiry is for the same reason that it was originally advocated: to help protect and guard against the use of superstition or personal bias (rather than evidence) as a basis for knowledge, though we have to acknowledge that the empiricist element does not guarantee much. But more substantively, we can justify the use of facts and observations with the use of a modified, distinctive definition of the term *objective*, one that distinguishes it from *objectivism*. Ricoeur (1977) made this distinction when he described both social action and written text as objective in the sense that, once performed (or written), both are "outside" of the actor, creator, or initiator. This attribute makes them available to the rest of the world, to the public. This sense of objectivity is consistent with our interpretation of knowledge production as a communal, intersubjective, dialogic examination or observation of facts and can be distinguished from objectivism, the assumption of a reality that is separate and distant from a subjective knower. In this way, "objectively" shared empirical evidence is part of the fusion of horizons that seems to be the beginning or basis of a viable postempirical epistemology. A final reason for preferring empirical to nonempirical work is that the rest of the world is still grounded in empiricist science. To convince others, to even talk to others, we need facts, observations, and data to support our arguments. As Weisstein (1979:187) said, "Evidence became a friend of mine."

CONCLUSION

We started this Introduction with a question of what constitutes knowledge. It seems appropriately feminist to end it with a request that knowledge address itself to the "big" but practical questions. Bowles (1983:42) said it well. "For me, that means, what do we need to know in order to survive? (This takes us to such 'problems' as nuclear power and ecology.) And, if we do survive, what do we have to know in order to live relatively peacefully and happily together? (This takes us to such 'problems' as the relationship between people of different sexes and races and classes.)"[20]

But enough talk *about* feminist methods. Let us consider some exemplary feminist inquiry. This book contains works by authors from various social science disciplines (sociology, history, anthropology, and political science).

In Part 1, the authors elaborate and develop some of the themes I have introduced. Included are contributions by Keller, who provides a well-developed and fascinating explanation for the masculine character of science itself; Westkott, whose work has already been discussed to some extent; Cook and Fonow, who very specifically and concretely describe feminist methodologies; and Anderson et al., whose presentation of oral history sets the stage for Part 2.

In Part 2, Gluck exemplifies feminist inquiry through oral history; Tsing presents a combination of anthropological fieldwork and feminist literary analysis; Ferree reviews some unusual survey and interview work with women workers; Kushner reanalyzes and reinterprets data on sex differences in suicide rates; Hyde challenges arguments for sex differences in cognitive abilities with a reanalysis of quantitative data; and Fishman and Kathlene present two kinds of linguistic analysis.

NOTES

1. "Postempirical" refers rather generally to a turning point in contemporary philosophy of science, epistemology, sociology of knowledge, and related fields. This turning point is characterized by work toward the development of an alternative to scientific methods for studying the social and cultural world. More detail and information about events leading up to this transition and the nature of the developing alternatives follow.

2. For accounts of the substantive impact feminist scholarship has had on various disciplines, see Du Bois et al. (1985), Farnham (1987), Langland and Gove (1983), Spender (1981), and Stacey and Thorne (1985).

3. See the chapter by Hyde in this volume for a challenge to the popular notion that men excel at math.

4. In contrasting foundationalism, defined by Hekman (1986:8) as belief in "an indubitable element of human existence that can 'ground' human knowledge" with relativism, I am following Bernstein (1983). He showed that the objectivism-relativism contrast is more relevant to contemporary epistemological issues than is the older objective-subjective dichotomy.

5. Freeman's work received the American Political Science Association's prize for the best work on women and politics in 1975.

6. Sometimes less and more objective data are called *soft* and *hard*, respectively. The hard-soft distinction, with its implicit evaluation that hard is better, is just one of many examples of genderisms in science (see Keller, 1985).

7. Some, but not all, writers in this tradition exempt knowledge about the physical world from this claim.

8. As an important part of what is called received, or generally accepted, knowledge, scientific methods and products can be seen as supporting the status quo, or serving the interests of the majority or dominant group. This does not mean that they always have done so. There are many historical and contemporary cases of scientists and scientific knowledge representing minority views, and opposing a nonscientific dominant view (for example, religious views that conflict with scientific views). However, science (along with its accompanying technology) has become a dominant worldview and to that extent serves someone's interests.

9. In the Einstein-Podolsky-Rosen (EPR) experiment as described by Capra (1982:83).

10. Perhaps this is what inspired the bumper sticker, which is currently popular, that reads, "Shit Happens," a phrase that belies the cause-and-effect assumption outlined earlier.

11. Some well-known examples of feminist inquiry that have this character include Kelly-Gadol (1976), Slocum (1975), Rubin (1975), Chodorow (1978), Dinnerstein (1976), Gilligan (1979), and Jaggar (1983).

12. Strathern (1987) is an exception to the widespread implicit or explicit adoption of this model. Her argument is developed in footnote 14.

13. The gender relevance of environmental policy and technology comes from the "women and nature," or the "nature, culture, and gender" literature, which really began with Simone de Beauvoir. This literature documents a tendency of many societies to associate women with nature and men with culture (the products of humans). Thus environmental policy that dominates and exploits the natural world is implicitly male, while ecologically sound policy is female (and, incidentally, found in most feminist utopias). Likewise, technology, insofar as it serves to dehumanize and distance us from nature, is masculine and not feminist. Also, we dominate and control nature through *science*, which is often defined as masculine (see Keller, this volume).

14. It is with respect to the challenge-and-resistance aspect of the paradigm shift model that Strathern (1987) disagreed with analyses of feminist scholarship as a paradigm shift. She argued that paradigms function differently in the natural and social sciences. In the social sciences many different perspectives are tolerated at the same time in the same discipline, or even subdiscipline, and paradigms come and go rather easily. In contrast, in the natural sciences, a single paradigm is generally accepted so that there is a more or less closed system, and new paradigms eventually replace older ones. The social sciences are much more open, and rather than being resisted, the feminist perspective is accommodated, not as a replacement but as another stance beside all the others.

Some of the problems raised by Strathern are resolved by first realizing that we are dealing with a process in progress. We do not know yet how it will end. Second, we can distinguish, as Stacey and Thorne (1985) did, between substantive transformation of theories or concepts, on the one hand, and the diffusion and acceptance of those new reconstructions by not-necessarily-feminist members of disciplines on the other. It is easy to identify the constructive aspect of feminist scholarship, whereas acceptance is uneven and slow.

15. Stacey and Thorne (1985) described characteristics of academic disciplines that seem to affect the overall depth of feminist transformation in a given discipline. Like Kuhn, however, they describe features that are internal to disciplines.

16. Though the cited authors mostly use the term feminist standpoint in the singular, they recognized, of course, that there are many different feminist standpoints. I use the plural to underscore that often overlooked fact.

17. Here Hartsock accepted the theories of Chodorow (1978) and Dinnerstein (1976) that a woman's sense of self is more relational and a man's is more separated, autonomous, and abstract. For more on this theme, see these authors' works and the chapters by Kathlene and Keller in this volume.

18. I do not endorse the practice of suttee; but I would like to point out that in order to endorse a relativistic stance about others' values and social practices and be consistent, one would have to apply this stance to all those practices, whether one agrees with them or not. In other words, it would seem somewhat inconsistent to tolerate women walking behind men but then draw the line at suttee. This is simply

imposing one's own values on another culture. Of course, I realize that women walking behind men is not as serious or harmful a practice as is suttee, but they are both practices that reflect women's lower social and political status. Wearing high heels does not have the same consequences as clitoridectomy, but both practices are body-deforming and related to gender.

19. Marx used the term *praxis* to distinguish between what one does and what one thinks and to distinguish revolutionary practice from other types of activity.

20. Bowles's statement might be considered a contemporary version of Tolstoy's statement, "The only question important for us [is] 'What shall we do and how shall we live?'" (cited in Bernstein, 1976:47).

REFERENCES

Aiken, Susan Hardy, Karen Anderson, Myra Dinnerstein, Judy Lensink, and Patricia Maccorquodale. "Trying Transformations: Curriculum Integration and the Problem of Resistance," *Signs: Journal of Women in Culture and Society*, Vol. 12, No. 2, 1987:255-275.

Annas, Pamela J. "New Worlds, New Words: Androgyny in Feminist Science Fiction," *Science-Fiction Studies*, Vol. 5, 1978:143-156.

Becker, Howard. *Sociological Work*. London: Allen Lane, 1971.

Bell, Colin, and Howard Newby. *Doing Sociological Research*. New York: Free Press, 1977.

Bem, Sandra L. "Probing the Promise of Androgyny," pp. 48-62 in A. G. Kaplan and J. P. Bean (eds.) *Beyond Sex-Role Stereotypes: Readings Toward a Psychology of Androgyny*. Boston: Little, Brown, 1976.

Bernstein, Richard J. *The Restructuring of Social and Political Theory*. New York: Harcourt Brace Jovanovich, 1976.

———. *Beyond Objectivism and Relativism: Science, Hermeneutics, and Praxis*. Philadelphia: University of Pennsylvania Press, 1983.

Bloor, David. *Knowledge and Social Imagery*. London: Routledge & Kegan Paul, 1976.

Bowles, Gloria. "Is Women's Studies an Academic Discipline?" pp. 32-45 in Gloria Bowles and Renate Duelli Klein (eds.) *Theories of Women's Studies*. London: Routledge & Kegan Paul, 1983.

———. "The Uses of Hermeneutics for Feminist Scholarship," *Women's Studies International Forum*, Vol. 7, No. 3, 1984:185-188.

Capra, Fritjof. *The Turning Point: Science, Society and the Rising Culture*. New York: Simon and Schuster, 1982.

———. *The Tao of Physics*. Toronto and New York: Bantam Books, Bantam Revised Edition, 1984.

Chodorow, Nancy. *The Reproduction of Mothering: Psychoanalysis and the Sociology of Gender*. Berkeley: University of California Press, 1978.

Dinnerstein, Dorothy. *The Mermaid and the Minotaur: Sexual Arrangements and Human Malaise*. New York: Colophon Books/Harper and Row, 1976.

Du Bois, Ellen Carol, et al. *Feminist Scholarship: Kindling in the Groves of Academe*. Urbana and Chicago: University of Illinois Press, 1985.

Eccles, Jacques. "Socializing Boys and Girls to Be Different," presentation sponsored by Women Studies Program, University of Colorado, Boulder, March 22, 1989.

Evans, Mary. "In Praise of Theory: The Case for Women's Studies," pp. 219-228 in Gloria Bowles and Renate Duelli Klein (eds.) *Theories of Women's Studies*. London: Routledge & Kegan Paul, 1983.

Farganis, Sondra. "Social Theory and Feminist Theory: The Need for Dialogue," *Sociological Inquiry*, Vol. 56, No. 1, 1986:50–68.

Farnham, Christie (ed.). *The Impact of Feminist Research in the Academy*. Bloomington: Indiana University Press, 1987.

Freeman, Jo. *The Politics of Women's Liberation*. New York: David McKay, 1975.

Frye, Marilyn. "Oppression," pp. 37–40 in Paula S. Rothenberg (ed.) *Racism and Sexism: An Integrated Study*. New York: St. Martin's Press, 1988.

Gadamer, Hans-Georg. *Truth and Method*. Translated and edited by Garrett Barden and John Cumming. New York: Seabury Press, 1975.

———. *Philosophical Hermeneutics*. Translated by David E. Linge. Berkeley: University of California Press, 1976.

———. *Dialogue and Dialectic*. Translated by P. Christopher Smith. New Haven: Yale University Press, 1980.

Gergen, Kenneth J. *Toward Transformation in Social Knowledge*. New York: Springer-Verlag, 1982.

Giddens, Anthony. *Profiles and Critiques in Social Theory*. Berkeley: University of California Press, 1982.

Gilligan, Carol. "Woman's Place in Man's Life Cycle," *Harvard Educational Review*, Vol. 49, No. 4, 1979:431–446.

———. *In a Different Voice*. Cambridge: Harvard University Press, 1982.

Gough, Kathleen. "Nuer Kinship: A Re-examination," pp. 79–121 in T. O. Beidelman (ed.) *The Translation of Culture (Essays to E. E. Evans-Pritchard)*. London: Tavistock Publications, 1971.

Habermas, Jurgen. *Knowledge and Human Interest*. Translated by J. Shapiro. London: Heinemann, 1970.

———. *The Theory of Communicative Action*. Boston: Beacon Press, 1984.

Haraway, Donna J. "Animal Sociology and a Natural Economy of the Body Politic, Part II: The Past Is the Contested Zone. Human Nature and Theories of Production and Reproduction in Primate Behavior Studies," *Signs: Journal of Women in Culture and Society*, Vol. 4, No. 1, 1978:37–60.

———. "In the Beginning Was the Word: The Genesis of Biological Theory," *Signs: Journal of Women in Culture and Society*, Vol. 6, No. 3, 1981:469–481.

Harding, Sandra. *The Science Question in Feminism*. Ithaca, N.Y.: Cornell University Press, 1986.

———. *Feminism and Methodology*. Bloomington: Indiana University Press, 1987.

Hartsock, Nancy C.M. "The Feminist Standpoint: Developing the Ground for a Specifically Feminist Historical Materialism," pp. 283–310 in Sandra Harding and Merrill B. Hintikka (eds.) *Discovering Reality*. Dordrecht, Holland: D. Reidel Publishing Co., 1983.

Heelan, Patrick. "Natural Science as a Hermeneutic of Instrumentation," *Philosophy of Science*, Vol. 50, 1983:181–204.

Hekman, Susan. *Hermeneutics and the Sociology of Knowledge*. Notre Dame, Ind.: University of Notre Dame Press, 1986.

Hesse, Mary. "In Defense of Objectivity," *Proceedings of the British Academy*, Vol. 58, 1972:275–292.

———. *Revolutions and Reconstructions in the Philosophy of Science*. Brighton, England: Harvester Press, 1980.

Horowitz, Irving L. *The Rise and Fall of Project Camelot: Studies in the Relationship Between Science and Practical Politics*. Cambridge: MIT Press, 1976.

Hubbard, Ruth, Mary Sue Henifin, and Barbara Fried (eds.). *Women Look at Biology Looking at Women: A Collection of Feminist Critiques*. Cambridge: Schenkman Publishing Co., 1979.

Jaggar, Alison M. *Feminist Politics and Human Nature.* Totowa, N.J.: Rowman and Allanheld; Sussex: The Harvester Press, 1983.

Jones, W. T. *The Classical Mind,* 2d ed. San Diego, Calif.: Harcourt Brace Jovanovich, 1970.

Kasper, Anne S. "Consciousness Re-Evaluated: Interpretive Theory and Feminist Scholarship," *Sociological Inquiry,* Vol. 56, No. 1, 1986:30–49.

Keller, Evelyn Fox. *Reflections on Gender and Science.* New Haven, Conn.: Yale University Press, 1985.

Kelly-Gadol, Joan. "The Social Relation of the Sexes: Methodological Implications of Women's History," *Signs: Journal of Women in Culture and Society,* Vol. 1, No. 4, 1976:809–823.

Klein, Renate Duelli. "How to Do What We Want to Do: Thoughts About Feminist Methodology," pp. 88–104 in Gloria Bowles and Renate Duelli Klein (eds.) *Theories of Women's Studies.* London: Routledge & Kegan Paul, 1983.

Kuhn, Thomas S. *The Structure of Scientific Revolutions.* 2d ed. Chicago: University of Chicago Press, 1970.

Langland, Elizabeth, and Walter Gove (eds.). *A Feminist Perspective in the Academy: The Difference It Makes.* Chicago: University of Chicago Press, 1983.

Longino, Helen, and Ruth Doell. "Body, Bias, and Behavior: A Comparative Analysis of Reasoning in Two Areas of Biological Science," *Signs: Journal of Women in Culture and Society.* Vol. 9, No. 2, 1983:206–227.

Lyotard, Jean Francois. *The Post-Modern Condition: A Report on Knowledge.* Translated by Geoff Gennington and Brian Massumi. Minneapolis: University of Minnesota Press, 1984.

MacKinnon, Catharine. "Feminism, Marxism, Method, and the State: An Agenda for Theory," *Signs: Journal of Women in Culture and Society,* Vol. 7, No. 3, 1982:515–544.

Nielsen, Joyce McCarl, and Jeana Abromeit. "Paradigm Shifts and Feminist Phase Theory in Women Studies Curriculum Transformation Projects," paper presented at the annual meeting of the American Sociological Association, San Francisco, Calif., August 1989.

Oakley, Ann. "Interviewing Women: A Contradiction in Terms," pp. 30–61 in Helen Roberts (ed.) *Doing Feminist Research.* London: Routledge & Kegan Paul, 1981.

Parlee, Mary Brown. "Feminism and the 'New Psychology,'" paper presented at the Center for the Study of Women and Society, CUNY Graduate Center, New York, May 1, 1986.

Polanyi, Michael. *Personal Knowledge: Towards a Post-Critical Philosophy.* New York: Harper & Row, 1958.

Reason, Peter, and John Rowan (eds.). *Human Inquiry: A Sourcebook of New Paradigm Research.* Chichester: John Wiley & Sons, 1981.

Reinharz, Shulamit. "Experiential Analysis: A Contribution to Feminist Research," pp. 162–191 in Gloria Bowles and R. D. Klein (eds.) *Theories of Women's Studies.* London: Routledge & Kegan Paul, 1983.

Ricoeur, Paul. "The Model of the Text: Meaningful Action Considered as a Text," pp. 316–334 in Fred Dallmayr and Thomas McCarthy (eds.) *Understanding and Social Inquiry.* Notre Dame, Ind.: University of Notre Dame Press, 1977.

Ritzer, George. *Sociology: A Multiple Paradigm Science.* Boston: Allyn and Bacon, 1975.

Roberts, Helen. *Doing Feminist Research.* London: Routledge & Kegan Paul, 1981.

Rosaldo, Michelle Zimbalist. "The Use and Abuse of Anthropology: Reflections on Feminism and Cross-Cultural Understanding," *Signs: Journal of Women in Culture and Society,* Vol. 5, No. 3, 1980:389–417.

Rosaldo, Michelle Zimbalist and Louise Lamphere (eds.). *Woman, Culture and Society.* Stanford, Calif.: Stanford University Press, 1974.

Rubin, Gayle. "The Traffic in Women: Notes on the 'Political Economy' of Sex," pp. 157–210 in Rayna R. Reiter (ed.) *Toward an Anthropology of Women.* New York: Monthly Review Press, 1975.

Schutz, Alfred. *Collected Papers,* Vol. 1. Edited and with introduction by Maurice Natanson. The Hague: Martinus Nijhoff, 1962.

_____ . *The Phenomenology of the Social World.* Translated by George Walsh and Frederick Lehnert. Evanston, Ill.: Northwestern University Press, 1967.

Slocum, Sally. "Woman the Gatherer: Male Bias in Anthropology," pp. 36–50 in Rayna R. Reiter (ed.) *Toward an Anthropology of Women.* New York: Monthly Review Press, 1975.

Smith, Dorothy E. "Some Implications of a Sociology for Women," pp. 15–29 in Nona Glazer and Helen Youngelson Waehere (eds.) *Woman in a Man-Made World,* 2d ed. Chicago: Rand McNally, 1977.

_____ . "A Sociology for Women," pp. 135–188 in Julia A. Sherman and Evelyn Tonton Beck (eds.) *The Prism of Sex: Essays in the Sociology of Knowledge.* Madison: University of Wisconsin Press, 1979.

Spender, Dale (ed.). *Men's Studies Modified: The Impact of Feminism on the Academic Disciplines.* New York: Pergamon Press Ltd., 1981.

Stacey, Judith, and Barrie Thorne. "The Missing Feminist Revolution in Sociology," *Social Problems,* Vol. 32, No. 4, 1985:301–316.

Stanley, Liz, and Sue Wise. *Breaking Out: Feminist Consciousness and Feminist Research.* London: Routledge & Kegan Paul, 1983.

Stimpson, Catherine R. "Our Search and Research: The Study of Women Since 1969," *Comment,* Vol. 14, May 1983:1–2.

Strathern, Marilyn. "An Awkward Relationship: The Case of Feminism and Anthropology," *Signs: Journal of Women in Culture and Society,* Vol. 12, No. 2, 1987:276–292.

Tanner, Nancy, and Adrienne Zihlman. "Women in Evolution, Part I: Innovation and Selection in Human Origins," *Signs: Journal of Women in Culture and Society,* Vol. 1, No. 3, 1976:585–608.

Tetreault, Mary Kay Thompson. "Feminism Phase Theory: An Experience-Derived Evaluation Model," *Journal of Higher Education,* Vol. 56, No. 4, 1985:363–384.

Theodorson, George A., and Achilles G. Theodorson. *Modern Dictionary of Sociology.* New York: Thomas Y. Crowell Co., 1969.

Toulmin, Stephan. "The Construal of Inquiry: Criticism in Modern and Post-Modern Science," *Critical Inquiry,* Vol. 9, 1982:93–111.

Weiner, Annette B. "Trobriand Kinship from Another View: The Reproductive Power of Women and Men," *Man,* Vol. 14, No. 2 (new series), 1979:328–348.

Weisstein, Naomi. "Adventures of a Woman in Science," pp. 187–204 in Ruth Hubbard, Mary Sue Henifin and Barbara Fried (eds.) *Women Look at Biology Looking at Women: A Collection of Feminist Critiques.* Cambridge: Schenkman Publishing Co., 1979.

Westkott, Marcia. "Women's Studies as a Strategy for Change: Between Criticism and Vision," pp. 210–218 in Gloria Bowles and Renate Duelli Klein (eds.) *Theories of Women's Studies.* London: Routledge & Kegan Paul, 1983.

Wolff, Janet. "Hermeneutics and the Critique of Ideology," *Sociological Review,* Vol. 23, No. 4 (new series), 1975:811–828.

PART ONE

Feminist Research Methods

1

Gender and Science

EVELYN FOX KELLER

*In this provocative article, Keller explains the masculine character of
science and scientific thinking. She builds on the subjective-objective
distinction that is basic in science and, using a sociological-
psychoanalytical perspective, describes the process by which the capacity
for scientific thought is developed and intertwined with the development
of emotional and sexual identity. This paper is important to the study of
feminist methods because it is a well-developed and articulate treatment
of the theme that scientific thinking itself is gendered.*

I. INTRODUCTION

The requirements of . . . correctness in practical judgements and objectivity in
theoretical knowledge . . . belong as it were in their form and their claims to
humanity in general, but in their actual historical configuration they are
masculine throughout. Supposing that we describe these things, viewed as
absolute ideas, by the single word 'objective', we then find that in the history
of our race the equation objective = masculine is a valid one [George Simmel,
quoted by Horney, 1926, p. 200].

Reprinted from *Psychoanalysis and Contemporary Thought: A Quarterly of Integrative and
Interdisciplinary Studies*, Vol. 1, No. 3, 1978:409–433. Copyright © 1978 by International
Universities Press, Inc. Used by permission of International Universities Press, Inc.

In articulating the commonplace, Simmel steps outside of the convention of academic discourse. The historically pervasive association between masculine and objective, more specifically between masculine and scientific, is a topic which academic critics resist taking seriously. Why is that? Is it not odd that an association so familiar and so deeply entrenched is a topic only for informal discourse, literary allusion, and popular criticism? How is it that formal criticism in the philosophy and sociology of science has failed to see here a topic requiring analysis? The virtual silence of at least the nonfeminist academic community on this subject suggests that the association of masculinity with scientific thought has the status of a myth which either cannot or should not be examined seriously. It has simultaneously the air of being "self-evident" and "nonsensical"—the former by virtue of existing in the realm of common knowledge (i.e., everyone knows it), and the latter by virtue of lying outside the realm of formal knowledge, indeed conflicting with our image of science as emotionally and sexually neutral. Taken seriously, it would suggest that, were more women to engage in science, a different science might emerge. Such an idea, although sometimes expressed by nonscientists, clashes openly with the formal view of science as being uniquely determined by its own logical and empirical methodology.

The survival of mythlike beliefs in our thinking about science, the very archetype of antimyth, ought, it would seem, to invite our curiosity and demand investigation. Unexamined myths, wherever they survive, have a subterranean potency; they affect our thinking in ways we are not aware of, and to the extent that we lack awareness, our capacity to resist their influence is undermined. The presence of the mythical in science seems particularly inappropriate. What is it doing there? From where does it come? And how does it influence our conceptions of science, of objectivity, or, for that matter, of gender?

These are the questions I wish to address, but before doing so it is necessary to clarify and elaborate the system of beliefs in which science acquires a gender—which amount to a "genderization" of science. Let me make clear at the outset that the issue which requires discussion is *not*, or at least not simply, the relative absence of women in science. While it is true that most scientists have been, and continue to be, men, the make-up of the scientific population hardly accounts, by itself, for the attribution of masculinity to science as an intellectual domain. Most culturally validated intellectual and creative endeavors have, after all, historically been the domain of men. Few of these endeavors, however, bear so unmistakably the connotation of masculine in the very nature of the activity. To both scientists and their public, scientific thought is male thought, in ways that painting and writing— also performed largely by men—have never been. As Simmel observed, objectivity itself is an ideal which has a long history of identification with masculine. The fact that the scientific population is, even now, a population that is overwhelmingly male, is itself a consequence rather than a cause of the attribution of masculinity to scientific thought.[1] What requires discussion is a *belief* rather than a reality, although the ways in which reality is shaped by our beliefs are manifold, and also need articulating.

How does this belief manifest itself? It used to be commonplace to hear scientists, teachers, and parents assert quite baldly that women cannot, should not, be scientists, that they lack the strength, rigor, and clarity of mind for an occupation that properly belongs to men. Now that the women's movement has made offensive such naked assertions, open acknowledgment of the continuing belief in the intrinsic masculinity of scientific thought has become less fashionable. It continues, however, to find daily expression in the language and metaphors we use to describe science. When we dub the objective sciences "hard" as opposed to the softer, i.e., more subjective, branches of knowledge, we implicitly invoke a sexual metaphor, in which "hard" is of course masculine and "soft," feminine. Quite generally, facts are "hard," feelings "soft." "Feminization" has become synonymous with sentimentalization. A woman thinking scientifically or objectively is thinking "like a man"; conversely, a man pursuing a nonrational, nonscientific argument is arguing "like a woman."

The linguistic rooting of this stereotype is not lost among children, who remain perhaps the most outspoken and least self-conscious about its expression. From strikingly early ages, even in the presence of astereotypic role models, children have learned to identify mathematics and science as male. "Science," my five-year-old son declared, confidently bypassing the fact that his mother was a scientist, "is for men!" The identification between scientific thought and masculinity is so deeply embedded in the culture at large that children have little difficulty internalizing that identification. They grow up not only expecting scientists to be men, but also perceiving scientists as more "masculine" than other male professionals, than, for example, those in the arts. Numerous studies of masculinity and femininity in the professions confirm this observation, with the "harder" sciences as well as the "harder" branches of any profession consistently characterized as more masculine.

In one particularly interesting study of attitudes prevalent among English schoolboys, a somewhat different but critically related dimension of the cultural stereotype emerges. Hudson (1972) observes that scientists are perceived as not only more masculine than are artists, but simultaneously as less sexual. He writes:

> The arts are associated with sexual pleasure, the sciences with sexual restraint. The arts man is seen as having a good-looking, well-dressed wife with whom he enjoys a warm sexual relation; the scientist as having a wife who is dowdy and dull, and in whom he has no physical interest. Yet the scientist is seen as masculine, the arts specialist as slightly feminine [p. 83.]

In this passage we see the genderization of science linked with another, also widely perceived image of science as antithetical to Eros. These images are not unrelated, and it is important to bear their juxtaposition in mind as we attempt to understand their sources and functions. What is at issue here is the kind of images and metaphor with which science is surrounded. If we can take the use of metaphor seriously, while managing to keep clearly in mind that it is metaphor and language which are being discussed, then we can attempt to understand the influences they might exert—how the use of language and metaphor can become hardened into a kind of reality. One way is through the internalization of these images by scientists themselves, and I will discuss more explicitly how this can happen later in the paper. As a first step, however, the imagery itself needs to be explored further.

If we agree to pursue the implications of attributing gender to the scientific mind, then we might be led to ask, with what or with whom is the sexual metaphor completed? And, further, what is the nature of the act with which this now desexualized union is consummated? The answer to the first question is immediate. The complement of the scientific mind is, of course, Nature— viewed so ubiquitously as female. "Let us establish a chaste and lawful marriage between Mind and Nature" wrote Bacon (quoted by Leiss, 1972, p. 25), thereby providing the prescription for the birth of the new science. This prescription has endured to the present day—in it are to be found important clues for an understanding of the posture of the virgin groom, of his relation toward his bride, and of the ways in which he defines his mission. The metaphoric marriage of which science is the offspring sets the scientific project squarely in the midst of our unmistakably patriarchal tradition. Small wonder, then, that the goals of science are so persistently described in terms of "conquering" and "mastering" nature. Bacon articulated this more clearly than today's self-consciousness could perhaps permit when he urged: "I am come in very truth leading you to Nature with all her children to bind her to your service and make her your slave" (Farrington, 1951, p. 197).

Much attention has been given recently to the technological abuses of modern science, and in many of these discussions blame is directed toward the distortions of the scientific program intrinsic in its ambition to dominate nature—without, however, offering an adequate explanation of how that ambition comes to be intrinsic to science. Generally such distortions are attributed to technology, or applied science, which is presumed to be clearly distinguishable from pure science. In the latter, the ambition is supposed to be pure knowledge, uncontaminated by fantasies of control. While it is undoubtedly true that the domination of nature is a more central feature of technology, it is impossible to draw a clear line between pure and applied science. History reveals a most complex relation between the two, as complex perhaps as the interrelation between the dual constitutive motives for knowl- edge—those of transcendence and power. It would be naïve to suppose that the connotations of masculinity and conquest affect only the uses to which science is put, and leave untouched its very structure.

Science bears the imprint of its genderization not only in the ways it is used, but in the very description of reality it offers—even in the relation of the scientist to that description. To see this, it is necessary to examine more fully the implications of attributing masculinity to the very nature of scientific thought.

Having divided the world into two parts—the knower (mind) and the knowable (nature)—scientific ideology goes on to prescribe a very specific relation between the two. It prescribes the interactions which can consummate this union, that is, which can lead to knowledge. Not only are mind and nature assigned gender, but in characterizing scientific and objective thought as masculine, the very activity by which the knower can acquire knowledge is also genderized. The relation specified between knower and known is one of distance and separation. It is that between a subject and object radically divided, which is to say no worldly relation. Simply put, nature is objectified. The "chaste and lawful marriage" is consummated through reason rather than feeling, and "observation" rather than "immediate" sensory experience. The modes of intercourse are defined so as to insure emotional and physical inviolability. Concurrent with the division of the world into subject and object is, accordingly, a division of the forms of knowledge into "objective" and "subjective." The scientific mind is set apart from what is to be known, i.e., from nature, and its autonomy is guaranteed (or so it has been traditionally assumed) by setting apart its modes of knowing from those in which that dichotomy is threatened. In this process, the characterization of both the scientific mind and its modes of access to knowledge as masculine is indeed significant. Masculine here connotes, as it so often does, autonomy, separation, and distance. It connotes a radical rejection of any commingling of subject and object, which are, it now appears, quite consistently identified as male and female.

What is the real significance of this system of beliefs, whose structure now reveals a quite intricate admixture of metaphysics, cognitive style, and sexual metaphor? If we reject the position, as I believe we must, that the associations between scientific and masculine are simply "true"—that they reflect a biological difference between male and female brains—then how are we to account for our adherence to them? Whatever intellectual or personality characteristics may be affected by sexual hormones, it has become abundantly clear that our ideas about the differences between the sexes far exceed what can be traced to mere biology; that once formed these ideas take on a life of their own—a life sustained by powerful cultural and psychological forces. Even the brief discussion offered above makes it evident that, in attributing gender to an intellectual posture, in sexualizing a thought process, we inevitably invoke the large world of affect. The task of explaining the associations between masculine and scientific thus becomes, short of reverting to an untenable biological reductionism, the task of understanding the emotional substructure that links our experience of gender with our cognitive experience.

The nature of the problem suggests that, in seeking an explanation of the origins and endurance of this mythology, we look to the processes by which the capacity for scientific thought develops, and the ways in which those processes are intertwined with emotional and sexual development. By so doing, it becomes possible to acquire deeper insight into the structure and perhaps even the functions of the mythology we seek to elucidate. The route I wish to take proceeds along ground laid by psychoanalysts and cognitive psychologists, along a course shaped by the particular questions I have posed. What emerges is a scenario supported by the insights these workers have attained, and held together, it is to be hoped, by its own logical and intuitive coherence.

II. THE DEVELOPMENT OF OBJECTIVITY

The crucial insight which underlies much of this discussion—an insight for which we are indebted to both Freud and Piaget—is that the capacity for objectivity, for delineating subject from object, is *not* inborn, although the potential for it no doubt is. Rather, the ability to perceive reality "objectively" is acquired as an inextricable part of the long and painful process by which the child's sense of self is formed. In the deepest sense, it is a function of the child's capacity for distinguishing self from not-self, "me" from "not-me." The consolidation of this capacity is perhaps the major achievement of childhood development.

After half a century's clinical observations of children and adults the developmental picture which emerges is as follows. In the early world of the infant, experiences of thoughts, feelings, events, images, and perceptions are continuous. Boundaries have not yet been drawn to distinguish the child's internal from external environment; nor has order or structure been imposed on either. The external environment, consisting primarily of the mother during this early period, is experienced as an extension of the child. It is only through the assimilation of cumulative experiences of pleasure and pain, of gratification and disappointment, that the child slowly learns to distinguish between self and other, between image and percept, between subject and object. The growing ability to distinguish his or her self from the environment allows for the recognition of a world of external objects—a world subject to ever finer discrimination and delineation. It permits the recognition of an external reality to which the child can relate—at first magically, and ultimately objectively. In the course of time, the inanimate becomes released from the animate, objects from their perspective, and events from wishes; the child becomes capable of objective thought and perception. The process by which this development occurs proceeds through sequential and characteristic stages of cognitive growth, stages which have been extensively documented and described by Piaget and his co-workers.

The background of this development is fraught with intense emotional conflict. The primary object which the infant carves out of the matrix of his/her experiences is an emotional object, namely the mother. And along with the emergence of the mother as a separate being comes the child's painful recognition of his/her own separate existence. Anxiety is unleashed, and longing is born. The child (infant) discovers his dependency and need— and a primitive form of love. Out of the demarcation between self and mother arises a longing to undo that differentiation—an urge to re-establish the original unity. At the same time, there is also growing pleasure in autonomy, which itself comes to feel threatened by the lure of an earlier state. The process of emotional delineation proceeds in fits and starts, propelled and inhibited by conflicting impulses, desires, and fears. The parallel process of cognitive delineation must be negotiated against the background of these conflicts. As objects acquire a separate identity, they remain for a long time tied to the self by a network of magical ties. The disentanglement of self from world, and of thoughts from things, requires relinquishing the magical bonds which have kept them connected. It requires giving up the belief in the omnipotence—now of the child, now of the mother—that perpetuates those bonds and learning to tolerate the limits and separateness of both. It requires enduring the loss of a wish-dominated existence in exchange for the rewards of living "in reality." In doing so, the child moves from the egocentricity of a self-dominated contiguous world to the recognition of a world outside and independent of himself—a world in which objects can take on a "life" of their own.

The recognition of the independent reality of both self and other is a necessary precondition both for science and for love. It may not, however, be sufficient—for either. Certainly the capacity for love, for empathy, for artistic creativity requires more than a simple dichotomy between subject and object. Autonomy too sharply defined, reality too rigidly defined, cannot encompass the emotional and creative experiences which give life its fullest and richest depth. Autonomy must be conceived of more dynamically and reality more flexibly if they are to allow for the ebb and flow of love and play. Emotional growth does not end with the mere acceptance of one's own separateness; perhaps it is fair to say that it begins there. Out of a condition of emotional and cognitive union with the mother, the child gradually gains enough confidence in the enduring reality of both him/herself and the environment to tolerate their separateness and mutual independence. A sense of self becomes delineated—in opposition, as it were, to the mother. Ultimately, however, both sense of self and of other become sufficiently secure to permit momentary relaxation of the boundary between—without, that is, threatening the loss of either. One has acquired confidence in the enduring survival of both self and other as vitally autonomous. Out of the recognition and acceptance of one's aloneness in the world, it becomes possible to transcend one's isolation, to truly love another.[2]

The final step—of reintroducing ambiguity into one's relation to the world—is a difficult one. It evokes deep anxieties and fears stemming from old conflicts and older desires. The ground of one's selfhood was not easily won, and experiences which appear to threaten the loss of that ground can be seen as acutely dangerous. Milner (1957), in seeking to understand the essence of what makes a drawing "alive," and conversely, the inhibitions which impede artistic expression, has written with rare perspicacity and eloquence about the dangers and anxieties attendant upon opening ourselves to the creative perception so critical for a successful drawing. But unless we can, the world of art is foreclosed to us. Neither love nor art can survive the exclusion of a dialogue between dream and reality, between inside and outside, between subject and object.

Our understanding of psychic autonomy, and along with it, of emotional maturity, owes a great deal to the work of the English psychoanalyst Winnicott. Of particular importance here is Winnicott's concept of the transitional object—an object intermediate between self and other (as, for example, the baby's blanket). It is called a transitional object insofar as it facilitates the transition from the state of magical union with the mother to autonomy, the transition from belief in omnipotence to an acceptance of the limitations of everyday reality. Gradually, it is given up,

> not so much forgotten as relegated to limbo. By this I mean that in health the transitional object does not "go inside" nor does the feeling about it necessarily undergo repression . . . It loses meaning, and this is because the transitional phenomena have become diffused, have become spread out over the whole intermediate territory between "inner psychic reality" and "the external world as perceived by two persons in common," that is to say, over the whole cultural field [Winnicott, 1971, p. 5].

To the diffuse survival of the "creative apperception" he attributes what, "more than anything else, makes the individual feel that life is worth living" (p. 65). Creativity, love, and play are located by Winnicott in the "potential space" between the inner psychic space of "me" and outer social space of "not-me"—"the neutral area of experience which will not be challenged" (as it was not challenged for the infant)—about which "we will never ask the question: Did you conceive of this or was it presented to you from without" (p. 12).

The inability to tolerate such a potential space leads to psychic distress as surely as the complementary failure to delineate adequately between self and other. "These two groups of people come to us for psychotherapy because in the one case they do not want to spend their lives irrevocably out of touch with the facts of life and in the other because they feel estranged from dream" (p. 67). Both inadequate and excessive delineation between self and other can be seen as defenses, albeit opposite ones, against ongoing anxiety about autonomy.

Emotional maturity, then, implies a sense of reality which is neither cut off from, nor at the mercy of, fantasy; it requires a sufficiently secure sense of autonomy to allow for that vital element of ambiguity at the interface between subject and object. In the words of Loewald (1951), "Perhaps the so-called fully developed, the mature ego is not one that has become fixated at the presumably highest or latest stage of development, having left the others behind it, but is an ego that integrates its reality in such a way that the earlier and deeper levels of ego-reality integration remain alive as dynamic sources of higher organization" (p. 18).

While most of us will recognize the inadequacy of a static conception of autonomy as an emotional ideal, it is easy to fall into the trap of regarding it as an appropriate ideal for cognitive development. That is, cognitive maturity is frequently identified with a posture in which objective reality is perceived and defined as radically divided from the subjective. Our inclination to accept this posture as a model for cognitive maturity is undoubtedly influenced by the definition of objectivity we have inherited from classical science—a definition rooted in the premise that the subject can and should be totally removed from our description of the object. Though that definition has proved unquestionably efficacious in the past, contemporary developments in both philosophy and physics have demonstrated its epistemological inadequacy. They have made it necessary for us to look beyond the classical dichotomy to a more dynamic conception of reality, and a more sophisticated epistemology to support it.

If scientists have exhibited a reluctance to do so, as I think they have, that reluctance should be examined in the light of what we already know about the relation between cognitive and emotional development. Elsewhere (Keller, manuscript) I have attempted to show the persistence of demonstrably inappropriate classical ideas even in contemporary physics, where the most dramatic evidence for the failure of classical ideas has come from. There I try to establish some of the consequences of this persistence, and to account for the tenacity of such ideas. In brief, I argue that the adherence to an outmoded, dichotomous conception of objectivity might be viewed as a defense against anxiety about autonomy of exactly the same kind as we find interfering with the capacity for love and creativity. When even physics reveals "transitional phenomena"—phenomena, that is, about which it cannot be determined whether they belong to the observer or the observed—then it becomes essential to question the adequacy of traditional "realist" modes for cognitive maturity as well as for reality. Our very definition of reality requires constant refinement as we continue in the effort to wean our perceptions from our wishes, our fears, and our anxieties; insofar as our conception of cognitive maturity is dictated by our definition of reality, that conception requires corresponding refinement.

III. THE DEVELOPMENT OF GENDER

What, the reader may ask, has all this to do with gender? Though the discussion has led us on a sizable detour, the implicit argument which relates it to the genderization of science should already be clear. Before articulating the argument explicitly, however, we need an account of the development of gender identity and gender identifications in the context of the developmental picture I have presented thus far.

Perhaps the single most important determinant of our conceptions of male and female is provided by our perceptions of and experiences with our parents. While the developmental processes described above are equally relevant for children of both sexes, their implications for the two sexes are bound to differ. The basic and fundamental fact that it is, for most of us, our mothers who provide the emotional context out of which we forge the discrimination between self and other inevitably leads to a skewing of our perceptions of gender. As long as our earliest and most compelling experiences of merging have their origin in the mother-child relation, it appears to be inevitable that that experience will tend to be identified with "mother," while delineation and separation are experienced as a negation of "mother," as "not-mother." In the extrication of self from other, the mother, beginning as the first and most primitive subject, emerges, by a process of effective and affective negation, as the first object.[3] The very processes (both cognitive and emotional) which remind us of that first bond become colored by their association with the woman who is, and forever remains, the archetypal female. Correspondingly, those of delineation and objectification are colored by their origins in the process of separation *from* mother; they become marked, as it were, as "not-mother." The mother becomes an object, and the child a subject, by a process which becomes itself an expression of opposition to and negation of "mother."

While there is an entire world which exists beyond the mother, in the family constellation with which we are most familiar it is primarily the father (or the father figure) toward whom the child turns for protection from the fear of re-engulfment, from the anxieties and fears of disintegration of a still very fragile ego. It is the father who comes to stand for individuation and differentiation—for objective reality itself; who indeed can represent the "real" world by virtue of being *in* it.

For Freud, reality becomes personified by the father during the oedipal conflict; it is the father who, as the representative of external reality, harshly intrudes on the child's (i.e., boy's) early romance with the mother—offering his protection and future fraternity as the reward for the child's acceptance of the "reality principle." Since Freud, however, it has become increasingly well understood that the rudiments of both gender and reality are established long before the oedipal period, and that reality becomes personified by the father as soon as the early maternal bond comes to be experienced as threatening engulfment, or loss of ego boundaries. A particularly pertinent discussion of this process is presented by Loewald (1951), who writes:

> Against the threatening possibility of remaining in or sinking back into the structureless unity from which the ego emerged, stands the powerful paternal force. . . . While the primary narcissistic identity with the mother forever constitutes the deepest unconscious origin and structural layer of ego and reality, and the motive force for the ego's 'remarkable striving toward unification, synthesis,'—this primary identity is also the source of the deepest dread, which promotes, in identification with the father, the ego's progressive differentiation and structuralization of reality [pp. 15, 17].

Thus it is that, for all of us—male and female alike—our earliest experiences incline us to associate the affective and cognitive posture of objectification with masculine, while all processes which involve a blurring of the boundary between subject and object tend to be associated with the feminine.

The crucial question of course is: What happens to these early associations? While the patterns which give rise to them may be quasi-universal (though strongest, no doubt, in our own form of nuclear family), the conditions which sustain them are not. It is perhaps at this point that specific cultural forces intrude most prominently. In a culture which validates subsequent adult experiences that transcend the subject-object divide, as we find for example in art, love, and religion, these early identifications can be counteracted—provided, that is, that such experiences are validated as essentially human rather than as "feminine" experience. However, in a culture such as ours, where primary validation is accorded to a science which has been premised on a radical dichotomy between subject and object, and where all other experiences are accorded secondary, "feminine" status, the early identifications can hardly fail to persist. The genderization of science—as an enterprise, as an intellectual domain, as a world view—simultaneously reflects and perpetuates associations made in an earlier, prescientific era. If true, then an adherence to an objectivist epistemology, in which truth is measured by its distance from the subjective, has to be re-examined when it emerges that, by this definition, truth itself has become genderized.

It is important to emphasize, even repeat, that what I have been discussing is a system of *beliefs* about the meaning of masculine and feminine, rather than any either intrinsic or actual differences between male and female. Children of both sexes learn essentially the same set of ideas about the characteristics of male and female—how they then make use of these ideas in the development of their gender identity as male or female is another question. The relation between the sexual stereotypes we believe in and our actual experience and even observation of gender is a very complex one. It is crucial, however, to make a vigilant effort to distinguish between belief and reality, even, or especially, when the reality which emerges is so influenced by our beliefs. I have not been claiming, for example, that men are by nature more objective, better suited for scientific work, nor that science, even when characterized by an extreme objectivist epistemology, is intrinsically masculine. What I have been discussing are the reasons we might believe all of the above to be true. These beliefs may in fact lead to observed differences between the sexes, though the question of actual differences between men and women in a given culture is ultimately an empirical one. The subsequent issue of how those possible differences might be caused by cultural expectations is yet a separate issue, and requires separate discussion. Without getting into the empirical question of sex differences, about which there is a great deal of debate, it seems reasonable to suggest that we ought to expect that our early beliefs about gender will be subject to some degree of internalization.

To return, then, to the issue of gender development, it is important to recognize that, although children of both sexes must learn equally to distinguish self from other, and have essentially the same need for autonomy, to the extent that boys rest their very sexual identity on an opposition to what is both experienced and defined as feminine, the development of their gender identity is likely to accentuate the process of separation. As boys, they must undergo a twofold "disidentification from mother" (Greenson, 1968)—first for the establishment of a self-identity, and second for the consolidation of a male gender identity. Further impetus is added to this process by the external cultural pressure on the young boy to establish a stereotypic masculinity, now culturally as well as privately connoting independence and autonomy. The cultural definitions of masculine as what can never appear feminine, and of autonomy as what can never be relaxed, conspire to reinforce the child's earliest associations of female with the pleasures and dangers of merging, and male with both the comfort and the loneliness of separateness. The boy's internal anxiety about both self and gender is here echoed by the cultural anxiety; together they can lead to postures of exaggerated and rigidified autonomy and masculinity which can— indeed which may be designed to—defend against that anxiety and the longing which generates it. Many psychoanalysts have come to believe that, because of the boy's need to switch his identification from the mother to the father, his sense of gender identity tends always to be more fragile than the girl's. Her sense of self-identity may, however, be comparatively more vulnerable. It has been suggested that the girl's development of a sense of separateness may be to some degree hampered by her ongoing identification with her mother. Although she too must disentangle herself from the early experience of oneness, she continues to look toward her mother as a model for her gender identity. Whatever vicissitudes her relation to her mother may suffer during subsequent development, a strong identification based on common gender is likely to persist—her need for "disidentification" is not so radical. Cultural forces may further complicate her development of autonomy by stressing dependency and subjectivity as feminine characteristics. To the extent that such traits become internalized, they can be passed on through the generations by leading to an accentuation of the symbiotic bond between mother and daughter (see, e.g., Chodorow, 1974).

It would seem, then, appropriate to suggest that one possible outcome of these processes is that boys may be more inclined toward excessive and girls toward inadequate delineation—growing into men who have difficulty loving and women who retreat from science. What I am suggesting, then, and indeed trying to describe, is a network of interactions between gender development, a belief system which equates objectivity with masculinity, and a set of cultural values which simultaneously elevates what is defined as scientific and what is defined as masculine. The structure of this network is such as to perpetuate and exacerbate distortions in *any* of its parts—including the acquisition of gender identity.

IV. THE DEVELOPMENT OF SCIENTISTS

Whatever differences between the sexes such a network might, however, generate—and, as I said earlier, the existence of such differences remains ultimately an empirical question—they are in any case certain to be overshadowed by the inevitably large variations that exist within both the male and female populations. Not all men become scientists, and we must ask whether a science which advertises itself as revealing a reality in which subject and object are unmistakably distinct does not offer special comfort to those who, as individuals (be they male or female), retain particular anxiety about the loss of autonomy. In short, if we can take the argument presented thus far seriously, then we must follow it through yet another step. Would not a characterization of science which appears to gratify particular emotional needs give rise to a self-selection of scientists—a self-selection which would, in turn, lead to a perpetuation of that characterization? Without attempting a detailed discussion of either the appropriateness of the imagery with which science is advertised, or of the personality characteristics which such imagery might select for, it seems reasonable to suggest that such a selection mechanism ought inevitably to operate. The persistence of the characterization of science as masculine, as objectivist, as autonomous of psychological as well as of social and political forces would then be encouraged, through such selection, by the kinds of emotional satisfaction it provides.

If so, the question which then arises is whether, statistically, scientists do indeed tend to be more anxious about their affective as well as cognitive autonomy than nonscientists. Although it is certainly part of the popular image of scientists that they do, the actual measurement of personality differences between scientists and nonscientists has proved to be extremely difficult; it is as difficult, and subject to as much disagreement, as the measurement of personality differences between the sexes. One obvious difficulty arises out of the ambiguity of the term scientist, and the enormous heterogeneity of the scientific population. Apart from the vast differences among individuals, characteristics vary across time, nationality, discipline, and, even, with degree of eminence. The Einsteins of history fail, virtually by definition, to conform to more general patterns either of personality or of intellect. Nevertheless, certain themes, however difficult they may be to pin down, continually re-emerge with enough prominence to warrant consideration. These are the themes, or stereotypes, on which I have concentrated throughout this paper, and though they can neither exhaustively nor even accurately describe science or scientists as a whole—as stereotypes never can—they do acquire some corroboration from the (admittedly problematic) literature on the "scientific personality." It seems worth noting, therefore, several features which seem to emerge from a number of efforts to describe the personality characteristics which tend to distinguish scientists from nonscientists.

I have already referred to the fact that scientists, particularly physical scientists, score unusually high on "masculinity" tests, meaning only that, on the average, their responses differ greatly from those of women. At the same time, studies (e.g., Roe, 1953, 1956) report that they tend overwhelmingly to have been loners as children, to be low in social interests and skills, indeed to avoid interpersonal contact. McClelland's subsequent studies confirm these impressions. He writes, "And it is a fact, as Anne Roe reports, that young scientists are typically not very interested in girls, date for the first time late in college, marry the first girl they date, and thereafter appear to show a rather low level of heterosexual drive" (1962, p. 321) (by which he presumably means sexual, thereby confirming, incidentally, the popular image of scientists as "asexual" which I discussed earlier). One of McClelland's particularly interesting findings was that 90% of a group of eminent scientists see, in the "mother-son" picture routinely given as part of the Thematic Apperception Test, "the mother and son going their separate ways" (p. 323)—a relatively infrequent response to this picture in the general population. It conforms, however, with the more general observation (emerging from biographical material) of a distant relation to the mother,[4] frequently coupled with "open or covert attitudes of derogation" (Roe, 1956, p. 215).

Though these remarks are admittedly sketchy, and by no means constitute a review of the field, they do suggest a personality profile which seems admirably suited to an occupation seen as simultaneously masculine and asexual. Bacon's image of a "chaste and lawful marriage" becomes remarkably apt insofar as it allows the scientist both autonomy and mastery[5] in his marriage to a bride kept at safe, "objectified" remove.

CONCLUSION

It is impossible to conclude a discussion of the genderization of science without making some brief comments on its social implications. The linking of scientific and objective with masculine brings in its wake a host of secondary consequences which, however self-evident, may nevertheless need articulating. Not only does our characterization of science thereby become colored by the biases of patriarchy and sexism, but simultaneously our evaluation of masculine and feminine becomes affected by the prestige of science. A circular process of mutual reinforcement is established in which what is called scientific receives extra validation from the cultural preference for what is called masculine, and, conversely, what is called feminine—be it a branch of knowledge, a way of thinking, or woman herself—becomes further devalued by its exclusion from the special social and intellectual value placed on science and the model science provides for all intellectual endeavors. This circularity not only operates on the level of ideology, but is assisted by the ways in which the developmental processes, both for science and for the child, internalize ideological influences. For each, pressures from the other operate, in the ways I have attempted to describe, to create distortions and perpetuate caricatures.

Neither in emphasizing the self-sustaining nature of these beliefs, nor in relating them to early childhood experience, do I wish to suggest that they are inevitable. On the contrary, by examining their dynamics I mean to emphasize the existence of alternative possibilities. The disengagement of our thinking about science from our notions of what is masculine could lead to a freeing of both from some of the rigidities to which they have been bound, with profound ramifications for both. Not only, for example, might science become more accessible to women, but, far more importantly, our very conception of "objective" could be freed from inappropriate constraints. As we begin to understand the ways in which science itself has been influenced by its unconscious mythology, we can begin to perceive the possibilities for a science not bound by such mythology.

How might such a disengagement come about? To the extent that my analysis rests on the crucial importance of the gender of the primary parent, changing patterns of parenting could be of special importance.[6] But other developments might be of equal importance. Changes in the ethos that sustains our beliefs about science and gender could also come about from the current pressure, largely politically inspired, to re-examine the traditionally assumed neutrality of science, from philosophical exploration of the boundaries or limitations of scientific inquiry, and even, perhaps especially, from events within science itself. Both within and without science, the need to question old dogma has been pressing. Of particular interest among recent developments *within* science is the growing interest among physicists in a process description of reality—a move inspired by, perhaps even necessitated by, quantum mechanics. In these descriptions object reality acquires a dynamic character, akin to the more fluid concept of autonomy emerging from psychoanalysis. Bohr himself perspicaciously provided us with a considerably happier image than Bacon's—one more apt even for the future of physics—when he chose for his coat of arms the yin-yang symbol, over which reads the inscription: *Contraria Sunt Complementa.*

Where, finally, has this analysis taken us? In attempting to explore the significance of the sexual metaphor in our thinking about science, I have offered an explanation of its origins, its functions, and some of its consequences. Necessarily, many questions remain, and it is perhaps appropriate, by way of concluding, to articulate some of them. I have not, for example, more than touched on the social and political dynamics of the genderization of science. This is a crucial dimension which remains in need of further exploration. It has seemed to me, however, that central aspects of this problem belong in the psychological domain, and further, that this is the domain which tends to be least accounted for in most discussions of scientific thought.

Within the particular model of affective and cognitive development I have invoked, much remains to be understood about the interconnections between cognition and affect. Though I have, throughout, assumed an intimate relation between the two, it is evident that a fuller and more detailed conception is necessary.

Finally, the speculations I offer raise numerous questions of historical and psychological fact. I have already indicated some of the relevant empirical questions in the psychology of personality which bear on my analysis. Other questions of a more historical nature ought also to be mentioned. How, e.g., have conceptions of objectivity changed with time, and to what extent have these conceptions been linked with similar sexual metaphors in other, prescientific eras, or, for that matter, in other, less technological cultures? Clearly, much remains to be investigated; perhaps the present article can serve to provoke others to help pursue these questions.

NOTES

1. For a further elaboration of this theme, see "Women in Science: A Social Analysis" (Keller, 1974).

2. See, e.g., Kernberg (1977) for a psychoanalytic discussion of the prerequisites for mature love.

3. To the extent that she personifies nature, she remains, for the scientific mind, the final object as well.

4. These studies are, as is evident, of male scientists. It is noteworthy, however, that studies of the relatively small number of female scientists reveal in women scientists a similar, perhaps even more marked, pattern of distance in relation to the mother. For most, the father proved to be the parent of major emotional and intellectual importance (see, e.g., Plank and Plank, 1954).

5. Earlier I pointed out how Bacon's marital imagery constitutes an invitation to the "dominance of nature." A fuller discussion of this posture would also require consideration of the role of aggression in the development of object relations and symbolic thought processes—an aspect which has been omitted from the present discussion. Briefly, it can be said that the act of severing subject from object is experienced by the child as an act of violence, and it carries with it forever, on some level, the feeling tone of aggression. For insight into this process we can turn once again to Winnicott, who observes that "it is the destructive drive that creates the quality of externality" (p. 93), that, in the creation and recognition of the object there is always, and inevitably, an implicit act of destruction. Indeed, he says, "it is the destruction of the object that places the object outside the area of the subject's omnipotent control" (p. 90). Its ultimate survival is, of course, crucial for the child's development. "In other words, because of the survival of the object, the subject may now have started to live a life in the world of objects, and so the subject stands to gain immeasurably; but the price has to be pain in acceptance of the ongoing destruction in unconscious fantasy relative to object-relating" (p. 90). It would seem likely that the aggressive force implicit in this act of objectification must make its subsequent appearance in the relation between the scientist and his object, i.e., between science and nature.

6. In this I am joined by Dinnerstein (1976), who has recently written an extraordinarily provocative analysis of the consequences of the fact that it is, and has always been, the mother's "hand that rocks the cradle." Her analysis, though it goes much further and much deeper than the sketch provided here, happily corroborates my own in the places where they overlap. She concludes that the human malaise resulting from the present sexual arrangements can be cured only by dividing the nurturance and care of the infant equally between the mother and the father. Perhaps that is true. I would, however, argue that, at least for the particular consequences I have discussed here, other changes might be of comparable importance.

REFERENCES

Chodorow, N. (1974), Family Structure and Feminine Personality. In: *Woman, Culture and Society*, ed. M. Z. Rosaldo & L. Lamphere, Stanford: Stanford University Press, pp. 43–46.

Dinnerstein, D. (1976), *The Mermaid and the Minotaur.* New York: Harper & Row.

Farrington, B. (1951), *Temporus Partus Masculus,* an Untranslated Writing of Francis Bacon. *Centaurus,* 1:193–205.

Greenson, R. (1968), Disidentifying from Mother: Its Special Importance for the Boy. *Explorations in Psychoanalysis.* New York: International Universities Press, 1978, pp. 305–312.

Horney, K. (1926), The Flight from Womanhood. In: *Women and Analysis*, ed. J. Strouse. New York: Dell, 1975, pp. 199–215.

Hudson, L. (1972), *The Cult of the Fact.* New York: Harper & Row.

Keller, E. F. (1974), Women in Science: A Social Analysis. *Harvard Magazine*, October, pp. 14–19.

————— (manuscript), Cognitive Repression in Contemporary Physics.

Kernberg, O. (1977), Boundaries and Structure in Love Relations. *J. Amer. Psychoanal. Assn.*, 25:81–114.

Leiss, W. (1972), *The Domination of Nature.* Boston: Beacon Press, 1974.

Loewald, H. (1951), Ego and Reality. *Internat. J. Psycho-Anal.*, 32:10–18.

McClelland, D. C. (1962), On the Dynamics of Creative Physical Scientists. In: *The Ecology of Human Intelligence*, ed. L. Hudson. London: Penguin Books, pp. 309–341.

Milner, M. (1957), *On Not Being Able to Paint.* New York: International Universities Press.

Plank, E. N., & Plank, R. (1954), Emotional Components in Arithmetic Learning as Seen Through Autobiographies. *The Psychoanalytic Study of the Child*, 9:274–293. New York: International Universities Press.

Roe, A. (1953), *The Making of a Scientist.* New York: Dodd, Mead.

————— (1956), *The Psychology of Occupations.* New York: Wiley.

Winnicott, D. W. (1971), *Playing and Reality.* New York: Basic Books.

2

Feminist Criticism
of the Social Sciences

MARCIA WESTKOTT

Westkott's frequently cited paper was one of the earliest to indicate the critical potential of feminist work to influence the social sciences. Her theses that knowledge is inherently dialectical and that feminist inquiry has emancipatory as well as critical power were referred to in the Introduction of this volume. This article develops these themes in a sophisticated analysis of the impact of feminist inquiry on content, theory, and method in the social sciences.

One of the struggles and, indeed, one of the sources of intellectual excitement in women's studies is the critical dialogue that feminist scholars create within the various traditional disciplines. These dialogues are not debates between outsiders and insiders; they are, rather, critical confrontations among those who have been educated and trained within particular disciplines. The feminist debate arises because some of these insiders, who are women, are also outsiders.[1] When women realize that we are simultaneously immersed

Reprinted with permission from *Harvard Educational Review*, Vol. 49, No. 4, 1979:422–430.
Copyright © 1979 by the President and Fellows of Harvard College. All rights reserved.

in and estranged from both our own particular discipline and the Western intellectual tradition generally, a personal tension develops that informs the critical dialogue. This tension, rooted in the contradiction of women's belonging and not belonging, provides the basis for knowing deeply and personally that which we criticize. A personally experienced, culturally based contradiction means that in some fundamental way we as critics also oppose ourselves, or at least that part of us that continues to sustain the very basis of our own estrangement. Hence, the personal struggle of being both insider and outsider is not only a source of knowledge and insight, but also a source of self-criticism.

As the debate becomes institutionalized within the academic sphere through women's studies programs and journals, it begins to develop its own critical traditions, which, in the social sciences, have been directed to issues of content and method. More specifically, the criticism has focused upon the invisibility or distortion of women as objects of knowledge, and upon conventional modes of establishing social knowledge. These issues of content and method are hardly fleeting matters, for they strike at the very foundation of the contemporary practice of social science. At the same time, the criticism also implies alternatives to contents and methods judged to be inappropriate. Criticism is not practiced in a vacuum; it is always criticism of something by someone. By clarifying what a social science is not or should not be, we can begin to realize what it can and should be. My intention is to adumbrate the alternatives that are implied by the criticism for the purpose of suggesting more appropriate (from a feminist perspective) approaches to social knowledge. My focus is upon themes and ideas rather than upon a paraphrasing of particular criticisms. I shall discuss first the criticism of and implied alternatives to *content*, then *method*, and finally *purpose* of social knowledge of women.

Among the major arguments that feminist criticism directs at social science is that it concentrates on the distortion and misinterpretation of women's experience. Women have not only been largely ignored in traditional approaches to knowledge[2]; where women have been considered at all we have been measured in masculine terms.[3] The concept of the human being as a universal category is only the man writ large. "Woman" is considered an abstract deviation of this essential humanity[4]; she is a partial man, or a negative image of man, or the convenient object of man's needs.[5] In any case, a woman is defined exclusively in terms of her relationship to men, which becomes the source from which female stereotypes emerge and are sustained.[6]

Moving beyond these stereotypes requires renaming the characteristics of women, not in terms of deviations from or negations of a masculine norm, but as patterns of human responses to particular situations.[7] In this view, masculinity and femininity are simply different human possibilities that have emerged historically. This understanding has led feminist scholars to rethink the concept of the person to include traditionally female characteristics.

Another strand of feminist criticism of content concerns the assumption that the human being and "his" social environment are mutually compatible.

According to this assumption, the personality is formed by and therefore reflects its social contexts. The male character structure and patriarchal culture mutually reflect and support one another through social, political, and economic institutions. For this approach to person and society to remain consistent, women and other deviants must either become invisible or their estrangement from, or failure in, such a society must be explained in terms of their "natural" inferiority. In calling attention to women's invisibility in social science and in rejecting the notion of women's natural inferiority, feminists have challenged the assumption that self and society are mutually reflective and supportive.[8] Instead, they have stressed the idea that girls and women have grown up and have lived in social contexts that are opposed to their needs as human beings. These social contexts, they argue, are patriarchal: through the organization of social relations, women are controlled by men and are culturally devalued. Feminist scholarship has attended to both the material base of that control[9] and to the cultural and psychological aspects of female devaluation. Recent work has focused on how family organization influences that devaluation at psychological—often uncon-scious—levels.[10] Whether a women manages to struggle against this sub-jugation or succumbs to it, or more likely both, in a patriarchical culture, she is still an outsider, an other, a marginal person, a deviant. In short, she is alienated.

By stressing female alienation in a male world, feminist scholars have shredded the happy functionalist assumption of a mutually supportive re-lationship between personality and culture. Moreover, they have suggested a theoretical approach to social knowledge that defines the socially constituted world "out there" as alien and opposing. Women's alienation from the man-made world suggests an alternative approach to social knowledge that is critical rather than functionalilst, emphasizing the discontinuities rather than the continuities, the oppositions and the contradictions rather than the coincidence between persons and social contexts.[11]

Most feminist criticism of social science methods is derived from the criticism of content. According to this criticism, the patriarchal bias is reflected in the ways in which questions about women are posed: the absence of concepts that tap women's experience,[12] the viewing of women as an unchanging essence independent of time and place,[13] and the narrowness of the concept of the human being reflected in limited ways of understanding human behavior.[14] Although these criticisms address methodological issues, they do not directly challenge the epistemological basis of mainstream social science. The epistemological criticism remains implied or sketchy, although exceptions exist, such as the work of Canadian sociologist, Dorothy Smith.[15]

Like the Marxist tradition within which she works, Smith's criticism directly challenges the norm of objectivity that assumes that the subject and object of research can be separated from one another through a methodological screen. The subject-object dichotomy in social science refers to the distinction between the person conducting the research and the person about whom knowledge is being developed. The ideal of objectivity was advocated by nineteenth century positivists, including Emile Durkheim, who argued that the object of social knowledge should be regarded as any other physical phenomenon and that the subject who conducts research must always be on guard not to let feelings "infect" research.[16] More recent versions of this ideal of objectivity have emphasized the importance of the universal application of social science methods as the best guarantee against the bias of subjectivity.

Marxists, especially those affiliated with the Institute for Social Research at Frankfurt,[17] criticized this ideology of objectivity and challenged the positivist idea of generalizing science and the notion that truth can be expressed in causal relations independent of time and place. They charged that positivist methods shatter and abstract concrete social relations into ahistorical relationships among things. Smith underscores this Marxist critique with a concern for women as agents of knowledge. She argues that the methodological norm of objectivity is itself socially and historically consti-tuted, rooted in an ideology that attempts to mystify the social relations of the knower and the known through procedures that appear anonymous and impersonal. This aura of objectivity can be maintained so long as the object of knowledge, the "known," can be an "other," an alien object that does not reflect back on the knower. Considering women only as *objects* of social knowledge fails to challenge this disassociation. Moreover, it is consistent with the wider cultural objectification of women, in which our basic humanness is denied, but our externally determined characteristics can be categorized and related to one another like other phenomena. It is only where women are also brought in as the *subjects* of knowledge that the separation between subject and object breaks down. Smith comments: "So long as *men* and the pronouns *he, his,* etc. appeared as general and impersonal terms, there was no visible problem. Once women are inserted into sociological sentences as their subjects, however, the appearance of impersonality goes. The knower turns out not to be 'abstract knower' after all, but a member of a definite social category occupying definite positions within the society."[18]

The specificity of the knower is revealed when women become subjects of knowledge, because women are not identified with the abstract human being but with particular deviations or negations of this abstracted universal. Women studying women reveals the complex way in which women as objects of knowledge reflect back upon women as subjects of knowledge. Knowledge of the other and knowledge of the self are mutually informing, because self and other share a common condition of being women.

This emphasis upon the idea that subject and object are humanly linked converges with the interpretive tradition in the social sciences. Like the Marxist tradition, the interpretive tradition dissents from the mainstream positivist emphasis upon objectivity.[19] It emphasizes instead the idea that social knowledge is always interpreted within historical contexts, and that truths are, therefore, historical rather than abstract, and contingent rather than categorical. The interpretive approach also assumes that these historical truths are grasped not by attempting to eliminate subjectivity but through the intersubjectivity of meaning of subject and object. This intersubjectivity does not mean the identity of subject and object, but rather their dialectical relationship. Thus the questions that the investigator asks of the object of knowledge grow out of her own concerns and experiences. The answers that she may discover emerge not only from the ways that the objects of knowledge confirm and expand these experiences, but also from the ways that they oppose or remain silent about them. Hence, the intersubjectivity of meaning takes the form of dialogue from which knowledge is an unpredictable emergent rather than a controlled outcome.

This feminist critique of conventional social science methods intersects with the Marxist and interpretive criticisms at the points where their methodologies reflect women's experience. The idea of grounding inquiry in concrete experience rather than in abstract categories is reflected in women's historical identification with the concrete, everyday life of people and their survival needs. The idea of knowledge as an unpredictable discovery rather than a controlled outcome is reflected in women's historical exclusions from institutions, where planned rational control is the mode of operation, and in women's historical identification with domestic spheres which have been less rationally controlled or predictable. And finally, the idea of knowledge emerging from a self-other dialectic is reflected both in the historical exclusion of women from educational institutions where knowledge has been transmitted through books and lectures and in women's participation in societies and friendships where social knowledge has emerged from dialogue, a practice recently exemplified by women's consciousness-raising and support groups.

These historical experiences of women reflect the particular social relations implied by Marxist and interpretive methodologies. Threading itself throughout the social contexts of women creating and gaining knowledge is an affirmation of the idea of the human being as fully and freely creating herself and the world in which she lives, a process which includes negotiating that creation through dialogue with others. It is this sense of humanism that feminist social science affirms in these other critical traditions that have preceded it.

The third criticism that feminist scholars direct against traditional social science actually prefigures the other two. Containing implications for both content and method, it is concerned with the purpose of the social knowledge of women. It certainly takes no more than a modicum of perception to realize that women have become the latest academic fad. As objects of knowledge, women have become marketable commodities measured by increasing profits for publishers and expanding enrollments in women's studies courses. While women are riding the crest of the wave which we ourselves have helped to create, it may be a rather sobering, albeit necessary, task to reflect on the ephemeral nature of the academic market in which we are now valued.

In this respect we have much to learn from the academic social-science exploitation of the poor, especially the Blacks, in the sixties. In the name of academic liberal concern and compensation the black ghetto was measured, analyzed, processed, dissected—in short, reduced to manipulable data that advanced the career interests of the investigators but did little to improve the plight of the investigated.[20] The fact that research on the black ghetto is now passé, although black ghettos continue to exist, and research on women is now *au courant* should give us pause. Once women have had "their day," once the academic market has grown tired of this particular "area," once the journals are glutted with information about women, minority as well as white women, how then shall we justify the importance of studying women? Shall knowledge of women also recede in the shadow of benign neglect?

The issue here concerns the exploitation of women as objects of knowledge. So long as we endorse the idea that the purpose of the study of women is justified solely in terms of our past exclusion as objects of knowledge, we inadvertently contribute to this exploitation as well as to its faddish nature. Women are an attractive subject to exploit so long as we hold that the purpose of social knowledge is simply getting more information. In social science's unrestrained pursuit of information, any new object of study that can generate mounds of data is of interest so long as it is a prolific source.[21] When the data are no longer new, the object of study loses its primacy.

Along with this flimsy market valuation of content is the problem of simply recording the present or past conditions of women. The methodological approach which recognizes as valid only the factual recording of what is allows no justification for attending to alternatives to present conditions. The effect of this approach is to justify the present. Ironically, in the practice of conventional social science,[22] this methodological conservatism is frequently accompanied by an ideology of social change. Hence, it is not at all unusual to see social scientists, who openly advocate social change, practicing a social science that on the epistemological level denies the possibility of that change.[23] Women's devaluation and the consequences of this devaluation are reinforced by a social science which records these conditions while systematically ignoring alternative possibilities. A depressing pall hangs over this litany of past and present subjugation of women, precisely because its methodological principles allow for no future that is not an extension of present facts.

This approach to knowledge, impoverished by a flat and rigid literalness, reinforces the exploitation of women as data-generating objects of research. The method mirrors the idea of the person as a passive recorder of social reality. It is assumed that neither the process of recording data, nor the object about whom the data are recorded, has any imaginative capacity to transcend the present. Both the recorder and the recorded, the researcher and the researched, must necessarily resign themselves to the apparently self-perpetuating facts, facts which one can amass but cannot change. Social science, conceived in this way and applied to women, is an extension of the more-equals-better principle: the more information about women the better. If past examples are reliable clues, the only result can be an academic discipline in which initial excitement soon slips into the drudgery and cynicism of the accumulation of information for its own sake.

Opposed to this social science *about* women is an alternative social science *for* women.[24] A social science for women does not exclude information about women, but informs the knowledge it seeks with an intention for the future rather than a resignation to the present. The intention is not an historical inevitability but a vision, an imaginative alternative that stands in opposition to the present conditions of the cultural domination of women and is indeed rooted in these conditions. This dialogue with a future suggests a social science that is not simply a doleful catalogue of the facts of patriarchy, but an opposition to the very facts that it discovers.

The tension between describing and transforming which is first perceived in the knower, the subject of knowledge herself, implies a concomitant tension in the object of knowledge. From this perspective, women as objects of knowledge are viewed not as passive recipients nor as active, confirming reflections of society. Instead, the tension which informs the method suggests a concept of women in society which also expresses a negation: women opposing the very conditions to which they conform.

This tension requires at the very least a reconsideration of the assumption in social science research that there is a basic continuity between consciousness and activity. Conventional social science research continues to assume a fit between consciousness and activity,[25] despite the recognition of the possibility of a discontinuity between consciousness and activity. The assumption reflects the condition of being a male in patriarchal society, a condition of freedom, which admittedly varies greatly by race and class, to implement consciousness through activity. Because this freedom has been historically denied to women, the assumption of a convenient parallel between consciousness and activity does not hold. The idea of women simultaneously conforming to and opposing the conditions which deny their freedom suggests a breach between consciousness and activity that does not exist, at least not in the same way, for the men who have had the power to implement consciousness through activity and to create the concepts that reflect that power.

Such a dissociation between conforming behavior and consciousness emphasizes the crucial importance of women's consciousness in patriarchal society in at least two respects. In the first place, consciousness can be viewed as it is split off from activity,[26] freed from conforming behavior, imagining and fantasizing oneself in a world freed from oppression. In short, consciousness can be viewed as women's sphere of freedom, a sphere that exists simultaneously with unfree, conforming behavior. This is a split that women poets and novelists have long recognized. Witness Doris Lessing's account of a woman lunching with her husband and his colleague: "Having handed them coffee and chocolate wafers, she set an attentive smile on her face, like a sentinel, behind which she could cultivate her own thoughts."[27] The thoughts that are hidden behind the appropriately silent, feminine smile tell us who this women is and who she could be. Historians have been discovering these thoughts in women's journals, memoirs, and letters. This is the area of women's creative imagination that mainstream social science with its methodological insistence on recording behavior has not tapped. To ignore women's consciousness is to miss the most important area of women's creative expressions of self in a society which denies that freedom in behavior.

Secondly, the idea of women's dissociation of consciousness from behavior suggests not only a freeing of consciousness, but also a tension between consciousness and behavior. Considering behavior alone is insufficient to understanding women in patriarchy, nor is it adequate to link women's behavior only to the dominant, male-created ideology. As Nancy Cott has shown, the meaning which women ascribe to their own behavior is reducible to neither the behavior itself nor to the dominant ideology.[28] It is derived from women's consciousness which is influenced by the ideas and values of men, but is nevertheless uniquely situated, reflective of women's concrete position within the patriarchal power structure. Finally, this emphasis on consciousness suggests that women's unique interpretation of their own conforming behavior affects that behavior in ways that are intelligible only through reference to women's consciousness itself.

The opposition to patriarchal domination within both subject and object, knower and known, is a profound expression of a longing for freedom from that domination. For those of us who are seeking knowledge of women, this idea of freedom can be expressed as a future intention which indicates to us which facts in the present are necessary to know. These facts, including those concerning the ways in which we may unreflectively participate in our own victimization, may not be convenient or comfortable for us. But facts, even difficult ones, become important sources of self and social knowledge as a means of creating a future free of domination. Without this sense of what knowledge is important for our liberation, we are in the situation of gathering any and all information we can about ourselves so long as it sells, and thus we exploit ourselves as objects of knowledge. The difference between a social science about women and a social science for women, between the possibilities of self-exploitation and those of liberation, is our imaginative capacity to inform our understandings of the world with a commitment to overcoming the subordination and devaluation of women.

The feminist criticisms of social science content, method, and purpose are not tightly integrated into an academic discipline. They are, rather, strands that are just beginning to emerge. What all three share is a dialectical approach to social knowledge. To emphasize the dialectics of self and other, person and society, consciousness and activity, past and future, knowledge and practice, is to approach social knowledge as open, contingent, and humanly compelling, as opposed to that which is closed, categorical, and human-controlling.

This is the exciting challenge and hope that feminist criticism brings to social science. As a result, women's actions are being reinterpreted and profoundly illuminated from the perspective of women's consciousness.[29] Social institutions such as motherhood are being re-examined for their patriarchal assumptions and are being countered with a vision of decent and humane parenting.[30] A psychology of women emphasizes its intention to be *for* women by not only explaining the conditions that affect the psychology of women and men, but also by exploring the bases from which those conditions can be transformed.[31] Self-knowledge and social knowledge are being creatively mediated in women's studies programs, through collaborative scholarly work, and in professional dialogue.[32]

The practice of these alternatives is not without its practical risks, especially for those who employ them within academic contexts where the model of mainstream social science is the unexamined standard. The dialogue concerning the criticism and its alternative practices has been limited primarily to women's networks, caucuses, and organizations. Yet it offers intellectual excitement and vitality to the practice of social science as a whole. To attend to the feminist criticism is to open the social sciences to both the feminist challenge and its hope.

NOTES

An earlier version of this paper was presented at the National Women's Studies Association First National Conference, 1 June 1979. I am grateful to Lee Chambers-Schiller for reading the original draft and discussing these ideas with me.

1. See Vivian Gornick, "Women as Outsiders," in *Women in Sexist Society: Studies in Power and Powerlessness*, ed. Vivian Gornick and Barbara K. Moran (New York: New American Library, 1971), pp. 126–144.

2. The invisibility of women in all disciplines is an early and recurrent theme of feminist criticism. See Nona Glazer, "General Perspectives," in *Woman in a Man-Made World: A Socioeconomic Handbook*, ed. Nona Glazer and Helen Youngelson Waehrer, 2nd ed. (Chicago: Rand McNally College Publishing, 1977), pp. 1–4; Sally Slocum, "Woman the Gatherer: Male Bias in Anthropology," in *Toward an Anthropology of Women*, ed. Rayna Reiter (New York: Monthly Review Press, 1975), pp. 36–50; Delores Barrancano Schmidt and Earl Robert Schmidt, "The Invisible Woman: The Historian as Professional Magician," in *Liberating Women's History: Theoretical and Critical Essays*, ed. Bernice A. Carroll (Urbana: Univ. of Illinois Press, 1976), pp. 42–54.

3. Naomi Weisstein, "Psychology Constructs the Female," in *Woman in Sexist Society*, pp. 207–224; Susan Carol Rogers, "Woman's Place: A Critical Review of Anthropological Theory," *Comparative Studies in Society and History*, 20 (1978), 123–162.

4. Carol C. Gould, "The Woman Question: Philosophy of Liberation and the Liberation of Philosophy," in *Women and Philosophy: Toward a Theory of Liberation*, ed. Carol C. Gould and Marx W. Wartofsky (New York: Putnam, 1976), pp. 5–44.

5. Caroline Whitbeck, "Theories of Sex Difference," in *Women and Philosophy*, pp. 54–80.

6. Dorothy Dinnerstein, *The Mermaid and the Minotaur: Sexual Arrangements and Human Malaise* (New York: Harper & Row, 1976) among others, has argued that female stereotypes are male creations based upon role-defined male-female relations. See also Janita H. Williams, "Woman: Myth and Stereotype," *International Journal of Women's Studies*, 1 (1978), 221–247; Linda Gordon, Persis Hunt, Elizabeth Pleck, Rochelle Goldberg Ruthchild, and Marcia Scott, "Historical Phallacies: Sexism in American Historical Writing," in *Liberating Women's History*, pp. 55–74; Michele Wallace, *Black Macho and the Myth of the Superwoman* (New York: Dial, 1979).

7. Jean Baker Miller, *Toward a New Psychology of Women* (Boston: Beacon Press, 1977).

8. See Greer Litton Fox, "Nice Girl: Social Control of Women through a Value Construct," *Signs*, 2 (1977), 805–817.

9. See Heidi Hartmann, "Capitalism, Patriarchy, and Job Segregation," *Signs,* 1 (1976), 137–169.

10. See Dinnerstein, *The Mermaid and the Minotaur,* and Nancy Chodorow, *The Reproduction of Mothering* (Berkeley: Univ. of California Press, 1978).

11. An excellent example of scholarship that illuminates such contradictions is Nancy F. Cott, "Passionlessness: An Interpretation of Victorian Sexual Ideology, 1790–1850," *Signs,* 4 (1978), 219–236.

12. Joan I. Roberts, "The Ramifications of the Study of Women," in *Beyond Intellectual Sexism,* ed. Joan I. Roberts (New York: David McKay, 1976), p. 8; Arlene Kaplan Daniels, "Feminist Perspectives in Sociological Research," in *Another Voice: Feminist Perspectives on Social Life and Social Science,* ed. Marcia Millman and Rosabeth Moss Kanter (New York: Doubleday, 1975), pp. 340–370.

13. Sheila Ryan Johansson, "'Herstory' as History: A New Field or Another Fad?" in *Liberating Women's History,* pp. 402–403.

14. Arlie Russell Hochschild, "The Sociology of Feeling and Emotion: Selected Possibilities," in *Another Voice,* p. 283.

15. Dorothy Smith, "Women's Perspective as a Radical Critique of Sociology," *Sociological Inquiry,* 44 (1974), 7–13; "Some Implications of a Sociology for Women," in *Woman in a Man-Made World,* pp. 15–22.

16. Emile Durkheim, *The Roles of the Sociological Method* (New York: Free Press, 1964), pp. 32–44.

17. See Jurgen Habermas, *Knowledge and Human Interests,* trans. Jeremy Shapiro (Boston: Beacon Press, 1971); Theodor W. Adorno et al., *The Positivist Dispute in German Sociology,* trans. Glyn Adey and David Frisby (New York: Harper & Row, 1976); Herbert Marcuse, *Reason and Revolution* (New York: Oxford Univ. Press, 1941).

18. Smith, "Some Implications of a Sociology for Women," pp. 16–17.

19. The relationship between Marxist and interpretive approaches is drawn in Janet Wolff, "Hermeneutics and the Critique of Ideology," *Sociological Review,* 23, NS (1975), 811–828.

20. Alvin W. Gouldner, "The Sociologist as Partisan: Sociology and the Welfare State," in *The Relevance of Sociology,* ed. Jack D. Douglas (New York: Appleton-Century-Crofts, 1970), pp. 112–148; Frances Fox Piven and Richard A. Cloward, *Regulating the Poor: The Functions of Public Welfare* (New York: Random House, 1971).

21. Eric Voegelin, *The New Science of Politics: An Introduction* (Chicago: Univ. of Chicago Press, 1952), p. 8.

22. The following critique of the conservatism of the practice of positivist social science has been influenced by the work of those associated with the Institute for Social Research at Frankfurt. See fn. 18.

23. Marcia Westkott, "Conservative Method," *Philosophy of the Social Sciences,* 7 (1977), 67–76.

24. In the constitution developed at its founding conference in 1977, the National Women's Studies Association affirmed the importance of this distinction. "Constitution of the NWSA," *Women's Studies Newsletter,* 5, Nos. 1 and 2 (1977), 6.

25. See esp. Talcott Parsons, *Toward a General Theory of Action* (New York: Harper & Row, 1951).

26. This argument has been made with regard to class consciousness by some Marxists. See esp. Georg Lukacs, *History and Class Consciousness: Studies in Marxist Dialectics* (Cambridge, Mass.: MIT Press, 1971), pp. 83–109.

27. Doris Lessing, *The Summer Before the Dark* (New York: Knopf, 1973), p. 14.

28. Nancy F. Cott, "Passionlessness," pp. 219–236.

29. See esp. Caroll Smith Rosenberg, "The Female World of Love and Ritual," *Signs*, 1 (1975), 1–29; and Nancy F. Cott, *The Bonds of Womanhood* (New Haven: Yale Univ. Press, 1977).

30. Adrienne Rich, *Of Woman Born: Motherhood as Experience and Institution* (New York: Norton, 1976).

31. Miller, *Toward a New Psychology of Women.*

32. See Deena Metzger and Barbara Meyerhoff, "Dear Diary (or Listening to the Silent Laughter of Mozart while the Beds are Unmade and the Remains of Breakfast Congeal on the Table)," *Chrysalis*, 7 (1979), 39–49.

3

Knowledge
and Women's Interests

Issues of Epistemology
and Methodology in Feminist
Sociological Research

JUDITH A. COOK AND
MARY MARGARET FONOW

Thus far we have discussed and presented feminist research methods in philosophical terms: we have considered it primarily as one among many different ways of knowing. Cook and Fonow describe in a lucid, well-organized manner the concrete elements, or "nuts and bolts," of feminist research methods. Many of the themes that were discussed in the Introduction and in the preceding paper by Westkott—the shift in focus to women, the importance of consciousness-raising and knowledge for women, and the transformational, or emancipatory, power of women studies—are concretely exemplified in this chapter. Although Cook and Fonow's thesis is based on work published primarily in sociological sources, it nevertheless captures the essence of feminist work in all social sciences. (They do not talk specifically about oral history, but it is treated in the following chapter.)

In this paper we are concerned with analyzing current issues in feminist methodology as they appear in the writings of scholars working within the discipline of sociology. We have chosen to limit our analysis to works which were published or produced during the past nine years in order to focus on the most recent developments in this area, and to assess the cumulative effects of earlier feminist critiques of sociological methods and the assumptions which underlie them (e.g., Bernard, 1973; Smith, 1974; Millman and Kanter, 1975). We have also decided to focus on literature which is explicitly sociological in its subject matter and authorship. This has involved excluding recent developments in feminist methodology within other social science disciplines such as psychology and anthropology (see special issues of the journals *Psychology of Women Quarterly* [Unger, 1981] and *Women's Studies* [Scheper-Hughes, 1983]), and in fields ranging from history and literature (see *The Prism of Sex: Essays in the Sociology of Knowledge* [Sherman and Beck, 1979]) to philosophy and metaphysics (see *Discovering Reality: Feminist Perspectives on Epistemology, Metaphysics, Methodology, and Philosophy of Science* [Harding and Hintikka, 1983]). This strategy has been chosen to enable a summary of the progress made by feminist sociologists in transforming the epistemological and methodological nature of their own discipline and to highlight areas in which changes are necessary but, as yet, unaccomplished.

THE CONCEPT OF FEMINIST METHODOLOGY

The very notion of feminist methodology is an elusive concept because we have been trained to think in terms of a positivist schema which equates the term "methodology" with specific techniques for gathering and analyzing information. Instead, our use of the concept mirrors that of Abraham Kaplan's treatise on the conduct of contemporary social inquiry, in which he proposes that methodology refers to the *study* of methods and not simply to the specific techniques themselves: "The aim of methodology, then, is to describe and analyze these methods, throwing light on their limitations and resources, clarifying their presuppositions and consequences, relating their potentialities to the twilight zone at the frontiers of knowledge" (1964:23). Thus, our analysis has taken a sociology-of-knowledge approach to the concept of

Reprinted from *Sociological Inquiry*, Vol. 56, No. 1, Winter 1986:2–29. Used by permission of the University of Texas Press.

feminist methodology by examining both its practice in actual research and its underlying epistemological assumptions (Stacey and Thorne, 1985).

To a certain extent, we have found it difficult to formulate a closed concept of feminist methodology in sociology because of the gap between how epistemological assumptions are discussed in the abstract and how they are articulated in the empirical research studies we examined. On the one hand, feminist methodology is often presented as consisting of a number of assertions about the nature of social reality and sociological inquiry; on the other hand, pieces of empirical research may incorporate only one, two, or perhaps three of these ideas. Thus, a question arises over which is the *real* feminist methodology. Is feminist methodology that which feminist reasearchers *do* or that which they *aim for?* We argue that, at least within the field of sociology, feminist methodology is in the process of *becoming* and is not yet a fully articulated stance. Attempts to impose premature closure on definitions of feminist methodology run the risk of limiting its possibilities by stipulating a "correct" set of techniques without adequate opportunity to examine a wide variety of other approaches for their feminist relevance.

Moreover, we have focused on attempts to develop a theory of feminist methodology as well as the actual practice of feminist methodology because of our belief that knowledge should not be limited solely to what exists at present. In other words, rather than confining our analysis to studies where feminist methodology has been employed, we think it is important to include literature exploring the potential applications and paths of development of this concept. Following Immanuel Kant's notion of criticism (1933), we view feminist methodology as incorporating a critique of social science which includes reflections on the sources and potentials of possible knowledge. So, like Marcia Westkott (1979), we reject the conservatizing limitation of a phenomenon to the factual recording of what is, suppressing the likelihood that liberating alternatives will be discovered.

Moreover, we recognize the problems in detaching epistemological analysis from its substantive base. We agree with Liz Stanley and Sue Wise (1983:181) that "abstract discourse" is of little help to feminist scholars without an understanding of "direct experience directly related to us" as women and as researchers. We do not feel, as do Stanley and Wise, that one is preferable to the other; our framework views them as different aspects of the same phenomenon. But we do feel that understanding feminist methodology in sociology involves attending to the linkages between how it is done and how it is analyzed, rather than focusing only on one or the other.

Thus, our notion of feminist methodology is one which has emerged out of our reading of sociological literature of two types. The first concerns feminist analyses of the epistemological assumptions which underlie different ways of knowing the social and of understanding women's experiences. This includes those researchers who employ the self-reflective process in examining and interpreting their methodological stances and practices in regard to feminist ideals. The second type of literature includes empirical research on gender asymmetry that we feel incorporates these feminist assumptions into the techniques and strategies used to gather and analyze data. We located both types by searching the methodology and gender listings in *Sociological Abstracts* for the years 1977 through 1985, and by our own general knowledge of research in the field of feminist scholarship. (For a recent bibliography on feminist methodology, see Reinharz, Bombyk, and Wright, 1983.) We selected particular works in order to maximize the varieties displayed by the field; we were not attempting to see which methods were *most frequently* used by feminist researchers. Instead, we were interested in examining the *variety* of research strategies which have been informed by feminist assumptions about the nature of social reality. Moreover, our search for empirical studies was guided by a concern with methodological innovation; thus, we sought out those studies which used strategies not typically employed in mainstream sociological research.

To summarize, then, our notion of feminist methodology includes more than just a focus on the research techniques of feminist scholars. As we have applied the concept, it encompasses two interrelated dimensions: (1) the epistemological ideas of feminist methodology found in literature analyzing its possibilities, and (2) the methodological practices of feminist methodology displayed in studies of gender domination and subordination. Because of a desire to avoid premature closure of the concept, we have not formulated a universal definition or set of necessary and sufficient criteria; we feel there is no "correct" feminist methodology within the field of sociology at this point in time. Finally, we are aware of the problems inherent in focusing solely on the abstract components of feminist methodology, thereby detaching epistemology from its contextual base in actual research studies. Because of this, we have concentrated on uncovering the interrelations between these two levels as well as within them.

With all of these issues in mind, the following section presents some basic principles that run throughout sociological analyses of feminist epistemology. While few feminist empirical studies incorporate every one of these principles, all acknowledge at least one or two. This latter point will be discussed in a second section on applications of feminist principles to approaches in empirical research.

Principles of Feminist Methodology

From a review of the literature we have identified five basic epistemological principles discussed by scholars who have analyzed feminist methodology in the field of sociology. They include (1) the necessity of continuously and reflexively attending to the significance of gender and gender asymmetry as a basic feature of all social life, including the conduct of research; (2) the centrality of consciousness-raising as a specific methodological tool and as a general orientation or "way of seeing"; (3) the need to challenge the norm of objectivity that assumes that the subject and object of research can be separated from one another and that personal and/or grounded experiences are unscientific; (4) concern for the ethical implications of feminist research and recognition of the exploitation of women as objects of knowledge; and (5) emphasis on the empowerment of women and transformation of patriarchal social institutions through research.

Acknowledging the Pervasive Influence of Gender. Attending to the significance of gender as a basic fact of social life involves a number of factors. First and perhaps foremost, women and their experiences, including but not solely their relations to men, are the focus of inquiry (Epstein, 1981). Thus, investigations employing feminist methodology view women through a "female prism" in "research devoted to a description, analysis, explanation, and interpretation of the female world" (Bernard, 1979:274). Often these investigations occur within a sphere that has been socially lived as personal so that feminist methodology does not deny or discount the subjective but rather seeks to validate the private, emotional interiorized, intimate world (MacKinnon, 1982).

A second aspect of this principle involves the recognition that much of what masquerades as sociological knowledge about human behavior is in fact knowledge about male behavior (Ward and Grant, 1984). Taking men as the normal subjects of research is a way of ignoring gender that results in equating the masculine with the universal (ASA Committee on the Status of Women in Sociology, 1980). Such unexamined assumptions regarding scientific objectivity often serve to obscure patriarchal bias at the very core of science (Cook, 1983). David Morgan (1981) proposes that academic discourse is, in reality, a male discourse hiding behind the labels of science, rationality, and scholarship. Since men dominate academic settings, where much research is carried out, they create a male scientific culture characterized by male sociability and grounded in an academic "machismo."

A third way of attending to gender is to locate the researcher as a gendered being (Eichler, 1980) in the web of social relations that simultaneously influences the analytical and interpretive procedures of sociology and shapes the life experiences of the researcher. For example, Dorothy Smith (1981:36) views social relations—the "regular, repetitive and differentiated work activities of individuals related to one another in modes to which property relations are central"—as the starting point for every analysis, so that explications of these relations allows the feminist researcher to understand the actions of another individual. In this way, the feminist investigator is able to locate herself as a subject in history so that her own vantage point arises from the same social relations that structure the everyday worlds of the experiences of those she studies. Understanding the common experiences of women researchers and women subjects in a society characterized by a marked degree of gender asymmetry enables the feminist researcher to bring women's realities into sharper focus.

To summarize, acknowledging the importance of gender in social life and social research means a variety of things to feminist sociologists. Specifically, it involves defining women as the focus of analysis, recognizing the central place that men have held in most sociological analysis, and viewing gender as a crucial influence on the network of relations encompassing the research act.

Focus on Consciousness-Raising. The concept of consciousness-raising is incorporated into feminist methodology in a variety of ways. The feminist consciousness of the researcher (and the researched), the use of consciousness-raising techniques as a research method, and the consciousness-raising potential of the research act are the three most salient features of this aspect of epistemology (Richardson, Fonow, and Cook, 1985).

As an outcome of being in society but not of society, feminist scholars inhabit the world with a "double vision of reality" which is part of their feminist consciousness (Stanley and Wise, 1983). Through this double vision "women's understandings of our lives are transformed so that we see, understand and feel them in a new and quite different way" at the same time that we see them in the "old way," enabling us "to understand the seemingly endless contradictions present within life" (1983:54). This ability to penetrate official interpretations of reality and apprehend contrary forces places feminists in a position to name, describe, and define women's experiences, in essence to conceptualize or in some cases reconceptualize social reality. At the methodological level, an awareness of the double consciousness that arises from being a member of an oppressed class (women) and a privileged class (scholars) enables feminist researchers to explore women's perceptions of their situation from an experiential base (Reinharz, 1983). According to Maria Mies (1983), if women's lives are to be made visible, "Feminist women must deliberately and courageously integrate their repressed, unconscious female subjectivity, i.e., their own experience of oppression and discrimination, into the research process" (1983:121). Because women and other exploited groups are forced, out of self-preservation, to know the motives of their oppressors as well as how oppression and exploitation feel to the victims, they are better equipped to comprehend and interpret women's experiences.

Scholars who possess the double vision of reality are also in a better position to understand various responses to oppression, particularly the contradictions between action and consciousness. Westkott (1979) maintains that the freedom to implement consciousness through activity will vary greatly by race, class, and gender. Thus, research methods which overemphasize quantification force the researcher to pose structural questions about action while ignoring the subjective dimension of behavior, as well as the contradictions between action and consciousness. Such an approach ignores the fact that women simultaneously oppose and conform to conditions that deny their freedom. However, this split between conforming behavior and consciousness opens the possibility of at least imagining one's freedom. In this way, "consciousness can be viewed as women's sphere of freedom, a sphere that exists simultaneously with unfree, conforming behavior," so that methodological overreliance on recording behavior and failure to tap the private terrain of consciousness neglects "the most important area of women's creative expression of self in a society which denies that freedom in behavior" (1979:429).

Consciousness-raising as a specific methodological tool has been advocated by a number of feminist sociologists (Mies, 1983; Stanley and Wise, 1983;

Reinharz, 1983). One way this can be done is to examine situations that typically produce changes in consciousness, such as divorce, unemployment, widowhood, infertility, rape, physical abuse, and sexual harassment. Studying crisis situations increases the likelihood that the researcher and subject will relate during a more self-conscious "click" moment. "Only when there is a rupture in the 'normal' life of a woman . . . is there a chance for her to become conscious of her condition" (Mies, 1983:125). The rupture with normalcy serves to demystify the "naturalness" of patriarchal relations and enables the subject to view reality in a different way.

Another application of this method is through the use of specific consciousness-raising techniques, such as role playing, rap groups, simulations, and psycho-drama, in a more self-conscious, deliberate manner. These approaches have provided feminist researchers with a way to tap women's collective consciousness as a source of data and have provided participants in the research project with a way to confirm the experiences of women which have often been denied as real in the past (Reinharz, 1983). Mies suggests a shift from individual interviews toward group discussions held over a period of time to obtain more diverse data and also to help female subjects "overcome their structural isolation in their families and to understand that their individual sufferings have social causes" (1983:128). Similarly, Thelma McCormack (1981) proposes the use of simulation to examine processes such as persuasion and problem solving in a controlled laboratory setting designed to encourage role flexibility and freedom from one's personal biography. She notes that simulation techniques enable women to ignore history in formulating their behavior and that such a method generates affective responses among subjects that result in consciousness-raising.

Finally, the research process itself can become a process of "conscientization" for both the researcher and the subjects of research. The methodology of conscientization has been borrowed from Paulo Freire and adapted to feminist analysis by Mies (1983). This problem-formulating method makes the objects of research the subjects of research. In the process of learning to perceive social, political, and economic contradictions, the people are motivated to take action against the oppressive elements of reality (1983:126). Thus, the outcome of research is greater awareness leading to social change.

In summary, then, the theme of consciousness-raising is a central tenet of feminist methodology in a variety of different forms. First, a researcher's feminist consciousness can serve as a source of knowledge and insight into gender asymmetry and how it is managed in social life. Second, consciousness-raising techniques can be used to elicit data from respondents while consciousness-raising life-course transitions provide an opportune context in which to examine women's worlds. Finally, the process of conscientization combines consciousness-raising and social change through encouraging politicization and activism on the part of research subjects.

Rejection of the Subject/Object Separation. Feminists have questioned the normative structure of science, including the canon of objectivity. Chief among their concerns are the rigid dichotomy between the researcher and the researched and the resulting objectification of women and tendency to equate quantification with value neutrality.

Epistemologically, feminist methodology rejects the assumption that maintaining a strict separation between researcher and research subject produces a more valid, objective account. One way in which feminists avoid treating their subjects as mere objects of knowledge is to allow the respondent to "talk back" to the investigator. An example of this is Ann Oakley's feminist paradigm for interviewing (1981) which seeks to minimize objectification of the subject as data by viewing the interview as an interactional exchange. In her framework, answering the questions of interviewees personalizes and humanizes the researcher and places the interaction on a more equal footing. The meaning of the interview to both the interviewer and the interviewee and the quality of interaction between the two participants are all salient issues when a feminist interviews women. Oakley also points out that interactive interviewing is an approach which documents women's own accounts of their experiences and allows the sociologist to garner knowledge not simply for the sake of knowledge itself but for the women who are providing information. Similarly, mechanical failure of her tape recorder led Helena Lopata (1980) to discover that, without a predetermined interview schedule, widows focused on subjects very different from those she had thought would be important. This feedback from respondents was then used to construct a better survey instrument, more responsive to the actual concerns of the women.

Within the tradition of action research, several feminist sociologists advocate a participatory research strategy which emphasizes the dialectic between researcher and researched throughout the entire research process, including formulation of research problem, collection of data, interpretation of findings, and implementation of results (Abdullah and Zeidenstein, 1978; Barndt, 1980; Fonow, 1985). The researcher's understanding of her connectedness to the experiences of the research subject through partial identification is labeled "conscious partiality" by Mies and becomes for her a way to replace mere "spectator knowledge," which emphasizes neutrality and indifference toward subjects' lives (1983:123).

Feminists have been pointed in their analysis of how this false dichotomy between subject and object obscures the political domination of women through their objectification in research. According to Smith (1979), feminists are in the unique position to understand how sociological methods conceal the social relations between the knower and the object. As researchers try to include women as subjects they cannot fail to notice how the practice of sociology transforms all actors into objects. "As women we become objects to ourselves as subjects. We ourselves, therefore, can look back as subjects constituted as objects in that relation, and in doing so, we disclose its essential contradiction" (1979:159). Feminist consciousness of the link between the knower and subject can not only serve to demystify objectivity and the objectification of women, but also extends our understanding of how the exploitations of women as data mirrors the treatment of women who contribute their specific skills and expertise to the research enterprise. Thus, women research assistants, secretaries, graduate students, and (often unnamed) spouses are manipulated and objectified through the research process (Nebraska Sociological Feminist Collective, 1982).

Feminist have also been critical of the tendency to equate measurement or quantification with objectivity. Numerous critiques of quantitative research techniques have been made by sociologists who have pointed out the potentials for distortion of women's experiences inherent in this approach. For example, Mildred Pagelow's analysis of research on battered women (1979) points out that current emphasis on statistical methods means that variables are often conceptualized according to what is most easily quantifiable rather than what is most theoretically important. Thus, woman battering is typically defined as referring only to physical violence, excluding psychological and verbal abuse because it is too difficult to measure quantitatively. Another example of quantitative objectification concerns the way statistics are kept by non-sociologists and then adopted uncritically by researchers who fail to explore sexist assumptions underlying the definitions of statistical categories (e.g., the fact that the FBI does not include marital rape as rape in its Uniform Crime Reports, or the fact that local police department statistics often blend wife abuse with other domestic violence crimes such as child abuse or sibling-to-sibling violence). Pagelow also explores how assumptions underlying the construction of many scales, inventories, and indexes are biased against women or include unsubstantiated claims. This is particularly the case when researchers use family violence scales, which equate a slap delivered by a man with a slap delivered by a woman, ignoring the obvious sex differences in the intensity of such violence and in the outcome of such abuse. She points out that, in general, the insistence that sociologists use only research instruments tested previously for validity and reliability in a large variety of populations often means insisting that they use out-dated scales and questions with underlying sexist biases. Finally, Ann and Robin Oakley's (1979) critique of the production and use of official statistics notes the necessity of distinguishing between the processes producing actual behavior and the processes producing statistics, since these are separate phenomena requiring different interpretations. For example, women may be erroneously categorized as "homemakers" after they have lost their jobs because they fail to report their status as "unemployed" given the lesser entitlement of women's jobs to unemployment benefits.

To summarize, rejection of the rigid dichotomy of subject and object has led sociologists to three paths of investigation. First, they have explored the fallacy that strict separation of researcher and respondent produces more valid, legitimate knowledge. Second, they have examined ways in which the research process obscures yet reinforces the subordination of women participants at every level. Finally, equation of quantification with objectivity has been critiqued by feminist scholars who point out that quantification has its own inherent biases and distortions.

Examination of Ethical Concerns. A concern with ethical issues is another characteristic of feminist methodology, and a number of scholars have tried to delineate the central tenets of a feminist ethic. The Nebraska Sociological Feminist Collective (1982) has developed a comprehensive analysis of issues they believe characterize such an ethic. They place professional ethical questions within the context of a feminist perspective that recognizes the oppression of women both within society and within the discipline of sociology.

One key element in this oppression is the use of language which perpetuates women's subordination. The generic use of masculine pronouns, application of offensive adjectives to women's experiences, and subsumption of women under male category labels (e.g., considering lesbian issues as part of the topic of [male] homosexuality) are just some of the ways language is used for social control. Further, a feminist ethic requires investigation into professional gatekeeping practices, particularly those which prevent publication and dissemination of feminist research through "mainstream" sociological channels (Eichler, 1981). Additional feminist issues regarding the gatekeeping process include the influence of gatekeeping on topic selection and research funding; the problems involved when feminists become gatekeepers; formulation and implementation of alternatives to the present gatekeeping system; and the effects of gatekeeping on feminists negotiating the processes of hiring, promotion, and tenure (Cook and Fonow, 1984).

Judith DiIorio (1982) discusses the ethical dilemmas of feminist praxis in feminist fieldwork. Interpretation of the feminist goal of social change becomes problematic when the researcher seeks to intervene in the lives of those she is trying to understand. Because much of feminist politics involves the personal and intimate lives of women and men, any intervention risks the possibility of disrupting relationships that are personally satisfying to the participants and perhaps materially necessary for survival. DiIorio discusses her female respondents in a participant-observation study of automotive van clubs:

> . . . they were working-class women whose economic independence under present structural realities was a virtual impossibility, and whose consciousness of survival strategies saw little hope external to that of marriage. Unless I could offer a means of altering the material realities of their existence in the here and now, I wondered what was to be gained by seeking to raise their consciousness concerning the injustices of heterosexism and their personal relationships. (1982:14)

Finally, feminist sociologists have addressed the ethics of dealing with research subjects' requests for assistance and information. Rather than viewing such requests as impediments to eliciting information, investigators have questioned the moral implications of *withholding* needed information. Ann Oakley (1981) confronted this issue in her study of childbirth and decided to forego the "correct" but ludicrous responses recommended by methodology texts:

> . . . strategies recommended in the textbooks for meeting interviewee's questions . . . advise that such questions as "Which hole does the baby come

out of?" "Does an epidural ever paralyse women?" and "Why is it dangerous to leave a small baby alone in the house?" should be met with such responses from the interviewer as "I guess I haven't thought enough about it to give a good answer right now," or "a head-shaking gesture which suggests that's a hard one" . . . Also recommended is laughing off the request with the remark that "my job at the moment is to get opinions, not to have them." (1981:48)

In summary, feminist methodology involves a concern with ethical issues that arise when feminists participate in the research process. These include the use of language as a means of subordination, the fairness of gatekeeping practices, interventions in respondents' lives, and withholding needed information from women subjects. Anticipating the consequences of research for the research subjects and the potential ethical issues involved are themselves problematic, and more attention to the development of a feminist ethics is in order. Along those lines, a recent issue of the journal *Humanity and Society* was devoted to the topic of feminist ethics, edited by the Nebraska Sociological Feminist Collective.

Emphasis on Empowerment and Transformation. Feminism is also likely to influence the researcher's view of knowledge itself. Central to many discussions of feminist methodology is the notion that the purpose of knowledge is to change or transform patriarchy (Acker, Barry, and Esseveld, 1983). For Westkott, producing a "doleful catalogue of the facts of patriarchy" is not enough (1979:429). Feminism is a vision of freedom as future intention and this vision must indicate which facts from the present are necessary knowledge for liberation. Description without an eye for transformation is inherently conservative and portrays the subject as acted-upon rather than as an actor or potential actor.

Feminist researchers are also aware that there is an audience for their knowledge, often comprised of individuals with conflicting expectations, intentions, and goals. Jean Lipman-Blumen (1979) discussed the special difficulties of the researcher's relationship to policy makers, community activists, other researchers, and the target group itself. Technical language, elaboration of obvious truths, conflicting findings, overly lengthy reports, political naiveté, unrealistic project time lines, and unresearchable questions are a few of the many problems caused by the mismatch between demands of policy and action and the results of inquiry. Though the problems can be dealt with by the investigator through a variety of strategies, Lipman-Blumen warns that all parties need to focus on workable implementation plans in order to translate knowledge into policy or action. Pagelow advocates the participation of the target group in the planning and the conduct of public policy research (1979). Her specific recommendations concern research on battered women and stress the advantages of involving women's shelters in the investigation process. She argues that shelters provide a client population of women and children potentially available for study, and that shelter staff are another source of information regarding both organization features and interpersonal group processes relevant to the delivery of services to shelter residents.

For Mies, social change is the starting point of science. In order to understand the content, form, and consequences of patriarchy the researcher must be actively involved in the fight against women's exploitation and oppression so that "in order to understand a thing one has to change it" (1983:125). Methodologically, this means the search for techniques which analyze and record the historical process of change and ultimately the transfer of such methodological tools to the subjects of research so they might confront their oppression and formulate their own plan of action. Thus, "the truth of a theory is not dependent on the application of certain methodological principles and rules but on its potential to orient the processes of praxis toward progressive emancipation and humanization" (1983:124). Feminist research is, thus, not research about women but research for women to be used in transforming their sexist society.

To summarize, an assumption of feminist methodology is that knowledge must be elicited and analyzed in a way that can be used by women to alter oppressive and exploitative conditions in their society. This means that research must be designed to provide a vision of the future as well as a structural picture of the present. This goal involves attending to the policy implications of an inquiry, and may involve incorporating the potential target group in the design and execution of a study. Finally, feminist methodology endorses the assumption that the most thorough kind of knowledge and understanding comes through efforts to change social phenomena.

Innovative Application of Research Strategies in Feminist Methodology

In order to address the topic of gender asymmetry using feminist epistemological assumptions, researchers have applied a variety of innovative approaches. Although most of these techniques and strategies have been used elsewhere for purposes not explicitly feminist, we argue that their innovative character is not in their formulation but in their application. In other words, what is unique about these studies is the way in which epistemological, methodological, and ontological concerns coincide, given their focus on sexual inequality through a lense shaped by the epistemological assumptions discussed earlier.

While no single investigation incorporates all five of these assumptions, most of the studies discussed in this section have employed at least two or three. However, we feel it is important to avoid equating the *number* of epistemological concerns addressed by a study with the *degree* of feminism of its methodology. We are *not* proposing an additive model of feminist methodology in which a study dealing with four epistemological issues is considered "more feminist" than one incorporating only three. In general, we feel there is little to be gained by this type of competitive comparison. Of greater interest and usefulness are the ways in which epistemology is related to research design, methods, and analysis, and the following will focus on these interconnections.

Visual Techniques. Several feminists have used methodologies such as photography and videotaping to collect and/or elicit data. For example,

Deborah Barndt (1980) used a photo-novela to study the development of social and political consciousness among Peruvian women who were participating in a literacy program. This photo-novela consisted of pictures of two different teaching styles, one authoritarian and the other participatory. The novela was developed in collaboration with teachers and coordinators from the program, and then shown to students who were asked to comment on the pictures' relevance for their own experiences with education and the larger community. In this way, Barndt sought to capture the development of critical social consciousness (conscientization) among Third World migrant women and to show how dialogical interactive educational programs could nurture such a consciousness. This, in turn, enabled Barndt to explore the ways in which reflection and action operate on two levels—the psycho-social and the structural—to stimulate the development of critical analyses of social and political responsibilities. By focusing on the reactions of four non-literate Peruvian women to the photo-novela, Barndt demonstrates how their comments indicate the growing political awareness accompanying learning how to read, as well as changes in the women's responses to their own life situations through both personal reflection and public action, such as a woman-organized strike for better village water conditions.

Likewise, Timothy Diamond (1977) used visual imagery to explore the notion that men and women inhabit different social worlds in which common linguistic structures assume different meanings for individuals, depending upon their gender. Subjects in this study were asked to play the common party game of charades, acting out titles of books and movies selected by the researchers (e.g., *Tender Is the Night, The Parent Trap, Sons and Lovers*). Diamond videotaped these visual images and analyzed them according to the sex of the actor, revealing the extent to which words may be internalized and enacted dissimilarly. For example, men and women exhibited differences in the ways they "imaged" terms referring to parenthood; men enacted the term as if they were members of a triadic unit of father, mother, and child while women indicated only a mother and child to form a dyad; moreover, women portrayed the ages of children as younger (usually babes-in-arms) while men portrayed children as physically older and larger (usually waist-high). Diamond related these findings to the nature of parenthood in contemporary American society where fathers are generally not active in nurturing young children and where the bond between mother and child is typically considered the major parental relationship, with the father-child relationship usually being less intense. Other examples of the use of visual imagery as a method for exploring gender asymmetry are Gillespie-Woltemade's use of pictures of gravestones to depict power inequalities in familial relationships throughout America and Europe (1980), and Flora's analysis of class and gender politics in Latin American photonovels (1984).

Returning to Barndt's research on Peruvian women, one can see that her methods and design reflected the assumptions discussed earlier. The study's focus on women's lives, the importance of consciousness-raising (in this case, Barndt talks about the raising of her own consciousness as well as that of the women in her study), the feedback of ideas and world views between the feminist researcher and her Third World women subjects, and an emphasis on the empowerment of women to address their problems and seek changes in their villages are all examples of how a feminist epistemology underlies her research agenda and its execution. Moreover, visual methodologies are often useful for probing the hidden arenas in which many women operate in day-to-day life, as well as for eliciting more personal and intimate responses from subjects, as can be seen in the work of both Barndt and Diamond. On the other hand, visual approaches are also well suited for capturing the more mundane and taken-for-granted aspects of social existence which are rich in implications, although usually ignored, as in the analysis of Gillespie-Woltemade. Thus, visual techniques offer a range of largely unexplored possibilities for feminist researchers.

Triangulation of Methods. Another feminist methodological strategy is that of triangulation, or the use of more than one research technique simultaneously (Merton, 1957). Usually, this involves employing at least one quantitative and one qualitative method so that findings from each may inform and complement the other (Cook, 1984). One recent example is a study of teaching styles and attitudes of male and female university professors which used timed observation of classroom situations, questionnaires completed by students, and open-ended interviews with professors to elicit data (Richardson, Macke, and Cook, 1980). This study found that the position of women in academia could best be understood through a multi-dimensional approach which focused on their teaching styles (observation), reactions to the teaching from students (questionnaires), and the women's own thoughts, feelings, and experiences about university teaching (interviews). An important insight which emerged from this study was that women in the college classroom faced a double bind in which they had to demonstrate their competence to win the respect and cooperation of "skeptical" students while simultaneously diffusing their authority in order to avoid negative sanctions from students for violating female role expectations. Another example is Rosabeth Moss Kanter's research on men and women in a large multinational corporation which used participant-observation, interviewing, questionnaires, and content analysis to understand gender inequality in this type of organizational setting (1977). Yet another example can be found in the work of Helen Roberts on relationships between women and their doctors which employed content analysis of medical records, interviews with patients, interviews with doctors, and content analysis of professional literature and medical journals (1981).

Given that certain types of methods may systematically prevent the elicitation of particular types of information (Millman and Kanter, 1975), and given that the vast majority of published research in sociology uses quantitative techniques (Spector and Faulkner, 1980), triangulation is an especially appropriate feminist strategy for two reasons. First, by ensuring that qualitative approaches are included it increases the ability to gather information that is missing from the discourse of sociological knowledge due to the over-emphasis on topics which can be studied through quantification. Second, triangulation allows feminist researchers to debunk the biased and distorted results of earlier studies by replicating their original methods (usually quantitative) and comparing these results with finds on the same topic using other methods (usually qualitative) (Cook, 1983).

Linguistic Techniques. Another feminist methodological strategy involves borrowing techniques commonly used by linguists to conduct conversational analysis. One example is Pamela Fishman's analysis of taped conversations between couples in their homes (1978), which focused on how verbal interaction both reflects and perpetuates hierarchical relationships between men and women. Fishman found that women were more active in ensuring continuance of interaction through asking questions about male-initiated topics, making supportive utterance ("mm's," "yeah's," "oh's"), and using attention beginnings ("this is interesting," "y'know") to elicit male partners' interest. On the other hand, men were more likely to assume a dominant role in conversation through the use of minimal response to indicate lack of interest and by making statements that indicated the men's assumption that their topic was interesting and would elicit a response. Her results led Fishman to conclude that "the people who do the routine (conversational) maintenance work, the women, are not the same people who either control or benefit from the process" (1978:405). Moreover, it appears that the technique of conversational analysis allows investigators to study the "trivial, mundane interactions" that comprise "much of the essential work of sustaining the reality of the world" (1978:398).

Another example of this type of analysis is the work of Carol Gardner on male-to-female street remarks in urban settings (1980). Using interviewing to elicit the examples that were analyzed, Gardner focuses on how breaches of the norm of inattention between strangers in urban environments function to reaffirm male dominance and reinforce female role requirements of politeness and passivity. For example, women are faced with a dilemma when they encounter the common coupling of a respectful greeting ("Good morning, miss") followed by an evaluative remark ("You sure have got great boobs"), leaving women feeling confused and gulled and unsure of how to respond. Other dilemmas occur when women are expected to conform to the female stereotype of politeness by ignoring the uninvited comment yet punished when they do so and in situations where women's normal behavior is treated as if it is out of role. Through her analysis, Gardner is able to focus, once again, on the role of the mundane, daily life experiences which both illustrate and perpetuate sexual subordination.

Textual Analysis. The study of written texts has been employed by investigators to address several feminist issues. One example of this is a paper analyzing gender biases in the works of sociologist Erving Goffman written by the Nebraska Feminist Collective (1982). The collective's strategy was for each member to select one of Goffman's major pieces and acquaint herself with it individually. Next, everyone circled words or passages from their selection that fell into one of four coding categories devised by the group. Following that, each member re-read the entire text and extracted sexist statements as well as more implicit and contextual problems of bias, such as problems of omission and tone. These selections were reviewed by the group as a whole, which acted as an informed panel of judges for evaluating the coding of words, passages, and context. Then, each member took responsibility for writing a section of the final paper, which was reviewed and edited by the entire group. The results of the analysis revealed five dimensions of sexism in the writings of Goffman: (1) exclusion of women as a category of analysis; (2) repeated use of overt sexist statements made by *other* authors to illustrate points; (3) overemphasis on women's manipulative nature; (4) reinforcement of traditional gender roles; and (5) stress on male-dominated sexual relationships. This kind of shared textual analysis enables researchers to analyze a wide range of written documents and allows for group discussion in the construction of coding categories and throughout the actual coding process.

Another type of textual analysis is performed by Dorothy Smith (1983), whose framework entails understanding the social relations that underlie the production of a text as well as the ways in which it is heard or read. In one example, she analyzes an account of how a set of friends come to define a women (K) as mentally ill (1978). Noting that a large amount of contextual information is needed to justify the label of mental illness, Smith looks for ways the account is structured to show K's behavior as anomalous or unexplainable by any set of rules. One device which sets up K's behavior to be interpreted as odd are "contrast situations" (1978:39). Here, a description of K's action is preceded by information which sets up her behavior as bizarre ("When asked casually to help in a friend's garden, she went at it for hours, never stopping, barely looking up") (1978:39). Another example is the "cutting-out operation" by which K is demonstrated to be on a different "wavelength" than those around her because she does not recognize things that are blatantly obvious to her friends. In another set of texts, Smith addresses the differential meaning of the assertions "she killed herself" and "she committed suicide" by analyzing passages from Quentin Bell's biography of Virginia Woolf, psychiatric case histories, psychiatric texts, and an autobiography (1983). Much of Smith's analysis focuses on how texts constitute an abstracted mode of separating experience from its relation to an acting, feeling, thinking subject by use of certain terms and grammatical and logical links indicating proper sequencing.

Refined Quantitative Approaches. Some feminist sociologists have turned their attention to refining and developing quantitative ways of measuring phenomena related to sexual asymmetry and women's worlds. A recent example of this is an article by Singleton and Christiansen (1977) describing the construction and validation of a shortform "attitudes toward feminism" scale. In developing an instrument consisting of five and ten items, the authors note that the final product can be used reliably in a wide range of research situations where economy requires brief measures of prejudiced and authoritarian attitudes toward women. Likewise, a study by Schuman et al.

(1981) examined the effects of context on survey responses to questions about abortion. These researchers compared responses to a general item about abortion (Should a pregnant woman be able to obtain an abortion if she is married and wants no more children?) and a more specific item (Should a woman be able to obtain an abortion in the case of a defect in the unborn child?) They found that agreement with the general item was significantly higher when it was not preceded by the more specific item, and consequently they proposed that, when the specific item was asked first, respondents may have assumed that the general question did not refer to cases of fetal abnormalities. Additionally, they note that this kind of context effect is especially likely when researchers try to summarize a complex issue with a single, general item, warning against the dangers of unreliable results in such cases. Additional examples of this approach include Mary Corcoran's study of sex differences in measurement error (1980) and attempts to redefine and reoperationalize indicators of labor force participation for Third World women who work in the informal and nontraditional sectors of their countries' economies (Dixon, 1982; Deere and de Leal, 1979).

Collaborative Strategies. Some feminist sociologists have adopted the collaborative or collective model of conducting research (MacKie, 1985). Mary Jo Deegan (1983) analyzes the histories of three feminist sociology collectives to which she has belonged, focusing on factors affecting success or failure in writing and publishing as well as longevity. It seems that the collective process has several advantages over traditional, individualistic ways of doing social science. First, opportunities for receiving feedback are considerably enhanced; Deegan's analysis itself was read and critiqued by all but two of the members of the three collectives she discusses. Second, members can nurture each others' professional development through acting as "peer mentors" by "sharing information on how to write papers, how to get them accepted at meetings, how to submit and publish papers, and, most importantly, how to think of ourselves as theorists" (1983:8). Part of this collegial relationship between members also involves making networking contacts with other feminists. Finally, working collectively has the important advantage of generating optimism about feminist sociology through stimulating participants to develop a feminist understanding of everyday life.

In one of their papers, members of the second collective analyzed by Deegan—the Nebraska Feminist Collective—describe their group approach to sociological inquiry. They note that the collaborative model is hindered by situations such as school changes, varying commitments to the profession, unequal access to resources, and academic standards that favor competitive, individualistic writings over cooperative, reflective ones. Despite these hinderances, however, members felt the feminist goal of a non-hierarchical group was successfully accomplished and that major methodological and interpretive decisions were shared throughout the analysis (1982).

Deegan believes that several factors contribute to the success of efforts to work collectively (1983). The need for face-to-face interaction requires that members live in the same geographical area. Additionally, it is easier if members are at the same career stage and share a common base of feminist knowledge, values, and interests. Another important aspect is development of a specific agreed-upon definition of the group project and recognition that a two-year commitment is necessary for accomplishment of most goals.

Another feminist collaborative effort is a volume of feminist theory and research called the *Midwest Feminist Papers,* published yearly by the Midwest Sociologists for Women in Society. The topic of each year's volume is different; a recent volume, edited by Judith Levy, S. Randi Randolph, and Judith Wittner, presents the life histories and personal accounts of women sociologists practicing over five decades of the discipline (1983). Overall, while the collaborative model for doing research is not exclusively feminist, it can provide a means for accomplishing goals which are crucial to the feminist perspective on research by promoting cooperative, egalitarian relations between women researchers and through sharing details about the process of data gathering and analysis with the audience.

Use of the Situation-at-Hand. One final type of methodology, more difficult to characterize than the others, involves using an already given situation as a focus for sociological inquiry or as a means of collecting data. That is, feminist scholarship often takes advantage of existing circumstances which are relevant to a particular topic of study or can be used to elicit information in a more naturalistic manner. This approach is often a way for women to creatively manage sexism in their own social environment by turning it into a topic for study or a means for consciousness-raising (Gurney, 1985). One example of this type of approach is the work of Liz Stanley and Sue Wise (1979), analyzing obscene phone calls that they received over a period of several years in which their names and home phone numbers were used on advertisements for local gay and lesbian groups. In discussing the great amount of stress induced by continually receiving such calls, the authors note that their decision to use them as data for research was one way of coping with the sense of personal assault they felt. Using a content analysis of transcripts of the phone conversations, Stanley and Wise construct a typology of the themes, preoccupations, and concerns revealed. Some calls emphasized violence and some contained specifically anti-lesbian hatred ("You need a whipping and then stringing-up in public as an example"), still others stressed heterosexual violence ("I'll bite you. You'd scream and you'd love it too"), while other callers viewed lesbianism as a turn-on, and still other men made the calls as a type of sex service request ("I've come now. Thanks"). The authors also reflect on their experiences in presenting the research results to others, particularly gay men, who were largely unsympathetic to the upsetting effects the calls had on the researchers.

The research of Stanley and Wise illustrates several of the feminist epistemological assumptions described previously. The study focused on lesbian women's experiences of homophobia; it dealt in detail with the consciousness-raising of the two researchers which resulted from both doing the study and reporting the results to unsympathetic male audiences. Finally, it involved the use of personal, grounded experiences as a source of data and method of interpretation.

Another example of using the situation-at-hand is the work of Giorlando and Pfau-Vicent (1982), who staged a feminist protest against a sexist fraternity fund-raising drive on a university campus and used the protest situation as a means for gathering data concerning men's and women's attitudes toward having parts of their bodies displayed as sexual objects. Still another illustration is the "small-action research project" discussed by Mies (1983:132), which grew out of informal discussions at a shelter for battered women and involved collecting and analyzing the life histories of shelter residents.

This type of feminist methodological strategy is particularly well suited to situations in which non-reactive data gathering is essential. Often, the research subjects in an already given situation have little control over the events because they have already occurred or occurred for some reason other than research. It is unlikely, for example, that the obscene phone callers in the Stanley and Wise study would have been so honest about their feelings toward women and lesbianism in an interview or questionnaire situation. Because feminist sociologists are often investigating topics of a controversial, emotional nature, use of the situation-at-hand is an especially appropriate and creative way of gathering and analyzing data.

To summarize, this section of the analysis has focused on innovative applications of feminist principles in developing methodological strategies to examine gender relations. Many of these approaches, such as visual methods, are particularly well suited for studying the informal, backstage, and hidden contexts in which women predominate. Other techniques, such as conversational analysis, are appropriate for exploring the mundane, taken-for-granted aspects of everyday life which help to sustain gender inequality through their very commonality. In addition, some of these approaches display a feminist concern for the dignity and welfare of the research subject, the audience, and the researcher herself, as in the case of collaborative strategies. In still other instances, the method used reflects an attempt to critique and refine previous ways of measuring concepts through either direct examination of previous concepts or operationalizations, or simultaneous use of a variety of methods as in triangulation. Finally, many of the techniques reveal especially creative ways of gathering data in a non-reactive manner, by using an already given situation, reflecting the sometimes controversial nature of feminist concerns.

SUMMARY AND CONCLUSIONS

After discussing several dimensions of the concept of feminist methodology, we turned to a description and analysis of both the epistemological ideas and methodological practices of feminist sociologists. There appears to be considerable interplay between ideal notions about how the social worlds of women should be studied and the innovative research techniques employed by those conducting empirical analyses. The following will illustrate the interrelations between the epistemology of feminist methodology and its substantive base in actual research studies.

Acknowledging the pervasive significance of gender entails several ideas, and the most uniquely feminist of these notions is that women are placed in the center of inquiry. Moreover, attending to the basic significance of gender involves accounting for the everyday life experiences of women which have been neglected by traditional sociology. Feminist sociologists are creating an understanding of the taken-for-granted, mundane aspects of social reality that oppress women and the daily occurrences which reinforce male domination. Thus, Pamela Fishman's study of routine conversational maintenance and Carol Gardner's work on street comments between strangers both explore aspects of women's daily experiences (promoting verbal interaction, encountering verbal harassment on the street) that help to establish and maintain gender inequality. Finally, acknowledging gender also involves exploring the effect of the research process on the feminist researcher and recognizing that gender influences the web of relationships comprising the research act. These aspects are apparent in the writing of the Nebraska Sociological Feminist Collective which includes discussion of their collective work processes, and the publication of the *Midwest Feminist Papers* which explores the life histories and research careers of feminist sociologists.

In addition to centering the inquiry on women, feminist methodology involves a concern with notions of consciousness, feminist consciousness, and consciousness-raising. A feature of this line of inquiry is recognition that the process of investigation can have a consciousness-raising effect on subjects and on the researcher herself. For example, Deborah Barndt's work with literacy programs among poor Peruvian women revealed that conscientization does not occur solely in one direction; her own understanding of the process of acquiring a critical consciousness changed as a result of her experiences with the women and their day-to-day lives. Similarly, Liz Stanley and Sue Wise found that the sexism of their subject matter (obscene phone calls) and the unsympathetic reactions of male colleagues (who found the calls sexually stimulating) forced them to prematurely terminate the study, led them to re-think their interpretation of the finds, and altered their relationships to men in general. The emphasis on consciousness-raising is related to its ability to uncover aspects of social reality that were not previously visible, tying in with feminist methodology's focus on the taken-for-granted. However, another reason for the concern with consciousness-raising is its potential for stimulating social change, relating it to yet another feminist epistemological notion. Finally, the idea of a feminist consciousness which sees both "apparent reality" and the contradictions underlying it stems from the experiences of feminist investigators who are continually forced to confront their own double consciousness in the process of conducting research.

Rejection of the artificial separation of subject and object has led feminist sociologists to question the strict dichotomy between researcher and women who are the focus of investigation. This has led to a re-examination of the assumption that more valid knowledge is produced when information is elicited in a format framed by the researcher's point of view. Instead, triangulation has been used to examine the same phenomenon using a variety of methods, so that feedback from the respondents' perspectives is incorporated into the findings. In this way, feminist sociology tries to avoid the complete objectification of women as data, so commonly found in the research process. Another dimension of the subject/object issue is a rejection of the traditional social science equation of quantification with objectivity. Thus, some feminist methodology involves refining statistical approaches, as in the study of sex differences in measurement error, and creating new numerical measures such as the shortform Attitudes toward Feminism Scale or indices of women's informal-sector labor market participation. In general, feminist attention to the problem of the dichotomous subject/object is resolved by including both (triangulation) or focusing on the subjective dimension, given the preponderance of "objective" studies and their questionable ability to tap many gender issues.

Feminist methodology in sociology is also concerned with the ethical issues that arise when women are involved in the research process. The use of language as a means of subordination is one dimension of this idea; certain vocabulary and styles of presentation can be used to discount or distort women's experiences. For example, Dorothy Smith's textual analysis of a student's account of her female friend's breakdown reveals how certain ways of linking ideas (called contrast situations) are used to pathologize the "troubled" woman's behavior and make it appear anomalous. Likewise, the Nebraska Collective's textual analysis revealed that "mode of irony" is used as a style of sociological presentation that often reinforces stereotypes of women as passive and manipulative. Other ethical issues addressed by feminist researchers include gatekeeping and its influence on access to scarce resources for research, withholding information from research subjects, and devising nonexploitative ways of approaching controversial topics. To some extent, the focus on ethical dimensions is related to the final epistemological assumption concerning knowledge and social change.

The transformative power of knowledge is emphasized in feminist methodology so that attention is paid to generating information that can be used to create alternatives to oppression. Deborah Barndt's work sought to study political consciousness-raising in the context of teaching women to read and, therefore, to better control their own lives and improve conditions in their villages. Rosabeth Moss Kanter's organizational research in a multinational corporation was conducted while she designed and implemented a training program to prepare women for management positions previously held only by men. Maria Mies' research on the life histories of residents at a battered women's shelter involved in organizing activities for battered women. Basically, then, this aspect of feminist methodology illustrates the principles that the most comprehensive type of knowledge results from attempts to change what one is investigating. Even if studies did not involve direct interaction with target groups of women, they generally contained an awareness of policy implications, where appropriate, or some sort of alternative vision of more liberating possibilities.

To conclude, feminist sociologists have analyzed feminist methodology and have engaged in feminist methodology and their discoveries and dilemmas should tell us something about the nature of women's social lives. The necessity of making the taken-for-granted problematic underscores women's location in the private, emotional backstage arenas. Similarly, women's low status position necessitates the uncovering of the mundane and devalued aspects of social life such as child-rearing and housekeeping. Because the nature of women's worlds is characterized by oppression, feminists often deal with controversial and emotion-laden topics. Formulating creative ways of handling the reactivity of topics such as woman battering, rape, and abortion have made some research designs especially clever and innovative. Also, the challenge of creating new and different types of relationships between the researcher and researched indicates the present extent of the separation women researchers feel from their women respondents. Finally, the diversity of ideas and techniques appears to stem from a tendency to choose methods to fit the research problem rather than vice versa.

ENDNOTE

An earlier version of this paper was presented at the 78th Annual Meeting of the American Sociological Association, Detroit, Michigan, 1983. The authors would like to thank the following people for their comments on an earlier draft of this paper: Marcia Texler Segal, Barrie Thorne, Pauline Bart, Laurel Richardson, and Nellice Gillespie-Woltemade. Address correspondence to Mary Margaret Fonow at: Center for Women's Studies, Ohio State University, 207 Dulles Hall, 230 West 17th Avenue, Columbus, OH 43210.

REFERENCES

Abdullah, T. A., and S. A. Zeidenstein. 1978. "Finding ways to learn about rural women: Experiences from a pilot project in Bangladesh." Sociologia Ruralis 18:158–176.

Acker, Joan, Kate Barry, and Joke Esseveld. 1983. "Objectivity and truth: Problems in doing feminist research." Women's Studies International Forum 6:423–435.

ASA Committee on the Status of Women in Sociology. 1980. "Sexist bias in sociological research: Problems and issues." ASA Footnotes 8:8–9.

Barndt, Deborah. 1980. Education and Social Change: A Photographic Study of Peru. New York: Kendall/Hunt Publishing Company.

Bernard, Jessie. 1973. "My four revolutions: An autobiographical history of the ASA." American Journal of Sociology 78:773–801.

———. 1979. "Afterword." In J. Sherman and E. Beck (eds.), The Prism of Sex: Essays in the Sociology of Knowledge. Madison: University of Wisconsin Press.

Cook, Judith A. 1983. "An interdisciplinary look at feminist methodology: Ideas and practice in sociology, history, and anthropology." Humboldt Journal of Social Relations 10:127–152.

Cook, Judith A., and Mary Margaret Fonow. 1984. "Am I my sister's gatekeeper?: Cautionary tales from the academic hierarchy." Humanity and Society 8:442–452.

Cook, Judith A. 1984. "Influence of gender on the problems of parents of fatally ill children." Journal of Psychosocial Oncology 2:71–91.

Corcoran, Mary. 1980. "Sex differences in measurement error." Sociological Methods in Research 9:119–217.

Deegan, Mary Jo. 1983. "Praxis in feminist sociology theory." Presented at the Midwest Sociological Society Annual Meeting, Kansas City, Missouri.

Deere, Carmen Diana, and Magdalena Leon de Leal. 1979. "Measuring rural women's work and class position." Studies in Family Planning 10:370–374.

Diamond, Timothy. 1977. "On the social structure of imagery: The case of gender." Ph.D. dissertation, Department of Sociology, Ohio State University, Columbus, Ohio.

Dilorio, Judith A. 1982. "Feminist fieldwork in a masculinist setting: Personal problems and methodological issues." Paper presented at the North Central Sociological Association Annual Meetings, Detroit, Michigan.

Dixon, Ruth B., 1982. "Women in agriculture: Counting the labor force in developing countries." Population and Development Review 8:539–566.

Eichler, Margrit. 1980. The Double Standard: A Feminist Critique of Feminist Social Science. New York: St. Martin's Press.

———. 1981. "Power, dependency, love and the sexual division of labour: A critique of the decision-making approach to family power and an alternative approach with an appendix: On washing my dirty linen in public." Women's Studies International Quarterly 4:201–219.

Epstein, Cynthia Fuchs. 1981. "Women in sociological analysis: New scholarship versus old paradigms." In E. Langland and W. Gove (eds.), A Feminist Perspective in the Academy: The Difference It Makes. Chicago: University of Chicago Press.

Fishman, Pamela. 1978. "Interaction: The work women do." Social Problems 25:397–406.

Flora, Cornelia Butler. 1984. "Roasting Donald Duck: Alternative comics and photonovels in Latin America." Journal of Popular Culture 18:163–183.

Fonow, Mary Margaret. 1985. "Women steelworkers confronting cutbacks and unemployment." Presented at the Society for the Study of Social Problems Annual Meetings, Washington, D.C.

Gardner, Carol Brooks. 1980. "Passing by: Street remarks and the urban female." Sociological Inquiry 3–4:328–356.

Gillespie-Woltemade, Nellice. 1980. "Visual sociology: Studying gender through tombstone inscriptions." Unpublished paper, Department of Sociology, Ohio State University, Columbus, Ohio.

Giorlando, Marianne Fisher, and Betty A. Pfau-Vicent. 1982. "Women's legs—men's legs: A feminist protest." Paper presented at the North Central Sociological Association Annual Meetings, Detroit, Michigan.

Gurney, Joan Neff. 1985. "Not one of the guys: The female researcher in a male-dominated setting." Qualitative Sociology 8:42–62.

Harding, Sandra, and Merrill B. Hintikka (eds.). 1983. Discovering Reality: Feminist Perspectives on Epistemology, Metaphysics, Methodology and Philosophy of Science. Boston: D. Reidel Publishing Company.

Kant, Immanuel. 1933. Critique of Pure Reason. Trans. Norman Kemp Smith. New York: Macmillan. (1781).

Kanter, Rosabeth Moss. 1977. Men and Women of the Corporation. New York: Basic Books.

Kaplan, Abraham. 1964. The Conduct of Inquiry: Methodology for Behavioral Science. San Francisco: Chandler Publishing Co.

Levy, Judith A., S. Randi Randolph, and Judith G. Wittner (eds.). 1983. "Life paths of women sociologists." Midwest Feminist Papers 3:1–84.

Lipman-Blumen, Jean. 1979. "The dialectic between research and social policy." In J. Lipman-Blumen and J. Bernard (eds.), Sex Roles and Social Policy. Beverly Hills: Sage Publishers.

Lopata, Helena Znaniecki. 1980. "Interviewing American widows." In W. Shaffir, R. Stebbins, and A. Turowetz (eds.), Fieldwork Experience: Qualitative Approaches to Social Research. New York: St. Martin's Press.

Mackie, M. 1985. "Female sociologists' productivity, collegial relations, and research style examined through journal publications." Sociology and Social Research 69:189–209.

MacKinnon, Catherine A. 1982. "Feminism, Marxism, method, and the state: An agenda for social theory." Signs 7:515–544.

McCormack, Thelma. 1981. "Good theory or just theory? Toward a feminist philosophy of social science." Women's Studies International Quarterly 4:1–12.

Merton, Robert K. 1957. "On manifest and latent functions." In R. Merton (ed.), Social Theory and Social Structure. New York: Free Press.

Mies, Maria. 1983. "Towards a methodology for feminist research." In G. Bowles and R. Klein (eds.), Theories of Women's Studies. Boston: Routledge and Kegan Paul.

Millman, Marcia, and Rosabeth Moss Kanter. 1975. "Editorial introduction." In M. Millman and R. Kanter (eds.), Another Voice. Garden City: Anchor Books.

Morgan, David. 1981. "Men, masculinity and the process of sociological enquiry." In H. Roberts (ed.), Doing Feminist Research. London: Routledge and Kegan Paul.

Nebraska Feminist Collective (Mary Jo Deegan, Barbara Keating, Jane Ollenburger, Sandy Kuenhold, and Sheryl Tillson). 1982. "The sexist dramas of Erving Goffman." Unpublished paper, Department of Sociology, University of Nebraska, Lincoln, Nebraska.

Nebraska Feminist Collective (Cynthia Trainor, Beth Hartung, Jane C. Ollenburger, Helen A. Moore, and Mary Jo Deegan). 1983. "A feminist ethic for social science research." Women's Studies International Forum 6:535–543.

Oakley, Ann. 1981. "Interviewing women: A contradiction in terms." In H. Roberts (ed.), Doing Feminist Research. London: Routledge and Kegan Paul.

Oakley, Ann, and Robin Oakley. 1979. "Sexism in official statistics." In J. Irvine, I. Miles, and J. Evans (eds.), Demystifying Social Statistics. London: Pluto Press.

Pagelow, Mildred Daley. 1979. "Research on woman battering." In J. Fleming (ed.), Stopping Wife Abuse. Garden City: Anchor Press.

Reinharz, Shulamit. 1983. "Experiential analysis: A contribution to feminist research." In G. Bowles and R. Klein (eds.), Theories of Women's Studies. Boston: Routledge and Kegan Paul.

Reinharz, Shulamit, Marti Bombyk, and Janet Wright. 1983. "Methodological issues in feminist research: A bibliography of literature in women's studies, sociology and psychology." Women's Studies International 6:437–453.

Richardson, Laurel, Mary Margaret Fonow, and Judith A. Cook. 1985. "From gender seminar to gender community." Teaching Sociology 12:313–324.

Richardson, Laurel, Anne Statham Macke, and Judith A. Cook. 1980. Sex-Typed Teaching Styles of University Professors and Student Reactions. Columbus: Ohio State University Research Foundation.

Roberts, Helen. 1981. "Women and their doctors: Power and powerlessness in the research process." In H. Roberts (ed.), Doing Feminist Research. London: Routledge and Kegan Paul.

Scheper-Hughes, Nancy. 1983. "The problem of bias in androcentric and feminist anthropology." Women's Studies 10:109–116.

Schuman, Howard, Stanley Presser, and Jacob Ludwig. 1981. "Context effects on survey responses to questions about abortion." Public Opinion Quarterly 45:216–223.

Sherman, Julia A., and Evelyn Torton Beck. 1979. "Introduction." In J. Sherman and E. Beck (eds.), The Prism of Sex: Essays in the Sociology of Knowledge. Madison: University of Wisconsin Press.

Singleton, Royce, Jr., and John B. Christiansen. 1977. "The construct validation of a shortform attitudes toward feminism scale." Sociology and Social Research 61:294–303.

Smith, Dorothy E., 1974. "Women's perspective as a radical critique of sociology." Sociological Inquiry 44:7–13.

———. 1978. "'K is mentally ill': The anatomy of a factual account." Sociology 21:23–53.

———. 1979. "A sociology for women." In J. Sherman and E. Beck (eds.), The Prism of Sex: Essays in the Sociology of Knowledge. Madison: University of Wisconsin Press.

———. 1981. The Empirical World as Problematic: A Feminist Method. Saskatoon, Saskatchewan: University of Saskatchewan Press.

———. 1983. "No one commits suicide: Textual analysis of ideological practices." Human Studies, in press.

Spector, Malcolm, and Robert R. Faulker. 1980. "Thoughts on five new journals and some old ones." Contemporary Sociology 9:477–482.

Stacey, Judith and Barrie Thorne. 1985. "The missing feminist revolution in sociology." Social Problems 32:301–316.

Stanley, Liz, and Sue Wise. 1979. "Feminist research, feminist consciousness and experiences of sexism." Women's Studies International Quarterly 2:359–374.

———. 1983. Breaking Out: Feminist Consciousness and Feminist Research. Boston: Routledge and Kegan Paul.

Unger, Rhoda Kesler. 1981. "Sex as a social reality: Field and laboratory research." Psychology of Women Quarterly 5:645–653.

Ward, Kathryn B., and Linda Grant. 1984. "The feminist critique and a decade of published research in sociology journals." Presented at the American Sociological Association Annual Meetings, San Antonio, Texas.

Westkott, Marcia. 1979. "Feminist criticism of the social sciences." Harvard Educational Review 49:422–430.

———. 1983. "Women's studies as a strategy for change: Between criticism and vision." In G. Bowles and R. Klein (eds.), Theories of Women's Studies. Boston: Routledge and Kegan Paul.

4

Beginning Where We Are
Feminist Methodology in Oral History

KATHRYN ANDERSON, SUSAN ARMITAGE,
DANA JACK, AND JUDITH WITTNER

Anderson et al. introduce oral history as being ideally suited to the purposes of feminist inquiry. The authors' development of the dialectical nature of female consciousness—for example, the realization that housework is considered work but yet not work—is especially well developed. They emphasize women as experts on their own behavior. Contrast this with traditional theories, which suggest that because of such things as unconscious motives and false consciousness, subjects cannot really know themselves. This chapter also realistically describes dilemmas experienced by the researchers themselves—for example, their need to generalize from particular experiences. Indeed, oral history itself is described as neither a psychological interview nor secondary documentation. Thus the oral historian walks a narrow line between these two. "Beginning Where We Are" is not just about feminist methods; these authors exemplify feminist self-scrutiny and awareness, both in their interdisciplinary collaboration and their sharing of the inside story of their research experiences.

Our means of knowing and speaking of ourselves and our world are written for us by men who occupy a special place in it . . . In learning to speak our experience and situation, we insist upon the right to begin where we are, to stand as subjects of our sentences, and to hear one another as the authoritative speakers of our experience.[1]

INTRODUCTION

Oral history is a basic tool in our efforts to incorporate the previously overlooked lives, activities, and feelings of women into our understanding of the past and of the present. When women speak for themselves, they reveal hidden realities: new experiences and new perspectives emerge that challenge the "truths" of official accounts and cast doubt upon established theories. Interviews with women can explore private realms such as reproduction, child rearing, and sexuality to tell us what women actually did instead of what experts thought they did or should have done. Interviews can also tell us how women felt about what they did and can interpret the personal meaning and value of particular activities. They can, but they usually do not.

Our fieldwork shows us that oral history has only skimmed the surface of women's lives. Women have much more to say than we have realized. As oral historians, we need to develop techniques that will encourage women to say the unsaid. We also need to move beyond individual accounts to make much more systematic use of our interviews. Here, then, we propose an interdisciplinary feminist methodology to achieve these goals.

This paper is the result of a series of collaborations. Initially, historians Kathryn Anderson and Susan Armitage worked together on the Washington Women's Heritage Project exhibit, which illustrated the everyday lives of women with photographs and with excerpts from oral history interviews. Their assumption was that Washington women shared a set of values—a female subculture—but this hypothesis proved more difficult to document than they had expected. Although both feminist scholarship and their own personal sense of self told them that relationships with others have always been a central component of female activity and identity, Anderson and Armitage found that existing oral histories provided very little direct support for this assumption. It was much easier to document activities than feelings and values. Surprised by this finding, each historian pursued the question further. Anderson's critical scrutiny of her own oral history interviews revealed a strong bias *against* just the sort of information we had hoped to find and led her to reformulate her questions and interview goals. Anderson turned to a colleague, psychologist Dana Jack, and found useful insights in her work and the work of other feminist psychologists. Thus our first interdis-

Reprinted with permission from *Oral History Review*, Vol. 15, 1987:103–127. An earlier version of this chapter was presented at the National Women Studies Association conference held in Seattle, Washington, in June 1985.

ciplinary connection was made, and we developed a perspective on women's historical activity that incorporated a methodology to explore and validate personal feelings.

While Anderson was thinking about personal experience, Armitage had begun to try to put women's experience into a wider context.[2] She was concerned, in particular, with finding a way to generalize from the individual to the common experience. She wondered how much the feelings and values of one individual woman can tell us about female values. Is there really a set of common feelings and values that women of a particular culture, class, or historical period can be said to share? Are there cross-class and cross-race commonalities? How can personal feelings be compared, without resort to sociological "schedules" and rigid interview formats? Just as Armitage was beginning to worry seriously about these questions, she was fortunate to find, in Judith Wittner, a feminist colleague who was thinking about similar questions within a sociological framework. Thus was forged the second interdisciplinary connection, as the life history tradition in sociology was brought to focus upon the wider questions raised by women's oral history.

The final collaboration brings us together to tell from our originally separate disciplinary perspectives how we have forged an interdisciplinary approach to the oral history of women's lives.

THEORETICAL FRAMEWORK

Recent feminist scholarship has been sharply critical of the systematic bias in academic disciplines, which have been dominated by the particular and limited interests, perspectives, and experiences of white males. Feminist scholars have insisted that the exploration of women's distinctive experiences is an essential step in restoring "the multitude of both female and male realities and interests" to social theory and research.[3]

Assembling women's perspectives seemed necessary to feminist scholars because women's experiences and realities have been systematically different from men's in crucial ways and therefore needed to be studied to fill large gaps in knowledge. This reconstitution of knowledge was essential because of a basic discontinuity: women's perspectives were not absent simply as a result of oversight but had been suppressed, trivialized, ignored, or reduced to the status of gossip and folk wisdom by dominant research traditions institutionalized in academic settings and in scientific disciplines. Critical analyses of this knowledge often showed that masculinist biases lurked beneath the claims of social science and history to objectivity, universal relevance, and truth.[4]

The injunction to study women's realities and perspectives raised methodological as well as substantive issues. Dominant ideologies distorted and made invisible women's real activities, to women as well as to men. For example, until recently it was common for women to dismiss housework as "not real work." Yet, unlike most men, women also experienced housework as actual labor, as a practical activity that filled their daily existence. In effect, women's perspectives combined two separate consciousnesses: one emerging out of their practical activities in the everyday world and one inherited from the dominant traditions of thought. Reconstructing knowledge to take account of women, therefore, involves seeking out the submerged consciousness of the practical knowledge of everyday life and linking it to the dominant reality.

The perspectives of two feminist scholars, Marcia Westkott and Dorothy Smith, have especially influenced our thinking about oral history. Westkott provides us with a basic approach to individual consciousness. She describes how traditional social science assumes a fit between an individual's thought and action, "based on the condition of freedom to implement consciousness through direct activity." But within a patriarchal society, only males of a certain race or class have anything approaching this freedom. Social and political constraints customarily have limited women's freedom; thus in order to adapt to society while retaining their psychological integrity women must simultaneously conform to and oppose the conditions that limit their freedom.[5]

In order to understand women in a society that limits their choices, we must begin with the assumption that what they think may not always be reflected in what they do and how they act. Studying women's behavior alone gives an incomplete picture of their lives, and the missing aspect may be the most interesting and informative. So we must study consciousness, women's sphere of greatest freedom; one must go behind the veil of outwardly conforming activity to understand what particular behavior means to her, and reciprocally to understand how her behavior affects her consciousness and activity.[6]

Dorothy Smith has argued that feminist sociology must "begin where we are" with real, concrete people and their actual lives if it is to do more than reaffirm the dominant ideologies about women and their place in the world. Smith suggests examining how these ideological forms structure institutions and shape everyday life; her "institutional ethnography" begins with the actual daily lives of women and moves from there to examine how their activities appear in organizational processes. As an example, Smith examines the articulation of two forms of women's work, mothering and teaching, to show in what ways the organizational processes of institutionalized education organize how women in these positions work with children, and the effect of institutional education in standardizing their activities, making them "accountable within the institutional context," and rendering invisible any education work that cannot be accounted for within the documentary record.[7]

From the point of view of feminist scholarship on women, therefore, oral history should involve more than simply gathering accounts from informants, itself a difficult process involving considerable skill. These bits of evidence we collect—subjectively reconstructed lives—contain within them formidable problems of interpretation. What theoretical conclusions to draw from these accounts is the additional and enormous task that oral historians face. Using the insights provided by feminist scholars, we explore in the following pages what it means to develop in oral history a feminist methodology situated in women's experiences and perspectives.

THE PROBLEM OF MEANING
(KATHRYN ANDERSON)

As I was interviewing women in Whatcom County for the Washington Women's Heritage Project, a public archive, my colleague Dana Jack was conducting confidential interviews with depressed women for a study of women's development. In the process of sharing what we were learning about women from their interviews, both of us gained valuable insights as to how women understand their lives.[8]

I became aware, as I reviewed my early interviews, that my research questions were more sophisticated than my interview questions; I had not probed deeply enough or listened attentively enough to satisfy my curiosity about how women interpret their existence.

Why have not historians, and especially historians of women, pursued the subjective experience of the past more rigorously? My own interviews and those of others show a definite preference for questions about activities and facts and a conspicuous lack of questions about feelings, attitudes, values, and meaning. Traditional historical sources tell us more about what happened and how it happened than how people felt about it and what it meant to them. As historians, we are trained to interpret meaning from facts. But oral history gives us the unique opportunity to ask people directly, How did it feel? What did it mean?

Activity is, undeniably, important to document; but a story restricted to action and things is incomplete. Oral history can tell us not only how people preserved meat but whether the process was fun or drudgery, whether it was accompanied by a sense of pride or failure. The unadorned story of what people did tells us more about the limitations under which they operated than the choices they might have made. With oral history we can go further, we can *ask* what the person would rather have been doing.

Reviewing my interviews, I have found that my training in the history of facts and action triumphed over my awareness of a decade of historical research pointing to the importance of relationships and consciousness in women's lives and kept me from hearing the reflections that women were clearly willing to share.

Although I asked what seemed at the time to be enlightened questions about relationships, I now see how often I shied away from emotionally laden language to more neutral questions about activity. My first interview with Elizabeth illustrates the point. We had been talking about her relationships with her mother and half sister when she offered the following:

> I practically had a nervous breakdown when I discovered my sister had cancer, you know; it was kind of like knocking the pins—and I had, after the second boy was born, I just had ill health for quite a few years. I evidently had a low grade blood infection or something. Because I was very thin and, of course, I

kept working hard. And every fall, why, I'd generally spend a month or so being sick—from overdoing, probably.

Instead of acknowledging and exploring further her reflections upon the physical and mental strains of her multiple roles, my next question followed my imperative for detailing her role on the farm: "What kind of farming did you do right after you were married?"

Elizabeth is a farm woman who was a full partner with her husband in their dairy farm and has continued an active role as the farm has switched to the production of small grains. Her interview has the potential of giving us valuable information about the costs incurred by women who combined child rearing and housework with an active role in the physical labor and business decisions of the farm. It also suggests something of the importance of relationships with family and close friends in coping with both roles. The interview's potential is severely limited, however, by my failure to encourage her to expand upon her spontaneous reflections and by my eagerness to document the details of her farming activity. Not until later did I realize that I do not know what she meant by "nervous breakdown" or "overdoing." The fact that other farm women used the same or similar terms to describe parts of their lives alerted me to the need for further clarification. Now I wish I had let her tell me in her own words of the importance of the relationship with her sister and why its possible loss was such a threat.

Later in the same interview I did a better job of allowing her to expand upon her description—only to deflect the focus from her experience once again. Elizabeth was telling me how hard it was to be a full partner in the field and still have full responsibility for the house:

This is what was always so hard, you know. You'd both be out working together, and he'd come in and sit down, and I would have to hustle a meal together, you know. And that's typical.

How did you manage?
Well, sometimes, you didn't get to bed till midnight or after, and you were up at five. Sometimes when I think back to the early days, though, we'd take a day off, we'd get the chores done, and we'd go take off and go visiting.

Was that typical? Neighbors going to visit each other after the chores were done?

While Elizabeth was telling me how she managed, I was already thinking about patterns in the neighborhood. My first question had been a good one, but by asking about what other people did, my next one told her that I had heard enough about her experience. The two questions in succession have a double message: "Tell me about your experience but don't tell me too much." Part of the problem may have been that even while I was interviewing women I was aware of the need to make sense of what they told me. In this case, the scholar's search for generalizations may have interfered with the interviewer's need to listen to an individual's experience.

If we want to know how women feel about their lives, then we have to allow them to talk about their feelings as well as their activities. If we see rich potential in the language people use to describe their daily activities, then we have to take advantage of the opportunity to let them tell us what that language means. "Nervous breakdown" is not the only phrase that I heard without asking for clarification. Verna was answering a question about the relationship between her mother and her grandmother.

> It was quite close since my mother was the only daughter that was living. My grandmother did have another daughter, that one died. I didn't know it until we got to working on the family tree. My mother was older than her brother. They were quite close. They worked together quite well when it would come to preparing meals and things. They visited back and forth a lot.

Her answer gave several general examples of how the closeness was manifested, but now I want to know still more about what Verna means when she describes a relationship as "close" twice in a short answer and what her perception of this relationship meant to her. My next question asked, instead, for further examples of manifestations: "Did they (grandparents) come to western Washington because your parents were here?"

Even efforts to seek clarification were not always framed in ways that allowed the interviewee to reflect upon the meaning of her experience. Elizabeth was answering a question about household rules when she was a child and commented: "My mother was real partial to my brother because, of course, you know that old country way; the boy was the important one." My question "How did her partiality to the brother show?" elicited some specific examples, but none of a series of subsequent questions gave her an opportunity to reflect upon how this perception affected her understanding of herself and her place in the family.

A final example from Verna's interviews illustrates the best and the worst of what we are trying to do. Her statement is the kind of powerful reflection upon her role as a mother that could only have emerged from a comfortable and perceptive interview. The subsequent question, however, ignores all of the emotional content of her remarks.

> Yes. There was times that I just wish I could get away from it all. And there were times when I would have liked to have taken the kids and left them someplace for a week—the whole bunch at one time—so that I wouldn't have to worry about them. I don't know whether anybody else had that feeling or not, but there were times when I just felt like I needed to get away from everybody, even my husband, for a little while. Those were times when I would maybe take a walk back in the woods and look at the flowers and maybe go down there and find an old cow that was real gentle and walk up to her and pat her a while—kind of get away from it. I just had to it seems like sometimes . . .

> *Were you active in clubs?*

Two realizations emerge from this somewhat humbling experience of recognizing the inadequacy of what, on other levels, are extremely useful interviews: (1) oral historians should explore emotional and subjective experience as well as facts and activities; (2) oral historians should take advantage of the fact that the interview is the one historical document that can ask people what they mean.

To accomplish the first of these, we need more and better questions about relationships of all kinds, questions that explore feelings of competency—when women feel good about what they have done and how they have done it—as well as feelings of incompetence, when they feel like failures or that things have gone wrong, and why. Oral historians need to be sensitive to women's perceptions of their choices and how they feel about their responses. We also need to be sensitive to what women value and why. When women reveal feelings or experiences that suggest conflict, we need to explore what the conflict means and what form it takes. Finally, we need general questions that allow women to reflect upon their experience and choose for themselves which experiences and feelings are central to their sense of their past.

The language women use to explore the above topics will be all the richer when they have ample opportunity to explain and clarify what they mean. We need to ask for explanations and examples of words and phrases like "support," "close," "sisterhood," "tomboy," "visiting," and "working together." With letters and diaries we can only infer what individuals mean by the language they use; with oral history interviews we can simply ask them.

The oral historian will never be as exclusively concerned as the psychologist with questions of self-concept and consciousness, but we can do much better than we have done to document questions of value and meaning in individuals' reflections upon their past. We must learn to help women to tell their own stories as fully, completely, and honestly as they desire.

LEARNING TO LISTEN (DANA JACK)

As I interviewed depressed women to try to understand their experience, I encountered a different set of problems from those described by Kathryn. My difficulty lay not in finding the "right" questions to ask, but in my ability to hear and interpret what women were saying about their psychological experience. The women told stories of the failure of relationships, and inability to connect with the person(s) with whom they wanted to achieve intimacy. These were the expected stories, predicted by existing models, and the temptation was to interpret the stories according to their agreement with or deviance from existing concepts and norms for "maturity" and "health." However, when the woman, instead of the researcher, is considered the expert on her own psychological experience, women's stories challenge existing standards and concepts. These norms are biased in their equation of maturity with self-reliance and autonomy, and are ideas impoverished by a history of male interpretation of female experience.

Within psychology, researchers have been reluctant to trust the reliability of subjective accounts of disturbed people, including depressed women. The reluctance is due to at least two major factors. First, the Freudian emphasis on the unconscious and the defensive maneuvers of the ego suggests that normal people's explanations for their behavior or emotions cannot be trusted. This stance holds true even more strongly in the case of psychopathology. The clinical view is that the person is repressing painful and/or threatening material and cannot give an accurate explanation of his/her psychological state; the person's behavior and emotions must be explained by experts. Thus the issue of interpretation becomes critical for the data we collect through oral interviews. Secondly, clinicians consider that the very nature of depressive illness causes the person to exaggerate the negative aspects of his/her life. Distortion becomes part of the illness, and women's descriptions of negative aspects cannot be considered as reliable. Again, the person has been eliminated as a valid interpreter of his/her knowledge. These two concerns have been called into doubt by research that independently verified the truth of depressed women's accounts by objective measures of outside events. Two studies, one by George W. Brown and Tirril Harris of depressed women,[9] and another by Deborah Belle of women in poverty,[10] have established the reliability of depressed women's descriptions of their lives.

The critical questions for oral interviewers are whose story is the woman asked to tell, who interprets it, and in what contexts? The subject's story (the data) is the result of an interaction between two people. The personality and biases of the researcher clearly enter into the process to affect the outcome. Is it the woman's understanding of her own experience that is sought, or is the researcher structuring the interview so that the subject tells a story that conforms to the researcher's orientation? If the goal of the interview is to encourage the woman to tell her own story, to speak in her own terms, then how one asks questions, and with what words, becomes critical to the outcome of the interview.

The oral interview not only allows women to articulate their own experiences but also to reflect upon the meaning of those experiences to them. It provides a picture of how a woman understands herself within her world, where and how she places value, and what particular meanings she attaches to her actions and locations in the world.

Oral interviews allow us to hear, if we will, the particular meanings of a language that both men and women use but which each translates differently. For women, the ability to value their own thought and experience is hindered by self-doubt and hesitation when private experience seems at odds with cultural myths and values concerning how a woman is "supposed" to think and feel. Looking closely at the language and the particular meanings of important words women use to describe their experience allows us to understand how women are adapting to the culture within which they live.

To explore women's experience of depression, I designed a longitudinal study that included interviews with a group of twelve women clinically diagnosed as depressed. Because I did not want to structure their thoughts about their experience of depression with my own ideas, I started with the question, "Can you tell me in your own mind what led up to your experience of depression?" Starting with their initial answers, I explored what they said using their own words to ask them to elaborate, or else I asked them to explain what they meant by a term.

Accepting the premise that we have a great deal to learn from women's stories about both their psychology and their history, how do we proceed with analysis? For me, the critical step was to learn to listen in a new way. As I listened to the woman's self-commentary, to her reflection upon her own story, I learned about her adaptation to the particular historical and relational world she was living in, especially her adaptation to the stereotypes to which she tried to conform. I listened with an awareness that the women's self-reflection is not just a private, subjective act. The categories and concepts we use for reflecting upon and evaluating ourselves come from a cultural context, one that has historically demeaned and controlled women's activities. So an exploration of the language and the meanings women use to articulate their own experience leads to an awareness of the social forces and the ideas affecting them. Observed from the outside through their behavior, depressed women are called passive, dependent, masochistic, compliant, and victimized by learned helplessness. Yet, agreeing with Marcia Westkott that we must go behind the veil of outwardly conforming activity in order to understand how behaviors affect women's consciousness and their self-concept, I found a different way to understand depression.[11] Basically, what became evident through listening to the women's self-reflection was the activity required in order to be passive, to live up to the stereotype of the "good" woman, particularly the good wife.

How do we listen to interviews without immediately leaping to interpretations suggested by prevailing theories? Content analysis provides the first step: it tells us what is there, what themes dominate the interviews. But the step that allows us to challenge existing formulations and to uncover what the women are feeling and saying is the step of exploring the dynamics of a person's thought through the use of language. By probing the meaning of the words women use to describe themselves and their experience, we can begin to employ an analysis of the social forces that affect their consciousness. In this way we can begin to understand Nancy Cott's observation that "the meaning which women ascribe to their own behavior is reducible neither to the behavior itself nor to the dominant ideology. It is derived from women's consciousness which is influenced by the ideas and values of men, but is nevertheless uniquely situated, reflective of women's concrete position within the patriarchal power structure."[12]

Women's concrete position as subordinates creates a possibility for self-evaluation that vacillates between "me" and "not me." On one level, women often accept the stereotypes that define them as dependent, passive, giving, compassionate and gentle. Yet these concepts are negatively valued in the wider society and are often impossible to live up to. Thus concepts that shape self-experience are often demeaning and self-alienating to women and at the same time are both valued and devalued by women who understand themselves in society's terms. With such a perspective on the woman's self-reflection, we can listen more perceptively to how she adjusts to her world and its expectations of her as a woman.

Listening to the women's interviews, I first noticed how they continually socialized their feelings: they judged not only how they were acting, but also how they were thinking and feeling.[13] The standard that they continually failed to meet (in their own minds) was a generalized image of how women *should* think and feel, informed by the wider culture and by the examples of their own families.

For example, psychologists consider depressed women to be overdependent upon their relationships for a sense of self and self-esteem. But if we look at how depressed women understand dependence, and how their evaluation of themselves as dependent affects their self-perception and their actions, the concept is cast in a new light. In a first interview with a thirty-three-year-old depressed woman, about seven minutes into the interview the following interchange occurred. The woman was talking about her feelings about herself, her problems, and how she felt she had "lost a lot of myself" through the activities of being a wife and a mother. In her self-understanding, the issue of dependence was central and problematic:

> You know, I'm basically a very dependent person to start with. And then you get me married and tied down to a home and not working . . .

Asked what she meant by dependent, she responded:

> I like closeness. I like companionship. I like somebody, and intimate closeness, even with a best friend. I was always so close to my mother. . . . I was used to that all through my childhood, having an intimate closeness . . . someone that shared my feelings, my fears, my doubts, my happiness, my achievements, my failures. And I've never had that with my husband. I can't talk to him on those levels. . . . He lives in a very concrete, day to day, black and white world. But I've always been used to channeling a lot of my energies into more deep levels of intimacy with people, and sharing. . . . And so I guess when I say I'm a dependent person, I guess I mean that I like having a closeness. I have a need for a deep intimate level of friendship with somebody.

> *How is that dependent?*
> Maybe it isn't. But I do have that need for closeness, and I've always, sometimes I've, sometimes I get frustrated with myself that I have to have that, you know. I look at other people that seem so self-sufficient and so independent and so—I don't know—I just have always needed a closeness. And maybe I identified that as dependency.

> *Does that have a negative kind of connotation to you?*
> It never used to, but since I've been married I realize it's kind of a negative thing to be that way. Because I've tried to bury that. And so I guess that has also contributed to a lot of my frustrations.

Saying that she "had been feeling that my need for intimacy and my need for that kind of a deep level of friendship or relationships with people was sort of bad," she began "to believe there was something the matter with me." In her attempt to "bury" her needs for closeness, she revealed the activity required to be passive, to try to live up to self-alienating images of "today's woman."

One sees how this woman's healthy capacity for intimacy, a hallmark of adult maturity, has been held up to her by the culture and by her husband as a weakness. Yet, women's capacity for intimacy, their orientation toward relationships, has recently been reinterpreted by feminist scholars as arising out of a developmental history which differs from that of males. The self-in-relation theorists consider that women and men have different ego capacities, strengths, and vulnerabilities based upon the fact that they form a gender identity either of sameness or difference in relation to the female primary caretaker. These revisionist theorists are redefining women's orientation toward their relationships as a central, positive, and crucial aspect of psychological development and functioning beyond childhood.[14] In the interview, one can also see how this woman has judged her feelings against a standard that says that to need closeness makes one dependent, that one should be able to be self-sufficient and autonomous. Further, she reflects upon her own experience, her capabilities, and her needs not from the basis of who she is and what she needs but in terms of how her husband sees her and how the culture sees her. This process of self-alienation is often deepened in therapy when the therapist identifies the woman's problem as being too dependent upon the husband and urges her to separate more and to do things for herself. Her capacity for closeness and intimacy goes unacknowledged as a strength and is presented to her as something that she must overcome in order to adjust to her relationship. Rather than a failure of the husband's response, the problem is identified as her "neediness."

For the researcher using oral interviews, the first step is to ask the meaning of words in order to understand them in the subject's own terms. If a researcher went into this interview with the traditional notion of dependence in mind, s/he would find the hypothesis that depressed women are over-dependent confirmed. Instead, when one listens, one hears how women use the language of the culture to deny what, on another level, they value and desire. We must learn to help women tell their own stories, and then learn to listen to those stories without being guided by models that restrict our ability to hear.

DEVELOPING THEORY FROM ORAL HISTORY (JUDITH WITTNER)

For very good reasons, oral histories have become important vehicles for research about women. Finding out about women's actual lives deepens the critique of existing knowledge by documenting the inadequacy of past assumptions. Often, women's life stories highlight the ways in which concepts and methods that claim the status of science in our respective fields are partial and subjective and make women's experience difficult to observe or to take seriously. Therefore, the seemingly simple task of description often forces us to give up old frameworks and develop new ones better grounded in women's realities. For example, until the 1970s sociologists routinely assumed that work and family relations were two separate domains, linked only by the common participation of employed fathers. But the analytic separation of work and family life obscured the character of the everyday lives of ordinary housewives. Sociologists studying housewives found that new conceptual frameworks were necessary to understand the tasks and situations that structured women's lives in households.

Women's life stories are equally important to theory building. As descriptions of social life from the vantage point of women accumulate, they show that we must change our theories of society to incorporate the activities and perspectives of women. Indeed, learning about these invisible and neglected areas of experience grounds our attempts to develop new understandings and helps us to formulate better social theories. If we are to reconstruct theoretical accounts of society by seriously including women, we must begin to situate each individual woman's life story in its specific social and historical setting and show how women's actions and consciousness contribute to the structuring of social institutions. We need to go directly to women to learn about their part in the production and reproduction of society. We cannot have adequate theories of society without them. The women interviewed by Anderson and Jack grappled with ideas about solitude and independence in the context of society-wide changes in women's situations and in their consciousness. Their conflicts expressed the meaning of contrasting and contradictory social pressures in personal terms. Their reports described how they understood the social relationships and institutions that made up the worlds they lived in and how they acted to preserve or restructure those relations. We need to show how the conflicts, hopes, and fears of these and other women spurred them to action or kept them from it, and what difference this state of affairs made to them and to the worlds they inhabit.

In pursuing these goals we should not be too quick to dismiss the insights of generations of scholars in our fields. Our research often teaches us to distrust the traditions and techniques of our respective disciplines and to argue that conventional divisions between disciplines are part of a system that deflects attention from women's settings and women's concerns. But often, I believe, we go too far in rejecting or ignoring research traditions that, despite their lack of direct concern with women, offer important ideas and research tools for women's studies. In order to build truly interdisciplinary approaches, it is important that we become familiar with these theories and methods so that we may adapt them to our own purposes.

For example, in my own discipline of sociology there have been significant attempts to overcome the influence of dominant ideologies by developing theories and methods of research that treat humans as active subjects and that consider the part meaning plays in social life. Despite the often greater visibility and prestige of abstract theories and quantitative analysis, the idea that meaning informs social action and is a critical element in its study has been a theme running through the history of sociology. Following Max Weber, this tradition is often referred to as the *verstehen* approach.

Sociologists in this tradition assumed that people's perspectives and subjective interpretations informed and organized their courses of action. They did not treat subjective orientations as biases to be eliminated from their studies, as did quantitatively oriented sociologists—quite the opposite. Subjectivity was central to their understanding of social action. In their view, people were constantly interpreting their situations and acting in terms of the meanings or perspectives they developed within particular situations and from specific positions within organizations and groups. They viewed society as a plurality of interacting and competing groups, each of which developed collective solutions to the problems encountered in their shared situations. In such a society there was no neutral vantage point but only the different viewpoints generated within variously situated collectivities. For example, Howard Becker has written:

> Italian immigrants who went on making wine for themselves and their friends during prohibition were acting properly by Italian immigrant standards, but were breaking the law of their new country (as, of course, were many of their Old American neighbors). Medical patients who shop around for a doctor may, from the perspective of their own group, be doing what is necessary to protect their health by making sure they get what seems to them the best possible doctor, but from the perspective of the physician, what they do is wrong because it breaks down the trust the patient ought to put in his physician. The lower-class delinquent who fights for his "turf" is only doing what he considers necessary and right, but teachers, social workers, and police see it differently.[15]

Sociologists such as Becker have focused upon how people actively dealt with situational contingencies and resolved the problems they met as they pursued their goals, using and changing these situations for their own purposes as well as adapting to them. According to this perspective, it was not structure that "determined" action. Rather, actors in similar situations were understood to develop shared perspectives or definitions of their situation and to act in terms of these definitions.

Subjective accounts were useful to sociologists for many of the same reasons that they are important in women's studies research today. Both oral historians and sociologists often depend upon these to uncover aspects of social life that had been socially invisible and to analyze and interpret social reality from a new vantage point. These sociologists were concerned with socially marginal people and groups such as women and with the theoretical understanding of marginalizing processes such as the production of deviant statuses. Certainly these substantive and theoretical concerns bring them close to students of women's lives.

Efforts to develop methods reflecting an interest in subjective meaning and those capable of providing an empirical foundation from which to

elaborate and refine the theory span the history of sociology in the United
States since World War I. Members of the first sociology department at the
University of Chicago developed the use of life histories and were also greatly
influenced by anthropological field techniques. Over time, these techniques
of participant observation were transformed into approaches suited to studying
groups and lifeways in urban settings. By the 1940s, quantitative methods
and grand theories dominated the field, and the use of personal accounts
declined. Still, many sociologists continued to base their research on subjective
accounts and wrote extensively on the theoretical and methodological issues
raised by these data. These sociologists have been called or call themselves
symbolic interactionists, naturalists, or humanists. Their work generally
includes the use of participant observation techniques and unstructured,
intensive interviews. Much of this work was published during the 1950s
and 1960s.[16] Today a growing number of sociologists have returned to this
literature for its approaches to collecting and analyzing subjective accounts.[17]

Several issues treated in this body of literature are useful as guides in
thinking through the problems of an oral history for women. First, interactionists showed why it was necessary to give up the claim that real science
is disinterested and neutral by linking meanings or "perspectives" to social
positions. Dominant perspectives were not "truer" to reality but were the
perspectives of dominant (more powerful, more legitimate) groups.[18] This
interactionist approach can help us to articulate more completely the sources
of women's alternative perspectives and to understand how women make
use of these alternatives in their everyday lives.

Second, interactionists treated the social order as a negotiated order
emerging out of social interaction. Social organization is the outcome of
this intentional action, as people collectively and individually try to work
out day-to-day solutions to problems they encounter in concrete situations.[19]
Their studies of the practical activities involved in the daily production of
social life should be of interest to us as we gather evidence about women's
daily lives and attempt to understand its significance as historical data.

Third, interactionists rarely saw subordinates as victims but rather looked
at how they carved out areas of autonomy despite their formal lack of power.
For example, Gresham Sykes showed that in certain respects it was inmates
who ran prisons, and guards who depended upon their cooperation to do
their jobs.[20] So, too, we must guard against regarding our informants as
passive victims, a perspective in direct contradiction to our desire to see
women as subjects actively constructing history.

Fourth, interactionists viewed society in terms of processes rather than
structures and viewed social institutions as the product of interaction over
time. As a result, they introduced history into their analysis of society. In
particular, they looked at biographies as historical accounts, detailing the
movements of individuals through institutions in patterned sequences, called
"moral careers" because accompanied by transformations in identity and
perspective.[21] By focusing attention on the dialectical relationship between
the construction of identities and the construction of institutions, the career

concept allowed sociologists to observe the process of "structuration" by moving analytically between personal accounts and institutional histories.[22] As we try to draw the connections between women's daily lives and the structures that limit and oppress them, surely such concepts will be useful additions to our methods and our thought.

I have barely touched upon some of the many suggestive ideas provided by this sociology. My object here has been to stress the value of a particular branch of sociology to the study of women and to suggest that oral historians acquaint themselves with this work. I do not intend to suggest that this literature has all the answers we are looking for. Indeed, it can be accused of the distortions and biases apparent in most scholarship that predates the feminist movement in academia. Certainly women's studies needs techniques that can help to show what has been taken for granted about women's lives and to provide sources of information to help us ask more relevant questions and undertake new lines of research. We must develop methods specific to our interests and problems. We need to construct our theories out of the actual experiences of women. Nevertheless, I believe that sociologists can teach us some of what we want to know about this work.

CONCLUSION (SUSAN ARMITAGE)

One of the assumptions shared by the authors of this paper is that there are profound differences in the ways that men and women view the world and their places in it. Fifteen years ago such an assertion by feminist scholars would have been virtually unthinkable. We were still so intimidated by Freud's famous dictum "biology is destiny" that the very notion of difference inevitably smacked of inequality; but as feminist scholarship has developed, and in particular as researchers have listened carefully to what they have heard in oral interviews, the *fact* of difference has become inescapable.[23] We are just at the beginning of knowing what that difference means. We do know, from a variety of sources, that women's sense of themselves in relationship to family and work is different from that of men. In the Washington Women's Heritage Project we identified this attitude in the high value women place on relationships; others have spoken of women's "embeddedness" in both family and work.[24] Historian Joan Kelly in one of her last articles explored the theoretical implications of this insight, calling it "The Doubled Vision of Feminist Theory."[25] Kelly challenged the nineteenth-century division of society into private and public spheres, arguing that "Women's place is not a separate sphere or domain of existence but a position within social existence generally." Recognizing women's true place leads to an awareness of the ways in which, for each gender, "our personal, social and historical experience is seen to be shaped by the *simultaneous operation of relations of work and sex*." Just as Westkott explored the "doubleness" of the individual female consciousness (as women simultaneously adapt to male social structures and reject them), so Kelly allows us to see the public roles of women as expressions of "doubleness" in which private and public concerns are always intertwined. As we unravel these meanings, we will understand much more fully than we do now not only how women have lived and understood their lives but how our social theory must change to accommodate this hidden reality.

Finally, the preceding pages show the growing complexity of feminist scholarship. Our paper includes critiques of accepted methodologies in history, psychology, and sociology. All three are revealed as inadequate to describe the reality of women's experience as we have come to understand it through many different kinds of feminist research in the past fifteen years. We certainly do not claim to understand fully the contours and complexities of women's lives, but we have enough knowledge to be certain that uncritical use of old methodologies will hinder rather than help our future investigations. Thus we regard it as essential that careful scrutiny be applied to the assumptions that we carry into the oral history interview. We propose a definite structuring of oral history methods to achieve the goals of feminist research. As Anderson and Jack have shown, we will not find out about women's consciousness unless we ask. We will need to incorporate considerable psychological awareness and listening skills into our interviews in order to succeed.[26] The stance we adopt toward our completed interviews is equally crucial. The desire of feminist researchers to make sure that women are the subjects and not the objects of study is laudable but difficult to accomplish. Here we need the sophisticated sociological awareness of the reciprocal relationships between individual and institution developed by interactionist sociologists and their followers. This range of skills makes it virtually mandatory that future women's oral history projects be conducted by interdisciplinary teams.

Why bother? Why not just continue our present uncritical interview methods? The answer, of course, is that they do not reflect the insights of the new feminist scholarship. The old methods will not tell us what we now know we can learn about women if we ask the right questions.

NOTES

1. Dorothy Smith, "Women and Psychiatry," in *Women Look at Psychiatry: I'm not Mad, I'm Angry,* ed. Dorothy Smith and Sara David (Vancouver: Press Gang Pub., 1975), 2.

2. See Susan Armitage "The Next Step," in Special Women's Oral History Two issue of *Frontiers: A Journal of Women Studies* 8 (1, 1983) 3–8.

3. Marcia Millman and Rosabeth Moss Kanter, *Another Voice: Feminist Perspectives on Social Life and Social Science* (New York: Anchor Press/Doubleday, 1975), viii.

4. See Dale Spender, *Men's Studies Modified: The Impact of Feminism on the Academic Disciplines* (Oxford, N.Y.: Pergamon Press, 1981).

5. Marcia Westkott, "Feminist Criticism of the Social Sciences," *Harvard Educational Review* 49 (November 1979): 422–30.

6. For a fuller explanation see Dana C. Jack, "Clinical Depression in Women: Cognitive Schemas of Self, Care, and Relationships in a Longitudinal Study" (Ph.D. diss., Harvard University, 1984), chap. 2.

7. Dorothy Smith, "A Sociology for Women," in *The Prism of Sex: Essays in the Sociology of Knowledge*, ed. Julia Sherman and Evelyn Beck (Madison: University of Wisconsin Press, 1979); and Smith, "Institutional Ethnography," unpublished manuscript, n.d.

8. Kathryn Anderson and others, interviews for the Washington Women's Heritage Project, Center for Pacific Northwest Studies, Western Washington University, Bellingham, Washington. In the following account, two interviews from the collection are cited: interview with Elizabeth Bailey, 1 July 1980; interview with Verna Friend, 31 July 1980.

9. George W. Brown and Tirril Harris, *The Social Origins of Depression: A Study of Psychiatric Disorder in Women* (London: Tavistock Publications, 1978).

10. Deborah Belle, ed., *Lives in Stress: Women and Depression* (Beverly Hills: Sage Publications, 1982).

11. Jack, "Clinical Depression in Women."

12. Nancy Cott, "Passionlessness: The Interpretation of Victorian Sexual Ideology, 1790–1850," *Signs* 4 (1978): 219–36, as explained by Westkott in "Feminist Criticism," 429.

13. Arlie Russell Hochschild, "Emotion Work, Feeling Rules, and Social Structure," *American Journal of Sociology* 85 (November 1979): 551–75.

14. See especially Nancy Chodorow, *The Reproduction of Mothering: Psychoanalysis and the Sociology of Gender* (Berkeley: University of California Press, 1978).

15. Howard Becker, *Outsiders: Studies in the Sociology of Deviance* (New York: Free Press, 1963), 14–15.

16. Members of the first sociology department at the University of Chicago wrote thousands of life histories during the 1920s and 1930s. An interesting treatment of Chicago life histories can be found in James Bennett's book *Oral History and Delinquency: The Rhetoric of Criminology* (Chicago: University of Chicago Press, 1981). Norman Denzin discusses the relation between symbolic interactionist theory and methods in *The Research Act: A Theoretical Introduction to Sociological Methods* (Chicago: Aldine Pub. Co., 1978). Everett Hughes provides important insights on how to study the connections between institutions and individuals in essays collected in *The Sociological Eye: Selected Papers*, 2 vols. (Chicago: Aldine Pub. Co., 1971). The work of his student Howard S. Becker has been centrally important to this tradition. See especially, *Sociological Work: Method and Substance* (Chicago: Aldine Pub. Co., 1970), a collection of his essays on method, and his introduction to Clifford Shaw's classic life history, *The Jack-Roller: A Delinquent Boy's Own Story* (Chicago: University of Chicago Press, 1966). Becker is credited with developing the labeling theory of deviance. David Matza defines and discusses "naturalistic" sociology in *Becoming Deviant* (Englewood Cliffs, N.J.: Prentice-Hall, 1969), in which he appraises the work of Becker and others. A bibliography that includes the work of many other sociologists employing subjective accounts can be found in R. Bogdan and S. Taylor, *Introduction to Qualitative Research Methods: A Phenomenological Approach to the Social Sciences* (New York: John Wiley and Sons, 1975). M. Hammersley and P. Atkinson, in *Ethnography, Principles in Practice* (London: Tavistock, 1983), provide a more recent annotated bibliography of ethnographic texts.

17. See, for example, Ken Plummer, *Documents in Life: An Introduction to the Problems and Literature of a Humanistic Method* (London: Allen and Unwin, 1983); A. Faraday and K. Plummer, "Doing Life Histories," *Sociological Review* 27 (November 1979): 773–92; Daniel Bertaux, ed., *Biography and Society: The Life History Approach in the Social Sciences* (Beverly Hills, Calif.: Sage Publications, 1981); Philip Abrams, *Historical Sociology* (Somerset, Eng.: Open Books, 1982); Clem Adelman, ed.,

Uttering, Muttering: Collecting, Using and Reporting Talk for Social and Educational Research (London: Grant McIntyre, 1981); and the previously cited Hammersley and Atkinson, *Ethnography, Principles in Practices.*

18. See Becker, "Whose Side Are We On?" in *Sociological Work* for a clear statement of this position.

19. Many studies describe how social order is negotiated on a daily basis by subordinates and superordinates in organizational settings. See, for example, Julius Roth, *Timetables: Structuring the Passage of Time in Hospital Treatment and Other Careers* (Indianapolis: Bobbs Merrill, 1963); Erving Goffman, *Asylums: Essays on the Social Situation of Mental Patients and Other Inmates* (New York: Anchor Press/ Doubleday, 1961); Gresham Sykes, *Society of Captives: A Study of a Maximum Security Prison* (Princeton, N.J.: Princeton University Press, 1958); Howard Becker, Blanche Geer, Everett Hughes, and Anselm Strauss, *Boys in White: Student Culture in Medical School* (New Brunswick, N.J.: Transaction Books, 1983); and Peter Berger, *The Human Shape of Work: Studies in the Sociology of Occupations* (New York: Macmillan, 1964).

20. Sykes, *Society of Captives.*

21. The career concept was first articulated by Everett Hughes in several essays collected in *The Sociological Eye.* See in particular his essay in that volume "Cycles, Turning Points, and Careers." Others who have commented on the concept or developed it in case studies include Howard Becker, "The Career of the Chicago Public School Teacher," *American Journal of Sociology* 57 (March 1952): 470–77; "Notes on the Concept of Commitment," *American Journal of Sociology* 66 (July 1960): 32–40; Howard Becker and Blanche Geer, "Latent Culture: A Note on the Theory of Latent Social Roles," *Administrative Science Quarterly* 5 (September 1960): 304–13; Howard S. Becker, Blanche Geer, and E. C. Hughes, *Making the Grade: The Academic Side of College Life* (New York: John Wiley and Sons, 1968); Howard S. Becker and Anselm L. Strauss, "Careers, Personalities, and Adult Socialization," *American Journal of Sociology* 62 (November 1956): 253–63; and three previously cited works: Becker et al., *Boys in White*; Goffman, *Asylums*; and Abrams, *Historical Sociology.*

22. Abrams, *Historical Sociology.*

23. The first major work clearly to take this as a premise was Carol Gilligan's *In a Different Voice: Psychological Theory and Women's Development* (Cambridge: Harvard University Press, 1982).

24. See in particular Barbara Noble and May Whelan, "Woman and Welfare Work: Demystifying the Myth of Disembeddedness," in *Sex/Gender Division of Labor: Feminist Perspectives* (Minneapolis: University of Minnesota Center for Advanced Feminist Studies and Women's Studies, 1983) and the papers of Italian feminists Luisa Passerini and Adele Pesce at the International Conference on Oral History and Women's History, Columbia University, November, 1983.

25. Joan Kelly, "The Doubled Vision of Feminist Theory: A Postscript to the 'Women and Power' Conference," *Feminist Studies* 5 (Spring 1979): 216–27.

26. For a clear explanation of the process of the psychological interview, see Pamela Daniels and Kathy Weingarten, *Sooner or Later: The Timing of Parenthood in Adult Lives* (New York: W. W. Norton, 1982), 315–22.

PART TWO

Exemplary Readings

5

Laura Ellsworth Seiler
In the Streets

SHERNA BERGER GLUCK

Imagine the U.S. political scene in the early 1900s: World War I was being fought, and President Wilson was being criticized for promoting U.S. participation in the war to defend democracy, on the one hand, and not supporting women's suffrage at home, on the other. A women's movement, active for more than fifty years, was in the final stage of its drive to obtain the right to vote for women. Then, as now, women's rights workers were not of a single mind. Liberals, conservatives, and radicals disagreed about the best means to get what they all wanted: suffrage. It was illegal then to give even information about birth control. This was the time of Laura Ellsworth Seiler, a relatively unknown woman who, while young, worked for women's suffrage, though she never dreamed of calling herself a feminist. Gluck's oral history of Laura Ellsworth Seiler is part of a larger project that involved interviews with five average, now elderly American women about their suffragist activities. Gluck's goal was to rescue from oblivion the noninstitutional, activist side of the earlier feminist movement, the side that will not be found in official histories, published memoirs, news clippings, and other written materials. Though all five women were more or less middle class and all were either expanding or challenging women's roles at the time, their lives are incredibly diverse. Thus Laura Seiler's story is not so much representative as it is exemplary.

As Tax (1985:9–17) pointed out in her introduction to the volume in which Gluck's chapter appeared, Gluck's work is unlike pre-1960 histories of the earlier women's movement. These early histories concentrated mainly on why the movement ended. Gluck's work, in contrast, has a celebratory tone, thus reflecting the importance of history as inspirational and visionary for future generations. This story reflects "the personal is political" theme of feminist inquiry: There is no sharp distinction between Laura Seiler's personal and public life. Gluck's documentation is minimally edited and without censorship. She lets the women speak for themselves, with the aid only of inserted news clippings to give the reader a better sense of the historical context.

Laura Ellsworth Seiler, at the age of eighty-two, though not an active participant in the current women's movement, closely follows its literature. She is particularly interested in vocational guidance for women as a result of her own long professional career. She has written a manual, as yet unpublished, on career management for women.

Laura is an attractive, perfectly coiffed, gray-haired woman who appears twenty years younger than her actual age. Her manner is very proper and businesslike, and her speech seems to bear the mark of lessons in elocution. Despite this outward formality and a clear reluctance to discuss her private life in any detail, Laura was quite cordial and eager to share her suffrage experiences.

When we recorded the first of two interviews in October 1973, Laura had just moved into a retirement facility in Claremont, California. Her apartment was tastefully and simply decorated with the artifacts obtained during her extensive travels. Among her books were several on the suffrage movement, a few on today's women's movement and a scrapbook covering her career in advertising. Though she is on congenial terms with the other inhabitants of the retirement facility, it is obvious that her life has been very different from the lives of most of the others and that her support of feminist goals is not shared by them.

Laura Seiler is an accomplished public speaker and a gifted storyteller; it is difficult to capture in print the marvelous vitality and perfect timing of her accounts. Nevertheless, it is hard to imagine that this well-groomed, dignified woman participated in that part of the suffrage struggle that today might well be called "guerrilla theater."

A PROPER BACKGROUND

All of my ancestors, on both sides, so far as I know, were in America before 1700. So it's a straight New England background until the generation in which I was born. My grandfather had a period of retirement because of a breakdown in health. When he decided to practice law again, he settled in Ithaca. It was a family joke that he moved to Ithaca because he had four daughters and a new college had just opened, that he moved to Ithaca to marry them off. Two of them did marry Cornell men. So even though they were in New York, I always thought of my family as New Englanders in exile. It seemed to me that they bore down more heavily on New England traditions than if they'd still been living there.

I was born in Buffalo in 1890, but when I was only six months old my mother and father separated and we moved to my maternal grandfather's household in Ithaca. My grandfather had been a judge, and though I don't think he was anything very important in the way of a judge, he was always called Judge Ellsworth. The household consisted of my grandmother and grandfather, a maiden aunt, my mother and the three of us children. I was the youngest. My sister was seven years older than I, and my brother five.

The house was very large. That was the day, of course, when you still had sleep-in servants. Down in the rather large, halfway basement was the dining room, a large pantry, a huge kitchen and what was called the maids' sitting room. It was called that because it was furnished so that they could have fun there. Beyond that, there was an enormous cellar. There was an outside entrance to the maids' sitting room so that their guests could come and go, and that's where the deliveries were made, too.

The first floor had a big central hall, a music room, a library, front and back parlors, and a very large bed/sitting room and bath for my grandfather and grandmother. On the other side was another bedroom with a room off it which was used for storage.

Up on the second floor there were one, two, three bedrooms and a bath in the front of the house, and what was then called the sewing room. Then you went down a flight of steps to a door, and there were one or two rooms for servants, and a big storage room, out of which came the most peculiar things when we had to break up the house (among others, a straw frame for hoopskirts). I don't think anything had been taken out of the room for twenty-five or thirty years.

When we first came home to my grandfather's, my mother was very ill, and for a while they weren't quite sure she was going to recover. But then she grew stronger. Of course, in those days it was unusual for a woman to be divorced, and I think that my mother, when she returned to the bosom of an orthodox Episcopalian family, was definitely made to feel it was improper; this living away from the husband was not the thing to do.

I definitely suffered very much when I was a small child because my sister told me, very early, that I must not ask my mother any questions about it. So I really hadn't the remotest idea where my father was or what was the matter with him. It bothered me a great deal. Some of the children might have had fathers who worked in Buffalo or someplace like that but they came home on weekends. I was the only one who had no father.

Of course, I have since thought that, in spite of the enormous disadvantages of not having a father, it was probably also partly responsible for my somewhat more friendly and less critical attitude toward men. I really never, in my family, encountered the thing known as a dominating male. My grandfather then was too old and too mellow, and, of course, charming with us children. He never was the tyrannical sort. I just grew up liking men and have never seen any cause to change my mind.

Grandfather was really the most important person in my group. When we moved into his house he was seventy-four and still practicing law. Later, after he retired, I used to spend a great many hours with him. He mostly sat about in a chair on the porch or in the house. My grandfather was what used to be called a "freethinker." He got his Phi Beta Kappa key back in 1835, when he was in Union Law School. In those days Phi Beta Kappa was an organization of freethinkers; that's what it means, its philosophy, the key of life. I can't remember any big lectures on ethical subjects, but I do think his attitude must have somehow been bred into me. It seems to me that very early in my life I realized that you didn't judge people by what they had, but by what they were. I have an idea that these things were offshoots of my grandfather's conversation and of other things that went on in the house.

My grandfather was a Democrat, and a Democrat in upstate New York was an oddity. He didn't think much of the local papers, so he always had the *Rochester Democrat* and *Chronicle* sent to him. It was a family custom to gather around the table in Grandfather's bedroom while Grandfather read the things he considered important that day. My older sister and brother sat in on these. I was too little—I knew that and never participated.

All the rest of the family were very orthodox Episcopalians, I should say. I can still remember my grandmother asking him to go to church and he, retorting with a grin, "No. I'm glad to pay for the pew, but you go and sit in it."

My grandmother was a rather protected Victorian woman. She was quite an attractive woman, rather small, and led a quite normal social life. My grandfather didn't like very well having people asked to meals. I remember that it had to be arranged with him beforehand, and there were not very many people he liked to have invited. Usually, when people came to the house they were calling on my grandmother, aunt and mother, and we entertained them at the front of the house. Only occasionally were they taken back to my grandfather's room.

I don't remember my grandmother going out to anything like club meetings. They went out to receptions, as they were called in those days. And I also remember that in the winter they had perpetually going what was called duplicate whist.

There were boards just big enough to hold four hands of cards under elastics. They had a series of them, I would guess probably twenty. As I recall, they had two tables always in the front parlor. And they played the boards all the way through, and kept track of their scores. The boards were shifted one to the right, so they went through again playing the hands their opponents had played, and then compared the scores at the end. That was called duplicate whist, and they did it all winter long.

One of my earliest and most charming recollections of my grandmother and grandfather was when I was quite small. Theoretically the door to my grandfather's bed/sitting room was always closed, and you knocked before you went in. But being small, I disregarded that and swung the door open and discovered my grandmother sitting on my grandfather's lap. I was so surprised. I'd never seen anything like that before in my life.

My mother's life was mostly concerned, of course, with us children. She wasn't too active outside the household, though since she had grown up in Ithaca she had plenty of friends. She didn't do anything special that I can recall in the way of church work, though we all went to church very regularly. One of my happiest recollections is that during Lent I always went with my mother, across the park where our church was, for the five o'clock Lenten services, which I enjoyed very much.

I didn't have any contact with my father or his family until I was eight when, for the first time, we were invited by my grandmother to spend the Christmas in Buffalo. That was the first time I ever saw my father. Then we also went back the year they had the Pan-American Exposition in Buffalo, in 1901. We spent almost the whole summer in Buffalo going to the fair every other day and staying with my grandmother and my father. That was about all, just very minimal contact.

My mother and father were originally just separated. My mother didn't get the divorce until 1900. My grandfather insisted she get it because he felt he wasn't going to live much longer, and wanted that all settled—for matters of the estate, I suspect.

My grandmother died of pneumonia very soon after she and my grandfather celebrated their golden wedding anniversary in 1899. That was a very exciting affair. My eldest aunt came back from St. Louis, where she lived. My grandfather retired about that time, when he was eighty-one or eighty-two. He died two years later, when he was eighty-four, in 1901. The last year or so, we had an old Civil War veteran who acted as companion to him, helping him around.

When we were growing up, it was always taken for granted that we would all go to college. My sister and I were really the first generation of women in my family to go to college. Mother had wanted to be a doctor, but they told her that she didn't have the physique for it. I think many girls were discouraged in that age by telling them that it was too strenuous and they could never do it. So she didn't go to college. She was always quite resentful, I think, that she hadn't. I don't think there was a finishing school in Ithaca in her days. I don't recall that she did anything in the way of a special school after she finished high school.

But we were all infected with the Cornell idea. My father had been a Cornell man, and also students frequently came to call on my sister. It was just taken for granted that we would all go to Cornell. We were always invited to parties at Sigma Phi fraternity, my grandfather's fraternity at Union. I think it was assumed that my sister, at least, would pursue a career. At that time she was utterly devoted to my grandfather, and she herself wanted to be a lawyer. I think she must have discussed it quite often with Grandfather. She abandoned the idea only after she took a year off between her junior and senior years in college and came down and worked for a year in New York. Then it was that she fell in love with Wall Street and decided that she preferred to go into the bond and stock business rather than be a lawyer.

While she was in school, she was determined to do well. She got the Phi Beta Kappa, too, and has always had my grandfather's key. I was so cross that there was only one large key, so that when I got mine, I bought the smallest one there was—it's about an inch long. I was furious that I couldn't have my grandfather's.

When my sister was a student at Cornell, Nora Stanton Blatch, Harriet Stanton Blatch's daughter and the granddaughter of Elizabeth Cady Stanton, was also a student there. They were great friends. I can remember Nora coming to dinner and much discussion of suffrage and so forth. Nora was in and out of our house in 1903 or 1904 when I was still in high school. So it was no surprise when my sister graduated that she should take a very active part in working for suffrage in New York.

I don't think my mother and aunt were much involved in these discussions, though my mother, being very maternal, was sympathetic about suffrage. I would never say that she was a confirmed suffragist; I don't think it would ever have occurred to her if her daughters hadn't been so much interested.

I remember something I thought was quite funny that happened when I was in high school. The speech teacher thought it would be highly instructive to have a debate on woman's suffrage. She picked out two girls, of which I was one, to do the affirmative, and two boys to uphold the negative. And we had a spirited debate before the school assembly. The really funny thing was that in the heat of rebuttal, I announced in firm tones, "The more responsibility you give women, the more they'll have," and there was a burst of howls from the audience, and I couldn't imagine for the moment what I'd said that was so funny. I heard about that for years afterwards.

Well, we won the debate, but then I was not especially interested in suffrage. I don't remember being interested in it again until I was in college. One day the boy that I was engaged to—somebody had said something about the law about suffrage—I heard him saying, rather smugly, "Laura doesn't believe in suffrage or any of that nonsense," and all of a sudden, I knew I did! That must have been around my junior year, and I forthwith started the Suffrage Club at Cornell among the coeds.

I didn't go to Cornell until 1908, though I graduated from high school in 1907; Cornell didn't take girls until they were seventeen, so I had to wait a year. I spent the winter of that year down in Panama, from about October till February. My father was an architect and he was the official estimator on buildings for the Canal Zone when they were building the canal. My grandmother had been down there with him, and he thought it would be very nice if I came down and spent the winter with my grandmother and him. So I did that, not doing anything special, just having a lot of fun.

I got back just in time to take the last semester in high school again and then I took some postgraduate work. The following autumn I went to the University. I took an arts course, as my sister had done. My brother was both an engineer and a naval architect. I took the number of courses in modern langugages to get by for my major. I just took the courses that interested me: evolution, comparative religions, lots of philosophy, some psychology. Every year, when I took my list of courses to be okayed by my faculty adviser, he would heave a large sigh and say, "I suppose if you don't intend to teach, it doesn't matter, because this is a salad course."

I got Phi Beta Kappa, for reasons that were a great surprise to me, since I had not especially concentrated on high marks. Meeting one of my professors coming up the hill one day, I expressed my surprise. He said, "Well, it was kind of a relief to be able to vote for somebody who hadn't always had her nose in a book."

I expected to do something after I graduated. My sister would never have let me get to that point without a definite idea that I was going to have a career. I wouldn't say that I had any clear idea, though, because years afterwards, when I was invited back to Cornell to make a vocational speech to girls, the dean of women said to me laughing, "Laura, do you know what you put on your application when you came in? As a freshman, you were asked what you intended to do. You put down that you intended to be a teacher, and the next question was why, and you said, 'Because they have such long summer vacations.'"

I definitely was engaged when I left Cornell, and I also was definitely planning to do something. You see, when my grandfather's estate was settled, it was divided evenly among his four daughters—except that he subtracted from my mother's part the very considerable sums of money that he had advanced to her during her most unsatisfactory marriage. So my mother with three children got very much less than the other three who had no children, which made it quite tough.

By the time we were ready to come down to New York, I don't think there was very much capital left. I always expected that I would be doing something in the way of earning a living, but I had no very definite ideas about it.

BECOMING AN ORGANIZER
FOR SUFFRAGE

It was while I was at Cornell that I became involved in the suffrage movement. It was a very natural thing for me to be interested in suffrage because of my sister's association with Nora Blatch. My sister graduated in 1908 and went to New York and was the vice president of the Women's

Political Union, which was, I think, the most militant of the national organizations. So by the time I went to Cornell, my sister was already working furiously for suffrage in New York.

I wasn't doing anything about it except reading some of the books. Of course, I took time off and went down and marched in the suffrage parade at my sister's behest. I think I probably marched with the Women's Political Union. That was, I think, the 1912 parade which Inez Milholland led, looking very beautiful, mounted on a white horse. There were also about a hundred men in the parade. Believe me, they had courage! Whoo! It took so much more courage for a man to come out for woman's suffrage than it did for a woman. They were quite remarkable.

There were not very many people interested in suffrage at that time. But, I started the Suffrage Club in 1912. I don't know whether it was my idea or whether my sister asked me to do it. I just called, or put up a notice, or something. I didn't live at the dormitory; I lived at home. I called a meeting in our general auditorium and explained to them about the suffrage movement.

Cornell at that time had only about three hundred women and some four thousand men. I'd say we probably had a pretty big club before we got through. And, of course, it went on after I left. I should guess that we must have had at least seventy-five, something like that. It was fairly popular with the women.

Of course, we were not very aggressive suffragists. We met in the women's dormitory and mainly just had meetings by ourselves. But after the group had been going for a while, we staged a debate. One of the men students came over to see me one day to say that his mother, who was a prominent anti-suffragist, was coming to visit him. He asked if I would like to arrange a debate while she was there. I was entitled to ask that one of the big auditoriums be set aside, and so I said, "Yes, I would."

I didn't think it was suitable for a person my age to debate his mother. This was fairly early in the suffrage movement and there was no suffrage group in Ithaca. If there was, I would have asked the head of that. But the Women's Club was vaguely interested in suffrage, so I consulted the president, the wife of an instructor and she agreed to debate. She was a very earnest young woman but not a skilled debater.

The woman who came from New York was a true *grande dame* indeed, with all the polished manner to go with debating. Sitting up on the platform, as chairman, I became congealed with horror because what was developing was a hair-pulling performance, sending the audience into fits of laughter. The woman from New York would say, "Now my esteemed opponent has said so-and-so," and the other woman, who was by then furious at the customary misleading statements that anti-suffragists specialized in, would say, "What she says is not so!" or, "That's a lie!"

I, of course, grew frantic realizing that the people in the audience, many of whom were townspeople as well as students, were going out to laugh their heads off. Certainly, it was going to do suffrage no good. I also knew

EDITORIAL

THE HEROIC MEN

The facts are all in print now about the masculine adherents of the woman suffragists who will march in the parade to-morrow. There will be 800 of them surely. They will represent every trade and profession except the clergy. This is clearly an oversight which should be rectified. There is no lack of clergymen ready to support the cause of votes for women. For the rest the list includes bankers, manufacturers, students, librarians, dentists, musicians, booksellers, journalists, as well as dancing teachers, egg inspectors, capitalists, watchmen, ladies' waistmakers — and authors. A lawyer will carry the banner, and a drum and fife corps will head the division.

This is important news and not to be trifled with. The men who have professed to believe in woman suffrage have always been numerous. But these men are going to do more than profess, they are going to march before the eyes of the more or less unsympathetic multitude. It is one thing to sit on the platform and smile at a woman's meeting, quite another to march behind a gaudy banner to the inspiration of the squeaking fife, in order to indicate one's belief in the right of women to the ballot. The men will be closely scanned, but they will not mind that. They will be called endearing names by small boys on the sidewalk. But doubtless they will study to preserve their gravity. They will not march as well as the women. Only trained soldiers can compete with the amazons in keeping step. There must be strong inducement to make men march in a woman's parade. Some may be looking for customers. We suspect both the waistmakers and the dentists, for instance. But the majority must firmly believe in the righteousness of the cause, and also in the value to it of their public appearance in line. They are courageous fellows. The march of the 800 may be renowned. We hope they will all hold out from Thirteenth Street to Carnegie Hall, and we extend to all the 800 our sympathy and admiration.

SUFFRAGE ARMY OUT ON PARADE

Perhaps 10,000 Women and Men Sympathizers March for the Cause.

STREETS PACKED FOR THEM

Cheers for the Women and Some Good-Natured Jesting at the Men.

AGED LEADERS APPLAUDED

They Rode in Flower-Bedecked Carriages— Women on Horseback and "Joan of Arc" Win Plaudits.

Part IX. of this morning's Times consists of four pages of pictures of yesterday's suffrage parade.

Ten thousand strong, the army of those who believe in the cause of woman's suffrage marched up Fifth Avenue at sundown yesterday in a parade the like of which New York never knew before. Dusty and weary, the marchers went to their homes last night satisfied that their year of hard work in preparing for the demonstration had borne good fruit.

It was an immense crowd that came out to stand upon the sidewalks to cheer or jeer. It was a crowd far larger than that which greeted the homecoming of Theodore Roosevelt and the homecoming of Cardinal Farley. It was a crowd that stood through the two hours of the parade without a thought of weariness. Women, young and old, rich and poor, were all banded into a great sisterhood by the cause they hold dear.

EDITORIAL

THE UPRISING OF THE WOMEN.

The parade on Fifth Avenue last evening of possibly 10,000 women of various ages, many of them young and personable, all surely representative of good types of womanhood, for they were obviously healthy and presumably intelligent, will be discussed from various points of view. Most of the comment it provokes will be humorous but amiable. Men generally view the woman suffrage movement calmly, seeming not to care much whether or not the women get the right to vote, and heeding little the consequences of the social revolution which would result from the triumph of the present agitation. A few men believe that the right of suffrage should be extended forthwith to the women. Our observation does not justify the inference that they are wise and thoughtful men, but they are certainly more admirable and entitled to more respect than the men who, believing the contrary, possessed of the knowledge that the vote will secure to woman no new privilege that she either deserves or requires, that the enfranchisement of women must inevitably result in the weakening of family ties, yet look upon the woman suffrage movement complacently and dismiss it with idle, trivial comment.

The situation is dangerous. We often hear the remark nowadays that women will get the vote if they try hard enough and persistently, and it is true that they will get, and play havoc with it for themselves and society, if the men are not firm and wise enough and, it may as well be said, masculine enough to prevent them. The agitation has been on foot for many years. One does not need to be a profound student of biology to know that some women, a very small minority, have a natural inclination to usurp the social and civic functions of men. But that is not true of a majority of the women in yesterday's parade, or of their thousands of sympathetic sisters who lacked the physical vigor, the courage, or the opportunity to join in the march. Their adherence to the cause is largely factitious, born of much agitation and much false theorizing. There are, however, unhappy creatures to whom the state of being a woman is naturally burdensome. Their influence would not count for so much if their less unhappy sisters, who have no real grievance against Mother Nature or society, would not give them countenance. There are numberless explanations of the conduct of otherwise nice and womanly women in this matter. There are few that can fairly be called "reasons."

We are told by some sages that education has made women discontented. It has made men discontented, too, for that matter. The equality of opportunity all men possess in this country has not allayed the discontent. There is no reason to suppose that the right to vote would allay feminine discontent. Granted the suffrage, they would demand all that the right implies. It is not possible to think of women as soldiers and sailors, police patrolmen, or firemen, although voters ought to fight if need be, but they would serve on juries and elect themselves if they could to executive offices and Judgeships. Many of them are looking forward to an apportionment of high offices between the sexes. This may seem preposterous to some of the men who chose to smile complacently at the aggressiveness of the women's rights adherents, but it is true. It is a state of things these men will have to cope with before they die if they do not arouse themselves and do their duty now.

We have said that the ballot will secure to woman no right that she needs and does not now possess. That is a true statement, and we hold that it is not debatable. Woman is thoroughly protected by the existing laws. Her rights as a taxpayer, a holder of property, are not in danger. Her dower rights are scrupulously upheld in the probate courts. In her pursuit of all the privileges and duties of men, however, she is deliberately endangering many rights she now enjoys without legal sanction. . . . It will be a sad day for society when woman loses the respect she now receives from all but the basest of men. Yet yesterday's parade demonstrates that she holds male courtesy in slight regard, or would, if we were willing to regard the parade as a demonstration of the feelings and opinions of all our women.

Millions of men labor all their years to keep up a home, of which a woman is mistress. Poor enough the home may be, and the measure of toil its upkeep demands of the man may age him prematurely and deprive him of all the freedom which he instinc-

tively desires. But most men throughout the civilized world have been doing their duty as husbands and fathers, as citizens, according to their lights. That the triumph of woman suffrage would tend quickly to change the point of view of these millions of plodding men is not to be doubted. If woman declares her independence, and forces the State to recognize it, the cry of the men will be "Let her uphold it and enjoy it as best she may." From the beginning "man that is born of woman" has been "of few days and full of trouble." Presumably he will continue to be born. Presumably he will continue to respect his mother, as ISHMAEL did. But with the opportunity afforded to him by the refusal of woman to recognize his manhood as a title of supremacy in the world's affairs, he will be at pains to avoid some of the troubles which he has hitherto regarded as part of his heritage.

This we hold to be inevitable. Let the women who are not yet avowed suffragists consider it. Above all, let the complacent multitudes of men who have accepted the full responsibility of citizenship consider it. There were, at most, 10,000 women in yesterday's parade. If their cause triumphs there will be 700,000 women voters in this municipality. Have the 10,000 thought much about the measure of influence they would exert if the whole number voted under the control of their associations and environment and as their intelligence impelled them to?

chairmen were supposed to keep their mouths shut, but I was a suffragist and I wasn't going to let this thing go down the river!

So I rose at the end and thanked both of them and then proceeded, rather crisply, I think, in about five minutes, to point out to them the difference between personality and causes. They could leave either confirmed in reaction with the anti-suffragists or planning to go ahead with the suffragists. And, as sometimes happens in those circumstances, I was so convinced that I was right that I felt about eight feet tall and I've never spoken better—with the result that I got an ovation at the end.

It did result in more women students joining our suffrage organization. All together it turned out well in the end, except that I received a letter of reprimand from my sister, who said, "Well, I hope you realize now all you did was to furnish an audience and a platform for an anti-suffragist." But I continued to believe that people should hear both sides of the story. It may not have been good maneuvering, but I thought it was the honest way to do it.

Then, in 1913, when I graduated, the Women's Political Union decided that it would be a very good thing for me to go and "organize," as they then called it, the two counties of Chautauqua and Cattaraugus in New York State. My mother, who was not a confirmed suffragist, but a very charming Victorian, went along to chaperone me.

Nobody had been in those western counties before. More work had probably been done up in Westchester and places like that, but I think perhaps mine was the first attempt to organize those western counties. They were basically manufacturing towns like Jamestown and Silver Creek and places like that. Of course, there was lots of farming in between. In those days, the population was much, much less than now, and they were small towns with one factory, let's say, or some kind of business in which people worked.

I had a little list given me of people thought to be sympathizers, and I was supposed to go in and organize them and leave a chapter of the Women's Political Union behind to go on working. Ahead of time, I had to send the newspapers a little publicity, telling them what it was going to be about. When I got there, I had to contact these women. In most of the small towns I had the names of three or four women who were thought to be sympathetic. Usually they were definitely upper-class or upper-middle-class, married and in their later thirties or middle forties. They were people who had traveled and for some reason or another had expressed some interest in suffrage. I don't recall any laboring-class women who were ever on that list.

That was very fortunate for us. We were trying to reach the local leaders in small towns and let them conduct the local organization work. It was called an organization trip, and that's just what it was. These contact women would arrange a house meeting for the purpose of forming a local group, and I would talk to the women there and provide them with the materials and tell them how to organize. Then it was up to them to do the local work on all classes.

Then, I had to make a street speech. That was in the days when you could still rent cars where the back went down. So we would rent a car and put an enormous white, green and purple banner across the back. The white was for purity, of course; the green was for courage; and the purple was for justice. That's supposed to be the explanation that we gave. The banner was a big one, and it covered practically the entire back. It made a very effective device for public speaking. Of course the most difficult moment for a street speaker is getting a crowd. As in all small towns, the most popular corner of the street was the one that held the bar. I always directed the chauffeur to stop just outside the bar.

My mother, who was small and charming and utterly Victorian and convinced that all good things started with the favor of the male, would go through the swinging doors, and say, "Gentlemen, my daughter is going to talk about suffrage outside, and I think you would be interested. I hope you'll come out." And just like the Pied Piper, they would all dump their drinks on the bar and come out and make the nucleus of the crowd.

I was always embarrassed to have to take up a collection. I was convinced they thought we put it in our own pockets. But Mother had no such qualms. She would circulate about giving out the pamphlets and holding out a basket and saying, "I'm sure you want to help the cause," and the folding money would come in. She was invaluable!

My speeches varied according to the type of town. In general, it was on the injustice against women and the fact, also, that the injustice affected men indirectly; it held down the wages of all of them if women were underpaid.

Once, in a small town, I had a very amusing experience. We'd been the guests in the house of a man who owned a factory, a very charming young man and his wife. I made a speech and, in the course of it, I reminded the crowd that the only way men had been able really to affect their wages and conditions was getting together into unions and bringing pressure to bear. A ripple of laughter swept the crowd and I couldn't imagine why until I got back to my host's home. He told me that he had spent all the last year fighting their efforts to form a union. So here I was, under his auspices, advising them to do it.

Well, things like that happened. And we also, of course, were aware that there were still dreadful conditions in factories in those days. We bore down on things of that sort. Child labor was by no means unheard of—any more than it is today. We focused on the importance of the vote to change these kinds of social conditions.

I did these street speeches in the evening, after dinner, in order to catch the men off work. The crowd would be mostly working-class men, the people you're likely to pick up in a street crowd, except for a few others that might just happen to be roaming around. In general, how much was due to my good mother, I don't know—I remember considerable enthusiasm for the speech and, also, a great deal of good-natured tolerance on the part of the men. And, as I say, rather good collections. I'm quite sure that that kind of campaigning did a lot of good because we reached people, I'm sure, who were not in the least interested in suffrage up to that moment.

On the whole, I think it was a successful tour. It bore fruit, definitely. We left behind a good nucleus of women who would then start in to plan and to work actively and to do things themselves. And, of course, it gave the central organization a chapter with which to work directly; the chapter could ask questions and get material to us, just the way a political organization would work.

Some of these women that I organized went on into quite extensive suffragist experiences. One of them, I remember, somewhat to my dismay, later joined Alice Paul's group and was hunger-striking in Washington.

I think we spent about six weeks in each of the counties, which made it about the first of September when we got back to New York. There was no question of where we were going. My sister was there, working on Wall Street. My brother was there, too, but I don't remember what he was doing. He had degrees in marine architecture and mechanical engineering. Though he wanted very much to do marine architecture, there was absolutely nothing like that going on when he left college.

I had been engaged and in October we married. At first we lived in the same apartment as my mother and sister. I was already working for the Women's Political Union and continued with that. My husband was not against my doing it. He was a charming man, a very gentle one, and a very open-minded one—a very good-natured person. I don't think, left to himself, that it would ever have occurred to him to advocate suffrage.

SUFFRAGE TACTICS IN
NEW YORK CITY

After we settled in New York, I went to work full time for the Women's Political Union. The president of the organization was Mrs. Blatch and my sister was the vice president. Mrs. Blatch, of course, was always in the office, which was just off Fifth Avenue on Forty-second Street, almost opposite the library. I think she was the only one of the officers who was at headquarters all the time. The others all had jobs of their own, of one kind or another, and were just serving on the board.

It was a fairly good-sized organization and, of course, we had many, many volunteers. As you know, most of the suffrage work was done by volunteers. Most were probably in their late thirties or early forties, though some were older. We had a large roster of very famous older women who came in and stuffed envelopes and did things like that.

My job was being head of the Speakers Bureau. I had had training in Cornell in public speaking. I was training speakers, giving them their assignments, as well as doing a lot of speaking myself. They were on a voluntary basis and some did much more speaking than others. We did have, especially at campaign times, a certain number of women who were just taken on and paid small sums, probably just enough to cover their expenses.

THE NEW YORK TIMES   NOVEMBER 5, 1911

CIRCULAR INCENSES WOMEN
AT A RALLY

Handed Out at the Doors, It Calls Suffragists
Destroyers of Homes.

NO NAME IS SIGNED TO IT

But Women's Political Union Speakers
Charge it to Cuvillier, on Whom the
Suffragists Are Making War.

There was an unexpected development at the women's big political rally in Alys Dancing Hall last evening, which marked the close of a campaign the Women's Political Union made to defeat Louis A. Cuvillier, candidate for Assemblyman in the Thirtieth Assembly District.

The development came through an anonymous leaflet handed to the people going into the rally. In large letters it announced that the women suffragists were "Destroyers of Home and Country," and "The Greatest Peril to Civilization and this Government."

You were supposed to be giving your time and yourself as much as you could afford. The secretaries, of course, were paid, and I might have been paid a small sum, too, but I don't remember.

The Women's Political Union was the most militant of the suffrage groups. Mrs. Blatch had been married to an Englishman and had lived in England for a time. We, as a society, were much closer to the English groups than were the other American suffrage organizations like Mrs. O. H. P. Belmont's Woman's Suffrage Organization or something like that, or Mrs. Catt's National American Woman Suffrage Association. These groups felt that what the women were doing in England was rather outrageous and they wanted no part of it. Mrs. Blatch, on the other hand, felt that the only way they were ever really going to get anywhere was to exert political pressure.

Consequently, the name of the organization was patterned after the English, which was called the Women's Social and Political Union, and there were friendly relations with the Pankhursts and with many other English people. Mrs. Pankhurst came over and addressed a large dinner meeting. Sylvia Pankhurst and Beatrice Forbes-Robertson also spoke and, I think, we raised money for them at one time or another.

The Englishwomen were very fond of talking about free unions and how their children were going to have hyphenated names. Like Havelock Ellis and his wife, they were going to have houses on opposite sides of the park. They felt that conventional marriage was not right, wasn't fair to women.

I was a little more conservative about things at the time and I felt the family had a place in society and I didn't go along with that. I thought it was kind of funny. But they took it all very, very seriously, you know. There was a whole cult of that sort of thing, especially in England. I think not to any great extent here.

I did meet a few women living in Greenwich Village at the time whom my sister knew, who were living with men without being married to them. You know, there was a certain amount of talk about it but they were still very valuable suffragists. They weren't making as much propaganda about it as the Englishwomen were. The attitudes of the Englishwomen reflected, of course, the much more difficult position of women in England than in America; American women have always had more freedom.

You may or may not recall that famous little curtain raiser of Ethel Barrymore's called *The Twelve-Pound Look*. That was marvelous. It played in England. The twelve-pound look was the cost of the typewriter with which the woman made herself economically independent from her husband— left him as soon as she learned to type. The twelve-pound look.

The Englishwomen generally were much more radically oriented than the Americans ever were. We did no chaining of ourselves to lamp posts, though the nearest approach came later with Alice Paul and her hunger strikers, in 1917. Mrs. Blatch was working on these things long before Alice Paul came into the picture at all. I think Alice Paul carried them to the extreme, and my impression is that she went far beyond anything Mrs. Blatch would have suggested herself.

What I have in mind when I speak of the Women's Political Union as being the most militant is that earlier, before Alice Paul's activities in Washington, we believed much more in demonstrations, in street speaking and in things of that kind, which I don't remember as being characteristic of the other organizations. For instance, we spoke on street corners every night of the week, using soapboxes with handles on them which every suffragette carried and plunked down on the curbstone. We had to have permits for speaking, but we got them from the police department. Now the other groups may have done street speaking, but if so, I wasn't conscious of it. They mostly spoke in halls. But we believed that you had to get to the people who weren't in the least interested in suffrage. That was the whole theory.

I would say that we had at least ten or twelve women out of our office speaking on street corners every night. As I recall it, there were always two women; one would be the speaker and the other would give out pamphlets and things of that kind. You carried the soapbox until you got to the corner. Of course, it was considered outrageous by many people for women to be speaking out on the street corners. Sometimes, depending on the neighborhood, those soapboxes on which we stood were rather dangerous little things. Things would be thrown down from the roofs. Sometimes stones would be thrown into the crowd. I don't remember anybody actually being seriously injured, but they weren't fun!

But there were lots of funny little things that went on, too. It wasn't all difficult. Once, a tiny little man in very shabby clothes, a clergyman from a parish somewhere out in the wilds of Long Island, came in and asked for a speaker for an evening meeting. Mrs. Blatch brought him out to me.

I had already assigned all my speakers for that evening, so I said I'd have to do it myself. My family was not exactly charmed by my taking these evening meetings, but I did when I had to. He said he would prefer a little older and more experienced woman. Mrs. Blatch came down hard on him and said, "Laura is one of our most experienced speakers," and went back into her office. He was a little crushed, but he began to explain to me how I had to get there. I had to change buses twice and so forth, and also that his wife was in a wheelchair; she'd been in an accident. She was very anxious to have me come out for supper.

After dinner we went over to the church and there was a small group of women. His wife was a very ardent suffragist and she had started this little group. The first thing he did was to ask me to play the Doxology [on the organ]. I had never opened a suffrage meeting with a Doxology before, but I was lucky enough to be able to play it and so I did. The women clustered around afterward and told me all about this wife and I said, "How come the Doxology?" They said, "Well, Mrs. whatever-her-name-was puts more faith in God than in politicians."

The organization was, of course, always trying to think of ideas which would get us publicity. Mrs. Blatch's whole idea was that you must keep suffrage every minute before the public so that it gets used to the idea and talk about it, whether they agree or disagree. It must be something that everybody was conscious of. I think she was quite right.

There were some women reporters who were very helpful to us, and they tried to get us all the publicity they legitimately could. But, of course, they didn't mind how ridiculous the thing was. One of the stunts was to make speeches from horseback.

One morning I was sitting in my office and they came bursting in from Mrs. Blatch's office and said to me, "You ride, don't you?" I said, "I haven't ridden since I left school." "But you do ride and you have a riding outfit? Well, so-and-so is ill. The horses are already ordered and we're going to ride down to City Hall park and make a speech, and you'll have to take her place."

You didn't argue in suffrage. You took orders! I went home and put on my riding habit and came back. By the time I got back, the horses were dancing out on Forty-second Street, very annoyed. I climbed on and they put big boards on the side of each horse announcing a meeting. Of course, the boards didn't please the horses; it hit them every time they moved.

All the sidewalks were lined with people and the buses were going by. There was much shouting at us. The policemen were furious with us for gumming up traffic. We got down to City Hall park just at noontime; it had been calculated that way.

Everybody came out from their offices, and Nora made a pretty powerful speech from her horse. Mine was behaving very badly by then. I began to say "Ladies and gentlemen," bouncing up and down. (They were English saddles and I'd never ridden in anything but an army or a Mexican saddle before.) Then, just as I was launching into my speech, I glanced across the square and there stood my astonished and astounded new husband.

At that very moment, a horrible little office boy jabbed a pin into my horse and she reared! I hung onto the front of this terrible English saddle and sawed on the curb bit and finally got the mare calmed down. But that was the end of my speech. We then took off back toward the office.

Between all the excitement and the saddle sores from not having ridden in a long time, I was in bed for a day. It was a little difficult to explain to my husband why suffragists had to make fools of themselves. That was the only time I remember specifically upsetting him.

Then we presently did another thing. They decided it would be nice to hire a motorboat and run up and down the shoreline yelling through a megaphone, "Suffrage votes for women," at all the men who were loading cargoes. I was assigned along with Nora for this job. We always took reporters with us when we did things. This time, women reporters evidently had rebelled and we got two men, both of whom were definitely anti-suffrage and *furious* at the assignment.

The man who was hired with the motorboat, which, by the way, was only ten or fifteen feet long, evidently had not been told what we were going to do. When we explained, he said, "Oh, what the men are going to say to you!" Of course, that was perfectly true. As soon as the men began understanding that we were yelling about votes for women, they made replies that you might expect. I acquired a good many four-letter words on that boat trip.

Meantime, as ferry boats went by everybody rushed to the side of the boat and the waves bounced us up and down. Then, a group of men going on a fishing trip thought that it was funny to annoy us. They went around us in circles, leaving each time, tremendous waves behind them until they almost swamped us. Both reporters, I remember, had to bail us out with their hats—just furious every minute. The whole excursion lasted about two or three hours. We were all exhausted and thought we were going to be submerged.

When we finally got back, Nora said, "Now see that you give us a good write-up." I looked all through the papers the next day. There was a *tiny* little paragraph in a column. A few days later I met one of the reporters who said he'd always hated suffragists. I said to him, "You certainly didn't do very well by us in the way of publicity." And he said, "Well, next time just get yourself drowned and I promise you the first page." So there were lots of funny things as well.

I don't remember the Women's Political Union actually endorsing anything outside its own interests. I don't think they could have; the women in it

were much too diverse. There were all kinds of women who believed in all
kinds of things. The only thing, you might say, that they all believed in
was that women ought to have the vote. So, for example, though many of
them were very interested and admired Mrs. Sanger very much, that would
be an entirely individual affair. She was quite a good friend of my sister's.

But there were many issues we *did* talk about. They were all interested
in child labor—which still existed. You may recall, that was the period of
the horrible Triangle Shirtwaist Fire[1] and all that sort of thing. We had a
very marvelous woman, Florence Kelley, who was on our board, who was
especially interested in the trade union movement for women.

There were plenty of other abuses of women, too. I remember when I
visited my sister for a summer vacation before I was through college. She
got me a press card to the old *Morning Telegraph*. The editor sent me on
assignments, one of which was the Hobo Convention at which [Eugene]
Debs was supposed to appear; he didn't because I think at that time he was
in jail. Bill Haywood came to the convention and spoke in place of Debs.
There were lots of reporters there.

We all held a little spoofy meeting when we discovered we were not
going to have Mr. Debs. Reporters made speeches and they asked "Sis
Hopkins"—which was me—to make one; we all wrote that up for the papers.
I remember that the *Morning Telegraph* published two versions of this, one
by the man and one by the woman—me—side by side.

What really reminded me of that was that, among other things, the editor
told me, for my own education, to visit the women's night court, which I
did. I was quite horrified at what seemed to me the disregard of women's
feelings and rights. I remember one case, especially. It was the trial of a
prostitute, and, no doubt, she was a prostitute. Her lawyer said something
about it was her word against the word of the policeman. There were no
witnesses. The judge said pontifically, "The word of an officer needs no
corroboration." I was enraged! That's the one thing I remember clearly out
of that assignment.

That attitude was, of course, general: women were viewed as second-class
citizens. There's no two ways about it. Their advice was not taken seriously
and their opinions were not given the same weight as those of men. I don't
think anybody argues about that anymore. It's still true, of course.

I don't know what all the individual women did in their street speeches.
I don't remember the moral superiority of women being borne down on
much. I do remember a great argument, following that same workers' meeting
I was supposed to write up. I went home with a woman who had been a
friend of my sister's, who was much more radical then I, and we fell into
a discussion of the single standard. I remember it very well because I was
a little shocked at the time. She said, "If we ever do get to have a single
standard, it'll be the men's standard and not ours." She spoke from experience,
and she was a newspaperwoman.

I don't remember women's moral superiority being especially emphasized.
In the first place, we had this little ultra-radical group within the movement.

I think it would have been a rather difficult argument to sustain. I certainly never used it in my speeches.

I used often to bear down on what I still believe: that there were certain things affected by politics about which men were relatively unfit to judge, such as things that concerned children, schools, similar things. I felt women should have a much larger voice in controlling these things, and that there were just naturally a whole lot of facets to be considered.

I remember once going to make a speech somewhere, and on the way up there on the train an idea occurred to me and I used it. I picked up a copy of the evening paper and held it up in front of them and took one headline after another and showed how the things talked about in that headline applied to women. I went all the way across the front page and there wasn't a single thing in the news in which women didn't have a stake. That was the thing we tried to get over.

I doubt very much that there was anything you could call a uniform position in our speeches. There was too much diversity among the women involved. I don't think you could have a uniform policy. We had all faiths and all types of people working for suffrage—most diverse. In fact, for me it was a liberal education, meeting the kind of people I'd never come into contact with before. Some of them were most admirable. Every once in awhile, they'd provoke some funny things.

The daughter of Robert Ingersoll had a house in Gramercy Park and they used to have little committee meetings there. Among others, one of the best workers in certain districts was a young Jewish girl from Russia, as I recall it. She attended a meeting one evening and took off her coat and gave it to the butler. Then she said, "Where is my check?" The butler said haughtily, "It won't be necessary, madam." Of course, that little story went all around with great entertainment.

But it's a very good example of the complete cross-section that we had in the suffrage movement, and I must truthfully say that I never saw any hint of snobbishness. There may have been some here and there, but it seemed to me that we all worked together for this one thing, without regard for anything else.

I was, for instance, assigned to make campaign speeches in the section that was run by this same girl. I went and I did exactly what she asked me, and she said very approvingly, "Well, it's nice to know you really take orders!" I said, "Of course, I came over, as my assignment, to do what you wanted done in this area." Evidently she had encountered others who hadn't been quite so cooperative.

But I do think that all kinds of women were working together for suffrage, with great unanimity on the whole. There was a great feeling of cooperation and admiration among the women who worked together.

I think many of the suffrage leaders, though, were very difficult to work with. It's quite understandable; you certainly have met plenty of what are colloquially called bossy women. They are apt to be women with a great deal of drive, women who get things done. They are very apt to be so sure that they're right that they don't want to waste time hearing arguments against their point of view.

Certainly Mrs. O. H. P. Belmont had a reputation of being difficult. I never worked for her. Certainly I think Mrs. Blatch was. From my point of view, she was very autocratic both in how she made decisions and the way she related to the workers. I violently disapproved of some of her policies. Considering that we were a women's organization, I felt that we should be especially fair in our treatment of employees.

I don't think that Mrs. Carrie Chapman Catt ever had that kind of reputation. I never heard that she did. I think she had very firm opinions, but I always gathered she was a person rather easy to get on with. And Anna Howard Shaw, of course, was a wonderful person. She spoke for us very, very often. I think of her as a national suffragist figure. She stands in my mind with a little group of very fine and prominent women who lent their support to suffrage, but I don't associate her with any special group.

Florence Kelley, too, was quite a marvelous person. I remember doing a brochure in which I had carefully dug out of the library all of the instances where women were discriminated against. When the pamphlet came out, Florence Kelley sent for me and she said, "I wonder if you have any idea how really unfair this pamphlet is?" "It's all there in black and white," I responded. "Yes," she said, "but so often there are the balancing laws against these." I remember her saying to me, "In addition to the dower rights,[2] there are the things called curtesy rights[3] which help to offset these. And that's true of all statements. It's true of all the statements you've made." I was crushed. What I had said was true, but it was not true in the sense of the whole truth. I think she impressed that on me forever more.

Actually, I left my job with the Women's Political Union because of my feelings towards Mrs. Blatch. I felt her very arbitrary and I didn't like her too well. So I didn't do the Speakers Bureau job for more than six months. But even after I left the organization, I spoke for them every so often— rather often, as a matter of fact.

FAMILY, WOMEN'S SUFFRAGE
AND A CAREER IN ADVERTISING

I left the Women's Political Union in 1914. Then I had to figure out what I could do. A friend of my sister's came over and they were consulting about what kind of business I could enter. Among other things my sister long before had told me, "Don't ever, ever, ever study stenography. What man studied stenography to get started in his job? You'll just get sidetracked, so be sure to say you just don't know it." So I didn't have that to offer to anybody.

I remember very well, this friend of my sister's said, "But you've been doing an awful lot of writing this summer." You see, I had sent advance releases, and then when I got through in the town, I gave them another big interview and a release. So I had been doing a whole lot of publicity writing. The friend said, "Why don't you try the advertising business? You can write copy quite well."

I didn't even know what advertising copy was; they had to explain to me that it was the text of the ad. She gave me a list of agencies and I called on some of them. I presume I looked exactly like Sis Hopkins, fresh down from the country. None of them was at all impressed. The agencies said they preferred people who had retail experience—women, that is.

Then I tried some of the department stores; no, they didn't have any time to try to train anybody like that. By then I got quite annoyed. The only store I hadn't called on was Macy's. I went in and demanded to see the advertising manager and told him about my experience trying to get a job in agencies and stores. And I said, "Now, I will come to work for you for ten dollars a week for two weeks. At the end of that time, both you and I ought to know whether I can write advertising copy." He was so flabbergasted that he hired me. At the end of two weeks, they were running the copy the way it was written. So then it became a real job.

I was there about six months and then I got pregnant. I hadn't really thought about a family, one way or the other; I certainly hadn't planned to have one at that time. My daughter was born in January of 1915, so I must have gotten pregnant quite soon, though I didn't quit work right away.

I was out of business until my daughter was about two and a half. I didn't do much outside the home; I was involved basically with the baby. We had moved out of my mother and sister's apartment, and we went to East Orange. Things were very tight. I've forgotten what my husband's salary was, but it was tiny. Of course, everything cost less in those days. My house allowance was five dollars, I remember, for food, and I wasn't a very good provider—knowing nothing whatever about it. When it got to be Friday, I remember nearly always we had to have cabbage because it was only five cents a head.

We had always had servants of some kind or another and I just never did have anything to do with running a house. I was very lucky because I had a marvelous black woman from Virginia, Emma, who came to work for me. Mother, as I recall it, paid for me to have Emma once a week. Emma told me later that I was the only woman for whom she ever washed in the morning and cleaned all the afternoon. I knew nothing whatsoever about domestic things.

I remember very well the day my sister said to me, fixing upon me a beady eye, "When are you getting back to business?" I, of course, felt mildly surprised, to say the least, and said, "How can I?" She said, "You *should* manage."

Presently, an apartment became vacant right across the hall in the place she was living with my mother. She immediately said, "This is the opportunity to move back here; then Mother can help and it will be much easier for you to get a maid." So that's what we did—moved across the hall from my mother and sister, and Emma came and stayed with us the whole time my baby was growing up. She was marvelous.

So, you see, my sister really shamed me into going back to work. I didn't think it was possible to both work and have a young child, but I discovered, of course, that it was. It was difficult, I have to say. Our apartment had these deep window seats, and I had to walk every morning past that front window on my way to the subway to work. My small daughter used to stand up in the window with the tears running down her cheeks. I used to feel like a dirty dog. It was very difficult. And, yet, I did think it was the right thing to do. My husband didn't make any fuss about my going back to work. I think he was probably rather pleased. He wasn't getting a very big salary in those days, and it was quite helpful to have a second salary.

I had decided I didn't want to go back to the department store field. I did try Macy's first, and I told them I wouldn't work after three o'clock in the afternoon (because that's when the baby came home from the park). Well, they wouldn't hear of that. "You can have hours off in the middle of the day," said one of them, who would like to have had me, "but you've got to be here to sign out with the rest of the employees, and sign in." I said, "Well, I'm going."

Then I began on the agencies again. Now, of course, I had a lot of good copy samples and I didn't any longer look like Sis Hopkins. But most of them would hear nothing about leaving at three o'clock in the afternoon— that was out. I got to one agency called the Federal Advertising Agency. It had nothing to do with the federal government; it had been named that because of the building they happened to be in. They had started out basically as a trade agency and were developing in the consumer field and they'd never had women except as file clerks or typists.

When I said this about three o'clock in the afternoon, the head of the copy department considered it awhile then said, "Well, we've never had a woman on the staff. Might as well try it. I like your copy." So I was taken on to work with the arrangement that I would go home at three o'clock every day.

After a relatively short time at copy writing, I was made what they called an account executive and did some copy still, but mainly edited other people's copy. I continued my suffrage activities, too, actually until we finally got the amendment through. I spoke occasionally, when they needed a speaker, especially in the evening. Also, when we were trying to get the state measure passed in New York, I took time off and had my daughter looked after and spoke continuously for the last two weeks.

I well remember the attitude of men—both in my office, the subway and on the street—the morning after that state measure was defeated. They openly jeered! There had never been any discussion about it before, in the office, but there were two or three men who took the occasion to make disparaging remarks the morning afterwards. "Well, I guess we know what we did to you yesterday!" and that kind of thing. But it was a passing phase.

Of course, many women I knew didn't believe in suffrage, either. An awful lot violently disapproved. They thought it a lot of nonsense. I didn't happen to number among my friends any ardent anti-suffragists who did anything about it. Most of them were just plain indifferent and thought it was a great waste of time, that it would just all be the same. And, you know, oddly enough, they anticipated what really happened. Most of my friends said, "This isn't going to make any difference; they're all going to vote the way their fathers and their husbands do anyway." You see, that was the burden of their song. As it happened, that's just about the way it turned out, unhappily.

But I remained interested and involved to the end. I remember when Alice Paul and her group started their demonstrations in 1917. I understood quite well the reasons she did it, and I wasn't ever disapproving. I remember being very horrified at what was done to the women, especially to this very delightful woman from Chautauqua County whom I had enlisted in suffrage and who was one of the hunger strikers. I think everybody was just sort of nauseated over the whole thing; it was so horrible, such a dreadful thing for the women to go through. But I also felt that it was a very admirable and probably a very valuable demonstration. There's no doubt about it, her effort is what precipitated the President's decision to bring the matter before Congress. I think we should give her due credit. I'm very sure that if Alice Paul hadn't carried on those demonstrations, it would have gone on years more before it ever got to the Congress.

I worked again during that final drive, and I do remember that there was a vast celebration when we finally had the federal amendment approved. Tennessee, I think, was the last one. But that spread over a long period of time. My daughter would have been five when that happened.

I don't have any recollection if the Women's Political Union survived after that. After I fussed with Mrs. Blatch and departed from them and when I went into business, I no longer was as close to them, organizationally speaking. I can't imagine, though, why they would have stayed on as an organization because there wouldn't have been anything for them to do, if you want to put it that way.

At that time, I think it hadn't occurred to a great many women that once they got the vote, the rest wouldn't be easy. I think most men felt that. I remember once, when watching at the polls, I was talking to a Tammany boss who was also watching. He said, "Of course I'm opposed to woman's suffrage. Once women get the vote, they can get practically everything they want."

That was more or less the attitude. It didn't occur to them that women's groups were going to break up as soon as the vote was won. They let their organizations go and most of them paid no further attention. A very few of them, of course, began to work in politics, but I think they were few and far between. From what I know, at least.

I didn't stay involved at all after we got the amendment, though I did belong to a couple of clubs and a certain number of business organizations, like the American Marketing Association. I joined the Women's Fashion Group fairly early; that was necessary. The clubs I belonged to were the

Women's City Club and the Town Hall Club. They were made up of women who definitely were the suffrage type.

There used to be a very interesting club of unusual women to which my sister belonged. One of these women had a big fuss with the head of that club—you can imagine they were all women with minds of their own—and she broke off and formed another organization. Later on, after it had been going for some years, my friend, Blair Niles, insisted on my joining that. It was called the Query Club, and was extremely interesting because of the women who belonged to it. Most of them were writers, and one woman was an explorer. They were all quite well-known women, as a matter of fact.

For a while I belonged to the Phi Beta Kappa Chapter in New York, but I got bored with that very quickly. I didn't do that very long. I never have been much of a joiner.

I did continue to do quite a lot of speaking during those years, too. I had to talk very often to boards of directors and things of that kind which you may or may not consider public speaking, but it falls into the same category. Once I went up to Cornell to speak to the coeds. And once I remember going to Philadelphia to address an advertising group. Things like that, but nothing else special.

Eventually I was made a vice president of the Federal Advertising Agency and the head of a department, mostly handling women's things, but not entirely. By then, we had plenty of other women, too. Many were in the copy department. I had several executive assistants. Also, women in other departments, like research, were assigned to me from time to time.

You know, up until World War II, I never did work past three o'clock in the afternoon! I enjoyed it. I could, by condensing my lunch hour, always go to matinées and do all kinds of things. It was very pleasant. Then, when personnel problems grew so difficult in the war, of course I was working till all hours myself.

After I'd been there some thirty years and they were giving me a testimonial dinner, one of the vice presidents stood up and said, "Well, I discovered in the records of the accounting department the other day that you were hired on a temporary basis. I would like to suggest that you be put on the permanent payroll."

I was extraordinarily fortunate. I sometimes think I worked for the only advertising agency I ever could have worked for. I had complete authority. The president discovered, after about five years, that if he'd just let me alone, I would make money for him. So he did exactly that. I was responsible to no one but my clients, really. I sent him memos about what we had decided to do but rarely consulted him in advance.

As I discovered in the course of my life, there were practically no other women in the advertising business who had any such degree of authority. In the big agencies, for instance, one or two of which flirted with me later on, I discovered that everything was *à la* committee; the plan went up here and had to be approved, and went up again and had to be approved. Of course, I couldn't possibly have worked that way. I discussed things with my clients, and came back and dictated the work reports, and got their okays on the estimates, and that was it! I wasn't discussing it with anybody, except occasionally with the research department.

This was very unusual, I must say. I began to appreciate how unusual it was, because sometimes my clients were the bosses of the women who were supposed to have authority. I knew, of course, from my work with their bosses that they didn't. That was particularly true of the women in the fashion group who were always supposed to be sort of heads in their own particular departments. But I discovered in working with them that all things they did had to be okayed, and I grew gradually to realize how unusual my opportunity was. I became a stockholder, eventually, and I was never really tempted to go to another agency.

I retired in June of 1948. I was worn out with the whole advertising business and I just stayed home for six years. I might have done a little writing here and there, but I didn't do much. I was utterly worn out. I had no idea of going back when I retired.

One day, one of my old clients, one of my smaller clients, as a matter of fact, called me up and was bitterly unhappy with his agencies, and had been ever since I retired. He asked if I would meet him at the Union League Club; he wanted to talk to me about something. I went, and he had his general manager there. He said, "I'm going to go to Europe on a buying trip and you can think about it while I'm gone, but I wish you'd go to some small agency, any one you pick, and make an arrangement with them to work only when you want to and as much as you want to, and take my account to them."

I thought about it. I had been fairly bored in the meantime, I may say. And so I did just that. I didn't go in at all in the months of July and August—we had a place in the country. I worked about three days a week the other months, perhaps four or five hours a day, whatever was necessary to handle his accounts, basically. I did some other things for them, too. That was for four years.

Then my husband was ready to retire. So I went too. We began to travel a great deal, mostly in Europe. My husband is a European and we had most of our friends over there. (I had, by the way, been divorced in 1928 and married my second husband in 1929.) We'd always been going back and forth. Right after he retired we spent the winter studying at the Instituto de Allende in Mexico, and then the summer at our place in Bucks County. The next year we went to California to try to make up our minds whether we wanted to live out here, and we drove all over. We ordered a cottage at Mount San Antonio Garden, and in 1960 we went abroad for a year until it was ready. We've lived in California since, though traveling a lot, until recently.

FEMINISM, SUFFRAGE
AND WOMEN'S LIBERATION

Looking back, I realize how great an influence my sister had on me. For instance, I don't think I ever would have taken public speaking in college if it hadn't been for my sister. She won the prize for the Woodford Oration for an original speech she titled "Men, Women and Human Beings." I came along and survived the competition and was, what they called, "on the stage"; I was one of the eight speakers on both the Eighty-sixth Memorial and the Woodford Oration. I didn't win either one of them, much to my sister's chagrin. The title for my original oration was "Crimes against Criminals."

Then, too, I think the emphasis on a career must have probably come from my sister. After all, she had gone ahead and done it and was getting to be quite well known. I certainly don't think I would have gotten those ideas growing up in Grandfather's house. In fact, I would think that the whole attitude of the family at that point would have been that you married and stayed home and had children. And if you were a maiden aunt, you would stay always in the home. I think it was assumed that my Aunt Lil would always live in my grandfather's house. I would say that that was the pattern of a perfectly orthodox Episcopal family.

Economics might have been a part of it, but unquestionably my sister would never have allowed me to think of living without doing some work. My daughter thinks that I would have climbed the walls if I had tried to stay home, but I think it would have been very easy for me to give up after I had the baby. I remember how taken aback I was when my sister suggested that I return to work. To her, of course, the arguments were absolutely unanswerable. She just is, and always was, a feminist. She did all kinds of things, including starting the Women's Bond Club on Wall Street.

I don't think it ever occurred to me to call *myself* a feminist. I was a suffragist. "Suffragist" is how we spoke of ourselves. It was mostly the newspapers, I think, that called us suffragette and that was an attempt to put us down. When you said "feminist," I thought of people like Olive Schreiner, Mrs. Pankhurst, Charlotte Perkins Gilman. They were so interested in the one thing that they hardly had time for other things. I think that always, all my life, I have always wanted to be interested in a great many things—just like my courses in college. Of course, that's the reason those women got things done, because they did channel all of their interests in one direction.

No, I never thought of myself as a feminist. In fact, all my life, until I was retired, I had more men friends than women. This was partly because of my choice of business. And I always got on extremely well with men. I have ascribed that, truly or not, to the fact that I grew up with absolutely no feelings of having been put down, as it were, by a male and I never have felt that way. Consequently, I don't have any of the bitterness that many women, I'm sorry to say, in women's lib have.

In spite of the fact that my sister was also very popular with boys, I think that, in some way, I associated "feminist" with a bitter anti-male position. I never thought of it, really, in college. I discovered very early that if you danced well and skated well—and I was a fancy skater—and did such things, that boys were also very pleased to discover that you could *think*. I was never brought up to feel that you had to pretend to be an imbecile to be attractive. I always got the kind of response I expected. The same thing was true in business. I can only remember twice when there was an attempt made to what you would call "put me down."

One of them, oddly enough, came about in a very curious way. I had become a little distressed at how rapidly the things we learned in college became obsolete. I wrote up to the president of Cornell and suggested that perhaps when twenty-five-year reunions came around it might be a very good idea to set aside at least one day and arrange workshops with the heads of departments, particularly the scientific departments, in which the changes had been the greatest, so that the alumni could be brought up to date. And they could say, "This is what you were taught in physics when you were in college; this is what we think now."

He thought it was a good idea, and he wrote down to the man who was the chairman of the twenty-five-year reunion of men that year. He came to call on me. He listened in a rather supercilious way to this idea, and when I was all through he said, "Where did you get the idea?" I said, "The same place where most of my ideas come from—out of my own head! Good evening." I was enraged. That is one of the few times I can remember. Otherwise, I have always found men very open and willing to meet you on your own grounds.

It's very hard to compare the modern women's movement to the original suffrage movement because today's movement is so much wider and deeper than suffrage. That was really a political job, and it was handled like a political job, more or less. This movement, now, I think, springs from much, much deeper grounds. It involves really women's estimate of themselves and what they feel they could contribute to the world.

I think that whereas women felt it definitely unfair that they couldn't vote, I think women now conceive of the inequality as something a great deal more serious than a personal affront. They realize that it has a lot to do with the kind of world we have and the mess we're in, and that the only valid hope for the future lies in *true* equality.

I think women have a lot of changing to do, too. I listen with *horror* at the chitchat that goes on in a normal group of women, and I'm not surprised that men make snide remarks about "girl talk." But that isn't true of the present movement. I'm talking mostly about women in my own age group. They're not going to change, and most of them are quite horrified, I think, at the changes the younger women want. Of course, it just so happens that I go along with the younger women, so I mostly have to keep my mouth shut.

Yes, I think this movement that's going on now goes back to the roots, to those early feminists. And they wrote well. Charlotte Perkins Gilman, for example. Olive Schreiner, of course, I always think of with special feeling because I felt that she, of perhaps all of them, had the least bitterness; she thought of it in terms of what it could become. I also felt that she was very much fairer to men.

I can't help reminding women that up to the time the suffrage amendment was ratified, *every single thing* that American women legally had, in terms of consideration, was *given* them by men. They had no way to get it. I think they were very unappreciative of how much they had actually been given because of men's own sense of justice.

That's one reason I get very impatient with women when they are too bitter. Perhaps if I'd had a different kind of life and different association with men, I too, would feel bitter. But I don't, and I think it's a great drawback because, as I have written my daughter, I look on bitterness as a kind of cancer of the heart. I think you get nowhere with it, and it's one of the most deadly things that one can give way to.

I think this is a major failing today. I'm astonished by some of the things I read. Now, how much they've been blown up by the media, of course, one doesn't know. And I'm far from saying that I'm silly enough not to know that a great many women have ample reason for the bitterness they feel. But I think it's a defect when you're working for equality. Many women felt very bitter in suffrage days, too—many of them, and with good reason. But it's never a help, that's my feeling.

I'm not particularly eager to make unkind comments about the women's movement today. I have every sympathy with their goals. It's just that when I hear them speak, I find so many of them strident and disagreeable. It's the old, old story; people don't really get outside themselves enough. I get very impatient with their bringing up individual grievances about things. I don't understand why they don't work more through groups of women.

I have very definite ideas about what they could be doing with groups of women that, as I see it, they are not doing. Women's groups seem to feel that they have to operate in a vacuum. If they belong to one little group that's dedicated to doing this particular thing, they're not at all concerned with what's going on out there and around. I think that's all wrong for this movement of women. I think that *every* woman's group has a stake in this movement, even though they are not organized to fight for *it*.

I don't care what the individual's special interest is in that group—she should have an overall interest in women. And every organization speaks with a louder voice than its individual members. If a group especially interested in a movement could only learn how important it is to approach other groups. If you say to them, "Look, we know that you give ninety-nine percent of your time to your project, but how about, just this once, writing a letter as an organization regarding this women's movement." I think they'd be rather surprised at the network of influence they could bring up.

That is what happened in suffrage, basically. We had a great deal of that. I'm amazed that modern women don't do more of it. They don't, from my point of view, make very good use of women as a whole. I mean, just think what a small number of women are ever going to get involved with NOW, for instance, compared to the number that sympathize with the overall aims and would be glad to lend their hands, perhaps to advocate the passage of a specific bill or something of that kind. Not to expect that they're going to spend much time with it, but that they are a group of women. They can take a vote and will probably be sympathetic to doing this little bit for equality. It would add up to a great deal.

It was quite interesting when we were doing the organizing, of course, to see which women in these very small towns could be interested. In general, it was the women with better educations. Once in a while, you got a woman from the blue-collar group, but not very often. And in some cases, you got women whose husbands definitely were not crazy about suffrage at all; they just said, "Well, if you want to, go ahead," even though they didn't really go along with it. In other words, they were mostly very substantial women—those who were willing to come right out for suffrage and form a suffrage group.

I think this movement today, though, involves all women, and I think that in a curious way women recognize that—even though they get awfully mad about the thing. Even the older ones who want to hang on to everything they have and not let anything go, even they, I think, have a certain sympathy with it. I have always felt that's why they are so nit-picking about the smaller things. In a way, I nit-pick myself, but I just feel that sometimes the women in today's movement are antagonizing a lot of people by some of the things they do. They shouldn't—just out of pure wisdom.

It's perfectly true that marriage has been one of our most stable institutions, but that's no reason that it can't be reexamined in the light of our present-day situation, and especially now that there is so much clamor for a decrease in population. I think it's awfully silly the way many women talk about these things.

However, to the young people belongs the future, and whether the older generation likes it or not, these things are all going to be reexamined and rearranged. At the moment, of course, I don't see very much possibility of creating a permissive institution which can offer the stability that marriage has offered us. I think it's going to be a very unhappy environment for children if we marry and divorce at such a rate as we're doing now. It *is* tough for children. They have enough things to learn about the world without having to adapt themselves overnight to a completely changed environment.

I would hope that a good many people would try it out; they have a nice name for the marriage that isn't legal, a colloquial name for it, which I've forgotten. At any rate, the Swedes have done this for years, tried out the thing first. Fine. But after they've tried it out, I would hope that people who had lived together for three or four years and found it companionable would go and get married before they have children. It seems awfully tough on the children to have their homes changed by divorce. These are things the younger generation are going to work out for themselves.

I heartily endorse the efforts of the modern women's movement. I think it's ridiculous that women shouldn't participate in government, and I'm very happy that we succeeded in electing that nice Mrs. Cohen to our City Council here in Claremont. We are now getting more women in such positions, all around. Of course, just getting them in where their faces show isn't the answer until they get some real authority and knowledge.

There is something to be said for the statements made by big organizations about minorities—that one of their troubles is not so much unwillingness to hire as the difficulty in finding qualified applicants. The same is true of women. That's changing, of course. I just hope that there is going to be a considerable change in the vocational advice that's handed out—beginning much earlier than college, way back in junior high. There isn't any reason on earth why girls shouldn't plan all kinds of careers. For example, if they find they're especially good at mathematics, for goodness sake, then let them do it! Let them take part in the new technology.

NOTES

[1.] In 1911, 146 young women perished in the Triangle Shirtwaist Fire. Locked in the shop, on the eighth floor of the building, and unable to escape the fire, they either leaped to their death or were consumed in the flames. This tragic episode did help to publicize the miserable working conditions in the sweatshops.

[2.] Dower rights refer to the legal right to a life estate in a husband's real property which a wife acquires by marriage for her use and the use of her children after his death.

[3.] Curtesy rights refer to the husband's life estate in his deceased wife's property.

6

The Vision of
a Woman Shaman

ANNA LOWENHAUPT TSING

Anna Lowenhaupt Tsing's fascinating account of a Meratus woman's creative transformation of tradition is exemplary feminist inquiry in more than one way. It is interdisciplinary, integrating feminist literary criticism with anthropological fieldwork. The analysis is subtle, nicely illustrating the role of the author's informed feminist perspective. Also, both the hermeneutic and emancipatory themes as well as the empirical criterion described in my Introduction to this book are well illustrated. Note especially the way Induan Hiling represents contradiction in the context of her own culture.

Adu hai,
Riding the horse of gaps, babe.
Swept by the wind,
Riding the horse of gaps, friend.
                              —Induan Hiling[1]

Among the Meratus Dayaks of South Kalimantan, Indonesia, shaman healers chant melodic invocations to the spirits and, rising to the sounds of drums and rattle bracelets, dance and sing of their supernatural travels.

Almost all Meratus shamans are men. Women as well as men may be accompanist singers who echo or answer shamans; but men hold the most prestigious and powerful performing roles.

At first glance, this situation seems familiar; in the United States, the most prestigious and powerful social roles are also predominated by men. Yet feminist anthropologists have shown how important it is to distrust this initial sense of similarity. To the extent that Meratus Dayak and U.S. systems of prestige and power are different, male and female rankings within these systems have an entirely different significance in each context. To understand gender inequalities, feminist analysis must consider separate structures and histories of inequality, as well as different ways of understanding *male* and *female* (Ortner and Whitehead 1981; Collier and Yanagisako 1987; Moore 1988).

Feminist anthropologists have paid special attention to the distinctive systems of symbols and meanings that groups of people bring to their interpretations of men's and women's roles. This is a crucial step in exploring cultural differences in the construction of gender. But insofar as the analysis ignores disruption and change to focus on cultural coherence, it can also support the troublesome assumption that these "cultures" we study are homogeneous and static. Indeed, these anthropological studies may unwittingly support ethnocentric ideas that only Euroamerican women have a history of challenging sexism, and, conversely, that Third World women are trapped by unyielding cultures until freed by Western ideas.

This chapter argues for the importance of culturally sensitive analyses of women who take exception and disrupt or transform cultural expectations. I focus on the spiritual expression of a Meratus woman shaman—an unusual woman, whose shamanic talents developed despite conventions that largely exclude women. (I have included her portrait as Figure 1.) I present her dream-inspired songs and pictures to explore the way these compositions, as a woman's work, interpret and revise the dominant Meratus shamanic tradition. I suggest that anthropologists pay attention to pieces like these compositions as innovative culture-producing commentary rather than looking only at their most conventional features.

My analysis is aided by the work of feminist literary critics. Creative innovation has long been a central concern of literary criticism, and since the 1970s, feminist litarary critics have used this tradition to shed light on women's literary innovations in the context of patriarchal constraints. Unfortunately, too often literary critics lose sight of the distinctive peculiarities of Euroamerican standards and consider their findings on gender differences and creative expression universal. Feminist literary criticism can advise anthropologists on how to think about exceptional women; at the same time, feminist anthropology reminds literary critics to attend to the cultural construction of both gender and creativity.

Several strands of feminist literary criticism are useful in discussing the work of Induan Hiling, the Meratus shaman. One approach in feminist criticism has shown how common female experiences and connections among

FIGURE 1   Induan Hiling performing. (Portrait by Elizabeth Fischbach)

women authors have influenced female creativity (see, for example, Moers 1976; Showalter 1977). A second approach has emphasized the influence of dominant male traditions on the creative productions of women. This scholarly work has suggested that in writing, women incorporate dominant conventions at the same time as they invert them, resist them, and transform them (see, for example, Gilbert and Gubar 1979). Finally, a third feminist critical approach has drawn on French literary theory to argue that male dominance is involved in the very means of expression that both men and women use, that is, language and particularly writing. Feminists using this approach have explored how female writing disrupts the masculinist structures basic to creative expression; female writing exposes and challenges writing's gender-asymmetric conditions (see, for example, Cixous 1980; Kamuf 1982). Each of these frameworks sheds light on the ways in which women's creative work can be shaped by, yet distinct from, the mainstreams of male-dominant cultural convention.[2] Taken together, these frameworks complement each other; I use each in turn to stimulate my inquiry of Induan Hiling's shamanic art.

Anthropologists have borrowed from literary criticism in other ways. Interpretive anthropology has looked for "textual" aspects of everyday understandings to show the interdependence and coherence of cultural meanings (Geertz 1973). Recently, some anthropologists have begun to explore how people bring varied interpretations, or "readings," to these everyday cultural texts (Bruner and Gorfain 1984). This chapter proposes that just as ordinary people "read" or interpret their culture, they also "write" or produce it. "Writers" positioned differentially by gender, class, race, age, or other lines of difference confront overlapping but distinct challenges as they incorporate, resist, and modify dominant conventions. This creativity both extends and disrupts lines of power and difference. I argue that anthropologists must extend the concept of culture to include appreciation of these multiple and sometimes contradictory culture-"writing" processes.

This kind of approach enriches the study of gender and male dominance cross-culturally. Studies of the cultural construction of gender have generally focused on local notions of male and female, or, to extend the textual metaphor of culture, what feminist literary critics have called "images of women" (and images of men). For example, anthropologists have argued that some cultures portray women as mediating between natural and cultural processes, while men are envisaged as being able to transcend nature (Ortner 1974). But this focus on cultural imagery is not always the most useful approach. In my fieldwork among Meratus Dayaks of the mountains of southeast Kalimantan (Indonesian Borneo),[3] I found that more important than images of women was the issue of who had access to politically significant expressive modes; women were disadvantaged not so much by what was said but by who got to speak.[4]

Although the imagery of Meratus ritual is generally gender balanced or gender neutral, the star performers and producers of ritual are almost always male. In this context the questions posed by feminist critics about women who manage to participate in purportedly universal creative traditions dominated by men seem particularly relevant. Under layers of conventional compliance, the work of these women can reveal a cutting edge of resistance.

The rest of this chapter extends this bridge between literary criticism and anthropology by looking at the ritual contributions of the Meratus shaman Induan Hiling. Her songs and pictures—the latter drawn in a context in which any kind of drawing or writing was unusual—provide a perceptive and challenging interpretation of Meratus shamanic tradition. They also offer a guide to the gendered basis of Meratus modes of expression.

GENDERED RESOURCES
FOR EXPRESSION

There is a connection from woman to woman, present to past, artist to artist, that is never spoken of. That connection is based on identification.
—Bernikow 1974:10

I first learned of Induan Hiling's spiritual work through a connection among unconventional women. Although we had known each other casually for some time, Induan Hiling only spoke to me of her inspiration when she heard of my close ties with another spiritual innovator, a woman named Uma Adang, who was leading a religious movement in a Meratus community a day's hike to the east.[5] Both Induan Hiling and I considered Uma Adang a sister, a mentor, and a remarkable leader. On the strength of this connection, Induan Hiling invited me to share her own spiritual revelations, curing experiences, and knowledge of *adat* customary law. She took out her pictures, showed me her songs and dances, and urged me to take her message to the United States.

Uma Adang was the first person to encourage Induan Hiling to take her spiritual calling seriously. Induan Hiling had not been sure of herself: Was she crazy or legitimately inspired? Uma Adang confidently directed her to view herself as a shaman-in-training. But despite her continued respect for Uma Adang's teachings, Induan Hiling never portrayed herself as a purveyor of Uma Adang's message. Her spiritual teachings, she insisted, came from her deceased father, once a well-respected shaman, who visited her in her dreams. Although she was encouraged by women, Induan Hiling was a student of the male-dominated central tradition.

Feminist literary critics have shown how women writers draw from one another even as their work fits neatly within the male-dominated canon. These critics have argued that women's creative work often develops from and extends a "female subculture." For anthropologists, this point seems almost commonplace, since anthropological studies of gender divisions in expressive culture have focused on the separation between male and female traditions (see, for example, Weiner 1976; Bell 1983; Ardener 1975; Herdt 1981). However, feminist literary critics also have shown that the "female subculture" of Western literature is neither autonomous from nor complementary to a "male subculture;" each woman's writing is intimately bound up with the *dominant* literary tradition, which rests mainly in the hands of men. This point should remind anthropologists that a separation between male and female cultural spheres cannot be breezily assumed, and, even in ethnographic contexts of gender segregation, it is useful to look at the gender relations upon which segregated expressive modes are predicated. The approach suggested by feminist critics explores the dynamic process in which men and women interact differentially with dominant cultural modes.

The Dominant Tradition in Meratus Shamanism

Meratus shamans (*balian*) chant and dance to summon spiritual beings to help with cures, taste the first rice, or protect the community from spiritual danger.[6] The accompanist singers paired with shamans (*pinjulang*) are often shamans' wives who learn their skills from their husbands.[7] In contrast to the enthusiastic self-presentation of shamans, *pinjulang* sometimes put a hand or a piece of their skirt over their mouths, muffling their own voices. Although some *pinjulang* are bolder and even claim to learn their skills from other women, they never summon spirits, sponsor ceremonies, or initiate a round of chanting within a ceremony.

Women are also participants in shamanic ceremonies in other ways: Both women and men help to prepare the ritual apparatus, bring their rice to be consecrated, and present themselves as patients for shamans to cure. Meratus ceremonies are never gender segregated, although the male shamans dominate center stage. Both women and men are essential in forming the audience, which is the spiritual community that creates the success of the performance.

Shamanic performances are occasions for socializing, eating together, and— in big community festivals—dancing, fighting, arranging love affairs, settling disputes, and visiting relatives. The importance of shamanic expression in the Meratus setting stems in part from its centrality in events in which both women and men reaffirm social and political affiliations. Shamanic performances also involve the recitation of long poetic chants, which map the shaman's travels through spiritual realms. Many women, as well as men, can knowledgeably discuss this poetic tradition. Unlike the exclusively male rituals of many parts of Melanesia, Australia, and the Amazon, Meratus shamanic ceremonies do not construct gender-segregated ritual spaces or commitments.

Most Meratus I asked would not rule out the possibility that a shaman could be a woman, even if they knew of no examples. But women have less access than men to both formal and informal training. Men are more likely than women to practice and play with ritual expression: Boys sing the drum beats that signify particular spiritual styles as they play by the river;[8] young men call out lines from the chants as they hike through the forest. Young men who want to become shamans can embark on a formal apprenticeship: They learn by sitting next to and dancing behind an experienced shaman. The apprentice repeats each line of the shaman's chant, committing it to memory. Some men also learn through dreams or spiritual encounters on lonely mountaintops or on great rocks in the middle of wild rivers.

Becoming a successful shaman involves more than expressive training: A shaman must use personal charisma and theatrical display to draw an audience for his ceremonies. The ability to combine a dramatic self-presentation with articulate knowledge of the tradition is especially important. Shamans can impress their audiences by fainting away from impassioned spiritual dialog; when possessed by dangerous spirits, they may growl and drink blood while crouched on all fours. A woman with extensive *pinjulang* experience may know a great deal about the chants. But knowledge alone cannot draw an audience, and without an audience, she has few opportunities to present herself as a spiritual authority.

The Women's Possession Movement

Men ordinarily dominate the dramatic center of ritual performances, so I was quite surprised when at one big festival a woman jumped up and began a wild dance around the ritual decorations, waving her arms and singing under her breath. As the festival proceeded over the next few days, a number of other women followed her example. I soon learned that episodes of women's possession had been sweeping across the mountains over the past few years, and people said they were spreading from one festival to the next. It was said that the women were possessed by *dewa* spirits who had been invited to the festival. Some women even continued possessed singing and dancing outside the festival context.

Senior shamans and other men described the movement as an epidemic of illness or craziness. They attempted to cure the affected women because, they said, otherwise the women might kill themselves by wandering off at night or stepping obliviously into a ravine. Since most of the women danced without a clearly articulated shamanic chant to explain their dancing, it was easy for the senior shamans to classify them as patients rather than as healers. A number of the women, however, spoke later not of being wordlessly possessed but of learning inspired teachings from this spiritual contact.[9]

Induan Hiling was first affected by uncontrollable singing and dancing about a year and a half before the episode I have just described. She remembers that her in-laws told her she was crazy. She had tended to agree until she consulted Uma Adang and, as a result, began to take her spiritual training seriously. She then realized that her deceased father was passing on his teachings through her dreams. Slowly, his teaching was augmented by other spiritual dream guides. As a shaman-in-training, Induan Hiling went beyond the women who danced and tranced inarticulately, with whom she originally identified, and her actions challenged standards of gender appropriateness in new ways.

Induan Hiling's Contribution

Induan Hiling vacillated between the labels of shaman and *pinjulang*. Sometimes she called herself a *pinjulang* to avoid presumptuousness; her influence was not yet great enough for her to claim to be a successful shaman. Yet she never meant her talents to serve as an accompaniment to a shaman's performance; her innovative work challenged shamans, not their *pinjulang* support. Her ambivalence about labels reflected her dependence on female resources as she attempted to enter the male tradition.

This ambivalence can be seen throughout Induan Hiling's work. She calls her songs *dunang*, the term used for the love songs and lullabies that both women and men sing and compose freely. But Induan Hiling's *dunang* have a spiritual rather than a romantic message; they describe a spiritual flight that puts her in the company of shamans and separates her from both the answering counterpoint of *pinjulang* and the teasing admiration of lovers. In the song fragment that begins this chapter, Induan Hiling rides a flying horse. In the fragment below, she chooses a flying cobra, a conventional familiar of Meratus shamans. The cobra's scales map her route of spiritual flight, as it extends both forward and back:

> The child of a cobra, babe,
> Soaring to the sun.
> If it has scales
> They cross across each other.
> The scales they point, babe,
> Where do they point, friend?
> They point to its tail,
> They point to its head,
> Those scales, babe.

Pinjulang sometimes describe themselves as supporting the shaman's flight or following him, but they never launch themselves. In contrast, Induan Hiling's song is that of a shaman. Yet the melody and the use of line markers like "babe" (*ding*, short for *ading*, "younger sibling"—used for romantic partners as well as children) show that this is the kind of song a woman could sing.

When I knew her in 1980 and 1981, Induan Hiling was in her mid-thirties, the married mother of three sons, and a central figure in a small swidden cluster that included her mother and sister as well as her husband and some of his kin. She was a soft-spoken, graceful woman, with no particular aspirations to use a male dramatic style. Yet she had embarked on a route of independent spiritual innovation. Only her close relatives and neighbors knew of her abilities at that point, but all agreed that she was on her way to more important achievements.

Induan Hiling stressed the importance of her creative connections to her deceased father, who was once an important shaman in the area. One of the first things she told me about herself was that her father had encouraged her to climb trees as a child, endowing her with an admired talent few women possess. Yet the development of her skills and influence also depended on the support of her mother and younger sister, both of whom lived next door. Both mother and sister are well-respected *pinjulang* with a thorough knowledge of ritual. Within the swidden cluster of which their households formed a central part, Induan Hiling's spiritual innovations provided a basis for aspirations to autonomy from the larger encompassing neighborhood.[10] There were no shamans within the cluster; instead, the women explored their own spiritual authority.

Induan Hiling's sense of her spiritual antecedents and mentors reflects her ability to use female resources while at the same time inserting herself within a male tradition. Of necessity, she uses conventions created by male shamans and appeals to male sources of authority for inspiration and legitimation. However, she also draws inspiration and support from other creative women.

INVERSIONS AND REVISIONS

We decided, therefore, that the striking coherence we noticed in literature by women could be explained by a common, female impulse to struggle free from social and literary confinement through strategic redefinitions of self, art, and society.

—Gilbert and Gubar 1979:xii

Induan Hiling's contributions proceed in dialog with dominant conventions of shamanism. At the time of my research her work had not unleashed a flood of change. But an analysis that assumed that her work merely reproduces social categories and reenacts cultural values would miss the tensions and breakthroughs of her innovations.

Unsubmissive and inspired women have made other appearances in the anthropological literature. A number of analysts have shown how women use possession or other ritual participation as an "oblique strategy" of protest (Lewis 1971:117; Kessler 1977). Yet because most anthropologists focus on predictably repetitive, nondisruptive female protest, their accounts too often take for granted the stability of local discourses of male dominance. Thus while functionalist and psychoanalytic analyses highlighted women's defiance of male authority in ritual (Gluckman 1963; Freeman 1968), these analyses ultimately dismissed women's challenges as a reaffirmation and restabilization of women's subordination through the expression of tensions. Interpretive approaches have looked more closely at local discourse on gender. For example, Kapferer (1983) has discussed Sinhalese beliefs that women are "natural" victims of possession and perpetrators of disorder. But because his analysis showed women as objects of cultural interpretation rather than as positioned subjects, it obscured the possessed women's role in negotiating new understandings of gender and inspiration. In such analyses, the women are seen through the eyes of conservative male elders, like those senior Meratus shamans who denied women's spiritual initiative by saying the women were victims of an epidemic illness. In contrast, my approach here avoids assumptions of social or cultural stability by exploring how an inspired woman's work contributes to a continually evolving discourse.

Induan Hiling's work draws eclectically from a set of familiar metaphors and genre conventions. As she uses pieces from one tradition to revise others, she creates products that—like the writings of Western women novelists and poets—seem open to multiple and sometimes contradictory interpretations. The following sections explore some of Induan Hiling's revisions and innovations, showing how her work contests conventional Meratus expectations of the links between gender and expression. Indeed, although Induan Hiling's work builds from the dominant Meratus tradition, it also interprets this tradition in a new way that is linked to her status as a woman creator.

Induan Hiling's Innovations: The Songs and Dances

> What shall be used, babe?
> Forging spurs,
> Finished in a day.
>
> —Induan Hiling

Induan Hiling inverts and revises both male and female expressive traditions in her song and dance repertoire. For example, male shamans use hand-held rattle bracelets to control rhythm and cue the drummer, while Induan Hiling puts rattling bells on her ankles, thus setting the rhythm with her steps without appearing to control it.[11] Her dance movements, featuring small, circumscribed steps and graceful body and arm movements, bear some resemblance to the secular women's festival dance. Male shamans tend to include much more prancing and stomping. But diverging from the slow, mincing gait of the women parading at festivals she moves to a lively and energetic rhythm, responding to her own inspired singing. Whereas women at festivals normally dance with their faces away from the audience, Induan Hiling dances with her face to the audience, thus dramatically unmuffling her voice.

As I mentioned earlier, Induan Hiling uses the melodic structure and refrains of love songs (*dunang*)—a comfortable, familiar medium for women. But she fills her songs with sacred imagery from the repertoire of shamans. One song she sang for me traces spiritual travel in a form almost identical to that found in conventional shaman's chants. In other songs, however, including the one I translate in the Appendix and quote throughout this chapter, she creates a hybrid genre.

In these songs Induan Hiling refers to the gendered metaphors of conventional love songs but transforms them in gender-free spiritual directions. In ordinary love songs, shining, golden, healthy but passive plants represent the beautiful women pursued by male suitors, who are portrayed as birds, wandering soldiers, and tree-cutters. In her songs Induan Hiling transforms the lovely but passive vegetation into an extremely active element: She sings of *swaying* fig trees and *singing* bamboos. Moving the vegetation even further out of the love song context, she omits the male half of the tree/bird and tree/tree-cutter contrast. The result is that vegetation becomes a metaphor for various aspects of *human* spiritual expression rather than for *women*.

The following fragment shows one complex set of associations for bamboo:

> There is a planting:
> A cut bamboo.

A bamboo that plays the flute
A bamboo that sings.
We cut if off
Touching the shoulders,
The scissored bamboo
Touching the waist.
Babe, the scissored bamboo,
The cut bamboo,
Where is it planted?
Where does it hang?

Bamboo is female in a number of love songs. To the extent that the bamboo in Induan Hiling's song carries female resonances, its activity in singing and playing the flute establishes it as a creative subject, not an object of courtship. Her dominant metaphor, however, is not of bamboo as woman but of bamboo as hair; this is a common shamanic reference for this (gender-neutral) spiritual attribute of the body. To make the move to *human* spirituality clear, Induan Hiling establishes the gender symmetry of her metaphor; as she explained it to me, she simultaneously invokes a male subject, whose hair is "touching the shoulders," and a female subject, whose hair is "touching the waist." She transforms a reference to women into a reference to spiritual experience that applies equally to men and women. Furthermore, she draws other ungendered metaphors into the portrait: She compares the bamboo to ritual streamers that are intricately "scissored" (actually, cut into designs with a knife) and finally "cut" (tied up) to close the performance; the bamboo is also, as earlier references in the song make clearer, the shamanic route itself, the pathway of spiritual expression. Thus Induan Hiling removes female resonances from the context of an asymmetrical male-female contrast and places them among spiritual references as features of a human spirituality that does not depend on gender difference.

The dualism of the objects in love songs is not entirely lost in this transformation, however. Induan Hiling's vegetation enters into a different opposition—with mountains and rocks rather than birds and tree-cutters. She explains mountains and rocks as representing an internal inspirational knowledge, the not-yet-articulated wisdom of origins. In contrast, her vegetation represents the ritual apparatus used in shamanic ceremony and the well-worn ritual practices within which shamans' chants emerge. Rocks and mountains contrast with vegetation as inspiration contrasts with tradition. Both elements, she implies, are needed for ritual efficacy; indeed, inspiration is articulated through tradition.

This complementarity is a motif repeated in much of her work. She sings of a fig tree on a mountain, which, as she explained, also refers to the hair growing on our heads:

On the summit of the mountain
There's a wild fig tree,
A hanging fig tree,
A swaying fig tree,

Hanging where
Swinging there
Our wild fig tree.

Elsewhere, she repeats the vegetation-mountain opposition in singing about bamboos on rocks and, using an image borrowed from "city people," of flowers on a table. This is *not* a gendered opposition. Transcending gendered love song imagery with non-gendered sacred text is essential to Induan Hiling's ability to cast her work as shamanism. Yet her use of the two-element opposition as a motif has its roots in the love song.

The Dream Pictures

Induan Hiling draws the same opposition into her dream pictures. Pictures are not a common form of Meratus creative expression; besides the scribblings of a few schoolchildren, almost no one writes or draws. Induan Hiling's dream-inspired drawings and "writings" transform and revise familiar themes into new mediums of spiritual expression. The complementarity of rocks and plants as text and ritual apparatus or inspiration and tradition is also key to these pictures' message.

Figure 2 is a drawing of a tree next to a rock. As Induan Hiling explained, the tree is a ritual stand complementing the rocks' written text, the scribbled lines that depict the internal knowledge of the shaman to be expressed in the chant. Although she herself could not read the message, she assured me that the scribbled lines in the rocks are "writing." (The English words on the side of the page do not represent "writing" in the same sense; I will return to them.) She features this kind of dream-dictated "writing" in a number of her drawings; in Figure 3, she has filled the page with it. She told me proudly how painstakingly she had drawn the "writing" in Figure 3; the work took longer than—in the local idiom—"enough time to smoke ten cigarettes." Although unreadable, this dream "writing" is a carefully written text.

Figure 2 presents the opposition between tree and rock, or tradition and inspiration, as symmetrical: Each element occupies one side of the page. Other drawings show further dimensions of Induan Hiling's vision of the complementarity between these opposed spiritual elements. In Figure 4 she has drawn a spiritual mountain as seen from above. Crisscrossing over the mountain like vines are the ritual decorations known as "walkways of the gods"; these represent the paths of articulated ritual expression. Her "writing" fills one open quarter of the mountain. Although visible only in this quarter, this is the inspirational text that energizes the whole mountain. In this drawing the vine-like "walkways of the gods" are ritual paths that provide the superficial expression of the inspired text of the mountain.

Figure 5 shifts focus entirely to the intricate flowering of ritual form. This drawing represents ritual decorations; Induan Hiling has shown them here as delicate and plant-like. Each lobe is a leaf; each leaf is beautified and empowered by marks that can be interpreted equally as ornamentation

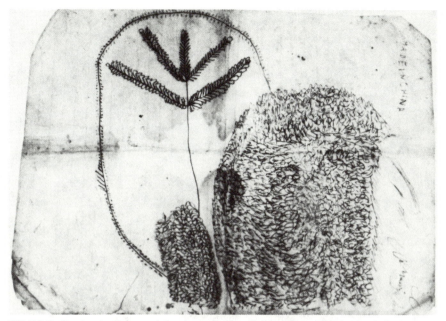

FIGURE 2   The bamboo altar and the shaman's text. (Original 6″ × 7½″ in blue ballpoint pen)

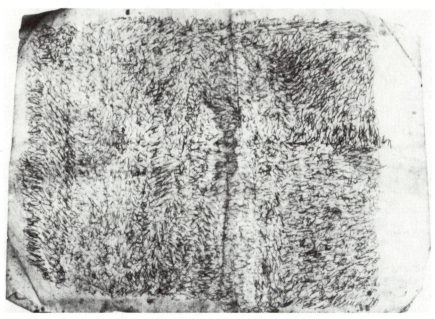

FIGURE 3   The shaman's book. (Original 6″ × 7½″ in blue ballpoint pen)

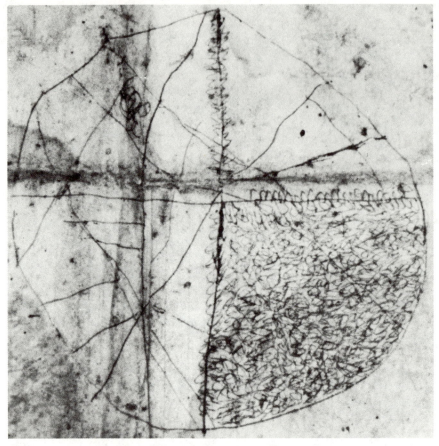

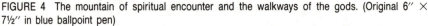

FIGURE 4 The mountain of spiritual encounter and the walkways of the gods. (Original 6″ ×
7½″ in blue ballpoint pen)

or text.[12] The text is thus encapsulated in the ritual apparatus. Although
each drawing combines elements of text and ritual in different ways, the
importance of a complementarity between inspiration and traditional form
is reiterated in each. Even Figure 3, in which the page is filled with inspirational
message, reminds us of the importance of ritualized form precisely because
it lacks any.

Induan Hiling's explanation of shamanism as inspiration externalized and
articulated through traditional form is both an innovative and perceptive
interpretation. Conventional shamanic apprenticeship encourages a reading
of the chants that stresses the endless elaboration of complexity and diversity
rather than oppositions. Mountains and vegetation are common symbolic
elements in shamans' chants, but nowhere else did I see the two elements
so clearly identified as complementary pairs, with such stably resonating

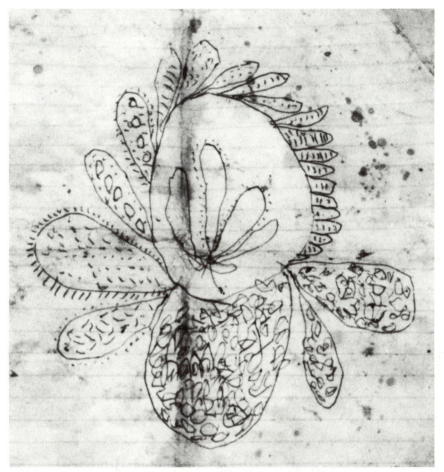

FIGURE 5 The ritual set-up. (Original 6″ × 7½″ in blue ballpoint pen)

reference to the possibilities of spiritual expression itself. Induan Hiling's interpretation of the tradition successfully clarifies a number of key elements: Her oppositions speak of the necessity for both shamans' chants and ritual decorations in a performance. They also recall linked images of primal knowledge and carefully learned tradition within the chants themselves as well as the complementarity of dreams and apprenticeship in learning. Yet her interpretation is also a challenging one, pointing to the possibilities of simplification and codification of that which shamans say can never be simplified or codified.

Induan Hiling's engagement with the dominant tradition of Meratus shamanism results in a perceptive interpretative framework. As a woman shaman, she has needed to forge original paths to achieve legitimacy. These

FIGURE 6 Flying over mountains, rocks, grass, and trees. (Original 6″ × 7½″ in red and blue pencil; tracing by A. L. Tsing)

paths have led her not only to innovative revisions, but also to imaginative and insightful views on Meratus shamanism.

THE CONDITIONS OF CREATIVE PRODUCTION

> [T]he aim is not to claim for women the rights and privileges traditionally the prerogative of men, but to demonstrate how representations by women display the grounds of representation and the fault-lines of radical difference.
> —Crosby 1984:256

Induan Hiling intends her drawings to be more than critical appraisals: They are encapsulations of or substitutes for performance. The drawings—particularly the more complex ones—are themselves rituals. Indeed, the contrast between picture or script as ritual and the more conventional male-dominated ritual performance suggests a new dimension of Induan Hiling's contribution: Her work makes evident the gendered grounds of Meratus ritual representation.

Induan Hiling presents a complete ritual performance—a curing ritual—in the complex drawing reproduced in Figure 6. She has drawn not only the mountain/vegetation opposition described above but also the shaman who brings together tradition and inspiration. On each side of the drawing are rocks; the triangles that dominate the landscape are mountains. On the rocks and mountains grow vegetation: At the peak of the darkest mountain is a wild fig tree with its fruits, a wild palm grows to its immediate left, and herbs and grasses are found near that mountain's summit, including the plant that appears to have drifted off the top. But she has also drawn the dreamer herself in the form of an airplane (on the left of the picture). The airplane is the dreamer who energizes and experiences the dream landscape. Meratus generally interpret airplanes as the vehicles of spiritual travel. Here the representation of spiritual travel empowers the drawing as a shamanic ritual. Induan Hiling's sister, who was suffering from leprosy, kept this picture as an aspect of her cure. The drawing is not meant as a reminder of a shamanic performance; it is itself a curing ritual.

The picture incorporates a number of key elements of more conventional performances, particularly with its addition of the spiritual travel of the shaman. Yet there are clearly significant differences between this picture and a conventional performance. Most importantly, perhaps, the picture offers no dramatic action. The picture flattens the performance, abolishing performance time.

The time of the performance involves not just duration but the capture of attention. A successful ritual establishes the centrality of the shaman within the attention of the audience. Indeed, the listeners often sleep, but if they did nothing but sleep, the ritual would be less effective. And the listeners might just sleep—despite the beauty of the dance, the decorations, and the poetry—except for unpredictable elements in the performance and the possibility for various kinds of dramatic upsets or excess. For example, if the ritual preparations are badly done, the spirit may be angry or even dangerous. Perhaps the shaman will be overwhelmed within his chant and fall into a faint, and it may be difficult to revive him. Unlike the decorations and the chants, these elements are never described as necessary to ritual— in fact, they involve messing up rather than following the rules—but these are key elements of performance time.

Dramatic upsets and excesses are also the performance elements most clearly associated with male experience and male political advantage. Outside of the context of shamanism, men much more than women use the threats and surprises of impressive speeches and angry outbursts to position themselves focally within social gatherings. When shamans improvise with their knowledge and ferocity, they call upon these dramatic talents to sustain the drawing power of the performance. This is not so much a matter of gender rules as of men's ability to go beyond the rules—and thus establish them (Tsing in press).

Most performances take at least an entire night. That performance time is significant for gender privilege is suggested by one male shaman's comment that women tend not to become shamans because they do not want to stay up all night. He was ignoring the fact that *pinjulang* do stay up to accompany the shaman. But there is a difference in the wakefulness of the shaman and the wakefulness of his woman accompanist: The attention of the former is also attention-drawing—wakeful for the audience—while the latter is awake merely for herself and for the shaman. The ability to wake up the audience, at least sporadically, is a crucial skill of the shaman.

Sometimes women can seize the dramatic center: The possessed women with whom Induan Hiling began her spiritual career manipulated audience attention with their wild dancing and bursts of spirit-inspired song. Without the women's dramatic excesses Induan Hiling might not have had a platform from which to rise. Yet most of the possessed women were willing to lend credence to shamans' views of them as patients rather than healers by representing themselves as inarticulate victims of spiritual power. As long as they were seen as patients, their dramatic performances did not threaten the men's preeminence. Furthermore, the most ritually knowledgeable women, the *pinjulang*, avoided possession; this reinforced the idea that women could be either knowledgeable (and shy) or else dramatic (and inarticulate) but not both knowledgeable and dramatic. Without gender-appropriate ways of bringing together dramatic self-presentation and claims to traditional knowledge, women have difficulty breaking into the mainstream of male-dominated spiritual expression.

Induan Hiling's work succeeds by sidestepping performance requirements that advantage men; thus even in its omissions it exposes gender asymmetries in the conditions of spiritual expression. In this regard, we also see some of the advantages she gains by using the love song format instead of the chant: If she feels more comfortable calling her chants *dunang* (love songs), it is perhaps because the performance requirements of the two forms differ significantly and not that she is unable to assemble a conventional chant. Whereas shamans must convene a formal ritual event to perform chants, love songs are sung while minding children, resting, and socializing with friends. Although both forms use an improvisational style that responds to context and audience as well as the intentions of the singer, the kind of audience attention shamanic chants and love songs seek is different: Love songs tease, flatter, soothe, and flirt, thus drawing attention to the subtle attractions of daily interaction; shamanic chants alternately amaze, wheedle, praise, pontificate, or startle in an attempt to convene a spiritual community around the performance of the shaman. Induan Hiling's innovation has been to use informal daily contacts—the audience of love songs—as a community to support spiritual leadership. Because public ritual performance privileges male expressive leadership, she ingeniously avoids it.

Her pictures even more clearly bypass performance requirements: They do away with performance entirely in favor of the codification of spiritual knowledge and authority. This codification has a number of significant features.

First, her drawings, unlike shaman's performances, are easily reproducible. Induan Hiling was happy to allow me to copy the drawings, and, in two cases, she requested my copy and gave me the original because my copy was on cleaner paper and seemed likely to last longer.[13]

Second, her drawings work toward an impersonal visual authority rather than the contextually grounded authority of shamanic dialog. Although shamans may claim to chant time-honored traditional poetry that cannot be altered, the performance in fact changes with the purpose of the ceremony and the particular moods and motivations of both shaman and audience. The drawings, in contrast, cannot change their shape as they are called into different contexts of healing (although, of course, the interpretations may change).

Finally, Induan Hiling's drawings claim the authority of script. "Writing" gives her message the permanence of an artifact and disengages it from performance politics. Furthermore, Induan Hiling's undecipherable writing collapses time in more ways than the loss of performance: It brings the power of mysterious origins to bear on the spiritual meanings of the present.

In all these aspects of codification, writing becomes a woman's project through which male privilege can be countered, evaded, and exposed. In avoiding the shaman's task of drawing an audience through unpredictability and drama, the "writings" show these performance elements as gender-asymmetrical conditions of expression. Her writing encodes a form of resistance to male performance privilege.

DISCUSSION

Induan Hiling's difficulty in breaking into the male-dominated domain of ritual performance has encouraged her to develop new forms of ritual—spiritual songs with love song melodies and pictures and texts that invoke the authority of codification rather than performance. Her empowering spirit familiar, "the horse of gaps," is her ability to weave her creativity in and out of the empty spaces of male-dominated modes of expression.

The feminist literary analysis that has alerted us to the significance of such empty spaces draws particularly from French feminists (for example, Marks and de Courtivron 1980). These literary critics have argued that because writing (in Western culture) is a male project, female writing finds itself in the gaps and the margins rather than the lines that codify male dominance. This feminist work has not differentiated writing from other modes of expression; the argument is that all signification is male-dominated, and writing is merely the most powerful example. In contrast, my analysis of Induan Hiling's "writing" points to distinctions between modes of expression, as each promotes gender-linked possibilities for creativity and empowerment within particular cultural contexts. Induan Hiling uses "writing" in the Meratus context to undercut male-biased performance requirements.

Induan Hiling's "writing," however, does not tempt me to construct a theory of an essential female expression—even one tailored for the Meratus context—like the pre-Oedipal *ecriture feminine* of Cixous (1980). Instead, it points me away from an analysis limited to gender to attend to the ways that the gender-specific features of any cultural project are determined within a particular class and ethnic situation. Indeed, Induan Hiling's dream writing draws from a source of authority that, while not extensively exploited by male Meratus shamans, is ultimately male dominated. Her writing invokes the authority of the written word as used by the government officials and Muslim traders and settlers who increasingly draw the parameters of Meratus possibilities.

Let me return to the disturbing "Made in China" on the margin of Figure 2. No one besides me in the Meratus Mountains could read that phrase; I imagine Induan Hiling copied it off of an item bought at market, perhaps a tin plate. Yet she knew it was an example of foreign writing—the powerful foreign writing, in any language, with any message, that motivated her commitment to the codification of Meratus tradition. Her dream of textualization grew within the challenge of competing foreign scripts. Indeed, just as dramatic excesses in performance reveal something of the conditions of shamanic expression, Induan Hiling's own marginal notes reveal something of the conditions of representation for her own project.

The very unreadability of her own written text—note that she *could* have formed letters—follows from its opposition to the foreign letters, also unreadable, but in a different sense. Meratus tell a story of a time when God handed out the Holy Books: The Meratus ancestor ate his, and thus he ensured both internal inspiration and its essentially unarticulated script. Similarly, perhaps the undomesticated fertility of Induan Hiling's plant-form ritual decorations reaffirms that Meratus tradition, while constrained, is yet by other standards wild. Gender assumes a secondary role as the project is guided by Induan Hiling's status as a Meratus Dayak, challenging and challenged by powerful literate foreigners on every side. In Figure 6, their words even have a central position, generating the text that replaces performance.

Induan Hiling explained the word in Figure 6 ("Astarama") as the name she had been given in the dream that generated this picture. She pronounced the name "Irama," as in Haji Roma Irama, a popular music star in Indonesia at the time. Roma Irama's posters were prominently displayed in homes and stores in the market towns surrounding the Meratus Mountains.[14] Meratus bachelors blasted his recordings over their tape decks for a few days after every market visit—until their cheap batteries ran out. In invoking Roma Irama, Induan Hiling portrays herself as combining the inspiration of a shaman with a rock star. The charismatic image of Roma Irama helps explain her use of love songs as shamanic text. Moreover, Roma Irama's name alerts us to Induan Hiling's stakes in a new, "modern" cultural identity for Meratus Dayaks. Induan Hiling creates a Meratus spirituality that she hopes can match that of the more powerful national Indonesian culture.

In making claims for her dream-inspired writing as spiritual expression, Induan Hiling leans on the prestige of literate outsiders with Holy Books and written traditions. Why have Meratus men not been drawn to "literate" codification? A comparison to another ethnic situation seems suggestive:

The use of writing as an ethnic marker and its links to gender division by the Tamang of Nepal has been nicely described by Kathryn March (1983).

For the Tamang, men and women have complementary and parallel ethnic codifications: Men write and women weave. Although the two media are opposed in metaphors that contrast male and female points of view, both weaving and writing express Tamang ethnic and religious solidarity and their distinctiveness from outsiders.

In contrast, Meratus male leaders in Induan Hiling's mountain area do not wish to press the distinctiveness of Meratus ethnicity; instead, they emphasize their similarities to and thus connections with foreign power to augment their leadership positions within the local community. The performances of both shamans and political leaders reproduce models of outside authority as Meratus understand these models. Male leaders generally do not pose the Meratus community *against* outside models, because this would undercut their leadership skills. Thus in this area there have been few male attempts to codify Meratus difference.

Women, on the other hand, have fewer opportunities for contact and communication with powerful outsiders, such as the market traders, government bureaucrats, and army men with whom the men forge ties. This has disadvantaged women as actors in community politics. Yet as ethnic tensions have increased with the loss of Meratus lands to neighboring Muslims and with the emerging threat of state resettlement to crowded border areas, a number of women have played key roles in reformulating Meratus ideas about local culture and particularly shamanism to pose an alternative to powerful outside models of "civilization" and "religion." Induan Hiling's early mentor, Uma Adang, is one outstanding example; indeed, Uma Adang influenced Induan Hiling to turn her work in this direction. In the last two verses of the song that I have been discussing Induan Hiling attempts to articulate Uma Adang's message about the importance of codified local custom and religion under an imagined state protection (Tsing 1987). This section of the song begins with the following lines:

Adu hai, let's sing,
Swept by the wind, and
Riding the horse of gaps, singing,
Counting custom and tradition
In 41 paragraphs.

Here Induan Hiling's "horse of gaps" takes her beyond male strategies to the formulation of a more codified and distinctive ethnic identity for Meratus. Induan Hiling's "writing" also makes its own contribution to this emerging discourse, where gender challenges and ethnic challenges meet.

*   *   *

Induan Hiling's work inserts itself within a tradition in which men predominate as star actors and speakers; and in its need to revise, sidestep, and transform that tradition, her work exposes some of the tradition's dependence on male privilege. Her work provides a critical interpretation of shamanic tradition in two senses: First, it provides an innovative reading of of convention; and, second, its inversions, revisions, and even omissions create through their imaginative resistance to this convention. In retreating from ordinary Meratus standards of performance and leadership, Induan Hiling challenges these standards and contributes to an emerging Meratus conversation on gender, creativity, and power.

NOTES

Research in South Kalimantan was carried out between 1979 and 1981 under the auspices of the Lembaga Ilmu Pengetahuan Indonesia and the sponsorship of Dr. Masri Singarimbun. Support was provided by fellowships from the National Institute of Mental Health and the Social Science Research Council. This article has benefited from readings by Jane Atkinson, Jim Fernandez, Janet Jacobs, Anne-Marie Mires, Beth Nelson, Renato Rosaldo, Alix Kates Shulman, Lynn Wilson, and Harriet Whitehead. Elizabeth Fischbach drew the portrait of Induan Hiling, which I reproduce with her permission. I am particularly grateful to Induan Hiling for sharing her work with me—and allowing me to share it with others.

1. Induan Hiling is a pseudonym for a Meratus Dayak woman whose name I have changed to protect her privacy. These lines are from one of Induan Hiling's inspired songs, the entirety of which I have translated in the Appendix. I have used fragments from this particular song throughout this chapter.

2. The following review articles were particularly useful in introducing me to the nuances of recent work in feminist literary criticism: Sternhell 1982; Crosby 1984; Kolodny 1980. Another useful introduction to feminist criticism is Moi (1985). Moi's analysis separated Anglo-American and French tendencies in feminist literary theory and criticized Anglo-Americans particularly for their author-centered humanistic vision, in which women's writing automatically reflects the "female" experiences of the author. In my chapter I argue that some of these Anglo-American approaches have at least some usefulness for contemporary cultural anthropology. The "texts" of cultures rather than authors have been the object of anthropological analysis, and thus the male-centered unity of anthropological texts can be disrupted by a focus on "authors" that allows us to look at how the heterogeneous interests of ordinary people influence the continuing formation of culture.

3. The Meratus have also been called *Bukit*, but they consider this a derogatory term. "Dayak" refers to non-Muslim indigenous people of Borneo.

4. The importance of Meratus performance standards in privileging men as political actors is discussed in an article titled "Gender and Politics in Meratus Dispute Settlement" (Tsing in press), which can be read as a companion piece to this chapter.

5. Uma Adang's movement is discussed in detail in Tsing 1987. Uma Adang "adopted" both Induan Hiling and myself—as well as numerous other fans—as siblings.

6. Meratus shamanic curing is described in Tsing 1988.

7. Conventions differ among the various shamanic styles associated with different Meratus regions. In Induan Hiling's area, women play the part of *pinjulang* in the most popular styles; in other styles, men tend to be *pinjulang* (also known as *patati*) as well as shamans.

8. Although in some Meratus shamanic styles women play the drums, in Induan Hiling's local area only men are drummers.

9. The women had divergent positions: Some seemed more comfortable with the illness attribution than others. Two were young and refused to speak about their

experience, thus bringing their behavior in line with the possessed behavior expected of children, regarded as common victims of *dewa* kidnapping. Several were close kin of *dewa* shamans, and their possession behavior—whether they called it illness or inspiration—seemed closely related to their other attempts to further these men's careers within the community. But a few of the most articulate told me with considerable self-assurance that they were receiving spiritual teachings.

10. Central mountain Meratus live in dispersed households and small swidden clusters, which affiliate to form neighborhoods of 5 to 30 families. Neighborhoods are political and religious communities; however, individual families and swidden clusters have considerable autonomy and are always free to join a different neighborhood or keep their affairs to themselves. Meratus community dynamics are discussed in Tsing 1984.

11. Among the Ma'anyan Dayaks of Padju Epat in Central Kalimantan, female shamans conventionally use rattling anklets (Alfred Hudson, personal communication). I do not know if Induan Hiling was aware of the Ma'anyan tradition.

12. A number of pieces of the ritual decorations for a shamanic festival are painted with plant-like designs. Decorated boards used in ritual stands are called *papan tulis*— "writing boards." Induan Hiling uses this identification of decoration and writing in this drawing.

Such an identification of decorated boards as "writing" is also found in the ritual practice of Central Kalimantan Ma'anyan (Hudson 1966). In other parts of Borneo, "writing boards" of rather different sorts are used to remind shamans of the stages of their chants (Harrison 1965). One source of Induan Hiling's ideas about writing is probably these common connections among decoration, "writing," and shamanic knowledge. Other sources involve Induan Hiling's interpretation of the power of Arabic and Western scripts.

13. The issue of reproducibility is also relevant to love songs: They can be copied more easily than shamans' chants because they are not so shrouded in secrecy and they pass easily from one singer to another. Induan Hiling was also aware of the mechanical reproducibility of recorded pop music, to which Meratus love songs are sometimes compared. (A number of young men have tape recorders on which they play tapes of the popular love songs called *orkes malayu*.) The last section of my chapter suggests how Induan Hiling combined her identification with local shamans with an emulation of national pop music heroes.

14. Roma Irama himself is a master of combining genres and transforming symbols. One of his then current posters shows him as a pious pilgrim in Arab dress before an Islamic prayer rug with a woman kneeling at his feet and his electric guitar in his hand. Another shows him with a bloody headrag—and his guitar—manning revolutionary barricades.

REFERENCES

Ardener, Edwin. 1975. "Belief and the Problem of Women." In Shirley Ardener, ed., *Perceiving Women*. New York: Wiley.

Bell, Diane. 1983. *Daughters of the Dreaming*. North Sydney: Allen and Unwin.

Bernikow, Louise. 1974. *The World Split Open: Four Centuries of Women Poets in England and America, 1552–1950*. New York: Vintage Books.

Bruner, Edward, and Phyllis Gorfain. 1984. "Dialogic Narration and the Paradoxes of Mosada." In Edward Bruner, ed., *Text, Play, and Story*. Washington, D.C.: American Ethnological Society.

Collier, Jane, and Sylvia Yanagisako, eds. 1987. *Gender and Kinship*. Stanford: Stanford University Press.

Cixous, Helene. 1980. "The Laugh of the Medusa." In Elaine Marks and Isabelle de Courtivron, eds., *New French Feminisms: An Anthology*. Amherst: University of Massachusetts Press.

Crosby, Christina. 1984. "Stranger than Truth: Feminist Literary Criticism and Speculations on Women." *Dalhousie Review* 64(2):247–259.

Freeman, J. Derek. 1968. "Thunder, Blood, and the Nicknaming of God's Creatures." *The Psychoanalytic Quarterly* 37(3):353–399.

Geertz, Clifford. 1973. *The Interpretation of Cultures*. New York: Basic Books.

Gilbert, Sandra, and Susan Gubar. 1979. *The Madwoman in the Attic*. New Haven: Yale University Press.

Gluckman, Max. 1963. "Rituals of Rebellion in South-East Africa." In Max Gluckman, *Order and Rebellion in Tribal Africa*. London: Cohen and West.

Harrison, Tom. 1965. "Borneo Writing." *Bijdragen tot de taal-, land-, en volkenkunde*. 121(1):1–57.

Herdt, Gilbert. 1981. *Guardians of the Flutes*. New York: McGraw-Hill.

Hudson, Alfred. 1966. "Death Ceremonies of the Padju Epat Ma'anyan Dayaks." In Tom Harrison, ed., *Borneo Writing and Related Matters*. Sarawak Museum Journal, Special Monograph No. 1, XIII (27), pp. 341–416.

Kamuf, Peggy. 1982. *Fictions of Feminine Desire*. Lincoln: University of Nebraska Press.

Kapferer, Bruce. 1983. *A Celebration of Demons*. Bloomington: Indiana University Press.

Kessler, Clive. 1977. "Conflict and Sovereignty in Kelantanese Malay Spirit Séances." In V. Crapanzano and V. Garrison, eds., *Case Studies in Spirit Possession*. New York: Wiley.

Kolodny, Annette. 1980. "Dancing Through the Minefield: Some Observations on the Theory and Politics of a Feminist Literary Criticism," *Feminist Studies* 6(1):1–25.

Lewis, I. M. 1971. *Ecstatic Religion*. Harmondsworth, England: Penguin Books.

March, Kathryn. 1983. "Weaving, Writing, and Gender," *Man* (new series) 18(4):729–744.

Marks, Elaine, and Isabelle de Courtivron, eds. 1980. *New French Feminisms: An Anthology*. Amherst: University of Massachusetts Press.

Moers, Ellen. 1976. *Literary Women*. Garden City, N.Y.: Doubleday.

Moi, Toril. 1985. *Sexual/Textual Politics: Feminist Literary Theory*. London: Methuen.

Moore, Henrietta. 1988. *Feminism and Anthropology*. Minneapolis: University of Minnesota Press.

Ortner, Sherry. 1974. "Is Female to Male as Nature Is to Culture?" in Michelle Rosaldo and Louise Lamphere, eds., *Woman, Culture, and Society*. Stanford: Stanford University Press.

Ortner, Sherry, and Harriet Whitehead, eds. 1981. *Sexual Meanings*. New York: Cambridge University Press.

Showalter, Elaine. 1977. *A Literature of Their Own*. Princeton: Princeton University Press.

Sternhell, Carol. 1982. *A Whole New Poetics Beginning Here: Theories of Feminist Literary Criticism*. PhD dissertation, Stanford University.

Tsing, Anna. 1984. *Politics and Culture in the Meratus Mountains*. PhD dissertation, Stanford University.

———. 1987. "A Rhetoric of Centers in a Religion of the Periphery." In Rita Kipp and Susan Rodgers, eds., *Indonesian Religions in Transition*. Tucson: University of Arizona Press.

———. 1988. "Healing Boundaries in South Kalimantan," *Social Science and Medicine* 27(8):829–839.

———. In press. "Gender and Performance in Meratus Dispute Settlement." In Jane Atkinson and Shelly Errington, eds., *The Paradox of Difference: Essays on Gender in Island Southeast Asia*. Stanford: Stanford University Press.

Weiner, Annette. 1976. *Women of Value, Men of Renown*. Austin: University of Texas Press.

APPENDIX
One of Induan Hiling's Songs

All of the song fragments discussed in the chapter are from this song.

The song	My commentary
Adu hai, Riding the horse of gaps, babe. Swept by the wind, Riding the horse of gaps, friend.	*Clearheaded in* *spiritual flights,*
Finished in a day— Forging spurs, babe, Finished in a day. The horse of distances.	*the shaman forges* *a spiritual* *route*
What shall be used, babe? Forging spurs Finished in a day.	
Used to circle and contain, babe— That striped cup The gilded one, babe, That striped cup The cup that is composed To circle and contain.	*and a message* *that protects* *and contains* *the community.*
Swept by the wind . . .	
The child of a cobra, babe, Soaring to the sun. If it has scales They cross across each other. The scales they point, babe, Where do they point, friend? They point to its tail, They point to its head, Those scales, babe.	*Going further* *in flight,* *the route is* *mapped out* *before and* *behind.*
Let's plant bamboo. I'll plant some. A clump of bamboo, A stick of bamboo, It may have hollow stems, It may have nodes, It may have a growing bud.	*A spiritual path* *is laid out* *as bamboo grows:*
Those stems, babe, Isn't it so? Half of them are tall, Half of them are small, Half of them are high, The growing buds, babe.	*Some paths go* *farther than* *others.*
Adu, it's we ourselves, Our own mountain, babe. The mountain called Jungku With two shoulders, Hanging there Swinging where On our own mountain.	*But all are* *ultimately* *based on* *knowledge of* *the self,*

(continues)

APPENDIX *(continued)*

The song	*My commentary*
On the summit of the mountain	*as hair grows*
There's a wild fig tree,	*from our heads.*
A hanging fig tree,	
A swaying fig tree,	
Hanging where	
Swaying there	
Our wild fig tree.	
Where does it sway?	
Where does it hang?	
Yes, it's you and I, babe.	
There is a planting:	
A cut bamboo.	
A bamboo that plays the flute	
A bamboo that sings.	
We cut it off	
Touching the shoulders,	
The scissored bamboo	
Touching the waist.	
Babe, the scissored bamboo,	
The cut bamboo,	
Where is it planted?	
Where does it hang?	
Adu hai, let's sing,	*The songs*
Swept by the wind, and	*of shamans*
Riding the horse of gaps, singing,	*recount*
Counting custom and tradition	*local custom,*
In 41 paragraphs.	*as protected*
The constitution of custom	*by the state,*
The law of tradition	
The prohibitions of the Basic Constitution.	
We'll stand on the center of the five National Principles	
To face our music in the world.	
Adu hai,	*and by the*
At the moment	*legitimacy of origins.*
When God stood up,	*For as law and custom*
And first took care of custom:	*were created*
The constitution of custom	*by God,*
The constitution of law.	*so, too,*
At the moment	*human breath*
When God the One	*("divided into two"*
(I mean, not that God,	*by the nostrils)*
Not that God—)	*and consciousness*
Stood up in the wind	*(that "named")*
It was divided into two	*were forged*
It was named	*within the*
—Even water was not yet named,	*ultimately*
Water was still one—	*undecipherable*
Du dat	*mystery of*
Jat sat	*original*
Dat jur	*knowledge.*
Dat say	
Dat	
Sut tup.	

7

Between Two Worlds
German Feminist Approaches to Working-Class Women and Work

MYRA MARX FERREE

The importance of considering social class as well as gender is illustrated in this chapter. Ferree's summary of recent research focuses on how factory-employed women in Germany work with, through, and around domestic/public distinctions. The dilemma presented is that of being responsible for home and housework in a society that puts greater value on exchange-value or paid work. The research subjects in this case cope by staying "between [the] two worlds." This account of working women from their own point of view—a view that challenges researchers' middle-class conceptual distinctions—helps us understand why some women resist some aspects of feminist agendas—for example, the socialization of housework. The author's work shows her awareness of the contradictions that are internal to the lives of these women respondents as well as of those that exist between the views of working-class and middle-class women.

There is no shortage of sociological research on women and work in the United States. It may seem strange, therefore, to suggest that we have something to learn about our own society from research done in West Germany. However, some sociologists there have approached the study of women and work from the bottom up, considering first the experiences and perspectives of working-class women.[1] Their focus integrates feminist theory with empirical data in ways that can be useful to American researchers struggling with similar problems.

The prominence of empirical data in this work raises legitimate questions about the comparability of West German and American women's experiences. Although these questions can only be answered conclusively when we have more data, there are broad similarities in German and American women's lives that encourage comparison. In both countries, about half of all adult women were in the labor force in 1980,[2] largely concentrated in specific sex-typed, underpaid occupations. In both countries, women continue to carry the primary responsibility for housework and child care. Both countries provide only minimal social support and services to employed mothers.

There are also differences, some of which have theoretical repercussions. First, there are no rapid increases in female labor force participation in West Germany to lure feminists into a belief that paid employment alone is an indicator of women's improved status. From 1925 to 1976, the female proportion of the German labor force has fluctuated between 35.8 and 37.2 percent, showing no clear trend over time.[3] In the United States, in contrast, the female proportion of the labor force rose from 22 percent in 1930 to 40 percent in 1976.[4] From an American vantage point, women's paid employment is part of a new reality that includes the second wave of feminism. But Germans are more likely to view women's labor force participation and their family responsibilities as aspects of the old reality that feminism must address.

Second, social class, rather than race, is a central issue for feminists in West Germany. Many German scholars begin from a perspective more fundamentally critical of capitalism and its impact on women's lives than that of most American researchers. Certainly there are exceptions on both sides of the Atlantic,[5] but German feminist sociologists are likely to be particularly attentive to the role of class when evaluating the status and aspirations of women.[6] American research on women's work usually displays a laudable reluctance to generalize about women factory workers from studies of women professionals. But in fact there are comparatively few empirical studies of American women factory workers, or of any other working-class women, from which to draw independent conclusions.[7] West German feminist research, in contrast, emphasizes the experiences and perspectives of women in working-class jobs.

As the many American studies of dual career families and women achievers have shown, professionals rarely doubt that the demands of the marketplace should take priority in determining where one lives, how one arranges one's schedule, and the extent of extraprofessional commitments in one's life. Putting work first is often studied as "work commitment," a value seen as necessary for women's individual success and as an essential prerequisite to their making significant inroads into male domains of privilege, prestige, and power. American scholars tend to see women's work commitment as feminist in effect, if not in intent.

Certainly professional women derive more rewards from their work than do working-class women. But American researchers—who are, of course, professionals—fail to acknowledge that these rewards may distort their view of work; they tend to use such benefits to justify their own priorities. Working-class women often do not share these priorities, and American scholars tend to describe these women's perspective as "traditional," "hierarchical," or "familistic"—which is to say nonfeminist to some degree.[8] Then researchers use class position to explain and justify this difference in values (Why should working-class women buy into the system when the rewards are so slight?). But the class-based double standard remains largely unquestioned.[9] In effect, American scholars (generously) excuse working-class women from sharing this (self-evidently good) interest in conforming to the demands of the workplace. Although working-class women's jobs undeniably involve a lifetime of exploitation as poorly paid workers, American researchers too readily assume that a paid job offers them nothing but this "extra" burden.[10] Distinguishing between women who want to work and women who have to work makes housework invisible and creates an imaginary boundary between types of women that follows class lines.

While not denying or minimizing the extent to which working-class women carry a double burden, some recent West German research asks how and why they do so, examining their choices and preferences as well as the conditions in which they struggle. The women in these studies emerge as participants who shape their own lives rather than as passive victims of sex and class oppressions.[11] These German feminists do not present labor force participation as a panacea, nor do they consider accommodation to the whims of the employer or the market a moral imperative. But they do challenge the assumptions that paid employment has nothing but money to offer working-class women and that such women would be liberated if freed from the necessity of having to work.

In the following four sections I offer an overview of some of the more significant of these studies, work representing the efforts of four separate research groups, in Munich, Frankfurt, Göttingen, and Hannover. In the final section of this essay, I suggest the utility of these studies for constructing a feminist sociology of work responsive to the concerns of women in working-class jobs.

THE DIVIDED LIFE: TWO MODES
OF WORK

Elisabeth Beck-Gernsheim argues that the occupational disadvantages of women, beyond those created by direct discrimination, cannot be attributed primarily to the familiar double burden of housework and paid employment.[12] Rather than seeing women as limiting their psychological involvement with their paid jobs because of their home responsibilities, Beck-Gernsheim views women as more deeply involved with the content of their work than are men but penalized for this interest in content. Concern over the content of the work helps to determine the nature of the jobs into which women are channeled and tends to make women less willing or able to fight for their economic interests. Beck-Gernsheim argues that, in the present system, caring about what one produces more than about one's financial return creates labor market disadvantages for the worker. Moreover, she presents evidence that an intrinsic work orientation—the sense of wanting a job that matches one's abilities and interests and wanting to do good work—remains important to women even though employers treat it as a deficiency (a lack of competitiveness, ambition, assertiveness) and use it to justify women's low pay and poor work conditions.[13] According to Beck-Gernsheim, women's collective stubbornness in adhering to an intrinsic orientation reflects no personal deficiency but rather the fact that there are whole sectors of the economy, as well as particular jobs, in which an intrinsic work orientation is essential and thus actively promote it. Work that deals directly with people is perhaps the clearest case of the match between women's interest in work and employers' interest in women.

As Beck-Gernsheim assumes, and as Ilona Ostner argues more explicitly, the present occupational structure is a product of the historical development of capitalism.[14] As occupations have developed, they have been differentiated from housework and other forms of use-value production by becoming increasingly specialized and abstract and so ever less concretely connected to the satisfaction of individual human needs. Because finding job satisfaction in meeting the needs of known others becomes less and less possible, more and more of the meaning of the job becomes invested in the economic and social rewards workers obtain. Thus, work is instrumental and must be viewed that way. But the closer the work remains to the direct satisfaction of the needs of known others, the more an instrumental view can actively interfere with one's performance of a job. Conversely, a competitive and instrumental view of employment will make responding to the others' needs frustrating and unpleasant for the worker.

Beck-Gernsheim and Ostner collaborated on a study of nursing as an occupation that illustrates their approach to sex differentiation.[15] They describe the ways in which male nurses are initially uncertain of and deficient in their ability to respond empathetically to the needs of individual patients but do develop this ability on the job. They also contrast the structure and demands of nursing as a paid occupation with the supplemental nursing that is done within families. This unpaid nursing is not romanticized—the caregiver often feels hostage to the needy person because of the close personal ties and unbounded time demands characteristic of direct use production. But paid nursing also exploits the worker. Employers of nurses benefit at low cost from the skills that women bring to the job, while nurses' concern for their patients as people is used to inhibit their demands for better pay and for recognition as professionals. Women themselves find paid employment as a nurse preferable to the unbounded demands of unpaid nursing but also emphasize the caring and giving elements of the job as essential rewards. In this analysis, sex-typed women's occupations are structurally located between the impersonality of pure market relations and the unmitigated personal pressures of pure use production.

Both Beck-Gernsheim and Ostner argue that in general women's interests, expectations, and skills focus on the direct satisfaction of the needs of others; men's do not. This sex-specific human capital is developed through socialization, not just in childhood, but in actual work experiences. Doing housework is among these work experiences. The use-value orientation developed in and for housework actually makes many women's occupations—including that of homemaker—uniquely rewarding but also deeply frustrating because the overall structure of the exchange-based economy restricts the extent to which these occupations allow the intrinsic satisfaction they promise. Positive evaluation of housework as an alternative form of work organization tied to a use-value ethic contrasts theoretically with a critical appraisal of its necessarily marginal and dependent character in an exchange society. Beck-Gernsheim argues that women are aware of both aspects; in doing women's work they are painfully marginalized, but they also resist accommodation to the prevailing exchange-value ethic.

Rather than seeing the combination of paid work and housework as simply a double burden, Beck-Gernsheim stresses that it creates a "divided life" in which women are torn between two modes of existence, neither of which is fully satisfactory. From this perspective, even professional work appears as an "essential aggravation": essential in that it secures the means of existence and also provides the opportunity to acquire and exercise specialized competencies in which one may rightfully take pride; an aggravation in that it limits and suppresses spontaneity, emotion, and all abilities and interests not occupationally relevant and subordinates personal realtionships to occupational demands, making them increasingly instrumental.[16] In a society organized around occupations, lack of paid employment is a psychological as well as an economic problem; in a society made up of human beings, reduction to the capacities used in one's job is equally problematic. Women recognize and experience this structural conflict in greater measure than do men. The division between housewife (use-value oriented) and worker (exchange-value oriented) is increasingly felt by individual women, rather than distinguishing between women and men or between two groups of women. For the most part, women's attempts to deal with this conflict have been individual rather than collective. Antagonism between women who have come to different resolutions is sharpened, as each feels the other does not understand the renunciations necessary or the rewards available in her way of life.

FACTORY AND FAMILY
IN CRITICAL PERSPECTIVE

Christel Eckart, Helgard Kramer, and Ursula Jaerisch approach the issue of structural conflict between housework and paid labor by analyzing how women factory workers define their interests and act to advance these interests.[17] The researchers construct a life-course perspective on the variety of ways in which housework and paid work come together to determine women's lives and consciousness. Their sample, therefore, includes women of a variety of ages and family situations. They interviewed seventy-one women who were pieceworkers in five firms in the electrotechnical and clothing industries—women in jobs that are among the most onerous, worst paid, and most insecure in the German economy.[18]

Not surprisingly, intrinsic interest in the work as Beck-Gernsheim and Ostner describe it is of little relevance to these women; few of them sought or trained for the kind of work they were doing.[19] Yet to describe these women as forced to work would also distort their situation. Eckart, Jaerisch, and Kramer describe instead a "family-centered instrumental orientation," not unlike that often ascribed to working-class men: the job is important, but primarily as a means of earning money, carrying out one's family responsibilities, and trying to achieve "the good life." These women factory workers differ from men primarily in that they see an alternate route to achieving these goals in marriage and the exchange of housework for economic support. Their low wages make both strategies crucial. Employment does not release them from dependence on family economic support (from parents, if not from husbands) nor does family support free them from wage earning. Women experience both dependencies as burdensome, yet they also find it personally important and rewarding to maintain both family and job.

Full-time housework is neither economically possible nor totally desirable for most of these women. Along with economic presures, motives like the desire to expand areas of competence and to interact with people outside the family also influence these women to enter and stay in the labor force. Such motives are not incompatible with an instrumental orientation: indeed, in a market economy, competence is largely measured by earnings. Paid work offers possibilities for more distanced and instrumental interaction than that available in the home; thus workplace ties provide a form of emotional relief greatly valued by these women. Romantic views of housework ignore the strains of use-value production that make such relief necessary for women at all class levels. The polarized conceptual model of "women who want to work" and "women who have to work" simply does not fit these women's experience.

Because women value their jobs, they do not wish to appear constrained at work by their family commitments, and so they minimize their real limits—personalize them as individual failings or else drive themselves to exhaustion. When unavoidable conflicts arise, the women bargain individually with their husbands or work supervisors in order to reach a resolution that enables them to keep on in their jobs. "Concessions" then keep women grateful to both their bosses, working hard in order to make it up to them, and unwilling to express other grievances. Women in different life stages have a variety of immediately urgent interests, which can undercut solidarity among women workers.

Although women's jobs are important to them, housework is no less so. Eckart, Jaerisch, and Kramer argue that housework is both an alternative means of securing an economic existence and a source of intrinsic reward in its own right. Both of these aspects of housework make it valuable to women and make employed women reluctant to concede responsibility for it. Eckart and her coauthors conclude that women have conflicting feelings about reducing the share of housework they do, despite the terrible burdens it imposes, and thus may resist changing the division of labor in the home. One crucial reason for this resistance is that return to the job of full-time housewife is a potential route of escape from the factory. Holding that alternative open by being the one who does the housework makes it possible to avoid seeing oneself as a factory worker for life. The prospect of someday being able to quit, like the prospect of retirement for working-class men, may help make the days and years of labor more endurable, even if full-time housework itself is also stressful. Second, housework is a way of making up to family members for the costs the mother or wife's job imposes on them; the less family members approve of her working, the more restitution she feels she owes them.[20] Third, and not least important, housework offers an alternative experience in and of itself. The work is closely tied to those for whom it is done and so offers intrinsic rewards these women do not find in the workplace. To bargain to change the division of labor and to calculate the exchange of effort and reward is to take an alienated stance to their housework and family relationship that these women experience as undesirable and self-defeating.

This view of housework provides insight into some women's reactions to feminist proposals for collectivization of, or pay for, housework. Eckart, Jaerisch, and Kramer asked directly about these issues and found considerable antipathy to both. The women they interviewed saw intimacy and housework as necessarily related and thus argued that collectivization would introduce new intimate ties, each generating its own irresistible demands on the what, when, and how of housework. Each person with whom housework is shared has a legitimate interest in how it is done; this, the women felt, creates pressure, not relief from responsibility. Pay for housework they saw as a threat: it objectifies and alienates the work, making it like their jobs, and introduces the control of the state or employer into the family and so reduces their own control over their work. Moreover, in their view full-time housework is already compensated by the avoidance of the factory it provides. If women choose to pursue the alternative of marriage as a means of support, then their husbands must be well enough off to afford it. Thus these women saw pay for housework as subsidizing husbands rather than wives and as transferring income to those who do not need it.

That family demands are defined as illegitimate in the workplace (even by unions) and that job demands are seen as equally illegitimate at home means that each woman has to represent herself in negotiations in both settings. Eckart, Jaerisch, and Kramer argue that women's real interest is in achieving a balance between the two qualitatively different types of work. This suggests that women are not backward or "unliberated" when they choose part-time work or other alternatives that advance this interest. Women's desire to reconcile and enjoy both forms of work has not been represented by unions or by feminists who define work commitment as essential for women's progress or even by feminists who define housework as an occupation like all others that should be done for a wage. Working-class women see no option but to bargain for accommodation individually rather than collectively, although this is ultimately to their disadvantage. They accept both the pressures of trying to do too much housework as the price they have to pay for not wanting to choose between unsatisfying alternatives. Because of this, women can be co-opted by particular concessions from husband or employer.[21] Feminist analysis itself, rather than appeals to "socialization" or "working-class values," is thus able to explain lesser support for feminism among working-class women.

SATISFACTION WITH
WORKING-CLASS JOBS

One of the most politicized issues in the discussion of working-class women is that of job satisfaction. Those who argue that women either ought to stay home, ought to work for pay, or ought to have a choice between these two "alternatives" advance evidence about women's satisfaction or dissatisfaction with their present work to justify their argument.[22] Women's attitudes toward paid work are presumed to be cause and consequence of their attitudes toward housework. Thus, working-class women who hate their jobs are assumed to prefer housework, while their strong sense of responsibility for their families rather than their work conditions is assumed to explain alienation from paid work. Conceptually, then, those involved in this discussion treat housework and paid work as occupying opposite poles of a single continuum, so that aversion from one must mean preference for the other.[23]

It is unusual to find studies of women's work that recognize what are actually two separate dimensions and relate job dissatisfaction to the actual conditions under which women work, rather than primarily to attitudes about work and family roles. Lother Lappe and Ilona Schöll-Schwinghammer collaborated on an extensive project that investigated conditions in a number of female sex-typed occupations and women workers' response to these conditions. Their research produced two related books. Lappe's book is based on the actual observation of a number of workplaces and on interviews with workers about what they actually do: Schöll-Schwinghammer's connects these work conditions to a variety of subjective responses.[24] They sampled factories rather than individuals and concentrated on firms and jobs within firms that employed a high proportion of women. They interviewed 500 women employees, of whom 372 were in production jobs and the remainder in data entry, other clerical jobs, and retail sales work.

Because Lappe and Schöll-Schwinghammer have measures of actual work conditions (the speed of the assembly line, the noise level, etc.), in addition to women's evaluations of their jobs, they are able to demonstrate convincingly that these work conditions directly relate to women's work attitudes. In cases where management characterized the women's work as "easy," the researchers found instead stressful conditions in which women had to maintain a fixed posture, focus on fine detail, or work at a pace faster than one task per minute. These conditions affect the extent to which women see their work as bearable over time. While 40 percent of the entire sample felt that they will be unable to keep working in their current jobs, this percentage varied for those in different occupations. Large appliance assemblers, for example, work on a slower line and have more diverse physical movements, which helps to explain why they can endure their work better and find it more satisfying than electronic components assemblers find theirs. In general, the women (unlike many men) are in jobs that do not allow them to conserve their strength, that make no allowances for the diminished physical capacities of aging workers, and in which, therefore, lifetime work commitment is unrealistic.[25]

Despite the stressful conditions of their jobs, nearly half the women find their work enjoyable in some respects, and an additional third find that other compensations at work make up for the negative aspects. The most dissatisfied workers are the low-level clerical workers (typists, data-entry clerks); 36 percent of clerical workers compared with 14 percent of the entire sample found nothing at all satisfying about their jobs. This can partly be explained by work conditions. The high noise levels and the monotony of clerical work interfere with the sustained attention demanded by the job (unlike assembly-line workers, clerical workers cannot talk or daydream while they work), and the set posture creates physical aches and pains. But the dissatisfaction is related to expectations as well. Clerical workers expect their jobs to be easier and more interesting than factory work and thus are less prepared to accept their actual work conditions. Also their greater job security and the appearance of choice in the sort of work they seek contribute to a less resigned attitude. Factory workers, on the other hand, consider their jobs merely better than unemployment and have lower expectations for both pay and satisfaction.

Housework adds to the stress in these women's lives as well; for example, women with more children find the same jobs more tiring. But relatively few of the women translate their difficulties into a preference for housework. They are divided in their opinions about whether they or full-time housewives have a better life (44 percent vs. 37 percent, respectively), and about whether the major advantage of paid work is the income (34 percent) or the social contacts and social recognition it affords (36 percent). The majority of the women do not see full-time housework as potentially satisfactory. But the combination of being overburdened at home and of working in stressful conditions on the job is the best predictor of a woman's desire to quit paid employment.[26]

Lappe and Schöll-Schwinghammer focus on the situational roots of working-class women's dissatisfaction with employment, rather than on "traditional attitudes" or on a family orientation presumed to be characteristic of the working class. Dissatisfaction thus defined cannot so readily be used to justify social policies that drive working-class women out of their jobs and back to their kitchen. This analysis highlights the extent to which the jobs themselves must be changed to make them physically endurable for longer periods of time and the pay increased to reflect the real difficulty of the work. However, the study does not examine the character of housework nor women's response to it in the same revealing detail. Although Lappe and Schöll-Schwinghammer make clear women's interest in remaining in the labor force, they do not recognize the ways in which housework, too, might be changed to women's advantage.

SERVING TWO MASTERS

One particularly fascinating study, conducted by a research team under the direction of Regina Becker-Schmidt, attempts to describe the burdens and rewards that working-class women find in housework as well as on the job.[27] Through analysis of sixty in-depth interviews (half with present factory workers, half with former factory workers, all of whom were caring for small children), the research team offers a dialectical understanding of the objective demands of work, both paid and unpaid, and the subjective reality of the worker, whose desires cannot be reduced to a simple preference for either paid work or housework. They argue that women are neither indifferent to, nor uncritically identified with, either type of work. Both positive and negative aspects of each type of work emerge through comparisons women draw between them as they actively shift their perspective ("As a worker I would like. . . . But as a mother I want. . . .").

Because these working-class women describe both fulfillment and disappointment in paid work and housework alike, their response can be characterized as fundamentally ambivalent to each. This ambivalence shows up in conflicting feelings (emotional ambivalence), inconsistencies of opinion (cognitive ambivalence), and in the wish to be in two places at the same time (divided will). Such genuine ambivalence is obscured by procrustean research designs that place respondents unequivocally into categories of either work or family orientation, and it is denied theoretically when either paid work or housework, or the choice between them, is presented as a route to liberation for women. Instead, the ambivalence of response to both forms of work suggests that both structures need to be changed, even if both are already, in their present forms, personally important to women.

This ambivalence is a fundamentally appropriate, though by no means necessary, response to the actual structural contradictions within and between the two qualitatively different types of work.[28] Becker-Schmidt and her co-workers argue that an unqualified preference for either paid work or housework requires the individual to deny the real problems or ignore the real rewards that exist in both forms of work, as well as in the combination of the two. They see ambivalence, the characteristic response of working-class women, as the best possible response to a situation fraught with structural contradictions.[29]

Such contradictions exist within each form of work as well as between them. Contradictions within paid work include, for example, the pressures to produce good, error-free work, on the one hand, and the pressure to produce as much as possible, on the other. Work structures induce workers to compete with each other in order to maintain performance, while at the same time leading them to cooperate with each other in order to sustain an integrated production process. As workers, women experience these and other contradictions in their jobs. Thus, time pressure and nervous stress make them want to quit but at the same time give them pride in being good workers who are able to meet the demands of a difficult job. Objective recognition and a sense of being useful and important exist simultaneously with physical exhaustion and a sense of being used up and exploited.

In their study, Becker-Schmidt and her team find that women combine awareness of exploitative work conditions with a certain distance from the situation. Since they proudly try not to be corrupted by the conditions into producing shoddy work or engaging in cut-throat competition, the need to compromise with conditions and to be indifferent to the work is a source of anger. The woman's sense of herself as a good worker and her empathy with the consumer who does not want a defective product stand in conflict with her desire to minimize the effort she must expend to earn a paycheck. Thus, she is constantly aware that she offers both human capital (skills and capacities brought to and developed on the job, which the job itself does not fully utilize) and commodity labor power (time and physical and psychic effort spent in exchange for a wage). She knows how wide the gap is between what she really can do and what she is expected and allowed to do on the job; from this awareness spring both resignation and resistance.

The contradictions within the home are no less intense than those in the factory, but they are qualitatively different. Personal relationships, for example, validate one's worth as a unique individual but also give psychological force to social demands for conformity; private ownership of goods (e.g., house, boat, car) creates an area of freedom in which one can act and exercise control but at the same time creates fear of losing these things and a sense of being held hostage by them; privacy in the home offers the security of the familiar and protection from oppressive forms of social control but also leads to boredom with the familiar and lack of social protection from oppression and violence.

Women experience housework itself in contradictory ways. It is work for known others, not alienated from its direct utility for the consumers ("a labor of love"), but it is simultaneously not recognized as work because it is identified with the family relationship ("being a mother"). The feeling of autonomy in structuring one's own workday, in being one's own boss, coexists with the strain of scheduling work in and around the time demands of school or work or the hours when stores are open and services available.[30] The quantitative time demands of housework conflict with qualitative expectations. Attempts to create schedules and to plan some measurable output for the time expended continually clash with attempts to respond to needs as they arise, to be sympathetic and patient. The housewife's sense of herself as "doing her own thing" coexists with her sense of being at the beck and call of others; being indispensable and thus important is the flip side of being always responsible and thus trapped. Whereas in paid work the tension between the self experienced as a capable person and as a commodity characterizes the structural contradiction, in housework the defining tension is between the self considered as an individual ego and as the "glue" that holds the family together.

The contradictions within each form of work are not resolved by combining the two, but the rewards and costs can be complementary. Difficulties that are acute in full-time housework (e.g., isolation, lack of recognition, absence of measurable output) are balanced by certain aspects of paid jobs (e.g., social ties with co-workers, tangible recognition in the form of a paycheck, production measured against a quota), while certain problems created by employment (e.g., close supervision, fragmentation of the work, anonymity) are complemented by aspects of housework (e.g., autonomy, an undivided work process, close personal relations).[31] Neither form of work appears as the sole villain in women's double day; neither constitutes a morally prior responsibility. Instead, these women are clearly interested in transcending a one-sided existence, even at the cost of assuming additional burdens.

But there are also contradictions between the two types of work. First, combining the two generates problems due to the sheer amount of work— the familiar problems of the "double day." Becker-Schmidt and her co-workers identify less obvious problems as well. For example, that housework and paid work are qualitatively different types of work is in itself stressful; combining the two forces women to shift gears psychologically. While the workplace is organized on the principle that time is money, work in the home requires one to spend time freely and respond to the needs of the moment. Thus, despite the severe time pressure in their overall workday, these employed women generally found it necessary to create a period of time when they returned from the factory before they faced the different sort of demands of children and housework, and vice versa. Second, the particular capacities and skills that women develop in each type of labor are often devalued or ignored by those for whom they work in their other life. This is experienced as a personal insult. In sum, these women discover specific costs in trying to move between two types of work and two types of relationship, even while they find it personally rewarding in other ways.[32]

CONCLUSIONS

The research reviewed here has several major implications for the study of women and work. One contribution is that it moves conceptualizations of housework and paid work out of the traditional mold of "either/or" to a consideration of the advantages and costs of "both/and" even for working-class women.[33] Although many feminist proposals for changes in social policy have acknowledged and affirmed the dual nature of women's work, much American scholarship implicitly accepts the standards of the market economy in evaluating the meaning of women's work. The idea that the value of housework can be enhanced by subsuming it within a cash nexus is only one example of the ways in which the criteria of capitalism are incorporated in even radical analyses. Other aspects of such production-centered analyses include seeing the family as merely the producer of commodity labor power, considering exchange and bargaining the fundamental way of conducting human relationships, and defining socialization as merely a process of induced conformity to social expectations. Families also produce human beings who are self-aware subjects and who possess a range of largely untested potential; human relationships can also be based on unalienated care-taking and care-giving; socialization is also the process of discovering the individual self in the face of social demands. Just as the dominance and exploitation that occur within families are properly exposed by the contrasts that emerge when women participate in workplace relations, so the dominance and exploitation of paid jobs are properly critiqued by standards of relationships formed in families.

According to these German researchers, working-class women are well aware of the negative aspects of their employment, but they do not translate this awareness into a desire to return to a life as a full-time housewife, farmer, or upaid family worker—use-value occupations many of them have directly experienced. The researchers are careful not to romanticize use-value production, intimate ties, and working-class community, and therefore transcend the dualistic stereotypes of "femininity versus feminism" that animate much contemporary debate. When paid work and housework are both examined critically, they emerge as different, but neither separate nor equal, modes of social relationship that carry distinct meanings. To be true to women's experience, scholars must recognize both the values and the costs of each. This suggests that when a theoretical or political focus on the rewards to be gained in either type of work obscures the rewards renounced in the other, the resolutions suggested will necessarily be insufficient and temporary.

Recognizing the qualitative differences between housework and family relations, on the one hand, and paid work and labor relations, on the other, makes possible a dialectical approach to women's experiences. By trying to serve two masters, patriarchy and capitalism, women try to escape the total domination of either one. But in this process new contradictions emerge that cannot be resolved without changes in both structures. Thus, neither patriarchy nor capitalism can be seen as either the root of or the route out of oppression without doing violence to the reality of working-class women's lives. Patriarchal assumptions are embedded in the structure of capitalism, and capitalist principles have come to shape the structure of families, but this is only half the picture. Capitalism also makes resistance to patriarchy possible, and patriarchy provides opportunities for resisting capitalism. Both freedom and oppression are inextricably mixed in both family and factory, and women's interests lie in refusing to be confined to either.

One special merit of the German studies is that they suggest why and how women's individual struggles with the contradictions of housework and of paid work result in locking women ever more tightly in the grip of patriarchy and capitalism. Women who seek to mitigate the strain of participating in two different work systems organized on two different sets of principles often seek out marginal positions—part-time work, structurally segregated use-value jobs, temporary employment—and then find that these alternatives are economically penalized. Yet to give up their interest in such alternatives would be to accept the very norms and values of capitalism that penalize them, just as giving up all interest in paid employment would be an accommodation to patriarchy. Some women do the former, some the latter; some resist both general concessions and make individual compromises. Part-time work illustrates this trap; evidence suggests that many women seek such work and see rewards in it even though they are also aware of the costs imposed.[34] Although these women's actions embody individual resistance to confinement in a single role, together these individual efforts to resist do nothing to relieve women's collective oppression—indeed, such efforts perpetuate their marginalization.

A second virtue of this research is that it combines close examination of the institutions and social relations that shape women's experiences with an extensive exploration of how working-class women themselves understand these structures. Each study is designed to take women as active subjects struggling to realize their interests; at the same time the research acknowledges the real constraints imposed on women and the ways in which these constraints influence women's understanding of their situation. In this sense, these studies provide four concrete and quite different examples of feminist methodology and suggest what an empirical sociology for women, to use Dorothy Smith's phrase, can offer.[35]

While middle-class professional women are relatively insulated from the costs capitalism imposes, as are working-class men from the costs of patriarchy, working-class women experience and must come to terms with both. Of course some insulation is hardly immunity; capitalism imposes costs on professional women as well. Although such women—and scholars are among them—are offered more rewards and so have more incentive to deny the real difficulties inherent in their work conditions, they can and sometimes do recognize these contradictions in their own experience and admit their own ambivalence about their work and home commitments. In this regard, professional women have a great deal to learn from working-class women. By giving voice to working-class women's experiences and by refusing presumptions of middle-class superiority, these West German sociologists have made a crucial contribution.

NOTES

I would like to thank Elisabeth Beck-Gernsheim, Regina Becker-Schmidt, Angelika Diezinger, Christel Eckart, Lerke Gravenhorst, Axeli Knapp, Helgard Kramer, Lothar Lappe, and Ilona Ostner for their hospitality and intellectual help as I worked through the implications of this material; Christine Bose, Valerie Carter, Roslyn Feldberg, Josef Gugler, Joan Huber, Pamela Roby, and Jane Wilkie for their constructive suggestions; the Zentralarchiv für empirische Sozialforschung for office space and assistance; and the Woodrow Wilson Faculty Development Fund, the German Academic Exchange Service, and the Connecticut Research Foundation, whose financial support made this work possible. This article was first presented at the American Sociological Association annual meeting in San Antonio, Texas, August 1984.

1. The category "working-class women" is not easy to identify. Any dichotomy based on male jobs (middle class/working class, professional/nonprofessional, white collar/blue collar) inevitably distorts by ignoring gender stratification in the labor force, while gender-based distinctions (female sex-typed/male sex-typed; traditional/ nontraditional) also ignore real differences in income, autonomy, and authority within each group. I use the term "working-class women" inclusively to refer to women whose jobs do not offer the rewards associated with male sex-typed white-collar work.

2. Deutscher Gewerkschaftsbund, Abteilung Frauen, Düsseldorf, *Frauenarbeit 1977– 80*, p. 27, states that 49.7 percent of German women aged fifteen to sixty-five were in the labor force in 1979; this compares with 50.8 percent of women sixteen and over in the United states in 1979 and 52 percent in 1982 (U.S. Department of Labor, *Employment in Perspective: Working Women*, Report 665, First Quarter, 1982 [Washington, D.C.: Government Printing Office, 1982]).

3. Brigitte Nauhaus, *Probleme der Frauenarbeitslosigkeit in der gegenwärtigen Krise* (Cologne: Pahl-Rugenstein Verlag, 1979), p. 4.

4. U.S. Department of Labor, *Women in the Labor Force: Some New Data Series*, Report 575, October 1979 (Washington, D.C.: Government Printing Office, 1979), p. 1.

5. Mechtild Brothun's study of women's work commitment fits into the American role-conflict framework (*Bedeutung der Berufstätigkeit von Frauen: Konfliktmanagement in komplexen Rollenkonfigurationen*, Forschungsbericht 2618 des Landes Nordrhein-Westfalen [Opladen: Westdeutscher Verlag, 1977]). Although there are significant American contributions to the development of a critical theory of women's work, most American empirical research that considers the joint effect of class and gender has been historical rather than sociological. See Pamela Roby, *Women in the Workplace: Proposals for Research and Policy concerning the Conditions of Women in Industrial and Service Jobs* (Cambridge, Mass.: Schenkman Publishing Co., 1981). A collection edited by Karen Sacks and Dorothy Remy brings together scholarship on working-class women and their jobs done from a critical perspective (*My Troubles Are Going to Have Trouble with Me* [New Brunswick, N.J.: Rutgers University Press, 1984]),

and Sally Hillsman Baker, "Women in Blue Collar and Service Occupations" (in *Women Working: Theories and Facts in Perspective*, ed. Ann Stromberg and Shirley Harkess [Palo Alto, Calif.: Mayfield Publishing Co., 1978], pp. 339–76) offers an overview of the empirical literature. See also Shirley Harkess, "Women's Occupational Experiences in the 1970s: Sociology and Economics," in this issue.

6. Whether all the sociologists whose work is discussed here can be described as feminist depends on one's definition of feminism. All incorporate feminist theory significantly in their research. I exclude East German research primarily because of differences in the work conditions and status of women in the German Democratic Republic. See Harry Shaffer, *Women in the Two Germanies: A Comparison of a Socialist and a Non-Socialist Society* (New York: Pergamon Press, 1981).

7. But see Ellen Rosen, "Between a Rock and a Hard Place" (paper delivered at the American Sociological Association annual meeting, Toronto, August 1981); Mary L. Walshok, *Blue Collar Women: Pioneers on a Male Frontier* (New York: Doubleday & Co., 1981); Sharon Harlan and Brigid O'Farrell, "Craftworkers and Clerks: The Effect of Male Co-Worker Hostility on Women's Satisfaction with Nontraditional Jobs," *Social Problems* 29, no 3 (February 1982): 252–65; Kathleen McCourt, *Working Class Women and Grass-Roots Politics* (Bloomington: Indiana University Press, 1977); Thomas Nowak and Kay Snyder, "Job Loss, Marital Happiness and Household Tension: Do Women Fare Better than Men?" (paper delivered at the Society for the Study of Social Problems annual meeting, San Antonio, August 1984); Kay Deaux and Joseph Ullman, *Women of Steel: Female Blue Collar Workers in the Basic Steel Industry* (New York: Praeger Publishers, 1983).

8. Susan Harding, e.g., contrasts the "egalitarian family strategy" of the middle class with the "hierarchical" strategy of the working class ("Family Reform Movements: Recent Feminism and Its Opposition," *Feminist Studies 7*, no. 1 [Winter 1981]: 57–76). Whether the middle class is really more egalitarian is debatable, as I argue in "Sacrifice, Satisfaction and Social Change," in Saks and Remy, eds. (n. 5 above); a shorter version appears as "The View from Below: Women's Employment and Gender Equality in Working Class Families," *Marriage and Family Review 7*, nos. 3–4 (Fall/Winter 1984): 57–75.

9. But see Harold Benenson's critique: "Women's Occupational and Family Achievement in the U.S. Class System: A Critique of the Dual-Career Family Analysis," *British Journal of Sociology 35*, no. 1 (March 1984): 19–41. Other American articles that challenge the prevailing perspectives are Lillian Rubin, "Why Should Women Work?" (University of California, Berkeley, Center for Study, Education, and Advancement of Women, 1981); Roslyn Feldberg and Evelyn Nakano Glenn, "Male and Female: Job vs. Gender Models in the Sociology of Work," *Social Problems* 26, no. 5 (June 1978): 524–38; Alice Kessler-Harris, "Review Essay: Women's Wage Work as Myth and History," *Labor History* 19, no. 2 (Spring 1978): 287–97.

10. But see Rubin; Myra Marx Ferree, "Working Class Jobs: Housework and Paid Work as Sources of Satisfaction," *Social Problems* 23, no. 4 (April 1976): 431–41, and "Working Class Feminism: A Consideration of the Consequences of Employment," *Sociological Quarterly* 21, no. 2 (Spring 1980): 173–84.

11. When this perspective, which parallels the anthropological view of the urban poor in the Third World, is brought to bear on working-class women in the United States, it is often by anthropologists. See Sacks and Remy, eds.

12. Elisabeth Beck-Gernsheim, *Der geschlechtsspezifische Arbeitsmarkt: Zur Ideologie und Realität von Frauenberufen* (Frankfurt am Main: Campus Verlag, 1981), and *Das halbierte Leben* (Frankfurt am Main: Fischer Taschenbuch Verlag, 1980); Beck-Gernsheim and Ilona Ostner, "Frauen verändern—Berufe nicht?" *Soziale Welt* 29 (1978): 257–87.

13. Historical evidence suggests that development of a capitalist earning ethic among men was a difficult and multigenerational process (Steven Dubnoff, "Gender, the Family and the Problem of Work Motivation in a Transition to Industrial Capitalism," *Journal of Family History* 4, no. 2 [Summer 1979]: 121–36). Beck-Gernsheim suggests that even today women remain marginal and are therefore more able to critique and reject the primacy of earnings in determining the value of a job. She also indicates that employers may exploit this orientation to block workers' organizing efforts. See also Hannah Creighton, "Tied by Double Apron Strings: Female Work Culture and Organization in a Restaurant," *Insurgent Sociologist* 11, no. 3 (Fall 1982): 59–64. Carole Turbin points out that the personal ties that may hinder initial organizing may later serve to sustain militancy ("Reconceptualizing Family, Work, and Labor Organizing: Working Women in Troy, 1860–1890," *Review of Radical Political Economics* 16, no. 1 [Summer 1984]: 1–16).

14. Ilona Ostner, *Beruf und Hausarbeit: Die Arbeit der Frau in unserer Gesellschaft* (Frankfurt am Main: Campus Verlag, 1978).

15. Ilona Ostner and Elisabeth Beck-Gernsheim, *Mitmenschlichkeit als Beruf* (Frankfurt am Main: Campus Verlag, 1979).

16. See, e.g., Beck-Gernsheim, *Das halbierte Leben*, pp. 9–10.

17. Christel Eckart, Ursula Jaerisch, and Helgard Kramer, *Frauenarbeit in Familie und Fabrik* (Frankfurt am Main: Forschungsbericht des Instituts für Sozialforschung, 1979). See also C. Eckart and H. Kramer, "Der Einfluss der Arbeit in der Familie auf die Möglichkeiten der Interessenwahrnehmung von Frauen in der Fabrik," *Beiträge zur Arbeitsmarkt- und Berufsforschung* 53 (Nuremberg: Institut für Arbeitsmarkt- und Berufsforschung, 1981), pp. 117–32; and Christel Eckart, "Arbeit als Interaktion" (paper presented at a conference on vocational education, Bremen, 1981).

18. One limitation of the studies reviewed here is that their subjects are ethnic Germans, even though the German labor force includes a substantial proportion of so-called *Gastarbeiter* of various nationalities. One estimate places the proportion of women wage earners who are of foreign nationality at 8 percent (Deutscher Ge-werkschaftsbund, *Frauenarbeit 1977–80*, pp. 31–32). Eckart et al. describe the factories from which their sample was drawn as employing 12–60 percent non-German women. From an American perspective the exclusion of the foreign-born women workers is an obvious shortcoming of these studies.

19. In fact many had once aspired to the sorts of female jobs Beck-Gernsheim and Ostner describe but had not been able to fulfill these aspirations. A study of unemployed teenage girls shows how the "its's just a job" orientation can be developed in the process of a job search, as working-class girls' desire for training and for an income that would make independence possible is repeatedly frustrated (R. Marquardt, A. Dietzinger, K. Dahlke, and H. Bilden, "Jugendarbeitslosigkeit und weibliche Normalbiografie" (research report, Munich, 1980, mimeographed); H. Bilden, A. Dietzinger, R. Marquardt, and K. Dahlke. "Arbeitslose junge Mädchen," *Zeitschrift für Pädagogik* 27, no. 5 [1981]: 677–95).

20. Eckart et al., p. 231.

21. That analysis by Eckart et al. of women's interest in housework, which incorporates women's resistance to capitalism, provides a counter to assumptions that the extent to which women remain responsible for housework is a direct indicator of the weight of patriarchy. Compare Heidi Hartmann, who ignores any interest women may have in keeping production home ("The Family as the Locus of Gender, Class, and Political Struggle: The Example of Housework, "*Signs: Journal of Women in Culture and Society* 6, no. 3 [Spring 1981]: 366–94). Recognizing the qualitatively different nature of paid work and housework, realizing women's interest in both, and

acknowledging how women are actively confronting the incompatible demands of these two systems are crucial steps for those concerned with the political mobilization of women (Eckart et al., pp. 188, 213–14, 363, 396–98). Some researchers argue that political programs, such as paid maternity leaves, that address these dual aspirations encourage women to see themselves as lifetime workers. See, e.g., Gisela Erler, Monika Jaekel, and Jürgen Sass, *International vergleichende Studie: Anpassungsprobleme zwischen Familie und Arbeitswelt* (Munich: Deutsches Jugendinstitut, 1982).

22. In West Germany and the United States the debate is sharpened both by governmental ideological support for "traditional" families and by a continuing high unemployment rate, which is often publicly blamed on women's employment.

23. In contrast, few assume that working-class men's higher job dissatisfaction predicts that they, more than middle-class men, are willing to assume responsibility for housework. The one-dimensional model also ignores the extent to which the use-value ethic of housework is also embedded within women's paid jobs. As Eckart et al. (pp. 55–56) and Ostner and Beck-Gernsheim explicitly argue, it is because of the market's sexual division of labor that the paid-work orientations of women are not inherently contradictory to a family-centered orientation.

24. Lothar Lappe, *Die Arbeitssituation erwerbstätiger Frauen: Geschlechtsspezifische Arbeitsmarktsegmentation und ihre Folgen* (Frankfurt am Main: Campus Verlag, 1981); Ilona Schöll-Schwinghammer, *Frauen im Betrieb: Arbeitsbedingungen und Arbeitsbewusstsein* (Frankfurt am Main: Campus Verlag, 1979).

25. On this point, see also Ruth Cavendish's study of a British auto parts factory (*Women on the Line* [Boston: Routledge & Kegan Paul, 1982]).

26. Nonetheless, 64 percent of the employed women with the greatest burden of work at home said that they preferred to be employed, and 32 percent thought they had a better life in general than did full-time housewives.

27. See Regina Becker-Schmidt, "Widersprüchliche Realität und Ambivalenz: Arbeitserfahrungen von Frauen in Fabrik und Familie," *Kölner Zeitschrift für Soziologie und Sozialpsychologie* 32 (1980): 705–25, "Entfremdete Aneignung—gestörte Anerkennung: Enteignungs- und Lernprozesse im Lebenszusammenhang erwerbstätiger Frauen" (Vortrag am 21. deutschen Soziologentag, Bamberg, October 1982); Regina Becker-Schmidt, Gudrun-Axeli Knapp, and Mechtild Rumpf, "Frauenarbeit in der Fabrik—Betriebliche Sozialisation als Lernprozess? Über die subjektive Bedeutung der Fabrikarbeit im Kontrast zur Hausarbeit," in *Beiträge zur Marxschen Theorie 14*, ed. H.-G. Backhaus et al. (Frankfurt am Main: Suhrkamp Verlag, 1981), pp. 52–74; R. Becker-Schmidt, Uta Brandes-Erlhoff, Ilse Lühring, and Beate Schmidt, "Familienarbeit im proletarischen Lebenszusammenhang: Was es heisst, Hausfrau zu sein," in Backhaus et al., eds., pp. 75–96; R. Becker-Schmidt, U. Brandes-Erlhoff, Marva Karrer, G.-A. Knapp, M. Rumpf, and B. Schmidt, *Nicht wir haben die Minuten, die Minuten haben uns: Zeitprobleme und Zeiterfahrungen von Arbeitermüttern in Fabrik und Familie* (Bonn: Verlag Neue Gesellschaft, 1982); R. Becker-Schmidt, U. Brandes-Erlhoff, M. Rumpf und B. Schmidt, *Arbeitsleben—Lebensarbeit: Ambivalenzkonflikte und Widerspruchserfahrungen von Fabrikarbeiterinnen* (Bonn: Verlag Neue Gesellschaft, 1983); R. Becker-Schmidt, G.-A. Knapp, and Beate Schmidt, *Eines ist zu wenig—Beides ist zu viel* (Bonn: Verlag Neue Gesellschaft, 1984).

28. From this theoretical perspective, an unqualified commitment to paid work is a deficiency, as it precludes valuing other positive aspects of life.

29. This perspective implicitly suggests a different approch to the analysis of survey data, one that would seek to identify holders of opinions that are inconsistent in terms of formal logic but make sense of an objectively inconsistent reality.

30. Time constraints are a much more difficult problem for West German women than for American women. Schools are half day, and stores keep short hours. The

scheduling problems this creates, especially for employed women, must be taken into account when comparing the level of social support for women's employment in the two countries.

31. While the Becker-Schmidt team does not pursue this issue in depth, their analysis would suggest that the aspects of housework experienced as rewarding by professional women might be in part quite different than those favored by working-class women. A scholar might find physical labor at home almost restful, while a factory worker surely would not.

32. Awareness of contradictions and their implications for subjective experience helps to direct research attention to issues such as the qualitatively different structure and meaning of time spent in housework and in other forms of subsistence production compared with time spent in paid work. See, e.g., Becker-Schmidt et al., *Nicht wir haben die Minuten* (n. 27 above); Heide Inhetveen, "Schöne Zeiten, schlimme Zeiten: Zeit, Geschichte, Biografien von Bäuerinnen," *Feministische Studien* 1, no. 1 (Fall 1982): 33–48; Ostner (n. 14 above), chap. 3. Other studies look at time from a life-course perspective (e.g., Ute Gerhard-Teuscher, "Aus aktuellem Anlass: Über Frauen-arbeitslosigkeit oder 'Wenn uns die Zeit unter den Füssen brennt,'" *Feministische Studien* 1, no. 1 [Fall 1982]: 127–36).

33. A widely cited example of the either/or approach is James Wright, "Are Working Women Really More Satisfied? Evidence from Several National Surveys," *Journal of Marriage and the Family* 40, no. 2 (May 1978): 301–14. See also my critique "Class, Housework, and Happiness," *Sex Roles* 11, no. 11/12 (December 1984): 1057–74.

34. Christel Eckart argues this point explicitly in "Die Teilzeitarbeit von Frauen: Eine prekäre Strategie gegen Einseitigkeit und Doppelbelastung," *Feministische Studien* 1, no. 1 (Fall 1982): 19–32. In contrast, Vicki Smith ("Women's Work Is Here to Stay: The Politics of Part-Time Employment" [paper presented at the conference "Women and Work in the 80's: Perspectives from the 1930s and 1940s," University of California, Berkeley, 1981]) describes the real costs of part-time work opportunities. Since most German unions are adamantly opposed to the expansion of part-time work, German feminists have more incentive to scrutinize carefully both its costs and its benefits.

35. Dorothy Smith ("A Sociology for Women," in *The Prism of Sex*, ed. Julia Sherman and Evelyn T. Beck [Madison: University of Wisconsin Press, 1979], pp. 135–87) speaks to the issue of connecting women's everyday experience to the macrosociological relationships that give it its particular form. She also makes several other theoretical points closely related to those raised here.

8

Women and Suicide in Historical Perspective

HOWARD I. KUSHNER

Kushner challenges and contradicts the widespread claim that there is a difference in the suicidal behavior of the two sexes. His analysis focuses on the meanings different people attach to suicide—those of the individual woman or man who attempts or commits suicide, those of the people who interpret the suicide's behavior, and those that are available in the larger culture. Thus Kushner's reanalysis illustrates the hermeneutic dimension in this body of research at several different levels: What appears at first glance to be an objective phenomena—one either does or does not attempt to commit suicide—is, after all, a matter of interpretation; and what appears to be a sex difference in the suicide rates of the genders reflects not only differences in interpretation but also sex-related differences in methods available for ending one's own life.

"Women," wrote William Knighton in 1881, "cling to life much more strongly than [do] men." In his widely republished article entitled "Suicidal

Reprinted from *Signs: Journal of Women in Culture and Society*, Vol. 10, No. 3, 1985:537–552. Copyright © 1985 by The University of Chicago. Used by permission of the author and The University of Chicago.

Mania," Knighton suggested that "religious restraints" and the possession of "a larger measure of that hope which springs eternal in the human breast" accounted for the fact that women "were less prone to commit suicide . . . than men."[1] Almost a century later, Louis Dublin concluded that "suicide . . . may be called a masculine type of behavior."[2]

Since the nineteenth century, investigators relying on official statistics have reported that men are much more likely to kill themselves than women are. In this article I will challenge that conclusion, suggesting instead that the portrayal of suicide as a male behavior tells us more about the assumptions that inform the collection of official statistics than it does about the conduct of women. I will review the statistical basis for the supposedly gender-specific nature of suicides commited in the United States and suggest that experts' focus on completed or "successful" suicides tends to distort our understanding of the suicides of women. I give an alternative explanation for the reported disparity between male and female rates of suicide completion, while exploring the broader social and economic implications involved in the continued assumption that women are less suicidal than men.

EPIDEMIOLOGY

Nineteenth-century statistics, both in the United States and Europe, suggest that women accounted for a very small percentage of completed or successful suicides. Crude rates for both Western European countries and the United States indicated that only one out of every four successful suicides was a woman.[3] Although official statistics, especially census returns, have been criticized for their inconsistencies and misrepresentations,[4] regional and local analyses have confirmed the official data.

For instance, a project to reconstitute the number of suicides in San Diego County over the past century from coroner's reports, death certificates, and newspaper accounts found that the ratio of women's successful suicides to men's was even lower than that reported in federal census returns.[5] Roger Lane's study of Philadelphia confirms and parallels the San Diego results.[6]

Interestingly, these studies have uncovered a consistent increase in suicide rates for women over the past hundred years. In 1880 women accounted for 12.8 percent of all completed suicides in San Diego County, even though they made up about one-half of the population. This percentage grew by approximately 10 percent of its base per decade. Thus, by 1970 women accounted for 37.6 percent of all suicides in San Diego County (table 1). In a century the rate had more than doubled for women from 6.7 per 100,000 (1880–1900) to 14.4 per 100,000 (1967–72). Roger Lane's Philadelphia study notes a similar trend. In the 1870s the suicide rate for white women in Philadelphia was 2 per 100,000. A century later, the rate reached 10.8 per 100,000—an increase of 540 percent.[7]

Nationally, this rise is reflected by a narrowing gap between male and female suicides over the past hundred years.[8] Researchers studying Alberta, Canada, have arrived at similar conclusions.[9] But while the differential between

TABLE 1
Suicides by Gender, San Diego County, 1880-1972 (%)

	1880–1900 (N = 148)	*1911–25* (N = 484)	*1938–42* (N = 207)	*1948–52* (N = 262)	*1967–72* (N = 1,294)
Men	87.2	85.0	75.4	74.4	62.4
Women	12.8	15.0	24.6	25.6	37.6

Source: San Diego County, California, Coroner's Reports, 1880–1972; Anita M. Muhl, "America's Greatest Suicide Problem: A Study of Over 500 Cases in San Diego," *Psychoanalytic Review* 14 (1927): 317–25, esp. 320; Aubrey Wendling, "Suicides in the City of San Diego, 1938–1942, 1948–1952" (San Diego State University, Department of Sociology, n.d.).

the numbers of men and women committing suicide has diminished, official statistics continue to report a much higher rate for men. In fact, no study has uncovered a greater incidence of suicide completion for women than for men in either the United States or Europe.

EXPLANATIONS

In the United States national mortality figures were first collected in the 1850 census, which was released in 1855.[10] However, before any substantial national data on the incidence of suicide were compiled or made public, experts had already assumed that motivations for suicide were gender specific. In a widely reprinted 1846 article, the *Whig Review* claimed that "in men, real or fancied impotence is very apt to induce self-destruction;—and among women, we cannot help always suspecting the dread of the consequences of secret loss of honor."[11]

By the mid-nineteenth century characterizations of women's suicides meshed with the ideology described by Barbara Welter as that of "True Womanhood, by which a woman judged herself and was judged by her husband, her neighbors, and society." Adherence to the virtues of "piety, purity, submissiveness and domesticity" translated into the belief that "a 'fallen woman' was a 'fallen angel,' unworthy of the celestial company of her sex." Loss of purity, according to the periodical press, "brought madness or death." And these dominant values, Welter argued, portrayed "Death Preferable to Loss of Innocence."[12]

Popular fiction reinforced this ideology. Toward the end of Nathaniel Hawthorne's *The Blithedale Romance,* the old yankee, Silas Foster, finally realizes what becomes obvious to readers in the previous chapter when they learn that Zenobia has been spurned by her lover Hollingsworth: "'And so you think she's drowned herself?' he cried. 'What on earth should the young woman do that for?' exclaimed Silas, his eyes half out of his head with mere surprise. 'Why, she has more means than she can use or waste, and lacks nothing to make her comfortable, but a husband.'"[13] Nineteenth-century fiction is littered with the corpses of such women. Whether it was Zenobia, Emma in Flaubert's *Madame Bovary* (1857), Anna in Tolstoi's *Anna Karenina* (1875), or Lili Bart in Wharton's *The House of Mirth* (1905), the cause was always the same: rejection after an illicit love affair led a despairing female to the only honorable (and predictable) resolution—self-murder.

Literary conventions aside—and this was, of course, a literary convention—the scenario gained credence from its similarity to nineteenth-century American newspaper articles about suicide by women. A hundred years ago the American press reported the details and backgrounds of most suicides in a manner that is uncommon today. For instance, in January 1890 the story of "A Depressive Girl's Suicide" headlined newspapers from coast to coast. A San Francisco newspaper read: "Gabrielle Oberbauer, a talented young crayon artist, shot herself, dead to-day in her apartment at 210 East Eighty-first street where her brother also lived. These two had become alienated from the other members of the family. Gabrielle had recently learned that William Brill, a wealthy glove manufacturer, who had been paying her marked attention, was about to marry another woman. This made her despondent and led to her suicide. Brill could not be seen today."[14]

Analysts based explanations of official statistics concerning women's lower suicide rates on the supposed differences between male and female motives. "In regard to sex," reported the *New York Times* in 1861, "only about one-fourth of the whole number [of suicides] were women . . . [even] though by the last census there is an excess of females over males . . . in New York." The newspaper went on to suggest that the even lower ratios for American women than for their European counterparts was due, in part, to "the greater facility of divorce" in the United States, since "a large proportion of female suicides attribute their act to domestic unhappiness." "Besides," explained the *Times*, "it is a well known fact that women possess greater courage and patience under misfortune than men, and less readily give way to despair and the vices consequent upon it."[15]

These views together formed a concept of female suicide as an individual emotional act, while male suicide rates were taken as a barometer of national economic and social well-being. Nineteenth-century experts like Albert Rhodes, relying on federal census returns, tied suicide by a woman to "her sexual organization." Rhodes explained the suicide differential this way: "The woman's mode of death is usually less violent. Copious weeping relieves the woman, and often saves her, while this relief is denied to man. Besides, when the hour for the act comes, her courage is apt to fail." When women commit suicide, Rhodes asserted, they do so for very different motives from those of men: "Women appear to be more subject to moral influences, such as disappointed love, betrayal, desertion, jealousy, domestic trouble, and sentimental exaltation of every description." Men, on the other hand, "are rather affected by trials of a material order, such as misery, business embarrassments, losses, ungratified ambition, the abuse of alcohol, the desire to escape from justice, and so on."[16]

Twentieth-century experts who have attempted to explain the reasons for the alleged sex-specific disparity in the suicide rate have simply made an interesting twist in the polarities implicit in nineteenth-century novels and newspaper reports. Dublin, who notes that "at every age period many more men than women kill themselves," suggests that suicide by women results from "maladjustment." Those women who commit suicide, Dublin asserts, must have experienced a "marked increase in . . . schooling and employment. . . . Greater economic and social independence . . . played a role." The therapeutic implications of his study are that to ensure mental health women should avoid such masculine activities as schooling and paid employment.[17]

A leading British suicidologist, Peter Sainsbury, explains the gender differential this way: "When the biological and social roles of the two sexes are compared, the female role appears more precisely, and her biological and social functions more harmonized." Males, on the other hand, are "less restricted by social conformity" and are encouraged to be individualistic and aggressive. A man is responsible "for [the] support and welfare of his family," and as a result, "he is more subject to the stresses of mobility and change." Thus, the "male's more arduous social role" explains "the marked liability of the male" for suicide as opposed to females.[18] Such analysis restates the belief that women are happier and more adjusted in their (easier) domestic roles than are men who bear the heavier social burden; indeed, when a woman kills herself, it is because she has attempted to act like a man!

The prestigious American Public Health Association's *Mental Disorders/ Suicide* quotes the Sainsbury analysis at length and endorses it, although the authors wonder, almost as an aside, why the rates differ so greatly between the genders "since women are exposed to some of the same factors" as men—for instance, social isolation, lack of employment, and loss of status.[19] Richard Davis's recent essay affirms its predecessors, concluding that "the greater the female labor force participation . . . the greater the rate of suicide."[20]

Thus, the dominant explanations for the lower incidence of suicide among women suggest that male suicide results from the stresses inherent in men's roles and responsibilities, while female suicide occurs when women deviate from their less conflicted roles and status. Those women who kill themselves after a man deserts them do so, according to these analyses, because they can no longer fulfill their social functions as mothers and wives.

Kathryn Johnson's "Durkheim Revisited" is the only study that does not tie lower suicide rates for women to their allegedly less stressful situation. Johnson agrees that "compared to men, women do not appear to have a great 'suicide problem.'" Noting that women historically "participate differently from men" in what Durkheim called "collective life," Johnson endorses the arguments of those who see women inhabiting "different social worlds" from men. She finds, however, that "married employed women have lower suicide rates than unemployed housewives," and suggests that the highest suicide rates are found among those women who are the most submerged in the family.[21] Yet since most women historically have inhabited the "social sphere" of the family, we would expect a much greater incidence of suicide among women than Johnson describes. Indeed, if she were correct, we might anticipate a declining rate for women as social and economic barriers begin to fall, while the opposite appears to be true. Although I do not necessarily disagree with Johnson's conclusions, I think her logic is tortured by her acceptance of the allegedly higher male suicide rate as fact when it is actually an assumption—one that the rest of this article will challenge.

ATTEMPTED VERSUS COMPLETED SUICIDES

All explanations, whether sexist or feminist in their assumptions, attempt to offer reasons for the apparently gender-specific nature of the suicide rate. In short, what is sought ultimately are the causes that lead individuals to take their own lives. For a variety of reasons, suicide studies tend to focus on the rates of successful or completed suicides.

Although we can never know for certain the extent of attempted suicide, most experts agree that for every one completed suicide there are six to eight attempts.[22] They indicate that women attempt suicide at a rate approximately 2.3 times greater than do men. On the other hand, men demonstrate the opposite trend; they complete suicide at a rate 2.3 times greater than women.[23] If the numbers of those attempting and completing suicide are added together, the rate differential between genders collapses.

Those who attempt suicide have not been included in most studies primarily because they are not recorded in official records. Researchers prefer to rely on tabulated statistics that can be measured, compared, and grouped in quantifiable categories.[24] Moreover, some sociologists defend this exclusion, claiming that "completers" and "attempters" are substantially distinct from one another. Ronald Maris, for instance, argues that these differences justify, if not demand, research that considers them separate groups. In particular, Maris focuses on the difference in intentions, asserting that attempters expect to be discovered and saved, while completers are less likely to place themselves in a position that allows for intervention in their actions.[25]

Even if Maris is correct, the procedures by which official suicide statistics are collected make no provision for differences in intent. In reality, experts who rely on successful suicide rates examine only outcome and not motive. Coroners, physicians, and others responsible for determining whether a particular death was a suicide are, moreover, already tied to an ideology that differentiates women's motives from men's. Such preconceptions are bound to influence collection of official statistics. Ironically, the very assumptions that inform judgments about individual suicides are presented as causes for the variations that are uncovered among them. A few nineteenth-century examples of this contradiction (chosen rather than current cases to avoid breach of confidentiality) help to demonstrate that suicide statistics cannot and do not measure individual intent.

There are many instances of persons who intend to kill themselves, but who, by chance, survive. Because official statistics only measure results, these cases are not counted as suicides. The suicide attempt of Anne Brewster, a thirty-two-year-old San Diego school teacher, in 1898 is one among many cases that exemplify the nature of official definitions. There was little question that when Brewster took a room at the Commercial Hotel and fired a pistol at blank range into her temple she expected to die. But the outcome was different: "Immediately afterward Miss Brewster burst from the room, holding a handkerchief to her right temple. . . . Miss Brewster pointed to a note lying on the table and said, 'There are the directions, I have shot myself.' To Mrs. Birdsall, who was immediately called, Miss Brewster said, 'I am tired of life. I want to end it all. That's the only reason.'"[26]

Brewster's note was the type that experts such as Maris identify as those left by individuals who intend to die:[27] "It is my earnest wish that my body be taken to the morgue and dispensed of from there—and not taken to my address. I wish the least possible expense and trouble. No funeral. No services." Both physicians who examined her "agreed that the bullet was imbedded in the brain . . . and that the chances for recovery were very dubious." Nevertheless, Brewster did not die, and thus her suicide attempt was ignored by those who measure such events.[28]

Others die from complications of a botched attempt. A person may not succumb to an intentional drug overdose but die later of a cause, such as pneumonia, brought on by the attempt. Generally, neither the coroner's report nor the death certificate will define the death as a suicide, because no matter how much the person's behavior had set up a chain of events leading to death, suicide was not the death's immediate cause. This distinction has special significance for women because they are more than twice as likely as men to employ poisons or drugs in suicide attempts.[29]

Clara Dudley, a thirty-four-year-old proprietor of "a house of ill-repute," attempted to commit suicide in 1899 "by swallowing a quantity of morphine." Dudley, according to newspaper reports, had "made previous attempts to commit suicide, having on one occasion, several months ago, inhaled gas. She was almost dead when the door of her room was burst open, and it was with the greatest of difficulty that she was brought back to life." In her latest try, reported the *San Diego Union*, Dudley lost consciousness, but according to her doctor, "she showed much improvement." Five days later Clara Dudley died of pneumonia brought on by her suicide attempt. Both the coroner's report and her death certificate list pneumonia as the cause of death. Officially, she and countless others like her are not recorded as suicides.[30]

Finally, official statistics cannot measure the difference between conscious and unconscious intentions. Who is to say that only conscious behavior constitutes a suicide? Dorcas Antle was a sixty-two-year-old widow who, only two months previously, had moved from Illinois to live with her son in Chula Vista, California. On April 21, 1895, Antle "took a dose of strychnine by mistake at 9 o'clock . . . and died in great agony twenty minutes later. She was in the habit of taking a sleeping powder upon retiring, but upon this occasion took a strychnine powder from the shelf and swallowed it." The county coroner ruled that the deceased died from "strychnine poisoning; the strychnine being administered by mistake." The coroner's evidence rested

on the deposition of Antle's son, a physician.[31] Of course, given the paucity
of available information, we cannot possibly determine whether Dorcas Antle
actually made an error. Nevertheless, as a recent widow and a new arrival
in California who suffered from insomnia, she fits the category of those at
high risk of taking their own lives.[32]

The case of Dorcas Antle raises another issue about the reporting of
suicide, especially as it relates to women. In this situation the coroner relied
on the testimony of Antle's son, a physician, to determine whether her
actions were suicidal or accidental. Children, even when they are physicians,
have a strong inclination to cover up a parent's suicide. Jack Douglas suggests,
moreover, that the impulse to gloss over the actual situation is endemic to
the reporting of suicide by women because "the meanings of male suicides
and of female suicides are different in Western societies." Social forces outside
the family, such as unemployment, are generally perceived as the cause of
men's suicides, while strains within the family are held responsible for
women's. When a woman commits suicide, Douglas argues, her husband has
"a much greater incentive . . . than a female in the same situation to attempt
to conceal the suicidal action."[33] The paradox is that although intention is
not reflected in or measured by official statistics experts use them to explain
motive. At best, these data tell us something about rates of suicide completion,
but they reveal nothing at all about intent.

However, if we combine completions and attempts, there is not now, nor
has there ever been so far as anyone can demonstrate, any gender-specific
difference in suicidal behavior. In fact, the evidence suggests that women
outnumber men in any final tabulation, because attempts are more frequent
than completions by as much as eight to one. And there seems to be no
substantial difference in behavior between many suicide attempts and those
suicides that official statistics report as completions. One cannot then argue,
as most of the literature does, that suicide is a male behavior.

LETHALITY OF METHOD

It may be that men are more often completers of suicide than women
because of differences between the sexes in suicide methods employed. Indeed,
lethality of method suggests itself as an area for further exploration. Existing
studies of the United States and Europe indicate that males choose more
lethal methods for suicide than females do.[34] In the United States the majority
of successful male suicides have employed firearms.[35] Such behavior also
shows historical consistency. In what must have been the first systematic
attempt to investigate suicide in the United States, E. K. Hunt found that
women chose less lethal methods than men. He reported that in 1843, 67.5
percent of male suicides selected highly lethal methods—using firearms,
cutting their throats, or hanging themselves—as compared with only 36.6
percent of successful women suicides. None of the women used firearms,
from which Hunt drew the conclusion that women have a "horror" toward
"the use of guns or pistols."[36]

The *American Journal of Insanity*'s analysis of the incidence of suicide in New York state in 1848 concluded "that females rarely have recourse to firearms . . . as a means of committing suicide. Hanging, drowning, and poisoning are the modes which they most frequently employ."[37] According to Rhodes's 1876 study, men who killed themselves showed "a tendency toward violent methods," while women selected "pacific" means for suicide. "Drowning and poisoning are the favorite modes of getting rid of life in the case of women," Rhodes found, and "throat-cutting, hanging, and shooting those of the men."[38]

A century later, Alan Marks and Thomas Abernathy still find "that female attempters and completers most often use drugs-poison while male completers most often use firearms."[39] In San Diego County approximately one-half of all successful male suicides for the past one hundred years have relied on firearms (table 2). National statistics reflect this same pattern.[40] In contrast, Hunt's 1843 study found that 63 percent of completed female suicides chose poisons.[41] The percentage of women who complete their suicides using firearms in San Diego County has varied, but it has remained well below the percentage who turn to poison. At the same time, studies of the nation as a whole find "an increasing proportion of women who are suiciding by firearms."[42]

Percentages can be misleading. To be convincing statistically, suicide completion rates should be compared to rates that measure the use of firearms per 100,000 of the living population. When this is done for San Diego County, the results are striking: over the last century, when the use of firearms by both men and women has increased, so has the rate of completed suicide (table 3). In San Diego County, at least, method rather than intention appears to separate male and female suicides, which suggests that studies dealing with suicidal motivation should not depend as heavily as they do on data that reflect only results and not intent.

"Method," argues Herbert Hendin, "cannot be understood without reference to the cultural context in which suicide occurs." In New York City, jumping from buildings accounts for 50 percent of suicides completed by blacks. "So much of the life of Harlem is lived in and on top of these tenements," writes Hendin, "that they occupy the conscious and unconscious life of their inhabitants and come to provide a tragic setting for black suicide."[43] He suggests that a similar analysis should be brought to bear on the relationship between firearms and female suicide completion. "The sociocultural acceptance of guns in the United States," Hendin believes, "is related to the frequency with which they are used for suicide."[44] This connection explains why men, whose use of firearms has greater social acceptance, generally are more likely than women to resort to guns. The exception that proves the rule is found in the American South. In that region, "where guns are most accepted as a part of the household," Marks and Abernathy find that "firearms are used by both sexes more frequently [for suicide completion] than in the rest of the country."[45] In European countries, such as Denmark, where suicide by firearms is far less frequent,

TABLE 2
Suicides by Method and Gender, San Diego County, 1880–1972 (%)

Method	1800–1900 Men (N = 129)	1800–1900 Women (N = 19)	1911–25 Men (N = 411)	1911–25 Women (N = 73)	1938–42 Men (N = 156)	1938–42 Women (N = 51)	1948–52 Men (N = 195)	1948–52 Women (N = 67)	1967–72 Men (N = 807)	1967–72 Women (N = 487)
Firearms	50.0	29.4	48.4	26.0	46.8	23.5	44.6	25.4	55.1	19.1
Poisons*	19.5	47.1	26.8	57.5	5.1	37.3	13.8	31.3	19.6	59.2
Hanging	10.9	0.0	8.3	12.3	12.2	9.8	15.9	13.4	8.8	6.8
Other	19.6	23.5	16.5	4.2	35.9	29.4	25.7	29.9	16.5	14.9

*Does not include asphyxiation by carbon monoxide but includes other gases.

Source: See table 1.

TABLE 3
Suicide Rates by Method and Gender, San Diego County, 1880–1972

Method	1800–1900 Men (N = 129)	1800–1900 Women (N = 19)	1911–25 Men (N = 411)	1911–25 Women (N = 73)	1938–42 Men (N = 156)	1938–42 Women (N = 51)	1948–52 Men (N = 195)	1948–52 Women (N = 67)	1967–72 Men (N = 807)	1967–72 Women (N = 487)
Firearms	21.3	1.9	32.6	3.1	17.3	3.0	13.4	2.8	13.1	2.7
All methods	42.5	6.7	67.3	12.0	36.5	12.6	29.8	10.7	23.8	14.4

Note: Rates are given per 100,000 population.

Source: See table 1.

men still complete suicide at about two to three times the rate of females. Moreover, throughout Europe without exception, men choose more lethal methods than women do and male use of firearms far exceeds that of women. Even in Denmark, where firearms are forbidden, 15 percent of male completers, as compared with 1 percent of females, used guns to kill themselves.[46]

These statistics should not obscure the main point: Although suicide methods influence rates of completion, "there is no relation between particular methods of suicide and suicide intent."[47] Differences in suicide completion rates between men and women are not derived from gender; rather they reflect the methods culturally and historically available to women. No student of history, particularly of women's history, should be surprised to learn that women have had less access to lethal technology than have men. To take this historic pattern as an indication of the emotional needs of women is to perform violence of a different sort. Moreover, limiting official statistics on suicide to completions ensures that suicidal behavior among women will be trivialized when compared with self-destruction among men.

CONCLUSION

The issues raised here go beyond setting the record straight. As long as suicide is seen as a male behavior, researchers will continue to locate its etiology in the "male sphere," with two general effects. First, the apparent fact of a gender-specific rate persuades clinicians and social scientists to continue to explain behavior in a sex-specific and pseudosociological framework. For these experts, the alleged maleness of suicide seems to suggest that the way for women to guarantee their own mental health and to avoid self-destruction is to accept traditional values, particularly those of the patriarchal family. The irony here, of course, is that the data indicate that "traditional values" have contributed to a much higher rate of attempted suicide by women than by men. This fact could be used to demonstrate that women are less content with their social condition than men are with theirs. Curiously, no suicide study has ever come to such a conclusion.

Second, viewing self-destruction as male behavior ensures that research on suicide will be conducted and funded in a manner that reinforces the assumptions described above. In a recent and well-publicized study, two labor economists, Morton Schapiro and Dennis Ahlburg, argued that "a 1% increase in the unemployment rate causes 318 more men to commit suicide a year in the United States." This government-funded, two-year project concluded that "the problem is most acute among men in the 15–34 age group who are faced with a tighter, more competitive job market. The study applies only to men," they said, "because they identify greater with their jobs than women."[48] Assumptions about who commits suicide led these researchers to ignore the impact of unemployment on women—indeed, to ignore women altogether in their investigation.

The study of suicide and suicidal behavior has implications that transcend the individual histories of those who take or attempt to take their own lives.

It provides another example of how allegedly objective social science research is influenced by experts' unconscious biases and unanalyzed assumptions. As long as researchers continue to focus on suicide as a male issue, not only will we know less about the causes of suicide but we will also continue to have a distorted view of social forces.

NOTES

Research for this article was supported in part by a grant-in-aid from the San Diego State University Foundation. I thank Kathleen Jones Bulmash and Carol R. Kushner for their comments and suggestions. Earlier versions of this essay were presented to "New Views on Women," San Diego State University, November 10, 1982; "Feminist Fortnight," Occidental College Women's Studies Program, Los Angeles, January 26, 1983; and the sixth annual scientific meeting of the International Society of Political Psychology, St. Catherines College, Oxford University, July 22, 1983.

1. William Knighton, "Suicidal Mania," *Littel's Living Age* (February 5, 1881), p. 430.

2. Louis I. Dublin, *Suicide: A Sociological and Statistical Study* (New York: Ronald Press, 1963), p. 23.

3. Ruth S. Cavan, *Suicide* (Chicago: University of Chicago Press, 1928), pp. 307–10.

4. Jack D. Douglas, *The Social Meanings of Suicide* (Princeton, N.J.: Princeton University Press, 1967), pp. 163–231.

5. Jay Mathews, "Darker Side of Sunny California: A High Suicide Rate under Study," *Washington Post* (December 26, 1981).

6. Roger Lane, *Violent Death in the City: Suicide, Accident, and Murder in Nineteenth-Century Philadelphia* (Cambridge, Mass.: Harvard University Press, 1979), p. 29.

7. Rates per 100,000 of the living population provide a more accurate indication of the extent of suicide in a given population than percentages. For San Diego rates, see sources listed for table 1. For Philadelphia rates, see Lane, p. 29.

8. Morton Kramer et al., *Mental Disorders/Suicide* (Cambridge, Mass.: Harvard University Press, 1972), p. 205.

9. Charles P. Hellon and Mark I. Solomon, "Suicide and Age in Alberta, Canada, 1951 to 1977: The Changing Profile," *Archives of General Psychiatry* 37 (May 1980): 508–9.

10. U.S. Bureau of the Census, *Mortality Statistics of the Seventh Census of the United States, 1850* (Washington, D.C.: A. O. P. Nicholson, Printer, 1855).

11. "Suicide," *American Whig Review* 6 (August 1847): 142; *Democratic Review* 34 (November 1854): 405–17; C. Nordhoff, "A Matter of Life and Death," *Harper's New Monthly Magazine* 18 (March 1859): 516–20.

12. Barbara Welter, "The Cult of True Womanhood: 1820–1860," *American Quarterly* 18 (Summer 1966): 151–55.

13. Nathaniel Hawthorne, *The Blithedale Romance* (1852; reprint, New York: Dell Publishing Co., 1960), pp. 269–70, 274–75.

14. *Alta California* (San Francisco) (January 2, 1890); *New York Times* (January 2, 1890).

15. "Suicides in New York City in 1860," *New York Times* (January 17, 1861).

16. Albert Rhodes, "Suicide," *Galaxy* 21 (February 1876): 192, 194.

17. Dublin (n. 2 above), pp. 23–25, 27–28.

18. Peter Sainsbury, *Suicide in London: An Ecological Study* (London: Chapman & Hall, 1955), p. 80.

19. Kramer et al. (n. 8 above), pp. 176–78.

20. Richard A. Davis, "Female Labor Force Participation, Status Integration and Suicide, 1950–1969," *Suicide and Life-threatening Behavior* 11 (Summer 1981): 111–23, esp. 123.

21. Kathryn K. Johnson, "Durkheim Revisited: 'Why Do Women Kill Themselves?'" *Suicide and Life-threatening Behavior* 9 (Fall 1979): 145–53.

22. Edwin S. Shneidman and Norman L. Farberow, "Statistical Comparisons between Attempted and Committed Suicides," in *The Cry for Help*, ed. Norman L. Farberow and Edwin S. Shneidman (New York: McGraw-Hill Book Co., 1961), pp. 24–37; Ronald Maris, *Pathways to Suicide: A Survey of Self-Destructive Behavior* (Baltimore: Johns Hopkins University Press, 1981), p. 268; Dublin (n. 2 above), p. 3; Herbert Hendin, *Suicide in America* (New York: W. W. Norton & Co., 1982), p. 49. Hendin sees the ratio as 10 to 1.

23. Shneidman and Farberow, p. 28; Maris, p. 243.

24. Mary Monk, "Epidemiology," in *A Handbook for the Study of Suicide*, ed. Seymour Perlin (New York: Oxford University Press, 1975), pp. 206–7; Douglas (n. 4 above), pp. 164–71.

25. Maris (n. 22 above), pp. 264–86.

26. *San Diego Union* (January 10, 1898).

27. Maris (n. 22 above), pp. 275–79.

28. *San Diego Union* (January 10, 1898).

29. Alan Marks and Thomas Abernathy, "Toward a Sociocultural Perspective on Means of Self-Destruction," *Suicide and Life-threatening Behavior* 4 (Spring 1974): 3–17, esp. 14.

30. *San Diego Union* (January 2, 1899), (January 7, 1899); San Diego County, California, Coroner's Reports, "Clara Dudley," January 6, 1899.

31. *San Diego Union* (April 22, 1895); San Diego County Coroner's Reports, "Dorcus Antle," April 22, 1895.

32. See Howard I. Kushner, "The Suicide of Meriwether Lewis: A Psychoanalytic Inquiry," *William and Mary Quarterly*, 3d ser., 38 (July 1981): 470–74, and "Immigrant Suicide in the United States: Toward a Psycho-Social History," *Journal of Social History* 18 (Fall 1984): 3–24.

33. Douglas (n. 4 above), p. 215. See also Kathleen Jones Bulmash, "Homicide in Nineteenth Century America: San Diego, a Case Study, 1870–1900" (paper presented to the Pacific Coast branch meeting of the American Historical Association, San Francisco, August 1982).

34. Maris (n. 22 above), pp. 269–70. Maris defines hanging, jumping, and use of firearms as highly lethal methods, and poisoning, cutting wrists, gassing, and most others as much less lethal. There is no necessary correlation between lethality and inflicted pain.

35. Dublin (n. 2 above), p. 41.

36. E. K. Hunt, M.D., "Statistics of Suicide in the U.S.," *American Journal of Insanity* 1 (January 1845): 225, 229–32.

37. George P. Cook, "Statistics of Suicide, Which Have Occurred in the State of New York from Dec. 1st 1847 to Dec. 1 1848," *American Journal of Insanity* 5 (April 1849): 302.

38. Rhodes (n. 16 above), pp. 192, 194.

39. Marks and Abernathy (n. 29 above), p. 11.

40. Kramer et al. (n. 8 above), pp. 216–17.

41. Hunt (n. 36 above), p. 229.

42. Marks and Abernathy (n. 29 above), p. 15; John L. McIntosh and John F. Santos, "Changing Patterns in Methods of Suicide by Race and Sex," *Suicide and Life-threatening Behavior* 12 (Winter 1982): 221–33.

43. Hendin (n. 22 above), pp. 148–49.

44. Ibid., p. 145.

45. Marks and Abernathy (n. 29 above), p. 15.

46. Grethe Paerregaard, "Suicide in Denmark: A Statistical Review for the Past 150 Years," *Suicide and Life-threatening Behavior* 10 (Fall 1980): 150–57. See also *World Health Statistics Report* (Geneva: United Nations, 1968), 21:6; Kramer et al. (n. 8 above), p. 220.

47. Hendin (n. 22 above), p. 145; Maurice Taylor and Jerry Wicks, "The Choice of Weapons: A Study of Suicide by Sex, Race, and Religion," *Suicide and Life-threatening Behavior* 10 (Fall 1980): 142–49; Paul Friedman, "Suicide among Police: A Study of 93 Suicides among New York City Policemen, 1934–1940," in *Essays in Self-Destruction*, ed. Edwin Shneidman (New York: Science House, 1967), pp. 414–49.

48. *Los Angeles Times* (October 25, 1982).

9

How Large Are Cognitive Gender Differences?

A Meta-Analysis Using ω^2 and d

JANET SHIBLEY HYDE

Behavioral scientists have tried for more than fifty years to document sex differences at the psychological level (for example, differences in personality attributes and cognitive abilities). Close analysis of the data used to support the general hypothesis of the existence of sex differences shows that there are few, if any, real differences at this level. Even aggression, traditionally considered male, or "masculine," behavior is not as exclusive to men as researchers and the public once thought it was. Yet researchers continue to try not only to document sex differences but to explain them. Thus some rather elaborate theories have been devised to explain a phenomenon that is nonexistent. Sociobiologists have carried this practice to an extreme, by stressing comparisons of males and females across species and ignoring those features of humans that differentiate them from other species—consciousness, a sense of self, and a sense of humor. Hyde's chapter is important because it challenges this tradition on its own terms—that is, she uses the style, format, and methodology of traditional science to show that sex differences in certain cognitive abilities are so small they are meaningless. ("Small" here means that a comparison of both women and men with respect to the ability in question shows almost similar distributions. See Hyde's Figures 1 and 2.)

To fully understand and appreciate this article, it is helpful to have some basic training in statistics. But those who do not should keep in mind the meaning of the term statistical significance. It does not necessarily mean that the difference between two groups (in this case, males and females) is a large one nor does it mean the difference is substantive. Even though evidence of statistical significance sometimes determines whether a study will be published, the determination of statistical significance depends to a great extent on the size of the sample: The larger the sample, the more likely a small or even miniscule difference between two groups will appear statistically significant. Further, the size, or magnitude, of a sex difference—that is, how much variation on a given attribute in a given population is due to sex (what Hyde calls effect size)—is an altogether different and separate statistical question than that of whether there is any difference at all. Hyde refers to the latter question as "hypothesis-testing." The point is that because of the nature of the methodology employed, sex differences in cognitive abilities (and in other individual attributes) have been greatly exaggerated—some might even say constructed—by the research process itself.

This note and Hyde's chapter refer to sex differences at the individual level, not to those at the social-structural, or interactional, level. There are sex differences in social patterns like the gender gap in earnings, sex segregation in occupations, and even some sex differences reported in this book—for example, Fishman's analysis of intimate conversation. These seem to be real differences in the sense that (1) their magnitude is greater than that for psychological differences of the kind Hyde is discussing and (2) they are partly explained by reference to ideological factors such as a culture's perceived differences about women and men. The discrepancy between evidence for sex differences at the individual level and those at the interactional and social levels itself needs to be explained.

Maccoby and Jacklin (1974) reviewed the enormous literature on psychological gender differences. In particular, they concluded that three cognitive gender differences were "well-established": Girls have greater verbal ability than boys, and boys have better visual-spatial ability and better mathematical ability than girls.

Sherman (1978) re-reviewed the evidence on cognitive gender differences and pointed out that even for these supposedly well-established differences, the magnitude of the gender difference was very small. For example, Maccoby and Jacklin (1974, Table 3.4) computed the magnitude of gender differences in verbal ability for a subset of studies providing sufficient data. Typically, the magnitude of the differences was only about .25 standard deviations. Sherman (1978, p. 43) noted that the proportion of variance (ω^2) accounted for by gender differences in verbal ability for the 1955 standardization of the WAIS (Matarazzo, 1972) was less than .01.

Meta-analysis is a technique for analyzing a body of research on a particular topic by statistical analysis of the analyses of the individual studies (Glass, 1976). It is becoming increasingly popular as a technique for evaluating a given area of research (for examples, see Hall, 1978; Kulik, Kulik, & Cohen, 1979; Smith, 1980; Smith & Glass, 1977). Typically, these studies use the measure

$$d = \frac{M_1 - M_2}{SD}$$

as a measure of the magnitude of differences between two groups, that is, as a measure of effect size.

The purpose of the present article is to reanalyze the studies on cognitive gender differences considered to be well-established by Maccoby and Jacklin (1974) and to determine the magnitude of these gender differences. Two measures of effect size were used: ω^2 (Hays, 1963) and d. Such an analysis is particularly important because the term "well-established" is often taken to mean "large." Maccoby and Jacklin's review has had a widespread influence, and their conclusions are cited in many introductory-level psychology texts. Thus, large numbers of people may have the impression that there are large gender differences in cognitive abilities. This, in turn, may affect practices such as vocational counseling. For example, a girl might be discouraged from a career in mathematics or science because of the "well-established" and "large" superiority of males in quantitative ability (despite repeated caveats in many texts about the great overlap in male and female distributions). Thus, it seems important to determine whether these "well-established" differences are in fact "large."

This study can be viewed as one example of a larger issue in psychological research: criticism of the hypothesis-testing approach and a suggested alternative, estimating the magnitude of effects. Cognitive gender differences are good examples because they are widely believed to be well-established, yet the size of the gender difference has rarely been estimated.

METHOD

Selection of the Data Set

The studies analyzed here are those listed in the Maccoby and Jacklin (1974) review. Thus, the studies reviewed on verbal ability are those listed in Tables 3.3. and 3.4 in Maccoby and Jacklin's book. The studies of quantitative ability are those in Maccoby and Jacklin's Table 3.5. The studies of visual-spatial ability are from Maccoby and Jacklin's Table 3.7. And, finally, the studies of field articulation (visual-analytic spatial ability) are from Maccoby and Jacklin's Table 3.8. These studies were chosen because they are precisely the studies that have led to the conclusion that these cognitive gender differences are "well-established."

Two restrictions were placed on the studies from those tables analyzed here. First, studies based on non-U.S. samples were omitted. It was seen as a reasonable goal simply to determine the size of gender differences in the United States. It seems quite possible that owing to differences in factors such as socialization practices or school curricula, gender differences present in one culture may not be present in another. Thus, inclusion of non-U.S. samples might only have clouded the picture. Second, a restriction of studies was made according to the age of subjects in the studies, based on the developmental nature of Maccoby and Jacklin's conclusions. In particular, they concluded that gender differences in verbal ability did not emerge until subjects were about 11 years of age. Thus, in an assessment of the magnitude of the established gender difference, it would be inappropriate to include studies based on subjects younger than 11 years of age. Hence, in Maccoby and Jacklin's Table 3.3, the study by Achenbach (1969) with 11-year-olds and all studies following it in the table are included. Similarly, Maccoby and Jacklin concluded that the gender difference in quantitative ability does not emerge until children are 12 to 13 years of age. Accordingly, the study by Hilton and Berglund (Note 1) including 10-, 12-, 14-, and 16-year-olds and all succeeding studies in Table 3.5 were included in the present review. Maccoby and Jacklin concluded that the gender difference in spatial ability was found consistently in adolescence and adulthood but not in childhood. Accordingly, the study by Nash (1973) with 11- and 14-year-olds and all succeeding studies in Table 3.7 were included in the analysis of visual-spatial ability here, and the study by Nash (1973) and all succeeding studies in Table 3.8 were included in the analysis of field articulation here.

Within the analysis of research on a particular cognitive ability, each study cited represents independent data. In cases in which longitudinal developmental data were presented, data from only one age-group are presented here. Only three studies were in this category, and in two of the three, the statistics were nearly identical at the different ages. In cases of cross-sectional developmental data, results from all appropriate ages were included. In addition, some studies included several different measures of the construct in question (e.g., verbal ability). In such cases, only one measure was included in the analysis in order to preserve the independence of the items in the data set. Only four studies were in this category, and one of them showed identical results for two measures. Of the remaining three studies, the measure showing intermediate results was reported.

It should be noted, however, that some studies are included in the analysis of two or more different abilities. For example, the study of Droege (1967) provided data on verbal ability, quantitative ability, and visual-spatial ability and thus is included in those three separate analyses.

Statistical Analyses

A number of measures of effect size are available (e.g., Craig, Eison, & Metze, 1976; Fleiss, 1969; Friedman, 1968; Hays, 1963; Tresemer, 1975). For each study, an attempt was made to compute two statistical measures of the magnitude of the gender difference. The first was ω^2 (Hays, 1963), which measures the proportion of the total variance in the population that is accounted for by gender differences. This measure is advocated by Fleiss (1969); see also Craig et al., 1976 for estimating the magnitude of effects. Its meaning is similar to the r^2 (proportion of variance accounted for) statistic in correlation and regression. Just as r^2 gives the proportion of variance in the criterion (Y) explained by the predictor (X), so ω^2 gives the proportion of variance in the entire distribution of scores that can be accounted for by gender differences (the remaining variance being due to within-gender variation and error of measurement). In the commonest cases, in which a t value or group means and standard deviations were presented, ω^2 was calculated using the following formula:

$$\omega^2 = \frac{t^2 - 1}{t^2 + n_1 + n_2 - 1}.$$

In the case of a two-factor design, the following formula was used:

$$\omega^2 = \frac{SS \text{ gender} - (c - 1) MS \text{ error}}{MS \text{ error} + SS \text{ total}},$$

where c = the number of levels of the gender factor, that is, $c = 2$ (Hays, 1963, p. 407). In the case of $t < 1$ or $F < 1$, ω^2 was set equal to 0. The statistic d is defined as the ratio of the difference between group means to the standard deviation of a group (the standard deviations of the two groups are assumed to be equal). It has been recommended for use in meta-analyses (e.g., Glass, 1976). In the present study, the standard deviation was defined as the average of the standard deviation for males and the standard deviation for females. Since the statistic assumes the standard deviations to be equal, the best estimate of that standard deviation is the average of the standard deviations of the two samples, male and female. Thus,

$$d = \frac{M_1 - M_2}{SD}.$$

The sign of d was set to be positive if the study yielded findings in the direction of the "well-established" difference and to be negative if the finds were in the opposite direction. For purposes of interpretation, Cohen (1969) considers a d of .20 small, a value of .50 medium, and a value of .80 large.

In cases in which the original reference provided insufficient information to compute either of these statistics (e.g., if only a significance level was reported), a letter was sent to the author at the address provided in the original paper or to a more recent address if provided by the APA Directory. The letter requested means and standard deviations for males and females and standard deviations for males and females and the *t* or *F* statistics. It was necessary to write such letters for 18 of the 53 different studies analyzed here. Thus, 34% of the studies provided insufficient information for a standard meta-analysis. Only seven responses to letters were received, and only two of these were able to provide the information requested. The remaining studies are listed as having no available ω^2 and *d* values in the tables.

RESULTS

Verbal Ability

The results for the 27 studies of verbal ability are shown in Table 1. As can be seen in that table, for those studies for which it was possible to compute ω^2 and *d*, both values tended to be low. The median value of ω^2 for verbal ability was .01; that is, gender differences accounted for only about 1% of the variance in verbal ability. The median value of *d* was .24. That is, the means for males and females were about one fourth of a standard deviation apart.

Quantitative Ability

The results from the 16 studies of quantitative ability are shown in Table 2. Once again, the values of ω^2 and *d* tended to be low. The median value of ω^2 was .01 for quantitative ability. The median value of *d* was .43.

Visual-Spatial Ability

The results from the 10 studies of visual-spatial ability are shown in Table 3. Three of those studies provided data for different samples at two different age groups. Hence, Table 3 can be considered to show 13 sets of data. The median value of ω^2 was .043. The median value of *d* was .45.

Field Articulation (Visual-Analytic Spatial Ability)

The results from the 20 studies of field articulation (typically measured by the Rod-and-Frame Test) are shown in Table 4. Two of the studies provided data for three separate age-group samples each, so that the number of data sets can be considered to be 24. The median value of ω^2 was .025. The median value of *d* was .51.

DISCUSSION

Magnitude of Gender Differences

The main conclusion that can be reached from this analysis is that the gender differences in verbal ability, quantitative ability, visual-spatial ability,

TABLE 1
Studies of Gender Differences in Verbal Ability

Study	Age	N	Difference	ω^2	d	Kind of Sample
Achenbach (1969)	11	159	None	NA	NA	5th and 6th graders
Cicirelli (1967)	11	641	None	NA	NA	6th graders, surban, middle-class, white
Weinberg & Rabinowitz (1970)	12–19	48	None	NA	NA	Hospital patients
Flanagan (Note 2)	14, 17	1,545	Females	NA	NA	Project TALENT data
Walberg (1969)	16–17	2,074	Females	.02	.33	High school physics students
Backman (1972)	17	2,925	Females	.33	1.40	Project TALENT sample
American College Testing Program (1976–1977)	18	45,222	Females	.02	.26	College freshmen
Rosenberg & Sutton-Smith (1966)	18–20	600	None	NA	NA	College sophomores
Bieri et al. (1958)	18–21	76	None	0	.19	Radcliffe women and Harvard men
DeFazio (1973)	18–21	44	None	0	NA	Selected for extreme scores on Hidden Figures Test
Feather (1968)	18–21	60	None	NA	NA	College students selected for extreme internal-external scores
Feather (1969)	18–21	165	None	NA	NA	College students
Koen (1969)	18–21	72	None	NA	NA	Harvard summer school
Laughlin (1969)	18–21	528	None	0	.03	College students
Marks (1968)	18	760	None	NA	NA	Penn State freshmen
Mendelsohn & Griswold (1966)	18–21	223	None	0	.16	College (Berkeley)
Mendelsohn & Griswold (1967)	18–21	181	None	0	NA	Berkeley undergraduates
Sarason & Minard (1962)	18–21	96	None	NA	NA	College
Very (1967)	18–21	355	Females	.04	.41	Penn State students
Rosenberg & Sutton-Smith (1964)	19	377	Females	.02[a]	NA	College students
Rosenberg & Sutton-Smith (1969)	19	1,013	Females	.04	NA	College students
Sutton-Smith et al. (1968)	19	1,055	None	NA	NA	College students
Bayley & Oden (1955)	29	1,102	Males	.01	.25	Gifted adults and their spouses
Blum, Fosshage, & Jarvik (1972)	84	54	Females	.06	.58	Longitudinal development sample
Gates (1961)	13	1,657	Females	.01	.22	Schoolchildren
Droege (1967)	18	6,167	Females	.01	.22	Representative sample of high school students
Matarazzo (1972)[b]	16–64	1,700	Females	.003	.12	WAIS 1955 standardization sample

Note: NA = not available (could not be computed from original paper, and author did not respond to request for further information or could not supply it). WAIS = Wechsler Adult Intelligence Scale.

[a]Percentage of variance accounted for was computed as $\phi^2 = x^2/N$.

[b]This study is not included in Maccoby and Jacklin's (1974) review; it is an additional large-scale study noted by Sherman (1978), included here because it is a major standardization study.

TABLE 2
Studies of Gender Differences in Quantitative Ability

Study	Age	N	Difference	ω^2	d	Kind of Sample
Hilton & Berglund (Note 1)	16	539	Males	NA	NA	College-bound students
Cicirelli (1967)	11	641	None	NA	NA	6th graders, suburban, white
Keating & Stanley (1972)	12–13	396	Males	NA	NA	Junior high students exceptionally gifted in math
Droege (1967)	18	6,167	Males	<.01	.06	High school students
Flanagan (Note 2)	14, 17	4,545	Males	NA	NA	Project TALENT data
Walberg (1969)	16–17	1,050	Males	.01	.43	High school physics students
Backman (1972)	17	2,925	Males	.17	.89	Project TALENT sample— high school students
American College Testing Program (1976–1977)	18	45,222	Males	.03	.35	College freshmen
Rosenberg & Sutton-Smith (1964)	19	377	None	.007[a]	NA	College students
Rosenberg & Sutton-Smith (1969)	19	1,013	Males	.005	NA	College students
Sutton-Smith et al. (1968)	19	1,055	None	NA	NA	College students
Rosenberg & Sutton-Smith (1966)	19	600	Males	NA	NA	College students
Bieri et al. (1958)	18–21	76	Males	.11	.72	Radcliffe women, Harvard men
Jacobsen et al. (1970)	18–21	136	None	.01	.27	College students
Sarason & Minard (1962)	18–21	96	None	NA	NA	College students
Very (1967)	18–21	355	Males	.06	.59	College students

Note: NA = not available.

and field articulation reported by Maccoby and Jacklin (1974) are all small. Gender differences appear to account for no more than 1%–5% of the population variance. The difference in means is only about one fourth to one half of a standard deviation (see Figures 1 and 2). Generally, it seems that gender differences in verbal ability are smaller and gender differences in spatial ability are larger, but even in the latter case, gender differences account for less than 5% of the population variance.

Practical Implications

What are the practical implications of the finding that these cognitive gender differences, although statistically reliable and replicable, are small? Two areas of practical concern are discussed below: vocational counseling

TABLE 3
Studies of Gender Differences in Visual-Spatial Ability

Study	Age	N	Difference	ω²	d	Kind of Sample
Nash (1975)	11–12	105	None	0	.04	6th and 9th graders, New
	14–15	102	Males	.04	.48	York public schools
Stafford (1961)	14–17	128	Males	.07	.60	High school students
Droege (1967)	18	6,167	Males	.04	.41	High school seniors
Flanagan et al. (Note 2)	14, 17	4,545	Males	NA	NA	Project TALENT data
Backman (1972)	17	2,925	Males	.14	.83	Project TALENT sample— high school students
Brisset & Nowicki (1973)	18–21	80	None	0	—	College students
Kidd & Cherymisin (1965)	18–21	100	Males	.045	NA	College students
Very (1967)	18–21	355	Males	.06	.52	College students
Davies (1965)	20–29	90	Males	.57	NA	Adult volunteers
	30–39	90	Males	.13	NA	
Sherman (1978)[a]	15	1,233	NA	.01	.25	High school math students
	16			.03	.37	

Note: NA = not available.

[a]This study was not included in Maccoby and Jacklin's (1974) review.

and explanation of observed gender differences in participation in certain occupations.

As noted in the introduction, there may be a temptation to use the findings of "well-established" gender differences in vocational counseling. The present analysis shows that gender is a poor predictor of one's performance on ability tests in any of these areas. Thus, presumably, gender would also be a poor predictor of performance on jobs requiring these abilities. Because the gender differences are small, one might question the wisdom of mentioning such differences in introductory psychology or child development texts that will be read by students who will eventually become teachers and guidance counselors and who may be prone to make the error of applying the findings of gender differences in their own counseling. At the very least, it would be important to stress how small the differences are and how unwise it would be to apply them in counseling a given individual.

The findings of gender differences in cognition have also been used in an explanatory way, in particular to account for gender segregation in some occupations. For example, only about 1% of engineers in the United States are women (Bird, 1968). Assuming that engineering requires a high level of spatial ability, can the gender difference in spatial ability account for the relative absence of women in this profession? The above finding of such a small gender difference would appear to argue that the answer is no. However, the question has now shifted from a discussion of overall mean differences in the population to differences at the upper end of the distribution. And

TABLE 4
Studies of Gender Differences in Field Articulation

Study	Age	N	Difference	ω^2	d	Kind of Sample
Nash (1975)	14	102	Males	NA	NA	9th graders, New York public schools
Weinberg & Rabinowitz (1970)	12–19	48	None	NA	NA	Hospital patients
Fiebert (1967)	12	30	None	.02	.49	Deaf subjects
	15	30	None	0	.30	
	18	30	Males	.06	.67	
Silverman et al. (1973)	18–22	30	Males	NA	NA	College students
Gross (1959)	18–25	140	Males	.22	1.16	College students
Stuart et al. (1965)	18–21	64	None	0	NA	College students and some noncollege high school graduates
Gruen (1955)	19–35	60	Males	.11	.77	Trained dancers
Schwartz & Karp (1967)	17	46	Males	.09	.85	Paid volunteers
	30–39	40	Males	.09	.71	
	58–80	34	None	.03	.51	
Bieri (1960)	18–21	60	None	NA	NA	College students
Bieri et al. (1958)	18–21	76	Males	NA	NA	Radcliffe women and Harvard men
Bogo et al. (1970)	18–21	97	Males	.12	.78	College students
Goldstein & Chance (1965)	18–21	26	None	0	NA	College students
Morf et al. (1971)	18–24	78	Males	.025	.40	College students
Morf & Howitt (1970)	18–27	44	None	0	.27	College students
Oltman (1968)	18–21	163	None	0	.17	College students
Sarason & Minard (1962)	18–21	96	Males	NA	NA	College students
Vaught (1965)	18–21	180	Males	.04	NA	College students
Willoughby (1967)	18–21	76	None	0	.18	College students
Gerace & Caldwell (1971)	25	40	Males	.08	NA	Adult volunteers
Blum et al. (1972)	64	43	None	.02	−.46	Aging twins (females scored higher)

Note: NA = not available.

relatively small mean differences can generate rather large differences at the tails of distributions, as the following sample calculation will show. Assume, conservatively, that the gender difference in spatial ability is .40 *SD*. Using *z* scores, the mean score for males will be .20 and the mean for females will be −.20. Assume also that being a successful engineer requires spatial ability at least at the 95th percentile for the population. A continuation of the *z*-score computation shows that about 7.35% of males will be above this cutoff, whereas only 3.22% of females will be. This amounts to about a 2:1

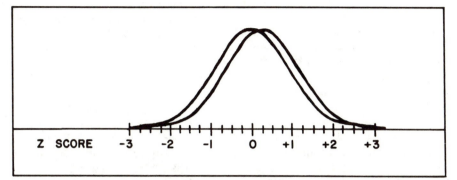

FIGURE 1 Two normal distributions with means .25 *SD* apart, that is, with a *d* of .25. This is approximately the magnitude of the gender difference in verbal ability.

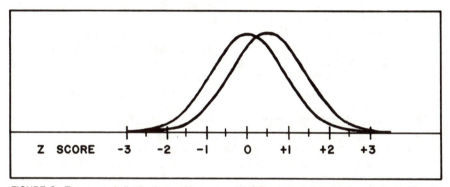

FIGURE 2 Two normal distributions with means .50 *SD* apart, that is, with a *d* of .50. This is approximately the magnitude of the gender differences in quantitative ability, visual-spatial ability, and field articulation.

ratio of males to females with sufficient ability for the profession. This could, therefore, generate a rather large difference although certainly not as large a one as the existing one.

The disparity would become even larger if one considered some occupational feat, such as winning a Nobel prize or a Pulitzer prize, that would require even higher levels of the ability. For example, suppose that spatial ability at the 99.5th percentile is now required. The same z-score calculations indicate that .85563% of males and .27375% of females would be above that cutoff, for an approximate 3:1 ratio of males to females. Once again, though, this is not nearly a large enough difference to account for the small proportions of women winning Nobel prizes. (The same computations could be used, recognizing the female superiority in verbal ability, to account for gender differences in the winning of Pulitzer prizes; once again, the gender difference in abilities would not, by itself, account for the observed difference.)

In sum, even small average gender difference in abilities can generate rather large differences in proportions of males and females above some high cutoff point that might be required for outstanding performance of some occupation. Nonetheless, the known differences in abilities are still too small to explain the observed occupational differences.

Sampling

In evaluating the existence and magnitude of cognitive gender differences, one important methodological issue deserves further discussion: sampling. It seems reasonable to define a cognitive gender difference as existing at a particular age if it is found to exist in a random sample of males and females of that age from a given culture (in this case, the United States). This definition is in contrast to that of Sherman (1978), who argued that gender differences are best studied on samples matched for prior relevant experience. For example, she has studied visual-spatial ability and quantitative ability in males and females who had taken the same high school math courses. The problem with this approach is that it may involve different percentages of the male and female populations and different cutoff points in their distributions. Essentially it confuses research on the existence of a gender difference with research on the cause of it. It would seem important first to establish the existence of a gender difference in random samples of the population, and then, if it exists, proceed to analyze its causes, whether biological or cultural or both.

With this definition of sampling in mind, brief descriptions of the samples involved in the gender differences studies can be found in Tables 1, 2, 3, and 4. Some of the deviations from ideal sampling are striking. For example, the study of verbal ability by Bieri, Bradburn, and Galinsky (1958) used as subjects Radcliffe female and Harvard male undergraduates. These subjects have surely already been selected for high levels of verbal ability, and the finding of no significant gender difference in the study is not at all surprising. Other obvious examples of problematic sampling occur in a study of verbal ability using Harvard summer school students (Koen, 1966), in another study of verbal ability using Berkeley undergraduates (Mendelsohn & Griswold, 1967), and in another study of verbal ability using high school physics students (Walberg, 1969). Finally, the study of quantitative ability by Keating and Stanley (1972) used junior high students who were exceptionally gifted in math and who initially were self-selected; doubtless, girls are less likely to self-select for high ability, particularly in a gender-inappropriate area such as math. Thus, many talented girls were probably lost from the sample. In defense of these studies, none was designed with the goal of normatively assessing the existence and magnitude of gender differences. Nonetheless, they have counted in the major tallies.

Indeed, the tough-minded might argue that all studies of college students are rendered irrelevant because the subjects have already had some prior selection on the basis of their cognitive abilities. If this rule is followed, few studies are left on the basis of which one can assess cognitive gender differences.

The more general point is that if one is to assess the existence and magnitude of cognitive gender differences, careful attention must be paid to sampling, and this has not been done in prior research or reviews.

A second point about sampling also needs to be raised. Some of the best studies from the point of view of random sampling are those that involve representative sampling of all high school students or all students in a given district. Such studies often involve enormous sample sizes. For example, the study by Droege (1967), which included measures of verbal ability, quantitative ability, and spatial ability, had a sample size of 6,167. Such a sample size increases the chance of finding a highly reliable gender difference that is very small and accounts for very little variance. Such sample sizes seldom appear in research in other meta-analyses (e.g., Hall, 1978; Smith, 1980). It seems that research on cognitive gender differences is particularly prone to the problems of enormous samples because cognitive gender differences can so easily be studied in large-scale research, such as standardization of tests. Thus, research on cognitive gender differences seems particularly prone to having large sample sizes that produce reliable but tiny differences.

Finally, the present findings may help to explain the lack of replicability in this area. If the true difference in population means for males and females is small, then one would expect that in repeated samplings, many would find no significant gender differences. This is precisely what one sees in Maccoby and Jacklin's tables. Further, the present findings explain why theories designed to explain the differences (e.g., brain lateralization theories) have met with little success and produce such conflicting data (Sherman, 1978). A small phenomenon will produce conflicting data in repeated sampling.

Recommendations

One problem that occurred in the process of doing the present analyses was the relatively high proportion of studies that provided insufficient information for ω^2 and d to be calculated. To facilitate more systematic assessment of gender differences, some journals have adopted the policy of requiring authors to report results of analyses of gender differences. However, if such analyses are to be complete, the magnitude of the differences also needs to be assessed. Based on the poor yield in response to letters requesting complete information for the present study, it seems important that such data be included in the original paper. Thus, a recommendation that emerges from this study is that journals encourage authors either to report ω^2 and/ or d values along with their analyses of gender differences or to report sufficient information (means and standard deviations for males and females and/or t and F statistics) so that ω^2 and d can be calculated. Such policies would seem to be important in order to avoid the assumption that gender differences that are well-established are also large, an assumption that the present review has shown to be false.

A more radical recommendation is also suggested by the present study. The results indicate that it is possible to have a moderately reliable psychological phenomenon (e.g., one that appears in 50% or more of published studies on the topic) that is nonetheless small. How many other areas of psychological research and theory are based on small effects that are assumed to be large and reliable because the size of the effect has never been evaluated? The radical recommendation, then, is that journals require reports of effect size such as ω^2 or d with all reports of significant results. Of course, a small effect might still be an important one. But at least the reader would have the option of deciding whether a significant effect was large enough to merit further attention, either in teaching or in research.

REFERENCE NOTES

1. Hilton, T. L., & Berglund, G. W. *Sex differences in mathematics achievement—a longitudinal study.* (Educational Testing Service Research Bulletin). Available from Educational Testing Service Research Bulletin). Available from Educational Testing Service, Princeton, N.J.

2. Flanagan, J. C., et al. *Counselor's technical manual for interpreting test scores* (Project TALENT). Palo Alto, Calif., 1961.

REFERENCES

Achenbach, T. M. Cue learning, associative responding, and school performance in children. *Developmental Psychology,* 1969, *1,* 717–725.

American College Testing Program. *College student profiles: Norms for the ACT assessment.* Iowa City: ACT Publications, 1976–1977.

Backman, M. E. Patterns of mental abilities: Ethnic, socio-economic, and sex differences. *American Educational Research Journal,* 1972, *9,* 1–12.

Bayley, N., & Oden, M. The maintenance of intellectual ability in gifted adults. *Journal of Gerontology,* 1955, *10,* 91–107.

Bieri, J. Parental identification, acceptance of authority, and within-sex differences in cognitive behavior. *Journal of Abnormal and Social Psychology,* 1960, *60,* 76–79.

Bieri, J., Bradburn, W., & Galinsky, M. Sex differences in perceptual behavior. *Journal of Personality,* 1958, *26,* 1–12.

Bird, C. *Born female.* New York: McKay, 1968.

Blum, J. E., Fosshage, J. L., & Jarvik, L. F. Intellectual changes and sex differences in octogenarians: A twenty-year longitudinal study of aging. *Developmental Psychology,* 1972, *7,* 178–187.

Bogo, N., Winget, C., & Gleser, G. C. Ego defenses and perceptual styles. *Perceptual and Motor Skills,* 1970, *30,* 599–604.

Brissett, M., & Nowicki, S., Jr. Internal versus external control of reinforcement and reaction to frustration. *Journal of Personality and Social Psychology,* 1973, *25,* 35–44.

Cicirelli, V. G. Sibling constellation, creativity, IQ, and academic achievement. *Child Development,* 1967, *38,* 481–490.

Cohen, J. *Statistical power analysis for the behavioral sciences.* New York: Academic Press, 1969.

Craig, J. R., Eison, C. L., & Metze, L. P. Significance tests and their interpretation: An example utilizing published research and ω^2. *Bulletin of the Psychonomic Society,* 1976, *7,* 280–282.

Davies, A. D. The perceptual maze test in a normal population. *Perceptual and Motor Skills*, 1965, *20*, 287–293.

DeFazio, V. J. Field articulation differences in language abilities. *Journal of Personality and Social Psychology*, 1973, *25*, 351–356.

Droege, R. C. Sex differences in aptitude maturation during high school. *Journal of Counseling Psychology*, 1967, *14*, 407–411.

Feather, N. T. Change in confidence following success or failure as a predictor of subsequent performance. *Journal of Personality and Social Psychology*, 1968, *9*, 38–46.

Feather, N. T. Attribution of responsibility and valence of success and failure in relation to initial confidence and task performance. *Journal of Personality and Social Psychology*, 1969, *13*, 129–144.

Fiebert, M. Cognitive styles in the deaf. *Perceptual and Motor Skills*, 1967, *24*, 319–329.

Fleiss, J. L. Estimating the magnitude of experimental effects. *Psychological Bulletin*, 1969, *72*, 273–276.

Friedman, H. Magnitude of experimental effect and a table for its rapid estimation. *Psychological Bulletin*, 1968, *70*, 245–251.

Gates, A. I. Sex differences in reading ability. *Elementary School Journal*, 1961, *61*, 431–434.

Gerace, T. A., & Caldwell, W. E. Perceptual distortion as a function of stimulus objects, sex, naivete, and trials using a portable model of the Ames distorted room. *Genetic Psychology Monographs*. 1971, *84*, 3–33.

Glass, G. V. Primary, secondary, and meta-analysis of research. *Educational Researcher*, 1976, *10*, 3–8.

Goldstein, A. G., & Chance, J. E. Effects of practice on sex-related differences in performance on Embedded Figures. *Psychonomic Science*, 1965, *3*, 361–362.

Gross, F. The role of set in perception of the upright. *Journal of Personality*, 1959, *27*, 95–103.

Gruen, A. The relation of dancing experience and personality to perception. *Psychological Monographs*, 1955, *69*(14, Whole No. 399).

Hall, J. A. Gender effects in decoding nonverbal cues. *Psychological Bulletin*, 1978, *85*, 845–857.

Hays, W. L. *Statistics*. New York: Holt, Rinehart & Winston, 1963.

Jacobson, L. I., Berger, S. E., & Milham, J. Individual differences in cheating during a temptation period when confronting failure. *Journal of Personality and Social Psychology*, 1970, *15*, 48–56.

Keating, D. P., & Stanley, J. C. Extreme measures for the exceptionally gifted in mathematics and science. *Educational Researcher*, 1972, *1*(9), 3–7.

Kidd, A. H., & Cherymisin, D. G. Figure reversal as related to specific personality variables. *Perceptual and Motor Skills*, 1965, *20*, 1175–1176.

Koen, F. Codability of complex stimuli: Three modes of representation. *Journal of Personality and Social Psychology*, 1966, *3*, 435–441.

Kulik, J. A., Kulik, C. C., & Cohen, P. A. A meta-analysis of outcome studies of Keller's personalized system of instruction. *American Psychologist*, 1979, *34*, 307–318.

Laughlin, P. R., Branch, L. G., & Johnson, H. H. Individual versus triadic performance on a unidimensional complementary task as a function of initial ability level. *Journal of Personality and Social Psychology*, 1969, *12*, 144–150.

Maccoby, E. E., & Jacklin, C. N. *The psychology of sex differences*. Stanford Calif.: Stanford University Press, 1974.

Marks, E. Personality factors in the performance of a perceptual recognition task under competing incentives. *Journal of Personality and Social Psychology*, 1968, *8*, 69–74.

Matarazzo, J. D. *Wechsler's measurement and appraisal of adult intelligence* (5th ed). Baltimore, Md.: Williams & Wilkins, 1972.

Mendelsohn, G. A., & Griswold, B. B. Assessed creative potential, vocabulary level, and sex as predictors of the use of incidental cues in verbal problem solving. *Journal of Personality and Social Psychology*, 1966, *4*, 423–431.

Mendelsohn, G. A., & Griswold, B. B. Anxiety and repression as predictors of the use of incidental cues in problem solving. *Journal of Personality and Social Psychology*, 1967, *6*, 353–359.

Morf, M. E., & Howitt, R. Rod-and-Frame Test performance as a function of momentary arousal. *Perceptual and Motor Skills*, 1971, *32*, 727–733.

Nash, S. C. *Conceptions and concomitants of sex-role stereotyping*. Unpublished doctoral dissertation, Columbia University, 1973.

Nash, S. C. The relationship among sex-role stereotyping, sex-role preference, and the sex difference in spatial visualization. *Sex Roles*, 1975, *1*, 15–32.

Oltman, P. R. A portable rod-and-frame apparatus. *Perceptual and Motor Skills*, 1968, *26*, 503–506.

Rosenberg, B. G., & Sutton-Smith, B. The relationship of ordinal position and sibling sex status to cognitive abilities. *Psychonomic Science*, 1964, *1*, 81–82.

Rosenberg, B. G., & Sutton-Smith, B. Sibling association, family size, and cognitive abilities. *Journal of Genetic Psychology*, 1966, *109*, 271–279.

Rosenberg, B. G., & Sutton-Smith, B. Sibling age spacing effects upon cognition. *Developmental Psychology*, 1969, *1*, 661–668.

Sarason, I. G., & Minard, J. Test anxiety, experimental instructions, and the Wechsler Adult Intelligence Scale. *Journal of Educational Psychology*, 1962, *53*, 299–302.

Schwartz, D. W., & Karp, S. Field dependence in a geriatric population. *Perceptual and Motor Skills*, 1967, *24*, 495–504.

Sherman, J. *Sex-related cognitive differences*. Springfield, Ill.: Charles C. Thomas, 1978.

Silverman, J., Buchsbaum, M., & Stierlin, H. Sex differences in perceptual differentiation and stimulus intensity control. *Journal of Personality and Social Psychology*, 1973, *25*, 309–318.

Smith, M. L. Sex bias in counseling and psychotherapy. *Psychological Bulletin*, 1980, *87*, 392–407.

Smith, M. L., & Glass, G. V. Meta-analysis of psychotherapy outcome studies. *Americand Psychologist*, 1977, *32*, 752–760.

Stafford, R. E. Sex differences in spatial visualization as evidence of sex-linked inheritance. *Perceptual and Motor Skills*, 1961, *13*, 428.

Stuart, I. R., Breslow, A., Brechner, S., Ilyus, R. B., & Wolpoff, M. The question of constitutional influence on perceptual style. *Perceptual and Motor Skills*, 1965, *20*, 419–420.

Sutton-Smith, B., Rosenberg, B. G., & Landy, F. Father-absence effects in families of different sibling compositions. *Child Development*, 1968, *39*, 1213–1221.

Tresemer, D. Measuring "sex differences." *Sociological Inquiry*, 1975, *45*, 29–32.

Vaught, G. M. The relationship of role identification and ego strength to sex differences in the Rod-and-Frame Test. *Journal of Personality*, 1965, *33*, 271–283.

Very, P. S. Differential factor structures in mathematical ability, *Genetic Psychology Monographs*, 1967, *75*, 169–207.

Walberg, H. J. Physics, femininity, and creativity. *Developmental Psychology,* 1969, *1,* 47–54.

Weinberg, S., & Rabinowitz, J. A sex difference in the Wechsler IQ Vocabulary scores as a predictor of strategy in a probability-learning task performed by adolescents. *Developmental Psychology.* 1970, *3,* 218–224.

Willoughby, R. H. Field-dependence and locus of control. *Perceptual and Motor Skills,* 1967, *24,* 671–672.

10

Interaction
The Work Women Do

PAMELA M. FISHMAN

Although there has been much documentation of male advantage at the macrostructural level (for example, the gender gap in earnings, sex segregation in the workforce, disparities of legal status between the sexes), such aggregate information sometimes does not seem very salient to one's everyday circumstances. Fishman's microsociological analysis of power shows the subtlety and ubiquitousness of male dominance in our culture. This work, which analyzes the text of transcribed conversations between intimates, is in the tradition of a perspective called "the social construction of reality." The social construction view stresses the processes by which society becomes the product of human consciousness and, at the same time, individuals become products of their society. One result is that humans are confronted with their culture without being aware that they created it. Fishman's work concretely captures these processes.

The oppression of women in society is an issue of growing concern, both in academic fields and everyday life. Despite research on the historical and economic bases of women's position, we know little about how hierarchy is routinely established and maintained. This paper attempts to direct attention to the reality of power in daily experience. It is an analysis of conversations between men and women in their homes. The paper focuses on how verbal interaction helps to construct and maintain the hierarchical relations between women and men.

Weber (1969:152) provided the classic conception of power as the chances of one actor in a social relationship to impose his or her will on another. Recently, Berger and Luckman (1967:109) have discussed power from a perspective which broadens the sense of "imposing one's will" on others. They define power as a question of potentially conflicting definitions of reality; that of the most powerful will be "made to stick". That particular people have the power to construct and enforce their definition of reality is due to socially prevalent economic and political definitions of reality.

Imposing one's will can be much more than forcing someone else to do something. Power is the ability to impose one's definition of what is possible, what is right, what is rational, what is real. Power is a product of human activities, just as the activities are themselves products of the power relations in the socio-economic world.

Power usually is analyzed macrosociologically: it cannot be solely a result of what people do within the immediate situation in which it occurs. What people do in specific interactions expresses and reflects historical and social structural forces beyond the boundaries of their encounters. Power relations between men and women are the outcome of the social organization of their activities in the home and in the economy. Power can, however, be analyzed microsociologically, which is the purpose of this paper. Power and hierarchical relations are not abstract forces operating on people. Power must be a human accomplishment, situated in everyday interaction. Both structural forces and interactional activities are vital to the maintenance and construction of social reality.

Recent work on gender and the English language shows that the male-female hierarchy is inherent in the words we use to perceive and name our world: the use of the male generic "man" to refer to the human species (Miller and Swift, 1976); the addition of suffixes ("authoress," "actress," "stewardess") when referring to female practitioners (Miller and Swift, 1976); the assymetrical use of first and last names (women are more often called by their first, men by their last, even when they are of equal rank (Thorne and Henley, 1975); women's greater vocabulary for sewing and cooking, men's for mechanics and sports (Conklin, 1974).[1] These studies of grammatical forms and vocabulary document the male-dominated reality expressed through our language.

Much less attention has been directed toward how male-female power relations are expressed in conversation.[2] By turning to conversation, we move to an analysis of the interactional production of a particular reality through people's talk.

This activity is significant for intimates. Berger and Kellner (1970:64) have argued that at present, with the increasing separation of public and private spheres of life, intimate relationships are among the most important reality-maintaining settings. They apply this arrangement specifically to marriage. The process of daily interaction in the marital relationship is, ideally:

> . . . one in which reality is crystallized, narrowed, and stabilized. Ambivalences are converted into certainties. Typifications of self and other become settled. Most generally, possibilities become facticities.

In these relationships, in these trivial, mundane interactions, much of the essential work of sustaining the reality of the world goes on. Intimates often reconstruct their separate experiences, past and present, with one another. Specifically, the couple sustain and produce the reality of their own relationship, and, more generally, of the world.

Although Berger and Kellner have analyzed marriage as a reality-producing setting, they have not analyzed the interaction of marriage partners. I shall focus upon the interactional activities which constitute the everyday work done by intimates. It is through this work that people produce their relationship to one another, their relationship to the world, and those patterns normally referred to as social structure.

WORK IN INTERACTION[3]

Sometimes we think of interaction as work. At a party or meeting where silence lies heavy, we recognize the burden of interaction and respond to it as work. The many books written on "the art of conversation" call attention to the tasks involved in interaction. It is not simply an analogy to think of interaction as work. Rather, it is an intuitive recognition of what must be accomplished for interaction to occur.

Interaction requires at least two people. Conversation is produced not simply by their presence, but also by their display of their continuing agreement to pay attention to one another. That is, all interactions are potentially problematic and occur only through the continual, turn-by-turn, efforts of the participants.

The work of Sacks and his followers (Sacks et al., 1974; Schegloff and Sacks, 1974; Schegloff, 1972) attempts to specify how conversationalists work to accomplish such things as beginnings and endings. They have ignored, however, the interaction between intimates. Schegloff and Sacks (1974:262) characterize intimates in home situations as "in continuing states of incipient talk." Thus, they contend that their analysis of the activities involved in opening and closing conversations, as well as those involved in keeping conversation going, do not apply to intimate conversations. But this perspective disregards the many conversations which do not begin with greetings nor end with good-bye's. If one sees a movie with friends, conversation afterwards does not begin again with greetings. In social gatherings lulls occur and conversation must begin anew. In any new setting in which conversation is possible, attempts at beginning, sustaining, and stopping talk still must be made. And these attempts must be recognized and oriented to by both parties for them to move between states of "incipient" and "actual" conversation.

In a sense, every remark or turn at speaking should be seen as an *attempt* to interact. It may be an attempt to open or close a conversation. It may be a bid to continue interaction: to respond to what went before and elicit a further remark from one's interlocutor. Some attempts succeed; others fail. For an attempt to succeed the other party must be willing to do further interactional work. That other person has the power to turn an attempt into a conversation or to stop it dead.

METHOD

The data for this study consists of fifty-two hours of tape-recorded conversation between intimates in their homes. Three couples agreed to have a Uher 400 tape recorder in their apartments. They had the right to censor the taped material before I heard it. The apartments were small, so that the recorders picked up all conversation from the kitchen and living room as well as the louder portions of talk from the bedroom and bath. The tapes could run for a four-hour period without interruption. Though I had timers to switch the tapes on and off automatically, all three couples insisted on doing the switching manually. The segments of uninterrupted recording vary from one to four hours.

The three couples had been together for varying amounts of time—three months, six months, and two years. The two couples who had been together the longest were recently married. All were white and professionally-oriented, between the ages of twenty-five and thirty-five. One woman was a social worker and the other five people were in graduate school. Two of the women were avowed feminists and all three men as well as the other woman described themselves as sympathetic to the woman's movement.

The tape recorders were present in the apartments from four to fourteen days. I am satisfied that the material represents natural conversation and that there was no undue awareness of the recorder. The tapes sounded natural to me, like conversations between my husband and myself. Others who have read the transcripts have agreed. All six people also reported that they soon began to ignore the tape recorder. Further, they were apologetic about the material, calling it trivial and uninteresting, just the ordinary affairs of everyday life. Finally, one couple said they forgot the recorder sufficiently to begin making love in the living room while the recorder was on. That segment and two others were the only ones the participants deleted before handing the tapes over to me.

I listened to all of the tapes at least once, many two or more times. During this period, I observed general features and trends of the interactions as a whole. Three transcripts were chosen from five hours of transcribed conversations for closer, turn-by-turn analysis of the progress of concrete, interactional activities. I chose these three because they were good examples of conversation that appeared to be problematic for the man, for the woman, and for neither.

PRELIMINARY EVIDENCE

Some evidence of the power relations between couples appeared while I was still in the process of collecting the tapes. During casual conversations with the participants after the taping, I learned that in all three couples the men usually set up the tape recorders and turned them on and off. More significantly, some of the times that the men turned the recorders on, they did so without the women's knowledge. The reverse never occurred.

To control conversation is not merely to choose the topic. It is a matter of having control over the definition of the situation in general, which includes not only what will be talked about, but whether there will be a conversation at all and under what terms it will occur. In various scenes, control over aspects of the situation can be important. The addition of a tape recorder in the home is an example of a new aspect to the routine situation. The men clearly had and actively maintained unilateral control over this new feature in the situation.

In this research, there is also the issue of a typically private interaction becoming available to a third party, the researcher. Usually the men played the tapes to censor them, and made the only two attempts to exert control over the presentation of the data to me. One case involved the "clicks" that are normally recorded when the recorder is turned off. Since more than one time segment was often on the same side of a tape, I relied on the clicks, as well as my sense of the conversations, to know when a new time segment began. One man carefully erased nearly all the clicks on the tapes, making it difficult to separate out recordings at different time periods.

The second instance was a more explicit illustration of male censorship. Early on, I made the error of asking a couple to help transcribe a segment of their tape. The error was doubly instructive. First, I saw that the participants could rarely hear or understand the problem areas any better than I even though they had been "on the spot," and were hearing their own voices. Second, the man kept wanting to know why I was interested in the segment, repeatedly guessing what I was looking for. At the time, I only knew that it was an example of decision-making and did not know specifically what I wanted. He never accepted this explanation. He became irritated at my continued attempt at literal transcription and kept insisting that he could give me the sense of what occurred and that the exact words were unimportant. He continued the attempt to determine the meaning of the interaction retrospectively, with constant references to his motives for saying this or that. It took hours to withdraw from the situation, as he insisted on giving me the help that I had requested.

The preliminary data suggest that the men are more likely than the women to control conversation. The men ensured that they knew when the tape recorder was on and, thus, when their interaction was available to a third party. They were unconcerned, however, if the women also knew. Further, in at least two cases they attempted to control my interpretation of the tapes.

FINDINGS: INTERACTIONAL STRATEGIES

Textual analysis revealed how interactants do the work of conversation. There are a variety of strategies to insure, encourage, and subvert conversation.

Asking Questions

There is an overwhelming difference between male and female use of questions as a resource in interaction. At times I felt that all women did was ask questions. In seven hours of tapes the three men asked fifty-nine questions, the women one hundred and fifty, nearly three times as many.

Other research (Lakoff, 1975) notes that women ask more questions than men. Lakoff has interpreted this question-asking as an indication of women's insecurity, a linguistic signal of an internal psychological state resulting from the oppression of women. But a psychological explanation is unnecessary to reveal why women ask more questions than men. Since questions are produced in conversations, we should look first to how questions function there.

Questions are interactionally powerful utterances. They are among a class of utterances, like greetings, treated as standing in a paired relation; that is, they evoke further utterance. Questions are paired with answers (Sacks, 1972). People respond to questions as "deserving" answers. The absence of an answer is noticeable and may be complained about. A question does work in conversation by opening a two part sequence. It is a way to insure a minimal interaction—at least one utterance by each of two participants. It guarantees a response.

Once I noted the phenomenon of questions on the tapes, I attended to my own speech and discovered the same pattern. I tried, and still do try, to break myself of the "habit," and found it very difficult. Remarks kept coming out as questions before I could rephrase them. When I did succeed in making a remark as a statement, I usually did not get a response. It became clear that I asked questions not merely out of habit nor from insecurity but because it was likely that my attempt at interaction would fail if I did not.

Asking "D'ya Know"

In line with the assumption that children have restricted rights to speak in the presence of adults, Harvey Sacks (1972) describes a type of question used extensively by children as a conversational opening: "D'ya know what?" As with other questions, it provides for a next utterance. The next utterance it engenders is itself a question, which provides for yet another utterance. The archetype is, "D'ya know what?" "what?" "Blahblah (answer)." Sometimes, of course, the adult answers with an expectant look or a statement like, "Tell me what." Whatever the exact form of that first response, the idea is that the first question sets off a three-part sequence, Q-Q-A, rather than a simple Q-A sequence.

Sacks points out that the children's use of this device is a clever solution to their problem of insuring rights to speak (at the same time, their use of this strategy acknowledges those restricted rights). In response to the "What?" the children may say what they wanted to say in the first place. Finding such three-part "D'ya know" sequences in interaction informs us both about the work of guaranteeing interaction and the differential rights of the participants. In the five hours of transcribed material, the women used this device twice as often as the men.

Attention Beginnings

The phrase, "This is interesting," or a variation thereof, occurs throughout the tapes. When conversation is not problematic, the work of establishing that a remark is interesting ideally is done by both interactants, not one. The first person makes a remark; the second person orients to and responds to the remark, thus establishing its status as something worthy of joint interest or importance. All this occurs without the question of its interest ever becoming explicit.[4] The use of "This is really interesting" as an introduction shows that the user cannot assume that the remark itself will be seen as worthy of attention. At the same time, the user tries single-handedly to establish the interest of their remarks. The user is saying, "Pay attention to what I have to say, I can't assume that you will." In the five hours of transcribed material, the women used this device ten times, the men seven.[5]

There are also many instances of "y'know" interspersed throughout the transcripts. While this phrase does not compel the attention of one's partner as forcefully as "this is interesting" does, it is an attempt to command the other person's attention. The phrase was used thirty-four times by the women and three times by the men in the transcribed conversations.

Minimal Response

Another interaction strategy is the use of the minimal response, when the speaker takes a turn by saying "yeah," "umm," "huh," and only that. Men and women both do this, but they tend to use the minimal response in quite different ways. The male usages of the minimal response displayed lack of interest. The mono-syllabic response merely filled a turn at a point when it needed to be filled. For example, a woman would make a lengthy remark, after which the man responded with "yeah," doing nothing to encourage her, nor to elaborate. Such minimal responses are attempts to discourage interaction.

The women also made this type of minimal response at times, but their most frequent use of the minimal response was as "support work." Throughout the tapes, when the men are talking, the women are particularly skilled at inserting "mm's," "yeah's," "oh's," and other such comments throughout streams of talk rather than at the end. These are signs from the inserter that she is constantly attending to what is said, that she is demonstrating her participation, her interest in the interaction and the speaker. How well the women do this is also striking—seldom do they mistime their insertions and cause even slight overlaps. These minimal responses occur between the breaths of a speaker, and there is nothing in tone or structure to suggest they are attempting to take over the talk.

Making Statements

Finally, I would like to consider statements, which do nothing to insure their own success, or the success of the interaction. Of course, a statement does some interactional work: it fills a space and may also provide for a response. However, such statements display an assumption on the part of the speaker that the attempt will be successful as is: it will be understood, the statement is of interest, there will be a response. It is as if speakers can assume that everything is working well; success is naturally theirs.

In the transcribed material, the men produced over twice as many statements as the women, and they almost always got a response, which was not true for the women. For example: many times one or both people were reading, then read a passage aloud or commented on it. The man's comments often engendered a lengthy exchange, the woman's comments seldom did. In a discussion of their respective vitas, the man literally ignored both long and short comments from the woman on her vita, returning the conversation after each remark of hers back to his own. Each time, she respectfully turned her attention back to his vita, "as directed." Listening to these conversations, one cannot conclude from the substance of the remarks that the man talk about more interesting things than the women. They take on that character by virtue of generating interaction.

INTERACTIONAL PROGRESS

The simple narration of the use of strategies obscures one important quality of interaction, its progression. The finding and frequency of strategies are of interest, but seeing the use of strategies in the developing character of interaction reveals more about the differential work done by the sexes.

In the transcript, a short segment of conversation is reproduced.[6] It is from the transcript originally chosen for analysis because the conversation appeared problematic for the woman. We can see why from the transcript: she documents her problems by the use of strategies that insure some type of response.

This segment is the beginning of an interaction during which the woman is reading a book in her academic specialty and the man is making a salad. The woman's opening remarks set up two "d'ya know" sequences, demonstrating her lack of certainty, before anything has been said, that the man will pay attention. A safe assumption, since the conversation never gets off

TRANSCRIPT

F: I didn't know that. (=)   Um you know that ((garbage disposal on)) that organizational
1
M: Hmmm? (=)

F: stuff about Frederick Taylor and Bishopsgate and all that stuff? (=)   ⌈In the early
2
M: UmHm ((yes))⌟

F: 1900's people were trying to fight favoritism to the schools (4)
3
M: That's what we needed. (18) I

F:
4
M: never did get my smoked oysters, I'm going to look for ((inaudible)) (14) Should we try the

---

F: OK. That's a change. (72) Hmm. That's very interesting. Did
5
M: Riviera French Dressing? (=)

F: you know that teachers used to be men until about the 1840's when it became a female occupa-
6
M:

F: tion? (2)   Because they needed more teachers because of the increased enroll-
7
M: Nhhmm ((no)) (=)

F: ment. (5)   Yeah relatively and the status (7)
8
M: And then the salaries started going down probably. (=)

F: ⌈There's two bottles I think⌉
9
M: Um, it's weird. We're out of oil again. ⌊Now we have to buy that⌋ ((whistling)) (8) Dressing

---

F: It does yeah. (76) That's really interesting. They didn't start
10
M: looks good. See? (2) See babe? (1)

F: using the test to measure and find the you know categorize and track people in American
11
M:

F: schools until like the early 1900's after the army y'know introduced their array alpha things
12
M:

F: to the draftees (?) And then it caught on with the schools and there was a lot of opposition right
13
M:

F: at the beginning to that, which was as sophisticated as today's arguments. The same argu-
14
M:

F: ments y'know (=)   But it didn't work and they came (4)   ⌈heh
15
M: Yeah (=)   Leslie White is probably right. ⌟

the ground. The "d'ya know" only solves the minimal problem of getting a response. She can not get a continuing conversation going.

Her second attempt at a conversation, in set 5, is a two-fold one, using both the "d'ya know" strategy and an attention beginning of "That's very interesting." This double attempt to gain his participation manages to evoke one statement of continuation out of him in set 8, but her follow-up calls forth only silence.

Her third attempt, in set 10, uses the attention beginning which had some small success the last time. She adds a few "y'know's" throughout her utterance, asking for attention. She finally achieves a minimal response, when she repeats something. Though she makes further attempts in the remainder of the interaction (not reproduced here), a conversation on the topic never does develop. After three or four more minutes, she finally gives up.

One might argue that because the man was making a salad he could not pay attention to the conversation. However, while still at work on the salad, the man introduces his own topic for conversation, remarking that then-President Nixon was a former lawyer for Pepsi-Cola. This topic introduction engenders a conversation when the woman responds to his remark. They go through a series of exchanges which end when he decides not to continue. This conversational exchange demonstrates the man was willing to engage in discussion, but only on his own terms.

The transcript demonstrates how some strategies are used in actual conversation. It also documents the woman working at interaction and the man exercising his power by refusing to become a full-fledged participant. As the interaction develops and she becomes more sure of her difficulties, she brings more pressure to bear by an increased use of strategies. Even so, she is only able to insure immediate, localized responses, not a full conversational exchange.

CONCLUSIONS

There is an unequal distribution of work in conversation. We can see from the differential use of strategies that the women are more actively engaged in insuring interaction than the men. They ask more questions and use attention beginnings. Women do support work while the men are talking and generally do active maintenance and continuation work in conversations. The men, on the other hand, do much less active work when they begin or participate in interactions. They rely on statements, which they assume will get responses, when they want interaction. Men much more often discourage interactions initiated by women than vice-versa.

Several general patterns of male-female interactional work suggest themselves. The women seemed to try more often, and succeeded less often than the men. The men tried less often and seldom failed in their attempts. Both men and women regarded topics introduced by women as tentative; many of these were quickly dropped. In contrast, topics introduced by the men were treated as topics to be pursued; they were seldom rejected. The women worked harder than the men in interaction because they had less certainty of success. They did much of the necessary work of interaction, starting conversations and then working to maintain them.

The failure of the women's attempts at interaction is not due to anything inherent in their talk, but to the failure of the men to respond, to do interactional work. The success of the men's remarks is due to the women doing interactional work in response to attempts by the men. Thus, the definition of what is appropriate or inappropriate conversation becomes the man's choice. What part of the world the interactants orient to, construct and maintain the reality of, is his choice, not hers. Yet the women labor hardest in making interactions go.

It seems that, as with work in its usual sense, there is a division of labor in conversation. The people who do the routine maintenance work, the women, are not the same people who either control or benefit from the process. Women are the "shitworkers" of routine interaction, and the "goods" being made are not only interactions, but, through them, realities.

Through this analysis of the detailed activity in everyday conversation, other dimensions of power and work in interaction are suggested. Two interrelated aspects concern women's availability and the maintenance of gender. Besides the problems women have generating interactions, they are almost always available to do the conversational work required by men and necessary for interactions. Appearances may differ by case: sometimes women are required to sit and "be a good listener" because they are not otherwise needed. At other times, women are required to fill silences and keep conversation moving, to talk a lot. Sometimes they are expected to develop others' topics and at other times they are required to present and develop topics of their own.

Women are required to do their work in a very strong sense. Sometimes they are required in ways that can be seen in interaction, as when men use interactional strategies such as attention beginnings and questions, to which the women fully respond. There are also times when there is no direct, situational evidence of "requirement" from the man, and the woman does so "naturally." "Naturally" means that it is a morally required and highly sanctionable matter not to do so. If one does not act "naturally," then one can be seen as crazy and deprived of adult status. We can speculate on the quality of doing it "naturally" by considering what happens to women who are unwilling to be available for the various jobs that the situation requires. Women who successfully control interactions are derided and doubt is cast on their status of female. They are often considered "abnormal"—terms like "castrating bitch," "domineering," "aggressive," and "witch" may be used to identify them. When they attempt to control situations temporarily, women often "start" arguments. Etiquette books are filled with instructions to women on how to be available. Women who do not behave are punished by deprivation of full female status. One's identity as either male or female is the most crucial identity one has. It is the most "natural" differentiating characteristic there is.

Whereas sociologists generally treat sex as an "ascribed" rather than as an "achieved" characteristic, Garfinkel's (1967, ch. 5) study of a transsexual describes one's gender as a continual, routine accomplishment. He discusses what the transsexual Agnes has shown him, that one must continually give off the appearance of being male or female in order for your gender to be unproblematic in a given interaction. Agnes had to learn these appearances and her awareness of them was explicit. For "normally-sexed" people, it is routine.

The active maintenance of a female gender requires women to be available to do what needs to be done in interaction, to do the shitwork and not complain. Since interactional work is related to what constitutes being a woman, with what a woman *is*, the idea that it *is* work is obscured. The work is not seen as what women do, but as part of what they are. Because this work is obscured, because it is too often seen as an aspect of gender identity rather than of gender activity, the maintenance and expression of male-female power relations in our everyday conversations are hidden as well. When we orient instead to the activities involved in maintaining gender, we are able to discern the reality of hierarchy in our daily lives.

The purpose of this study has been to begin an exploration of the details of concrete conversational activity of couples in their homes from the perspective of the socially structured power relationship between males and females. From such detailed analysis we see that women do the work necessary for interaction to occur smoothly. But men control what will be produced as reality by the interaction. They already have, and they continually establish and enforce, their rights to define what the interaction, and reality, will be about.

NOTES

An earlier version of this paper was presented at the 1975 ASA Meetings, San Francisco. I am indebted to Harvey Molotch, under whose encouragement I began the research. I am grateful to Myrtha Chabrán, Mark Fishman, Drew Humphries, Linda Marks, Florence Tager, and Susan Wolf for their support, discussions, and criticisms throughout work on this and earlier drafts, and to Malcolm Spector for his comments on the final version.

1. An excellent summary and analysis of this literature can be found in Thorne and Henley's introduction to their book, *Language and Sex: Difference and Dominance* (Thorne and Henley, 1975). Miller and Swift's (1976) encyclopedic work, *Words and Women*, catalogues the innumerable ways our language upholds the inferior position of women.

2. A notable exception is the work on interruptions in conversation by West (1977), West and Zimmerman (1977), and Zimmerman and West (1975). Hirschman (1974, 1973) has also examined the interactive production of language in male-female settings.

3. Throughout this paper, I use the terms interaction and conversation interchangeably, although it is not meant to suggest that conversation covers all the essential components of interaction.

4. The notion that joint expression of interest is a necessary feature of conversation is discussed by Garfinkel (1967:39–42).

5. Unlike the use of questions and "D'ya know," which were randomly scattered throughout the transcripts, six of the seven male usages occurred during one lengthy interaction. The conversation had been chosen because it was one of the very few cases when the man was having trouble maintaining interaction. In contrast, four of the female usages were from one transcript and the other six were scattered. My impression from listening to all the tapes was that a complete count would show a much larger proportion of female usage than the ten to seven figure indicates.

6. The numbers in parentheses indicate number of seconds of a pause. "(=)" means the pause was less than one second. My own comments on the tape are in double parentheses. M and F stand for male and female speaker, respectively. The conversation is presented in paired exchanges, sections 1–15. The sections ideally would be joined up in ticker tape fashion and would read like a musical score. Brackets between lines indicate overlapping talk.

REFERENCES

Berger, Peter and Hansfried Kellner. 1970. "Marriage and the construction of reality." Pp. 50–72 in Hans Peter Dreitzel, ed., Recent Sociology No. 2. London: MacMillan.

Berger, Peter and Thomas Luckmann. 1967. The Social Construction of Reality. New York: Anchor Books.

Conklin, N.F. 1974. "Toward a feminist analysis of linguistic behavior." The University of Michigan Papers in Women's Studies 1(1):51–73.

Garfinkel, Harold. 1967. Studies in Ethnomethodology. Englewood Cliffs, New Jersey: Prentice-Hall.

Hirschman, Lynette. 1974. "Analysis of supportive and assertive behavior in conversations." Paper presented at Linguistic Society of America.

————. 1973. "Female-male differences in conversational interaction." Paper presented at Linguistic Society of America.

Lakoff, Robin. 1975. Language and Woman's Place. New York: Harper Colophon Books.

Miller, Casey and Kate Swift. 1976. Words and Women. New York: Anchor Press.

Sacks, Harvey. 1972. "On the analyzability of stories by children." Pp. 325–345 in John Gumperz and Dell Hymes, eds., Directions in Sociolinguistics: The Ethnography of Communication. New York: Holt, Rinehart and Winston.

Sacks, Harvey, Emmanuel Schegloff and Gail Jefferson. 1974. "A simplest systematics for the organization of turn-taking for conversation." Language 50: 696–735.

Schegloff, Emmanuel. 1972. "Sequencing in conversational openings." Pp. 346–380 in John Gumperz and Dell Hymes, eds., Directions in Sociolinguistics: The Ethnography of Communication. New York: Holt, Rinehart and Winston.

Schegloff, Emmanuel and Harvey Sacks. 1974. "Opening up closings." Pp. 197–215 in Roy Turner, ed., Ethnomethodology: Middlesex, England: Penguin Education.

Thorne, Barrie and Nancy Henley. 1975. Language and Sex: Difference and Dominance. Rowley, Massachusetts: Newbury House.

Weber, Max. 1969. The Theory of Social and Economic Organization. New York: Free Press.

West, Candace. 1977. "Against our will: Negotiating interruption in male-female conversation." Paper presented at New York Academy of Science meeting of Anthropology, Psychology and Linguistics Sections, October 22, New York, New York.

West, Candace and Don Zimmerman. 1977. "Women's place in everyday talk: Reflections on parent-child interaction." Social Problems 24:521–529.

Zimmerman, Don and Candace West. 1975. "Sex roles, interruptions and silences in conversation." Pp. 105–129 in Barrie Thorne and Nancy Henley, eds., Language and Sex: Difference and Dominance. Rowley, Massachusetts: Newbury House.

11

A New Approach to Understanding the Impact of Gender on the Legislative Process

LYN KATHLENE

In the pilot study on which the following work is based, Kathlene proposed an instrumental-contextual typology to describe the public policy orientations of state legislators. This typology, which is outlined in Appendix A of her chapter, is a development of and provides empirical evidence for the psychoanalytically based hypothesis that women are more "connected" and men more "autonomous" in their basic relations to others and to the external world. Formulated by Chodorow and others, this widely cited theory is also used by Keller in her explanation of the masculine nature of science in Chapter 1 of this text.

This chapter features discourse analysis of legislative committee discussions and debates about specific legislative bills at each stage of the lawmaking process. The approach is multimethodological, including both qualitative and quantitative data and analysis at both the micro- and macropolitical levels, and it is multidisciplinary, representing political science, linguistics, and feminist theory. The focus is on "voice" and feminist interpretation.

Too often, focusing on women in a discipline like political science amounts to adding sex/gender as one of many quantitative variables, focusing only on women's issues, or being concerned solely with the sex ratio of a decisionmaking body. Kathlene's project examines gender as a meaningful and integral part of the political process itself.

For many of us, studying the political impact of gender is an uneasy merging of feminist critical theory with conventional quantitative methodology. Living in the age of post-positivist critiques and feminist calls for tapping into the personal, we are all well versed in the pitfalls of our methodological groundings. Yet we continue to search for "statistically significant" differences between women and men. In part, this is a pursuit of legitimacy (Klein 1983; Westkott 1983): The scholar needs to produce research on women that is at least methodologically sound (that is, acceptable for publication). In part, the researcher has implicitly adopted the epistemological premises underlying our de-gendered liberal theory (Steuernagel 1987; Jones 1988; Elshtain 1981; Dinnerstein 1976; Diamond and Hartsock 1981; Bordo 1987). And, partly, there is simply a practical problem; the lack of methodological alternatives congruent with feminist principles (Du Bois 1983; Mies 1983), especially for larger political studies. Interview and observational data suffice for small case studies and produce rich, in-depth knowledge; but the criticism of these methods (that they produce particularized rather than generalized results) is not without merit.[1]

Sometimes we attempt to overcome these problems by rethinking our variable selection. Our research designs are informed by a fundamentally different view of the political process as we redefine what is political, such as not accepting the artificial separation of the public and private sphere (Diamond and Hartsock 1981; Elshtain 1981). Through our feminist sensibilities, we expect not only to produce a base of research on women but also to find the unique contributions women offer our society. The body of literature on women and politics continues to grow and spur new efforts. But we have yet to adequately uncover many theoretically important aspects of female political participation and nonparticipation (Jones 1988) because our methodologies force us to describe women's experiences in terms of male behaviors (Klein 1983; Jones 1988; Kathlene 1989). Moreover, the concept of "gender" embodied in the studies of women and politics has

This chapter is a revised version of a paper prepared for the Annual Meeting of the Midwest Political Science Association, Chicago, Illinois, April 13–16, 1989. The author gratefully acknowledges the financial support of the Center for the American Woman and Politics (CAWP), a unit of the Eagleton Institute of Politics at Rutgers University; the views expressed in this chapter are those of the author and do not necessarily reflect those of CAWP. The author thanks Susan Clarke and Barbara Fox for design and methodological discussions, and Andrea Bender, Greg Goin, Alaurice Tafoya, and Laura Taylor for assistance in data collection and transcription.

often served only to replace the words "women" or "sex" (Jones and Jonasdottir 1988; Steuernagel 1987) rather than to represent the holistic concept of "women's culture . . . the social relations between and among the sexes" (Jones and Jonasdottir 1988:6). Only through research that is both theoretically and methodologically sensitive to the complex reasoning processes and attitudinal orientations arising from cultural sex socialization will the political impact of gender be uncovered and understood (Chodorow 1974; Gilligan 1982; Jones 1988; Kathlene 1989).

To this end, I offer a discussion and an example of one comprehensive multidisciplinary approach to studying the impact of gender on legislative policymaking. It is an approach that recognizes both macro- and micro-level pressures that model institutional and personal responses in the political environment. Theoretically, it assumes that women and men are not equal partners in the political or social world and that women and men are differentially affected by societal conventions. It emphasizes the subject as the "voice" of knowledge by systematically listening and analyzing word usage and verbal interaction in legislative committee hearings, floor debates, and personal interviews. The methodological theory is grounded in contemporary hermeneutics examined through the lenses of critical theory (Gadamer 1975; Geuss 1981; Habermas 1984), and the mechanics of the method are those used in sociolinguistics, aided by text-based concordance computer programs. The use of natural language analysis to reveal cultural values, attitudinal approaches, and situational responses (Ochs 1983; Forgas 1985; Ochs and Schieffelin 1986; Moerman 1988), in conjunction with quantitative methods to define broad trends set within a critique of institutional processes, provides a comprehensive approach to discovering not only the impact of gender but also the particular behaviors that display gender differences.

THEORETICAL DESIGN

In an earlier pilot study, two attitudinal constructs were developed to represent different approaches to policymaking under the broad themes of individualism and interdependence that have been found to be or theorized to be gender related by numerous scholars (see, for example, Chodorow 1974; Noddings 1974; Miller 1986; Dinnerstein 1976; Brooks-Gunn and Matthews 1979; Schaef 1981; Gilligan 1982; Gluck 1987). These constructs, labeled instrumentalism and contextualism, were used to guide and critique the analysis of verbal responses in personal interviews.[2]

This research project expands upon the theoretical and methodological framework by examining the policy effects or consequences of differing policy orientations. It challenges the assumption that gender impact lies only in, or even mainly in, the number of feminist- or women-centered bills enacted. It argues that differing gender-related orientations will have an impact on a wide range of issues, not just "women's issues." It also challenges the assumption that the effects of gender lie in the number of women legislators, and it emphasizes the importance of institutional bias and process in mediating potential gender effects.

The research attempts to answer three major questions:

1. Can a policy typology be developed that accurately distinguishes the significant and substantive differences between legislation informed by a contextual orientation and legislation informed by an instrumental orientation?[3]
2. Do legislators with contextual orientations sponsor legislation that differs in significant ways from legislation sponsored by legislators with more instrumental orientations?
3. Do bills characterized by these different policy orientations generate distinctive patterns of response and reaction in the legislative process?

With regard to number 3, it is hypothesized that the explicit procedures and implicit rules and norms of legislative bodies are conducive to the passage of legislation informed by instrumentalist orientations but may impede the introduction and passage of legislation congruent with contextualist perspectives (Ferguson 1984, 1987; Cohn 1987). As a consequence, contextual policymakers may be under pressure to conform by sponsoring instrumentally oriented bills. Additionally, the contextually oriented bills may be rejected or transformed during the legislative process more frequently than the instrumentally oriented ones.

A MULTIMETHOD APPROACH

A multiple method and/or flexible research approach to studying gender has been suggested by numerous feminist scholars (Klein 1983; Jayaratne 1983; Steuernagel 1987). Flexibility refers to the willingness of the researchers to change or choose the methodological approach *after* the data collection has begun, especially when they discover unanticipated results that would not be adequately captured by the original research design (Klein 1983; Mies 1983). This approach embraces the notion of the researcher as a "participant-observer," in the words of Hans-Georg Gadamer (1975): It recognizes the continuous learning process, devalues the dichotomous subject/object distinction, and allows for a more open research approach.

The research project in progress on the Colorado legislature reflects both a multiple method approach and a flexible design.[4] The main methodological focus of the research is the systematic language analysis of committee discussions and debates of legislative bills at each stage of the process, beginning with the introduction by the sponsor of a bill in the first committee hearing and ending with the final floor debate in the House. Twenty percent of the bills (n=69; see Appendix B) introduced during the 1989 session were taped and transcribed.[5] Additionally, all 65 House members were interviewed (22 females, 43 males). Each 45-minute interview was taped and will also be transcribed.

Although the examination of natural language within the context of institutional factors remains the focus of the research, over the course of the data collection it became apparent that other institutional factors needed to be accounted for in order to accurately judge the effects of gender. These factors include not only the general rules and norms functioning within a legislative body but also the particular new laws governing the Colorado legislature. Additionally, each committee had its own internal dynamic and a chairperson's leadership style seemed to complicate these dynamics.

Beyond the contextual environmental factors and language analysis, the demographics of each legislator are being gathered along with the outcome of all bills introduced this session (n=349) in order to identify larger patterns that may be linked to the analysis of interview and committee hearing transcripts. Hence, this research not only develops a linguistic approach to studying gender impact on public policy but represents a reformulating, multiple method approach to legislative research in general.

Environmental Factors: Contextual Analysis

General Legislative Processes: Consideration of the legislative context that representatives work within is absolutely essential if we are to understand how the institution itself molds political behavior and interacts with gender. General as well as particular legislative processes need to be incorporated into the analysis. For example, a general process might include the parliamentary procedure used to discuss and amend bills. Is it important to be highly proficient in the procedure and its specialized discourse in order to be an effective legislator? Are the policy agendas of the less skillful ones impeded?

Another extremely (but not obviously) important factor that often determines the early course of a bill is its title. If a title is very broad, "unfriendly" amendments (those opposed by the sponsor of the bill) can fundamentally change the substance of the bill. This situation arose in regard to a bill entitled "Concerning Court Actions," which was originally designed to protect the state against damage claims made by lawyers filing civil suits for reclamation of property seized during felony arrests. Through a series of complicated parliamentary procedures (one representative offered the sponsor's amendment to narrow the title, then immediately proceeded to offer a substitute amendment, and then an amendment to the substitute amendment—all to force the vote of his amendments prior to the sponsor's amendment), an unfriendly amendment that would have raised the dollar maximum in small claims court to $20,000 (ten times the current maximum of $2,000) was narrowly defeated. Obviously, this had nothing to do with the original intent of the bill, property seizure, but the amendments did fall under its title. The committee also rejected the title amendment, and the sponsor asked the committee to postpone her bill indefinitely because "If we leave the broad title on there, the bill could substantially change from what our original intent was." And as a supporting witness of the original bill remarked, "A title of this sort is of great concern to all of us in the court process, and you've seen just a taste of it."

A similar outcome can also occur if the bill is titled too narrowly. A committee can agree with the content of a bill but have one reservation in the wording or the approach. If the bill is too narrowly titled, a "friendly" amendment (one the sponsor of the bill accepts) that clears up an ambiguity or committee concern cannot be properly motioned and voted on. In such a case, a committee will often kill the bill because it is unable to adequately alter the bill despite the sponsor's support of the committee's desires.

Understanding and taking into account the title of the bill or the degree of parliamentary formality can be an important determinant in analyzing the outcome of a bill. If one finds that women's bills or certain issue areas appear to be treated similarly, incorporating the effect of the title on the amendment procedure or the formal/informal rules followed during the committee debates could be essential in understanding the strategies employed by the sponsor of the bill and the committee members.

Particular Legislative Processes: Every legislature or political institution will have its own particular rules. Recognizing and incorporating these facts allow the researcher to avoid misinterpreting events.

In November 1988 the citizens of Colorado passed two amendments that directly affected the legislative process. The most significant was dubbed the GAVEL (Give a Vote to Every Legislator) amendment. This amendment prevented (1) pocket vetoes by the speaker and committee chairs and (2) binding caucus votes. Proponents of GAVEL claimed that the current majority party (which was then Republican) was abusing its power and circumventing the democratic process by allowing legislative leaders to kill a bill before the bill was heard in committee. Before GAVEL, the speaker and every committee chair had the option to veto a bill prior to its being heard. Under this arrangement, the speaker would benefit the most by assigning his closest allies to chair positions. However, with GAVEL invoked, the speaker and the chairs lost their singular power. In 1989, to legally bypass the effects of GAVEL, the speaker "loaded" two committees with his closest allies and assigned bills he strongly disliked to one or both of the "killing committees." Hence, it was not uncommon to see bills "misassigned" (which was justified as "balancing the workload" among committees); for example, a daycare bill was heard by the Agricultural, Livestock and Energy Committee (and postponed indefinitely).

This bypass has important negative and, perhaps surprisingly, positive implications for understanding the impact of gender. In another example, one female-sponsored bill required insurance companies to pay for mammography screening. In a rare move, the female legislators from both parties banded together and used their influence (particularly through the strong Republican females) to get the bill "misassigned" to the Business Affairs and Labor Committee (headed by a female chair) as opposed to the Health, Environment, Welfare and Institutions Committee (headed by a male chair who has a record of opposing mandatory health benefits). Perhaps only in a year when misassignments were common could the women route their bill to a more favorable committee.[6] In this instance, the women used this process to their advantage.

We can see that in order to gain an understanding of the effect of gender within the context of the environment it is not sufficient to simply count the number of female-sponsored or feminist/women-centered bills that get proposed and enacted. Examining whether female-sponsored bills or women's/ feminist issues get killed more often than other bills is but the tip of the iceberg of understanding the potential of gender impact. We also need to know whether they were killed because of committee misassignment (Did a great number of these bills get routed to killing committees?). If this was the case, can we conclude that one or more powerful legislators who oppose certain types of legislation have more impact than other factors, for example, the percent of men versus women legislators? And, if this was the case, does it make more sense to focus our efforts on revamping institutional arrangements that impede gender impact rather than, say, trying to elect more women to a legislature that successfully hinders their impact?

Committee Dynamics and Personal Styles: Committees have differing internal dynamics depending on the membership and, importantly, the chairperson's style. How elective politicians operate in their working environment is a crucial area of research long overlooked by political scientists (Fenno 1988). From my observations and initial examinations of legislative transcripts, the two women chairpersons (of the Business Affairs Committee and the Education Committee) have a more informal style (with regard to parliamentary procedure), are open to extended testimony, and encourage committee questions, and intervene less than their male counterparts (women chairpersons tend to direct the committee debates but not get involved in the substantive arguments). How these differing dynamics affect witness testimony (Does a more open environment encourage more people to testify or speak more freely?) and the interaction between committee members and each witness as well as among the committee members themselves (Will more consensus emerge as issues are fully debated?) are examples of potentially significant gender impacts. The central question is, How are women using their positions of power and what differences does this use make on our public policies?[7]

Broad Behavioral Patterns: Statistical Analysis

Most political studies and, consequently, most political studies of gender impact rely heavily on quantitative methodologies. These methods are excellent tools for revealing many types of macrolevel trends but usually do not explore reasons for the trends, especially when the data were not originally collected by the analyst. As I pointed out in previous sections, understanding will always be limited when the data and researcher stand removed from the political context.

In this project, standard demographic data were included to ascertain if personal factors influence policy orientations or legislative success. In addition, all 349 bills introduced in the house in 1989 were coded according to the sponsor's sex, number of cosponsors, issue area, visibility (determined by number of newspaper articles), controversy (determined by coding editorials in the two major metropolitan-area papers), committee assignment, number of committee assignments, appropriateness of committee assignment(s), fiscal impact, amendments, committee outcome, and passage by the House. These variables will be cluster-analyzed to develop a bill treatment typology. This typology will then aid in determining if women's bills or if certain issue areas (perhaps some will be "women's issues") are treated differently. Moreover, simple statistics on these variables will help untangle multiple effects if, say, a high percentage of bills with a state fiscal impact get postponed indefinitely. Under such findings, we will want to look more closely at the passage/ defeat of women's bills, keeping fiscal impact in mind. A bill's success may not be gender-related, per se; it may be based on fiscal conservatism (although if women's bills more often have fiscal impacts it may say something about either women's issue areas or their policymaking approaches).

Verbal Interactions: Discourse Analysis

The multiple approaches previously discussed function mainly as descriptors of the environment where verbal interactions take place. It is the presumption of this research project that language reveals where gender differences and impact lie. Of course, language is not just words but is about action, influence and persuasion, the transmission of values, and learning from others. Language is verbalized thought. Through it we come to new understandings about our historical roots, share common experiences, solve problems, consider the normative implications of our behavior, and set a course for the future. To analyze human behavior without examining what we say is to deny the importance of that which is essentially human about humans. It is precisely our ability to engage in reasoning through discursive intercourse that speaks of humanity (Gadamer 1975).

From the perspective of hermeneutics, we have much to learn about human behavior through language, which is seen "as the mode of access to meaning . . . [of] not only texts but signs and symbols of all sorts, social practices, historical actions and works of art" (Warnke 1987:8). Sociolinguists share a similar perspective—that everyday words both reflect and create cultural values (Ochs 1983; Ochs and Schieffelin 1986; Moerman 1988). A detailed analysis of word usage and word meaning enables the researcher to answer the *why* questions behind observed behavior (Gilbert and Abell 1983) and, for our purposes, to document and understand how the underlying socially imposed sex-based norms are played out in the political process.

Analyzing language for gender impact requires utilizing a "theory of gender," operationalized through the attitudinal constructs developed in the pilot study along with sociolinguistic findings of differing situational and gendered speech patterns (see, for example, Williams and Giles 1978; Smith 1979; Kramarae 1982; Hoppe-Graff et al. 1985; Gallois and Callan 1985). How issues get framed and which images are invoked is directed by the words used to describe the situation. A case in point is Carol Cohn's (1987) analysis of U.S. defense intellectuals' specialized discourse of nuclear weaponry and policy options. That discourse conjures up images of sex, domination, domestic bliss, creation, and God—but never unimaginable suffering, death of millions, and destruction of life as we know it. Cohn argued that only through this disembodied discourse are we able to pursue the nuclear arms race. Moreover, learning the discourse and subsequently conversing in it seductively transform one's own positions. Her point is that without the words to transmit the values, the values cannot exist in the discussion.

Through natural language analysis, we will look at how issues are framed, what values are being invoked, and which approaches are successful in terms of enacting legislation. If women are bringing different priorities (Thomas and Welch 1989) to the legislative process, we expect to "hear" these different values espoused during committee discussions. In this way, the impact of gender goes beyond sponsorship of bills to the everyday interactions and decisions that mold all public policy.

EXAMPLES OF
NATURAL LANGUAGE ANALYSIS

The purpose of this section is to describe exactly how a concordance program works, present copies of the output (see Appendixes C, D, and E), and discuss some interesting patterns found as concrete examples of language analysis.

A concordance program[8] has two main features: It can rank list the number of times a given word is used and measure the percentage of text it occupies (see Appendix C); and it prints out, in alphabetical order, identical words in a limited context format (known as Keyword in Context, or KWIC) along with identification of the speaker and other pertinent information enabling the researcher to easily locate the specific passage within the full interview (see Appendix D).

The concordance can be used in numerous ways. The committee hearing transcripts can be combined and/or divided into subsets on the basis of issue area of the bill, committee, outcome (passed or killed), speaker, sex of the speaker, party affiliation of the speaker, or any combination of characteristics. There is no limit to the internal labels that can be encoded within the transcript (see Appendix E). Retrieving subsets or combinations of hearings allows one to test theories of gender differences and institutional pressures, both through a simple comparison of frequently used words and the examination of words in context. Another useful feature of the KWIC is the sequential order of the keywords—a particular word, along with the limited context, will be displayed in the sequential order found in the original text, which gives an immediate visualization of "pick-up" words (those words or issues that do or do not get used by other speakers). Additionally, one can examine rates of initiation—that is, who brings up the major points first.

An initial examination of three "finished" bills revealed some interesting patterns.[9] The most obvious pattern in all three bills was the relative absence of female committee member voices; the number was well below what would be expected based on the high percentage of females present during each of the hearings (the Judiciary Committee was 45 percent female; the Education Committee was 56 percent female). Moreover, during all three of these hearings, the committee were chaired by females (the Judiciary Committee has a female vice-chair; the Education Committee has both a female chair and vice-chair). If the women were not talking, is there evidence that they were listening better? It seems so—at least in the one male-sponsored bill on domestic abuse. By looking at initiation and pick-up patterns, we found that women were not focusing on the issue as framed by the sponsor and all male witnesses (the most predominantly used words were abuse, domestic abuse, permanent basis, emergency basis, personal basis, restraining order, protective order, emergency order, temporary order, permanent order, temporary relief, emergency relief). Rather, the negative testimony of one male witness invoked two females to pursue his main points (best interests of child, parent's rights, visitation rights) and in the end they successfully amended the bill in light of these problems. The amendments did not fundamentally change the bill but they added a dimension that was missing in the original version. The women incorporated language to address the "best interests of the child" and required the court to make a determination of "visitation for the non-custodial parent." Without these amendments, the courts would have automatically awarded temporary child custody for thirty days to the person who filed the domestic abuse complaint. Although most domestic abuse situations would result in the female receiving temporary custody, these two women believed that was an oversimplistic solution (possibly not always in the best interests of the child), and left the issue of visitation legally unsettled.

Another pattern found throughout the three committee hearings was the frequent use of qualifiers in declarative statements by women. When addressing the same issues, women were more likely to qualify their remarks with words like "if," "perhaps," "probably," "it might be," "at times." The higher incidence of use of qualifiers by females has been found in previous studies (Lakoff 1973) and is sometimes interpreted as a lack of broad experiences or a lack of self-confidence (see the discussion in Kramer 1975). However, our theory of gender hypothesizes that qualifiers represent the acknowledgment of interrelations, complexity, and an unwillingness to oversimplify. Two questions arise: (1) Do qualifiers represent contextual thinking? (2) Does language that is riddled with qualifers open or close discussions and in what situations do these outcomes occur?

Examination of the sponsor's introductions revealed three different patterns. In the male-sponsored bill that passed out of committee (subsequently referred to as Mpass) the sponsor's introduction was somewhat lengthy (350 words), and he repeatedly mentioned certain keywords describing his bill, which were subsequently picked up and repeated by all the male witnesses but not the female witness or the female committee members. In the female-sponsored bill that was postponed indefinitely (Fkill), the sponsor's introduction was longer (404 words) and also repeatedly mentioned certain keywords, but none of these words were picked up by the witnesses or committee members. And last, in the female-sponsored bill that passed out of committee (Fpass), the sponsor had a significantly shorter introduction (257 words), invoked keywords only once, which were subsequently picked up and repeatedly used by witnesses and committee members, and then ended with a summary (116 words), which again invoked, just once, the keywords of the bill.

Whether these styles set the stage for bill treatment cannot be ascertained at this point; however, when we examine the bill treatment within the context of other potentially mitigating factors, we are led to the interesting question of whether passage of women-sponsored legislation is marked by differing reception to verbal and logistic approaches. Such mitigating factors include those that were found to be relatively equal among the bills (for example, all bills dealt with crime; all bills dealt with modifying current procedures; none of the bills had a fiscal impact; all the sponsors were seasoned Republicans in their third or fourth term) plus other factors that were similar between the Mpass and Fkill but were different from Fpass (for example, sponsors of both Mpass and Fkill had lined up only one witness from their district to testify in favor of it whereas the sponsor of Fpass had lined up 4 witnesses from around the state; both Mpass and Fkill hearings took nearly the same amount of time, about 1 hour and 15 minutes whereas the hearing for Fpass was only 30 minutes long; Fkill and Fpass were heard by the same committee). More pointedly, do women need to make a stronger case for their issues (for example, have more witnesses, get straight to the point, and take less time)? And are more witnesses enough, or are some witnesses more credible than others?

As it turns out, the sponsor of Fpass is highly successful (83 percent of her bills were passed out of first committee) and she always followed a certain pattern. She began with a relatively short, unemotional, even detached introduction, touching on only the broadest issues and leaving the explanation of the bill's substance to her witnesses (all of whom were orchestrated so as not to repeat issues). Her first and last witness was always male. This sponsor arrived to the committee with amendments in hand, thereby focusing committee discussion on issues over which she had control. Even this limited data raises new questions such as (1) Is this a female pattern of success? and (2) Is it also a general pattern of success or do men have a wider variety of successful approaches available to them? These are but some of the issues that are uncovered through discourse analysis and, I hope, with the addition of all the data, will be better understood.

SUMMARY

Just as cultural sex-socialization is extremely complicated and played out in unforeseen behaviors, so, too, would be the resultant impact of gender on our public policies. This research project attempted to tap into those behaviors and attitudes through the systematic examination of verbal interactions during public policy formation. Gender impact has the potential to go beyond the sponsorship of bills (although this is very important) and to affect policy through the values and concerns women and men bring into the discussions of bills. Also, through language analysis, personal and group styles can be examined to determine whether gender impact is occurring through positions of power and/or particular group dynamics. It was hypothesized that the institution with its rules and norms will favor certain styles and that these styles may impede or lessen gender impact.

The research in progress of representatives in the Colorado state house is a multiple method approach, combining contextual environmental factors, demographic data, a typology of bill treatments, and finally, a systematic examination of the verbal interactions to ascertain the many subtle but potentially important impacts of gender on our public policies.

NOTES

1. General trends are not to be confused with the notion of universal principles. Rather, findings that transcend the particular would represent common strategies, discourses, or interests that arise from shared gender experiences. For example, if women think in terms of needs and interrelations in contrast to the dominant male notions of rights and individuality, we might be able to use generalized findings to address the process by which these values become operationalized and are received in the political realm. Descriptions of individual approaches of female political elites in small case studies cannot transcend the particular. Whether we should strive to meet the traditional methodological standards of political science is not the issue here. Rather, feminists find themselves caught between seeing, hearing, and describing individual approaches or using the methodology of large samples, which is incapable of seeing and hearing individuals, in an effort to find the extensive (rather than the particular) impact of gender on our political institutions.

2. For a detailed description of the attitudinal constructs, see Kathlene (1989). For a brief summary, see Appendix A.

3. A contextual orientation focuses on the *needs* of individuals, recognizing differing social, economic, and personal circumstances that require context-sensitive responses. An instrumental orientation focuses on *justice* for individuals, recognizing that conflicting claims are fairly solved through the application of impartial rules and laws. For a more in-depth discussion, see Kathlene (1989) and Lyons (1988).

4. The research project "Gender, Public Policy and the Legislative Process" is funded by the Center for the American Woman and Politics, Eagleton Institute of Politics, Rutgers University, directed by the author in collaboration with Susan E. Clarke, Center for Public Policy Research, University of Colorado at Boulder, and Barbara A. Fox, Department of Linguistics, University of Colorado at Boulder.

5. The selection of bills was based on a wide range of issue areas and committee assignment (9 out of a possible 11 committees are represented in the data) in order to test for institutional bias and gender impact beyond women-oriented issues.

6. A bill mandating a health-care benefit could properly be assigned to the Business Affairs and Labor Committee; however, this normally would occur, if at all, after being heard in the Health, Environment, Welfare and Institutions Committee (HEWI). In this case, HEWI was bypassed completely. In the second reading of the bill on the House floor (after the bill had successfully passed the Business Affairs committee),

the chair of HEWI argued vehemently against the bill because of the rising cost to employers "whenever the state mandates a particular health benefit." The sponsor countered "that we cannot paint all mandated benefits with the same brush" because early breast cancer detection not only would save lives but in the long run would also save health-care dollars. The bill passed the third reading in the House on a 56 to 7 vote. It subsequently passed the Senate and was signed by the Governor in April 1989.

7. In our group project meeting in October 1988, the Center for the American Woman and Politics (CAWP) organized an evening roundtable discussion that included the research grant recipients and four women in politics (Patricia Price Bailey, a Carter appointee to the Federal Trade Commission; Joan Anderson Growe, an elected secretary of state serving her fourth term in Minnesota; Ruth Messinger, New York City Council member since 1978; and Anne Scarlett Perkins, a member of Maryland's House of Delegates since 1979). These women discussed their experiences of and impressions about gender differences in the political process; they emphasized the need not only to analyze issue areas and the number of bills sponsored by females but to examine how women are using their power and affecting the process itself. According to them, seasoned women politicians may actually sponsor less legislation, using instead their positions of power to advance female causes. Basically, they said we need multiple measures to adequately capture the broad range of gender impacts.

8. The concordance program we used was developed by Mike Preston, director of the Center for Computer Research in the Humanities, University of Colorado, Boulder, and Sam Coleman, group leader, Mass Storage Group, Lawrence Livermore Laboratory, California. Documentation of the "Unicorn" package, written by Katherine Livornese, Discussion Paper No. 20, is available through the Center for Public Policy Research, University of Colorado at Boulder. Currently, the software runs only on mainframe Cyber systems but a PC version is underway. Other text retrieval PC programs are currently available with differing capabilities. The Oxford Concordance PC Program, from Oxford University Computing Services, has features similar to the Unicorn package.

9. The three bills were (1) "Concerning Restraining Orders to Prevent Domestic Abuse," sponsored by a male Republican, heard in the Education Committee, committee-amended and passed out to the floor with a favorable recommendation; (2) "Strengthen Crime Victim Compensation Act," sponsored by a female Republican, heard in the Judiciary Committee, sponsor-amended and passed out to the floor with a favorable recommendation; and (3) "Concerning Court Actions," sponsored by a female Republican, heard in the Judiciary Committee, challenged by a male committee member who attempted unfriendly amendments, then postponed indefinitely.

REFERENCES

Belenky, Mary Field, Blythe McVicker Clinchy, Nancy Rule Goldberger, and Jill Mattuck Tarule. 1986. *Women's Ways of Knowing: The Development of Self, Voice, and Mind.* New York: Basic Books.

Bordo, Susan. 1987. "The Cartesian Masculinization of Thought." In Sandra Harding and Jean F. O'Barr, eds., *Sex and Scientific Inquiry.* Chicago: University of Chicago Press.

Brooks-Gunn, Jeanne, and Wendy Schempp Matthews. 1979. *He and She: How Children Develop Their Sex-Role Identity.* Englewood Cliffs N.J.: Prentice-Hall.

Carroll, Susan J. 1985. *Women as Candidates in American Politics.* Bloomington: Indiana University Press.

Chodorow, Nancy, 1974. "Family Structure and Feminine Personality." In Michelle Zimbalist Rosaldo and Louise Lamphere, eds., *Women, Culture and Society.* Stanford: Stanford University Press.

Cohn, Carol. 1987. "Sex and Death in the Rational World of Defense Intellectuals." *Signs: Journal of Women in Culture and Society* 12:687–718.

Diamond, Irene, and Nancy Hartsock. 1981. "Beyond Interests in Politics: A Comment on Virginia Sapiro's 'When Are Interests Interesting?' The Problem of Political Representation of Women." *American Political Science Review,* 75:717–721.

Dinnerstein, Dorothy. 1976. *The Mermaid and the Minotaur.* New York: Harper Colophon Books.

Du Bois, Barbara. 1983. "Passionate Scholarship: Notes on Values, Knowing and Method in Feminist Social Science." In Gloria Bowles and Renate Duelli Klein, eds., *Theories of Women's Studies.* Boston: Routledge & Kegan Paul.

Elshtain, Jean Bethke. 1981. *Public Man/Private Woman.* Princeton: Princeton University Press.

Fenno, Richard F., Jr. 1988. "Congressional Research: Ideas for the Next Generation." *Extensions* (Summer):4–5.

Ferguson, Kathy E. 1984. *The Feminist Case Against Bureaucracy.* Philadelphia: Temple University Press.

———. 1987. "Work, Text, and Act in Discourses of Organization." *Women and Politics* 7:1–21.

Flammang, Janet A. 1985. "Female Officials in the Feminist Capital: The Case of Santa Clara County." *Western Political Quarterly* 38:95–118.

Forgas, Joseph P. 1985. *Language and Social Situations.* New York: Springer-Verlag.

Gadamer, Hans-Georg. 1975. *Truth and Method.* English translation by G. Barden and J. Cumming. New York: Crossroad Publishing.

Gallois, Cynthia, and Victor J. Callan. 1985. "Situational Influences on Perceptions of Accented Speech." In Joseph Forgas, ed., *Language and Social Situations.* New York: Springer-Verlag.

Geuss, Raymond. 1981. *The Idea of Critical Theory.* Cambridge: Cambridge University Press.

Gilbert, Nigel B., and Peter Abell. 1983. *Accounts and Action.* Aldershot, Hampshire: Gower.

Gilligan, Carol. 1982. *In a Different Voice: Psychological Theory and Women's Development.* Cambridge: Harvard University Press.

Gluck, Hazel Frank. 1987. "The Difference." *State Government* 60:223–226.

Habermas, Jurgen. 1977. "A Review of Gadamer's *Truth and Method.*" In Fred R. Dallmayr and Thomas A. McCarthy, eds., *Understanding and Social Inquiry.* Notre Dame, Ind.: University of Notre Dame Press.

———. 1984. *The Theory of Communicative Action, Vol. 1, Reason and the Rationalization of Society.* English translation by T. McCarthy. Boston: Beacon Press.

Hoppe-Graff, Siegfried, Theo Herrmann, Peter Winterhoff-Spurk, and Roland Mangold. 1985. "Speech and Situation: A General Model for the Process of Speech Production." In Joseph Forgas, ed., *Languge and Social Situations.* New York: Springer-Verlag.

Jayaratne, Toby Epstein. 1983. "The Value of Quantitative Methodology for Feminist Research." In Gloria Bowles and Renate Duelli Klein, eds., *Theories of Women's Studies.* Boston: Routledge & Kegan Paul.

Jones, Kathleen B. 1988. "Towards the Revision of Politics." In Jones and Jonasdottir, eds., *The Political Interests of Gender.* London: SAGE Publications.

Jones, Kathleen B., and Anna G. Jonasdottir. 1988. "Introduction: Gender as an Analytic Category." In Jones and Jonasdottir, eds., *The Political Interests of Gender.* London: SAGE Publications.

Kathlene, Lyn. 1989. "Uncovering the Political Impacts of Gender: An Exploratory Study." *Western Political Quarterly* 42:397–421.

Klein, Renate Duelli. 1983. "How to Do What We Want to Do: Thoughts About Feminist Methodology." In Gloria Bowles and Renate Duelli Klein, eds., *Theories of Women's Studies.* Boston: Routledge & Kegan Paul.

Kramarae, C. 1982. "Gender: How She Speaks." In Ellen Bouchard Ryan and Howard Giles, eds., *Attitudes Towards Language Variation.* London: Edward Arnold.

Kramer, Cheris. 1975. "Women's Speech: Separate but Unequal?" In Barrie Thorne and Nancy Henley, eds., *Language and Sex: Difference and Dominance.* Rowley, Mass.: Newbury House.

Lakoff, Robin. 1973. "Language and Woman's Place." *Language and Society* 2:45–79.

Lyons, Nona Plessner. 1988. "Two Perspectives: On Self, Relationships, and Morality." In Carol Gilligan, Janie Victoria Ward, Jill McLean Taylor, and with Betty Bardige, eds., *Mapping the Moral Domain.* Cambridge: Harvard University Press.

Mies, Maria. 1983. "Towards a Methodology for Feminist Research." In Gloria Bowles and Renate Duelli Klein, eds., *Theories of Women's Studies.* Boston: Routledge & Kegan Paul.

Miller, Jean Baker. 1986. *Toward a New Psychology of Women.* Boston: Beacon Press.

Moerman, Michael. 1988. *Talking Culture, Ethnography and Conversation Analysis.* Philadephia: University of Pennsylvania Press.

Noddings, Nel. 1974. *Caring: A Feminine Approach to Ethics and Moral Education.* Berkeley: University of California Press.

Ochs, Elinor. 1983. "Cultural Dimensions of Language Acquisition." In Elinor Ochs and Bambi B. Schieffelin, eds., *Acquiring Conversational Competence.* Boston: Routledge & Kegan Paul.

Ochs, Elinor, and Bambi B. Schieffelin. 1986. *Language Socialization Across Cultures.* Cambridge: Cambridge University Press.

Reinharz, Shulamit. 1983. "Experiential Analysis: A Contribution to Feminist Research." In Gloria Bowles and Renate Duelli Klein, eds., *Theories of Women's Studies.* Boston: Routledge & Kegan Paul.

Schaef, Ann Wilson. 1981. *Women's Reality.* Minneapolis: Winston Press.

Smith, P. 1979. "Sex Markers in Speech." In Klaus R. Scherer and Howard Giles, eds., *Social Markers in Speech.* Cambridge: Cambridge University Press.

Steuernagel, Gertrude A. 1987. "Reflections on Women and Political Participation." *Women and Politics* 7:3–13.

Thomas, Sue, and Susan Welch. 1989. "The Impact of Gender on Activities and Priorities of State Legislators." Paper presented at the annual meeting of the Midwest Political Science Association, April 13–16, 1989, Chicago, Ill.

Thorne, Barrie, and Nancy Henley. 1975. *Language and Sex. Difference and Dominance.* Rowley, Mass.: Newbury House.

Warnke, Georgia. 1987. *Gadamer: Hermeneutics, Tradition and Reason.* Stanford: Stanford University Press.

Westkott, Marcia. 1983. "Women's Studies as a Strategy for Change: Between Criticism and Vision." In Gloria Bowles and Renate Duelli Klein, eds., *Theories of Women's Studies.* Boston: Routledge & Kegan Paul.

White, Stephen K. 1988, *The Recent Work of Jurgen Habermas: Reason, Justice & Modernity*. Cambridge: Cambridge University Press.

Williams, J., and H. Giles. 1978. "The Changing Status of Women in Society: An Intergroup Perspective." In Henri Tajfel, ed., *Studies in Intergroup Behavior*. London: Academic Press.

APPENDIX A
Summary of Attitudinal Orientations, Main Attributes

Instrumentalism	Contextualism
• views self as autonomous	• views self in connection with community/others
• sees human interactions as separate and competitive	• sees human interactions as part of a continuous web of relationships
• distinguishes between objective and subjective knowledge: favors objective	• integrates objective and subjective knowledge; believes both have "bias"
• main focus is protecting individual's rights	• main focus is addressing needs
• separates the public and private spheres	• sees the interaction between the public and private spheres

APPENDIX B

Titles of Bills Taped and Transcribed for Analysis (n = 69; approximately 110 hours of committee and floor debates)

Bills Sponsored by Females	Bills Sponsored by Males
1. Insurance coverage for mammography screening	1. Insurance company change of domicile
2. School costs of community placement	2. Housing authorities powers
3. Establish full-day kindergartens	3. Domestic abuse restraining orders
4. Employment termination at higher education	4. Historic properties tax credit
5. State trooper retirement benefits	5. Classified employees of school districts
6. Dishonored negotiable instrument holder	6. PUC authority to regulate utilities
7. Disabled children home-care program	7. School Dropout Prevention Act
8. Mentally retarded tax exemption	8. Credit services organizations practices
9. Discharge of water pollutants	9. Deputy voter registration officers
10. Medical benefits for children	10. Pet animals for experimentation
11. Temporary juvenile holding facilities	11. Branch banking
12. Public schools of choice	12. Increase in estate tax
13. Adult high-school diplomas	13. Disabled voters voting access
14. Certification of nurse aides	14. Concerning crimes
15. Property tax relief	15. Improvement of air quality
16. Encourage opportunities for child care	16. Matching funds for volunteer firefighters
17. Concerning court actions	17. Health care professionals
18. Water-well contractors licenses	18. Wildlife management funding
19. Pesticide applicator liability insurance	19. Payment of claims by conservator
20. Grand jury statute modification	20. Accommodations accessibility for dogs
21. Quality of care incentive allowance	21. Electronic fund transfers
22. Audits of the Regional Transportation District	22. Rural Health Care Commission
23. Emergency needs of the homeless	23. Discovery in criminal proceedings
24. Equal access to library services	24. Enforcement of support obligations
25. Health Data Commission reports	25. Decentralization of home health services
26. Exceptions from psychotherapy rules	26. Fire and police group life insurance
27. Alcohol-related vehicular offenses	27. Revision of statutes
28. Strengthen Crime Victim Compensation Act	28. Reparation payments and social services
29. Medical waste management	29. Stationary source fees
30. Violating campaign contributions limits	30. Child care expenses and income tax
31. Superfund implementation	31. Acquisition of Chaffee County lands
32. Concerning custody proceedings	32. Accumulation of hazardous waste
	33. Tax on interstate telecommunications
	34. Infectious waste disposal
	35. Gang-related crimes
	36. Reporting child abuse
	37. Minimum security facilities

APPENDIX C

Example of Rank Frequency Word List of Committee Hearing on Domestic Abuse

1.) 155 (2.41%)
  I

2.) 127 (1.97%)
  YOU

3.) 82 (1.27%)
  NOT

4.) 81 (1.26%)
  WE

5.) 78 (1.21%)
  CUSTODY
  IF

6.) 60 (0.933%)
  ORDER

7.) 57 (0.886%)
  COURT
  WOULD

8.) 50 (0.777%)
  CHILD
  THINK

9.) 46 (0.715%)
  GOING
  REP
  THATS

10.) 45 (0.700%)
  DAYS

11.) 44 (0.684%)
  ALL
  CONTROL
  THERES

12.) 41 (0.637%)
  BILL
  THEY

13.) 40 (0.622%)
  DOMESTIC
  JUDGE
  ONE
  TEMPORARY

14.) 39 (0.606%)
  CARE

15.) 38 (0.591%)
  ABUSE
  CHILDREN
  OTHER

16.) 35 (0.544%)
  NO

17.) 34 (0.529%)
  CAN
  JUST

18.) 33 (0.513%)
  DO

19.) 32 (0.498%)
  STATUTE

20.) 31 (0.482%)
  COULD
  THIRTY

21.) 30 (0.466%)
  RIGHT

22.) 29 (0.451%)
  GET

23.) 28 (0.435%)
  ISSUE

24.) 27 (0.420%)
  BECAUSE
  COMMITTEE
  PARTY
  WORD

25.) 26 (0.404%)
  DAY
  SOME

26.) 25 (0.389%)
  JUDGES
  NOW
  RESTRAINING
  TIME

27.) 24 (0.373%)
  ANY
  COUNTY
  DISTRICT
  FIRST
  THEN
  WILL

28.) 23 (0.358%)
  COME
  DONT

29.) 22 (0.342%)
  ME
  SHOULD
  TAKE

30.) 21 (0.326%)
  DOES
  STANDARD
  UP

30.) 21 (Cont.)
  VERY
  WELL

31.) 20 (0.311%)
  FACT
  GO
  HEARING
  IM
  LIKE
  MORE
  ORDERS
  SECOND

32.) 19 (0.295%)
  EMERGENCY
  MAKE
  PERIOD
  SEVEN

33.) 18 (0.280%)
  HOME
  MY
  ONLY
  PARENT
  PROBLEM
  SAY

34.) 17 (0.264%)
  BEST
  INTEREST
  QUESTIONS
  TWO

35.) 16 (0.249%)
  MATTER
  MCINNIS
  MOTION

36.) 15 (0.233%)
  GRANT
  PAGE
  STATE
  VISITATION

37.) 14 (0.218%)
  BEFORE
  CASES
  MAY
  MINOR
  THANK YOU
  THEM
  WHETHER

38.) 13 (0.202%)
  CASE
  CERTAINLY
  DEAL
  SAYS

39.) 12 (0.187%)
AMENDMENT
CHAIRMAN
CHILDRENS
LOOK
MIGHT
MOVE
OKAY
OUR
SECTION
WANT
WAY
YOUR
YOURE

40.) 11 (0.171%)
BASIS
EVEN
KNOX
LANGUAGE
LAW
LINE
MADAM
PARTIES
PERMANENT
PUT
SITUATION
THREE
US
WHATS
YES

41.) 10 (0.155%)
ACTION
AMENDMENTS
BELIEVE
CALL
CANT
CODE
CONTINUED
D
DOESNT
FAMILY
HERNANDEZ
HOW
ISSUES
KNOW
MATTERS
MEANS
NEED
PEOPLE
POINT
PROTECTION
READ
SEE
THINGS

42.) 9 (0.140%)
APPROPRIATE
AWARD

42.) 9 (Cont.)
CONCERN
DID
GOT
HE
HEARD
INCLUDE
IVE
LEAST
MADE
PART
REQUEST
SHALL
SIDE
SOMETHING
THEYRE

43.) 8 (0.124%)
ASK
AWARDED
CLEAR
COURTS
DECISION
DEFINED
DIFFERENT
EVER
EX-PARTI
FRONT
HAPPENS
INVOLVED
LAST
MOST
PARAGRAPH
PLEASE
REALLY
REASON
SEEMS
SOMEBODY
THING
ZORBY

44.) 7 (0.109%)
ACT
ADD
ADDRESS
AUTHORITY
BACK
COMES
CONTINUE
DANGER
GIVE
GOOD
MUCH
NEXT
NOTHING
OBJECTION
PERSON
PRESENT
REGARDING
RELATIONS

APPENDIX D
Example of Concordance Output in KWIC Format of Committee Hearing on Domestic Abuse

```
CHILD (Cont.)
    WIT m2 a 1071 68   right regarding this child, and we want this
    WIT m2 a 1071 73   that  they  do  have  the right to take that
    WIT m2 a 1071 90   they  have  always  been the caretaker of the
    WIT m2 a 1071 90   they've  stayed  at  home  and cared for the
    WIT m2 a 1071101   that  the  other  parent would never see the
    WIT m2 a 1071105   it.  so  long." There's no right to see your
    WIT m1 p 1071 53   entering matters in the best interest of the
    WIT m1 p 1071 59      abuse  to  the  plaintiff  or  to a minor
    WIT m2 a 1071  4   alleged  to  have been abused, and there's a
    WIT m2 a 1071  5   been  abused, and there's a child who is the
    WIT m2 a 1071  6   of  the  husband  she  could  be awarded his
    WIT m2 a 1071  5   orders. So, anything that has to do with the
    WIT m2 a 1071  7   any reason that it has to be in here. If the
    SWEN f cm 1071 2   children's code that would take care of that
    MCIN m s 1071  1   at  that time? I don't believe so unless the
    SWEN f cm 1071 2   it follow that we should have, say where the
    WIT m2 a 1071  9      in  there  in  order  to  make sure the
    WIT m2 a 1071 20   these  decisions,  giving  custody  of  the
    WIT m2 a 1071 22   of a problem if you don't make sure that the
    WIT m2 a 1071 30   no  direction  here  to  say  what does the
    WIT m2 a 1071 33   might  be  the  person  whose  cared for the
    WIT m2 a 1071 33   person  whose  cared for the child, takes the
    WIT m2 a 1071 35   be  the  more  appropriate custodian for the
    WIT m2 a 1071 36   that.  We  don't  look  at  all to what the
    WIT m2 a 1071 38   be wrong. We ought to be looking at what the
    WIT m4 a 1071  5   issues.  This is in the best interest of the
    WIT m4 a 1071 12   extensive  around  the  best interest of the
    WIT m1 p 1071 23   it  is  in  fact  the  best interest of the
    TUCK f cm 1071 4      referring  to  the  best  interest  of the
    TUCK f cm 1071 2   to  be  used  is in the best interest of the
    MCIN m s 1071  3   control  will be in the best interest of the
    STAFF 1071     3   control shall be in the best interest of the
    STAFF 1071     5   days  shall  be  in the best interest of the
    MCIN m s 1071  4   124.  14-10-124  is the best interest of the
    TUCK f cm 1071 2   the  terminology in the best interest of the
CHILDREN (38)
    MCIN m s 1071  9      or  injuring  one  party  or  the minor
    MCIN m s 1071 12   temporary  care  and  custody  of  the minor
    WIT m1 p 1071 31   from the family home and granting custody of
    WIT m2 a 1071 36   But no decision regarding custody concerning
    MCIN m s 1071 19   of the problems on the domicile of the minor
    MCIN m s 1071 20   we  need  to  address  what happens with the
    MCIN m s 1071 21   I  deal  with  on  a personal basis involves
    MCIN m s 1071 22   involves children. The abuse is not with the
    MCIN m s 1071 23   abuse  is between the spouses, but there are
    WIT m2 a 1071  3   says that it could be in care and custody of
    SWEN f cm 1071 2   say  "awarding  temporary  care" of any minor
    WIT m2 a 1071  2   for  all  the alleged problems that refer to
    WIT m2 a 1071  3      there  are  emergency  pickup  orders  for
    WIT m2 a 1071  3   emergency  pickup orders for children if the
    WIT m2 a 1071 14   to  happen  all  the time whether or not the
    MCIN m s 1071  2   understand that. The children's code, if the
    MCIN m s 1071  4   where  the  dispute is not from abuse of the
    MCIN m s 1071  4   is  not  from  abuse  of  the children. The
    MCIN m s 1071  6   obviously  they  can't live together. So the
    MCIN m s 1071  7   children,  something  has to happen with the
    MCIN m s 1071  3   as a part of this, "this can not happen. The
    MCIN m s 1071  3   The  children  can not be taken care of. The
    MCIN m s 1071  4   court generally does grant visitation if the
```

child to be prevented from going to saudi arabia or to south
child out of the state or out of the country. There's no way We're
child, that they've stayed at home and cared for the child, been
child, been the one to take them to the doctor, to school, and to
child. All of a sudden if each spouse could come with this order
child. There's no right to visitation. There's no right to contact.
child. Certainly that's an impact. This statute has the same thing.
child, and you also find that unless restrained and enjoined, you
child who is the child upon prior marriage of the husband she could
child upon prior marriage of the husband she could be awarded his
child too in that action. Other questions? Rep swenson. Would it be
child can be handled under the children's codes. There's clearly
child is in fact in danger, I think the question is if there's in
child at that time? I don't believe so unless the child is in
child is in danger. That's correct. So then would it follow that we
child should go? No. When we just say, awarding temporary care... I
child under these kind of circumstances because I think the other
child based upon only hearing one side of it, that's a very serious
child is going to continue to have contact with the other parent.
child need. It might be that the parent who has been abusive and it
child, takes the child to school every day, does all the things for
child to school every day, does all the things for them and would
child, and there's nothing in here that addresses that. We don't
child needs. All we look at is has there been abuse? That seems to
child needs not what's going on between the parents. [tape switch]
child. The domestic violence coalition does not have a position on
child. And this legislature has dealt with those through
child and refer to the subsection in the domestic code so it has a
child, and it would appear to me that would be appropriate to add
child. I was making some notes on that, and they're Not complete.
child. Let's be sure harriet has this written down. And then i'll
child and control of any minor children of either party involved
child according to the .... Now is that how you intended it to be
child to the dissolution act. In the district court, that's the
child as defined in or something, so at least that the words are

children of other party. It does, it can exclude a party from a
children for a period not to exceed 30 days. Now that's one point
children have been in the district court in domestic relation cases
children was being made until they could get into the district
children. Finally let me say again, we need to address what happens
children. Most of the cases that I deal with on a personal basis
children. The abuse is not with the children. The abuse is between
children. The abuse is between the spouses, but there are children
children involved, and we need to address that short of going into
children of either party which means that if the wife is the one
children? Care, control is what you're saying is not defined. And
children because there are emergency pickup orders for children if
children if the children are in danger. There are provisions for
children are in danger. There are provisions for emergency custody
children are in danger. That, I think, is the basis of the concern.
children are in danger. And you have cases where the dispute is not
children. The children aren't in danger. But the two spouses,
children aren't in danger. But the two spouses, there's abuse going
children, something has to happen with the children while we try to
children while we try to get a cooling off period. And that's what
children can not be taken care of. The children will be here..."
children will be here..." and so on and so forth. Are there further
children aren't endangered by the abusing spouse. Rep knox. On that

APPENDIX E
Example of Formatted Text of Committee Hearing on Domestic Abuse

MCIN m s 1071

```
          m
          r
          4
          ed
          i
```

```
 1    Madam chairman hb 1071 concerns restraining orders to
 2    prevent domestic abuse. There's some deal of confusion in the
 3    current statute. So what this bill is an attempt to do is to
 4    clarify and streamline the statutes for domestic abuse protection
 5    so that the confusion is erased from the statutes. It provides
 6    that the county district courts be given authority to issue a
 7    permit, temporary restraining orders to prevent domestic abuse.
 8    It specifies that such orders can include restraining a party
 9    from threatening or injuring one party or the minor children of
10    other party. It does, it can exclude a party from a family home
11    for a period of not to exceed 30 days. It also can award
12    temporary care and custody of the minor children for a period not
13    to exceed 30 days. Now that's one point of contention about
14    this statute. Some judges in our state believe that on issuing
15    these kinds of orders you cannot award temporary care and custody
16    of the minor child. Other judges believe that under the current
17    statute you can make such an award. So we want to clarify that
18    and allow a temporary custody and care of the minor child for a
19    period not to exceed 30 days. It also requires that a motion
20    for a temporary restraining order take precedent over all other
21    matters on the docket. And that's important because of the
22    kind of crowded dockets we have and of course usually the
23    emergency situations of domestic abuse brings up. It also
24    provides some information on the service of citation and requires
25    the judge to make a temporary restraining order to prevent
26    domestic abuse if the evidence exists. That's just a very
27    brief summary of it. Madam chairman, with your permission I
28    think I can save the committee some time, certainly can get the
29    questions answered much more professionally by calling up my
30    first witness, my first and only witness, judge zorby who is a
31    current judge on the bench that helped me draft, though quite
32    frankly did most of the drafting of the bill, if that would be
33    fine.
```

FAAT f c 1071

```
          f
          r
          6
          ed
```

```
 1    That would be fine. Judge zorby would you join us?
 2    Certainly, rep knox.
```

Contributors

Kathryn Anderson, Women Studies and Fairhaven College, Western Washington University, Bellingham, Washington

Susan Armitage, Department of History and American Studies Program, Washington State University, Pullman, Washington

Judith A. Cook, School of Social Service Administration, The University of Chicago, Chicago, Illinois

Myra Marx Ferree, Department of Sociology, University of Connecticut, Storrs, Connecticut

Pamela M. Fishman, Executive Director of the Prospect Park Alliance, Brooklyn, New York

Mary Margaret Fonow, Center for Women's Studies, Ohio State University, Columbus, Ohio

Sherna Berger Gluck, Department of History, California State University, Long Beach, California

Janet Shibley Hyde, Department of Psychology, University of Wisconsin, Madison, Wisconsin

Dana Jack, Fairhaven College, Western Washington University, Bellingham, Washington

Lyn Kathlene, Department of Political Science, University of Colorado, Boulder, Colorado

Evelyn Fox Keller, Women Studies Department and Department of Rhetoric, University of California, Berkeley, California

Howard I. Kushner, Department of History, San Diego State University, San Diego, California

Anna Lowenhaupt Tsing, Anthropology Board of Studies, University of California, Santa Cruz, California

Marcia Westkott, Women Studies Program and Department of Sociology, University of Colorado, Boulder, Colorado

Judith Wittner, Department of Sociology, Loyola University, Chicago, Illinois